Ernest
Hemingway

SEVEN DECADES OF CRITICISM

Ernest Hemingway

SEVEN DECADES OF CRITICISM

Edited by
Linda Wagner-Martin

Michigan State University Press
East Lansing

Michigan State University Press
East Lansing, Michigan 48823-5202

06 05 04 03 02 01 00 99 98 1 2 3 4 5 6 7 8 9 10 11 12

Designed by Nicolette Rose
Cover photo credit: C. M. Zoehrer, courtesy of the John F. Kennedy Library

Library of Congress Cataloging-in-Publications Data

Ernest Hemingway: seven decades of criticism/edited by Linda Wagner-Martin.
         p.   cm.
    Includes bibliographical references.
    ISBN 0-87013-489-2 (alk. paper)
    1. Hemingway, Ernest, 1899-1961—Criticism and interpretation.
I. Wagner-Martin, Linda.
PS3515.E37Z58676   1998
813'.52—dc21   98-42861
                                                                    CIP

III. The Response to the Later Works

IV. The Response to *The Garden of Eden*

V. The Inevitable Consideration of Hemingway's Biography

CONTENTS

For Susan Beegel,
for her work with *The Hemingway Review*,
and for the memory of
Paul Smith

INTRODUCTION

When Hemingway was young, he lived all year long for the early July day when his fashionable mother, Grace Hall Hemingway, took him and his sisters by train and then by horse and wagon from the staid Chicago suburb of Oak Park, Illinois, to the (comparative) wilds of Horton Bay on Walloon Lake in Michigan. The lake country of mid-Michigan meant outdoor adventures—fishing, canoeing, swimming, hiking and, later, hunting and trapping, and being friends with the Indians who made their living from the lake and forests. It meant dirty fingernails and a fishy smell, a fast-maturing body that in this terrain legitimately could skip bathing. In many ways, it meant freedom from the orderly and well-mannered doctor's household, a home in which Hemingway's mother earned her spending money—and kept her professional reputation alive—by giving music lessons. As the first boy born to the Grace Hall-Clarence Hemingway marriage, Ernest Miller Hemingway dealt daily with a talented (and hearty) older sister, and three younger sisters. Not until Leicester arrived fifteen years after Ernest was born was there another boy in the Hemingway family.

Large but not particularly tough, a bit crude in his tastes and manners, Ernie Hemingway tried to figure out how to be a real man in turn-of-the-century, middle-class America. The culture was filled with the emblems of propriety—treasured objets d'art from Europe, gilt-framed photographs of austere patriarchs, carefully embroidered doilies placed meticulously on chair arms, and a lovingly polished piano lit by graceful, expensive piano lamps. Church choirs were sites of adolescent romance, and well-stocked public libraries marked the upwardly mobile suburb, one where nice people valued education and artistic endeavors like china painting and after dinner musicales; and religious practices let the world know that God was in His heaven and, therefore, all was right with the world.

Hemingway wasn't sure that approaching the realities of life could be handled quite so simply. Though he lived in Oak Park, he saw Chicago. He read the city papers; he bummed through suburbs less pristine than his own. He started to understand that there was a slightly saccharine gloss to the world as his parents saw it, and he early on became suspicious of abstract notions of right and wrong, the efficacy of firm belief systems, and class-mandated morality. Abstractions always stuck in Hemingway's throat. As he later had Frederic Henry reflect in *A Farewell to Arms*, "I was always embarrassed by the words *sacred, glorious,* and *sacrifice* and the expression *in vain*. We had heard them, sometimes standing in the rain almost out of earshot, . . . and I had seen nothing *sacred*, and the things that were *glorious* had no *glory*. . . ."[1] While Hemingway admired Teddy Roosevelt in his rough rider days, he also saw that machismo might not be the only viable attitude for a would-be realist writer.

He wrote, constantly. Hemingway published fiction in the high school literary magazine, and was on the staff of *The Trapeze*, the school's weekly paper. He penned cynical-sounding editorials and brusque sports stories; he mimicked Ring Lardner's attempts at crass humor, a literary form intended to shock the educated elite. And when the children of his parents' friends prepared for college, it suited Hemingway, instead, to go into the real world and become a newspaperman. His initial journalistic career lasted only a few months.

That same thirst for experience drove him to leave the Kansas City *Star* and, in the winter of 1917, join the Red Cross ambulance corps on the Italian front; like John Dos Passos and e. e. cummings, the young Hemingway wanted to be where life was happening. Badly wounded with shrapnel injuries to his legs, he recuperated for months in Italian hospitals, and then came home—to face a winter or two of recovery on his own. At twenty, Hemingway chose to spend the winter alone, living in a room in Petosky, Michigan, rather than in his father's home in Illinois. Being a writer, Hemingway found, was an arduous and sometimes depressing job, especially when wounded legs stiffened in the cold and the veteran who seemed so mature grew just plain tired of pain and isolation.

Hemingway's nineteen summers living his adventures in the Michigan lakes and woods, and his one winter working through his angst and anxiety about his injured body, marked his fiction irrevocably. Many of the drafts of the short stories he was to write in Paris during his halcyon apprenticeship there, the highly successful stories of *In Our Time* and *Men Without Women*, show that his fiction is often set in Michigan (and then, in later versions, changed to less provincial, more international settings). One of his most urban stories, flavored with what seems to be the Chicago sports scene, is "The Killers," a narrative that—as the manuscript opening shows—was originally set in the author's familiar mid-Michigan locale.

> It was very cold that winter and Little Traverse Bay was frozen across from Petosky to Harbor Springs. Nick turned the corner around the cigar store with the wind blowing snow into his eyes. He stopped and looked down the street, saw the ice smooth inside the breakwater and piled high and white outside with the sun on it. . . . The wind blew the snow off the drifts in a steady shifting against his face but he stood and looked at the frozen bay in the sunlight and watched the sun on the high hills on the other side.[2]

Whether Hemingway is describing the icy winter beauty, or, more frequently, recollecting the warm green havens he frequented during those childhood and adolescent summers, he writes specifically—and beautifully—about the world that nourished him as he grew. For instance, from "The Last Good Country," Hemingway wrote about his place:

> They were coming down a long hill when they saw sunlight ahead through the tree trunks. Now, at the edge of the timber there was wintergreen growing and some partridge berries and the forest floor began to be alive with growing things. Through the tree trunks they saw an open meadow that sloped to where white birches grew along the stream. Below the meadow and the line of the birches there was the dark green of a cedar swamp and far beyond the swamp there were dark blue hills. There was an arm of the lake between the swamp and the hills. But from here they could not see it. They only felt from the distances that it was there.[3]

The evocative intimacy of place well-remembered marks this, and many other of Hemingway's descriptions of that boyhood world. Too soon lost, like most of our own adolescent fantasies, Hemingway's memories of Michigan may have provided the undergirding for the mournful yet objective tone he achieved so early—and maintained throughout his best writing.

Life is not simple, Hemingway's writing reminds the reader, even though it has its moments of simplicity—and through them, its beauty.

The pervasive question for the editor of this *Seven Decades* collection of criticism about the writings of Ernest Hemingway—whether he is defined as Michigander, Mid-westerner, expatriate, or resident of Key West, Cuba, Idaho, or the world—is *why* his writing lasts so well. If Hemingway's fiction does evoke the early century's simplicity, what else besides nostalgia does it provide the reader here at the very end of that twentieth century? Centennial thoughts, themselves, are bound to be nostalgic, even wistful. July 21, 1899—Ernest Hemingway's birth day. We memorialize that date, as readers around the world honor it. Yet there is nothing that smells of the lamp in what is occurring today in Hemingway criticism: recent essays and books show to good advantage some of the most exciting critical thinking of the 1990s.

The reason Michigan State University Press felt justified in bringing out this third volume of critical response to Hemingway's writing—following the *Five Decades* and *Six Decades* collections which were published in the 1970s and the 1980s—is that critics both mature and newly trained have in the 1990s found fresh patterns, unpredictably complex insights, throughout Hemingway's fiction. In fact, that work seems to be bursting out of the carefully constructed parameters that early academic criticism had provided. While many of us were taught to look for the code hero, the stoic if put-upon man whose impact lasted beyond his mortal quest, many other readers thought that same patient and long-suffering character was a bit of a bore. While the concept of heroism was changing during these past seventy years, as fewer and fewer Robert Jordans sacrificed their lives for some other country's battle, different Hemingway characters emerged as interesting. Rather than Robert Jordan, perhaps, Frederic Henry—who in *A Farewell to Arms* deserted from another non-U.S. military action—posed a challenge to readerly critics. Or, more to the point, rather than yet another Hemingway male character, readers came to be increasingly fascinated by—and increasingly skeptical of—the author's women characters. More than a shift in focus from one gender to the other, readers and critics were finding themselves interested in scenes, and entire themes, that they had not noticed in earlier readings. Hemingway's fiction, for the 1990s reader, came to bear little resemblance to those same texts which critics at mid-century had analyzed with such relentless thoroughness. But if *A Farewell to Arms* was not the same novel as it had been for Lionel Trilling during the 1940s, then what kind of metamorphosis had taken place? Was the difference in effect to be found in the reader, in the reader's training, in the work, and/or in the cultural expectation of both the text and—not incidentally—the author?

When Trilling wrote about Hemingway soon after the close of World War II, very few students were able to study the then-contemporary writer in any classroom. Still very much alive, Hemingway had become an icon of *Life* magazine and radio interviews; academic study avoided—was prohibited from studying—still living authors. In place of tough and text-based criticism, then, based on a critic's real familiarity with works, literary criticism had more in common with philosophy. Trilling, for example, talks about the meaning of literature as it can be assessed primarily in terms of ideas. While he dislikes the work of Thomas Wolfe ("an emotional writer"),[4] John Dos Passos, and Eugene O'Neill (the latter because they believe "they have conquered the material upon which they direct their activity"), this astute critic senses something different—and praiseworthy—about the writing of both William Faulkner and Ernest Hemingway. But how can Trilling describe that difference? First, by commenting on what he calls these two writers' "living reciprocal relationship with their work." He judges this relationship by the two men's intensity, and says as if conclusively, "when they are at their best they give us the sense that the amount and intensity of their activity are in a satisfying proportion to the recalcitrance of the material." For Trilling, the writers are taking on both subjects and themes that are not only germane to life, but reflective of its intellectual—and emotional—complexity.

Trilling privileges Hemingway's early stories on the basis of their emotional truth. While he seems to discount Faulkner's subject matter as being so completely Southern that it remains less accessible, he is willing to compare Hemingway's fiction to that of Tolstoy and Dostoevski. He waxes especially enthusiastic about the American writer's "negative capability, this willingness to remain in uncertainties, mysteries, and doubts," a stance that is not unintellectual but rather the most intellectual (or perhaps the most philosophical) of all postures. As Trilling heads for his more prominent argument—that American writers have seldom been philosophical, or certainly not religious in any formal sense, he leaves Hemingway behind and continues his march into more expected meditative ground. The hint of existentialism marks this postwar prolegomenon, but it is interesting that Trilling's best examples of the fusion of the emotion with the intellect—and one aspect of what he sees as the newly modern—place Faulkner and, particularly, Hemingway squarely in the center of what is coming. As he says modestly, "The subject is extremely delicate and complex and I do no more than state it barely and crudely. But no matter how I state it, I am sure you will see that what I am talking about leads us to the crucial issue of our literary culture."

John Raeburn was to explore more fully than any other critic what Ernest Hemingway's role in that literary culture came to be. *Fame Became of Him, Hemingway as Public Writer* (1984) suggests that at least part of Hemingway's fiction and non-fiction developed reflexively, in response to the responses of readers who applied the moral principles of philosophical judgment to his creations. Raeburn thinks it is crucial to understand that Hemingway also identified himself as a modern, a complex writer who did not blink at the truth as he saw it, interpreted it, and wrote about it; and that in so doing, he took on the common modernist role of cultural priest. He not only took on that role, he actively sought it. Each of Hemingway's stories, novels, and nonfiction essays and books were undertaken with a moralistic—and a moralizing—purpose: most of the time, he wrote to instruct. Or he at least *seemed* to be writing to instruct. As Raeburn points out, "If we regard the nonfiction as sketches toward an autobiography, however, we must remember that this is a public autobiography. Whether these public revelations squared with the 'real' personality of Hemingway is a fascinating question, but the answer must remain problematical because of the difficulty of determining the 'real' Hemingway."[5]

The larger questions of identity buried under the author's aesthetic pronouncements, and drawing from the ages-old concept of what good writing was to be, Hemingway would have been entirely at ease with Trilling's linkages between literature and philosophy. Mark Spilka has added to our understanding of how traditional Hemingway was, and of how rooted in the nineteenth century, in both British and American cultures, the American modernist remained; part of that intractable rootedness stemmed from the fact that Hemingway continuously thought of himself as an intellectually imposing literary celebrity. A deeper part, as Spilka points out in *Hemingway's Quarrel with Androgyny*, resulted from his privileging the great (read, old and traditional) literatures. Hemingway could never truly become an innovative modernist writer because in his heart he wanted to become a latter-day Rudyard Kipling, or even an Emily Brontë.[6]

Had criticism stopped with exploring Hemingway's relationship to past American writing, to literature as it co-existed with philosophy, and to the writer's own carefully-achieved celebrity, there would be little need for the several volumes in this series. But after Hemingway's death by suicide in July of 1961, critical opinion began to change. Insidiously, like a poisonous gas, the fact of his taking his own life—no matter how ill or depressed he had come to be—began to color readers' reaction to his work. So long as the code formulae remained in place, the actuality of the writer's life—and then his unexpected death—undermined what his various fictions supposedly taught. How "undefeated" could the Hemingway legend remain, now that the author was dead? How bravely could Santiago bring in that stripped skeleton, when his own eyes showed him that bones meant nothing? And if the reader could remember back to the sexually-demolished Jake Barnes of Hemingway's first novel, what a travesty the title—*The Sun Also Rises*—became.

In addition to the biographical dimension, which—because of Hemingway's celebrity prominence—could hardly be ignored, the canon of literary criticism was also changing rapidly. Readers and scholars had moved from the philosophical practices that Trilling represented through the New Critical, Brooks-and-Warren emphases (which had benefited Hemingway's texts because they could so profitably be read closely) to a more probing interrogation of less why a fiction was written as it was, to why it was written at all. Once deconstruction and structuralism/formalism merged with currents of reader response, no single author could dominate the study of modern letters. In fact, because that single author (i.e., Ernest Hemingway) was so likely to dominate such a study, critics seemed bent on unseating him from his long-established prominence. When Jane P. Tompkins chose Hemingway's *The Sun Also Rises* to illustrate how dramatically personal criticism could open (or violate, or at least change) a text, in what is otherwise a moderate survey of the approaches of David Bleich, Norman Holland, Gerald Prince, and Wolfgang Iser, she challenged years of interpretations of the novel. In her essay "Criticism and Feeling," Tompkins admits to being bothered from the opening of the novel by the treatment Hemingway as author gives Robert Cohn (often, just "mean" in intention), Cohn's mistress Frances, and Jake Barnes' date, "a whore, whom he treats with such condescension that I'm sure I was right about his attitude towards women. All he can seem to talk about is the state of her teeth; he obviously doesn't regard her as a person at all."[7]

Prior to this essay, the academic approach to Robert Cohn was that he deserves neglect, if not condemnation: after all, he worships Brett, and what is worse, he shows his feelings. The Hemingway code hero, as readers have understood him, must be stoic, must tough it out. Tompkins' point is that good criticism, like good living, demands emotion. Yet here the only character in *The Sun Also Rises* who is capable of feelings—at least of showing them—is maligned, by everyone else in the cast of characters. United in what may be a kind of anti-Semitism as well (but it is 1977, and few readers were keen to find prejudice in the recently-hallowed modernist texts), Hemingway's positive characters—in Tompkins' view—are the objectionable ones. As she continues, even as Jake and Brett are trying to make love in the cab, she as reader doesn't care about their pain: "instead of feeling sorry for Jake and his awful wound and his doomed amour, I find his appeals for pity incredibly adolescent and full of bad faith. And so it goes. Bill Gorton seems to me just such another spoiled, overgrown lout; the fishing trip to Burguete, despite its beauty, an irresponsible attempt to escape into childhood; the worship of Pedro Romero an adolescent's dream of glory; Brett's vaunted stoicism at the goring of horses and torture of bulls a display of human arrogance and cruelty; and the image of murder as sexual intercourse—the sword driven into the heart of the bull—just what I would expect from a man who feels about women the way Hemingway does."[8]

Given the times, Tompkins' reading is surprising, going beyond any simple feminism or gendered approach (note that she includes Brett in her repulsion); but the critic quickly feels that she has been "too personal" and therefore re-shapes her approach back into her critical paradigm. This she terms Hemingway's "repressive technique," explaining that just plain suspicion on the part of the reader—just plain dislike of what appear to be the author's manipulations—is not in itself adequate basis for critical judgment. What her essay presents, then, is a ground of the process of judgment formation; she has shown the reader how to enact an opinion, and how to gather arguments to support that initial opinion. While Tompkins' view of Robert Cohn and Jake Barnes has remained a minority position, its existence led to some sense that even the standard interpretations of the primary modernist writers were open to interrogation.

Whereas Tompkins' view in 1977 struck the general reader as radical, Toni Morrison garnered a similar response in 1992 when she chose to use Hemingway's fiction—along with Willa Cather's—to illustrate the way some American writers relied on the African American presence for thematic contrast and emphasis. In *Playing in the Dark, Whiteness and the Literary Imagination*, Morrison positioned critics to read Hemingway for his uses of "Africanism." *To Have and Have Not* is here read in terms of the author's choices of naming the black, or referring to him as "nigger;" but more to the point, of identifying the African as representative of "outlaw sexuality." As Morrison explains, "Here [*To Have and Have Not*] we see Africanism used as a fundamental fictional technique by which to establish character. Within a milieu that threatens the dissolution of all distinctions of value—the milieu of the working poor, the unemployed, sinister Chinese, terrorist Cubans, violent but cowardly blacks, upper-class castrati, female predators—Harry and Marie (an ex-prostitute) gain potency, a generative sexuality. They solicit our admiration by the comparison that is struck between their claims to fully embodied humanity and a discredited Africanism. The voice of the text is complicit in these formulations: Africanism becomes not only a means of displaying authority but, in fact, constitutes its source."[9] In Morrison's reading, Hemingway's *The Garden of Eden*—in its published version—becomes a labyrinth of Africanist tropes (especially hair and skin eroticism) that give confused gender and racial signals to any reader.

With similar intensity, in 1994 John W. Crowley forced readers to revise the traditional complacency about drinking that fuels Hemingway's narrative in *The Sun Also Rises, To Have and Have Not, The Garden of Eden* and other of Hemingway's fictions. In *The White Logic, Alcoholism and Gender in American Modernist Fiction*, Crowley describes what he calls "the drunk narrative," a pattern that occurs often in modernism: "Hemingway uses drinking . . . to establish a hierarchy of moral merit for his characters."[10] Frequently in this author's fictions, the best and most noble of personae are the good drunks. And drunkenness carries with it "the threat of gender uncertainty . . . the male rummy is as unmanly as Brett [in *The Sun Also Rises*] is unwomanly." What makes Crowley's assessment significant for Hemingway critics is that he locates drinking as one of the essential male bonding devices, a means by which Hemingway's characters stave off the threats of homosexuality, but then concludes that "the strongest bonds among men are formed less by means of alcohol than in spite of it. Drinking as a proof of manhood is ultimately motivated for Hemingway by the power and presence of women beyond the charmed male circle." As critics pose new issues, and re-interpret texts readers thought they had heard the last word about, we are reminded of Tompkins' earlier comment that "works of literature lead a life of their own, which they receive, in part, from each generation of readers that comes to them."[11]

❦

This third collection of critical essays on Hemingway's work illustrates implicitly the truth of that statement. In the past ten years, the quality and range of criticism on Hemingway's writing has improved/increased dramatically. Part of this impetus comes from the activity of the 600-member Hemingway Society, with its biennial international conferences which attract worldwide attention. Part comes from the more critically sophisticated editorship of *The Hemingway Review*, the society's journal, which has recently attracted the best of current scholarship. Another part is the continuing interest in the Hemingway works that have seen posthumous publication, *A Moveable Feast* in 1964, *Islands in the Stream* in 1970, and—most controversial—*The Garden of Eden*, edited and shortened for its 1986 publication. It is this latter book, a novel that suggested that Hemingway was less rigorously heterosexual than he claimed, that has been the focus of a great deal of recent scholarship; accordingly, this collection includes a discrete section of six essays on that work.

Part of readers' fascination with Hemingway today is the natural return—after years of dedication to William Faulkner as the premier American modern novelist—to the writer who had always been paired with him, even in the collection of the Nobel Prize for Literature. In the popular mind, Hemingway had always remained superior to Faulkner, not the least because of his stylistic influence on the kind of writing that grew to become an entire genre, the laconic, hard-boiled mystery and/or detective novel. We have few such important naturalists in modern fiction, with descriptions of lands and oceans foreshadowing today's informed ecological concerns. And as the writer of great, if tragic, love stories, Hemingway has contributed his remarkable language to cartoons, greeting card legends, and borrowings in serious contemporary fiction; most recently, Hemingway as icon of the world's great writer saw a few of his post-World War I letters become the text for a commercially produced film, *In Love and War*.

In some academic circles, Hemingway's work lives as much through the secondary criticism devoted to it as through its valid existence as text. The best criticism changes the lenses, and thereby gives readers new ways of reading, seeing, visualizing the art. It is in the interaction between the literature and its criticism that Hemingway's *œuvre* remains most vital.

This collection begins, as did the others, with early responses to Hemingway's work. Gertrude Stein's praise for the first book, *Three Stories and Ten Poems* in 1923, points the way for other international literary figures, including D. H. Lawrence, whose 1927 commentary also appears. Novelist

Wright Morris writes carefully about what Hemingway meant to him, and to other writers of his generation. But except for Terrence Doody's remarkable 1974 treatment of Hemingway's style in *The Sun Also Rises*, the other twenty-two essays have been published since 1988. *Seven Decades* is truly representative of that splendid criticism being enacted during the past decade.

Such a concentration has been possible, largely, because of the generous coverage of *Ernest Hemingway: Five Decades* and *Ernest Hemingway: Six Decades*. Those two earlier collections included work by Edmund Wilson, E. L. Doctorow, Paul Goodman, Malcolm Cowley, William Faulkner, John Wain, Robert Penn Warren, Daniel Fuchs, Claude McKay, Dorothy Parker, Paul Rosenfeld, Nelson Algren, and countless superb Hemingway scholars— Carlos Baker, Frederick I. Carpenter, Harold M. Hurwitz, Keneth Kinnamon, Alan Holder, John Reardon, Michael Reynolds, Peter Lisca, Richard Bridgman, Richard P. Adams, Joseph J. Waldmeir, Robert O. Stephens, C. Hugh Holman, Larzer Ziff, John J. Teunissen, Scott Donaldson, Sam S. Baskett, James Hinkle, Bernard Oldsey, Gerry Brenner, Joseph M. DeFalco, James and Gwen Nagel, Robert A. Martin, and others.[12] One of the principles of selection for this edition has been that writers whose essays appeared in the first two collections would be placed on a secondary list, while writers not previously included would be given preferred treatment. I have been very fortunate in securing permission to use essays by some of the outstanding current Hemingway scholars, and one of the most surprising results of this principle has been the difference in proportion of male and female critics represented. Nearly all critics included in both the earlier books were male— a statement that reflects on the sexual composition of scholars and teachers in post-secondary institutions as much as it does on the composition of collective Hemingway scholars. The *Seven Decades* collection, in contrast, is comprised of more than 40 percent women scholars' work.

Hardly a frivolous statistic, the fact that so many top women scholars are writing about Hemingway, helping readers to see new facets of the supposedly-macho artist's work, is another answer to the question of readership: why has Hemingway's fiction and nonfiction continued to attract readers by the thousands? Whether it be in Lisa Tyler's stunning intertextual reading of Hemingway's fiction and Brontë's, or in Susan Beegel's medical assessment of the writer's probable illness, or in Pamela Smiley's linguistic-based reading, or in Amy Strong's application of Toni Morrison's aesthetics to Hemingway's early fiction, these women critics' perceptions bring innovative ways of focusing on familiar texts and familiar biographical problems. I regret having to omit work by Nina Baym, Sandra Spanier, Cathy N. Davidson, Wendy Martin, and Bernice Kert; but the essays by Debra Moddelmog and Jamie Barlowe-Kayes reassess boundary positions for critics female and male in ways that are unexpectedly inclusive. I regret, too, having to omit sections from books by James Phelan (*Narrative as Rhetoric*), Rose Marie Burwell (*Hemingway: The Postwar Years and the Posthumous Novels*), and Nancy Comley and Robert Scholes (*Hemingway's Genders, Rereading the Hemingway Text*), but another principle of selection was to avoid anthologizing chapters from readily-accessible books.

Once again, it has been a pleasure to work with the staff of Michigan State University Press. I hope this continuation of the press's "decades" series, so valuable at its inception nearly 40 years ago, provides significant, and even exciting, ways of thinking about Hemingway's writing. For the practice of criticism bears no small resemblance to the practice of writing itself, and as Hemingway told George Plimpton in the deservedly famous *Paris Review* interview, "If a writer stops observing he is finished. But he does not have to observe consciously nor think how it will be useful. Perhaps that would be true at the beginning. But later everything he sees goes into the great reserve of things he knows or has seen."[13] Critics and readers, too, benefit from new observations, new insights, new approaches to the most beloved of texts and authors.

Linda Wagner-Martin
Chapel Hill, North Carolina

Notes

1. Ernest Hemingway, *A Farewell to Arms* (New York: Charles Scribner's Sons, 1929), 184–85.
2. Ernest Hemingway, Manuscript of "The Killers," John F. Kennedy Library, Hemingway Room/Archive.
3. Ernest Hemingway, "The Last Good Country," in *The Nick Adams Stories* (New York: Charles Scribner's Sons, 1972), 91.
4. Lionel Trilling, "Contemporary American Literature in Its Relation to Ideas," in *The American Writer and the European Tradition*, edited by Margaret Denny and William H. Gilman (Minneapolis: University of Minnesota Press, 1950), 146; other citations from the same essay, pp. 147, 148, and 150.

5. John Raeburn, *Fame Became of Him, Hemingway as Public Writer* (Bloomington: Indiana University Press, 1984), 15. The whole biographical industry regarding Hemingway and his work treats aspects of this dilemma; the interested reader might well begin with the first biography (Carlos Baker, *Ernest Hemingway: A Life Story* [New York: Charles Scribner's Sons, 1969]) and move through Sheldon Norman Grebstein (*Hemingway's Craft* [Carbondale: Southern Illinois University Press, 1973]), Anthony Burgess (*Ernest Hemingway and His World* [New York: Charles Scribner's Sons, 1978]), and Robert E. Fleming (*The Face in the Mirror, Hemingway's Writers* [Tuscaloosa: University of Alabama Press, 1994]) to the four-volume biography by Michael Reynolds, the first book of which is *The Young Hemingway* (Oxford: Basil Blackwell, 1986).

6. Mark Spilka, *Hemingway's Quarrel with Androgyny* (Lincoln: University of Nebraska Press, 1990); see Richard Lehan, "Hemingway Among the Moderns," in *Hemingway In Our Time*, edited by Richard Astro and Jackson J. Benson (Corvallis: Oregon State University Press, 1974), 191–212.

7. Jane P. Tompkins, "Criticism and Feeling," *College English* 39, no. 2 (October 1977): 173–74.

8. Ibid., 174–75.

9. Toni Morrison, *Playing in the Dark, Whiteness and the Literary Imagination* (New York: Vintage Books, 1992), 80.

10. John W. Crowley, *The White Logic, Alcoholism and Gender in American Modernist Fiction* (Amherst: University of Massachusetts Press, 1994), x, 51, 57, 62. See also Donald W. Goodwin, *Alcohol and the Writer* (New York: Penguin, 1990), and Tom Dardis, *The Thirsty Muse, Alcohol and the American Writer* (New York: Ticknor & Fields, 1989).

11. Tompkins, "Criticism and Feeling," 178.

12. See Linda Welshimer Wagner, ed., *Ernest Hemingway: Five Decades of Criticism* (East Lansing: Michigan State University Press, 1974), and Linda W. Wagner, ed., *Ernest Hemingway: Six Decades of Criticism* (East Lansing: Michigan State University Press, 1987). Also, Linda Wagner-Martin, ed., *New Essays on The Sun Also Rises* (Cambridge: Cambridge University Press, 1987).

13. Ernest Hemingway, quoted in "An Interview with Ernest Hemingway," by George Plimpton, *Five Decades of Criticism*, 35.

PART I

The Response to the Earliest Works

REVIEW OF HEMINGWAY'S *THREE STORIES AND TEN POEMS*

Gertrude Stein

Three stories and ten poems is very pleasantly said. So far so good, further than that, and as far as that, I may say of Ernest Hemingway that as he sticks to poetry and intelligence it is both poetry and intelligent. Rosevelt [*sic*] is genuinely felt as young as Hemingway and as old as Rosevelt. I should say that Hemingway should stick to poetry and intelligence and eschew the hotter emotions and the more turgid vision. Intelligence and a great deal of it is a good thing to use when you have it, it's all for the best.

Reprinted from Chicago Tribune *(Paris edition), November 27, 1923.*

IN OUR TIME: A REVIEW

D. H. Lawrence

In Our Time is the last of the four American books, and Mr. Hemingway has accepted the goal. He keeps on making flights, but he has no illusion about landing anywhere. He knows it will be nowhere every time.

In Our Time calls itself a book of stories, but it isn't that. It is a series of successive sketches from a man's life, and makes a fragmentary novel. The first scenes, by one of the big lakes in America—probably Superior—are the best; when Nick is a boy. Then come fragments of war—on the Italian front. Then a soldier back home, very late, in the little town way west in Oklahoma. Then a young American and wife in post-war Europe; a long sketch about an American jockey in Milan and Paris; then Nick is back again in the Lake Superior region, getting off the train at a burnt-out town, and tramping across the empty country to camp by a trout-stream. Trout is the one passion life has left him—and this won't last long.

It is a short book: and it does not pretend to be about one man. But it is. It is as much as we need know of the man's life. The sketches are short, sharp, vivid, and most of them excellent. (The "mottoes" in front seem a little affected.) And these few sketches are enough to create the man and all his history: we need know no more.

Nick is a type one meets in the more wild and woolly regions of the United States. He is the remains of the lone trapper and cowboy. Nowadays

---

Reprinted and excerpted from Calendar of Modern Letters *(April 1927) review of* Nigger Heaven, Flight, *and* Manhattan Transfer, *along with* In Our Time.

he is educated, and through with everything. It is a state of *conscious*, accepted indifference to everything except freedom from work and the moment's interest. Mr. Hemingway does it extremely well. Nothing matters. Everything happens. One wants to keep oneself loose. Avoid one thing only: getting connected up. Don't get connected up. If you get held by anything, break it. Don't be held. Break it, and get away. Don't get away with the idea of getting somewhere else. Just get away, for the sake of getting away. Beat it! "Well, boy, I guess I'll beat it." Ah, the pleasure in saying that!

Mr. Hemingway's sketches, for this reason, are excellent: so short, like striking a match, lighting a brief sensational cigarette, and it's over. His young love-affair ends as one throws a cigarette-end away. "It isn't fun any more."—"Everything's gone to hell inside me."

It is really honest. And it explains a great deal of sentimentality. When a thing has gone to hell inside you, your sentimentalism tries to pretend it hasn't. But Mr. Hemingway is through with the sentimentalism. "It isn't fun any more. I guess I'll beat it."

And he beats it, to somewhere else. In the end he'll be a sort of tramp, endlessly moving on for the sake of moving away from where he is. This is a negative goal, and Mr. Hemingway is really good, because he's perfectly straight about it. He is like Krebs, in that devastating Oklahoma sketch: he doesn't love anybody, and it nauseates him to have to pretend he does. He doesn't even *want* to love anybody; he doesn't want to go anywhere, he doesn't want to do anything. He wants just to lounge around and maintain a healthy state of nothingness inside himself, and an attitude of negation to everything outside himself. And why shouldn't he, since that is exactly and sincerely what he feels? If he really *doesn't* care, then why should he care? Anyhow, he doesn't.

FROM THE WASTE LAND TO THE GARDEN WITH THE ELLIOTS

Paul Smith

W ritten in the cruelest month of 1924, Hemingway's cruelest short story, "Mr. and Mrs. Elliot," has long embarrassed many critics into silence, while others, shuddering with distaste, have dismissed it as an incomprehensibly aggressive assault on a comparatively inoffensive target—the very minor expatriate poet, Chard Powers Smith. Here, for the first time, critic Paul Smith provides compelling textual, biographical, and literary reasons to believe that this story is far more complex and well worth a second look. Smith argues persuasively that in "Mr. and Mrs. Elliot" Hemingway, as was his wont, was attempting to combat the powerful literary influence of T. S. Eliot with sexual and artistic insults, with a satirical punch below the belt. Smith's essay views the story as a sophisticated satire not only of the Chard Powers Smiths and the Tom Eliots, but of the social and literary pretensions of well-heeled expatriates. It further underscores "Mr. and Mrs. Elliot's" significance as Hemingway's earliest exploration of the tortuous relationship between an artist's sexual and creative impulses, and as an almost uncanny prediction of the sexual triangle that would

---

Reprinted with permission from Hemingway's Neglected Short Fiction, New Perspectives, *ed. Susan F. Beegel (Tuscaloosa: University of Alabama Press, 1989), pp. 123–29.*

destroy the author's first marriage and echo in the despairing pages of his posthumously published novel, The Garden of Eden.

❦

"Mr. and Mrs. Elliot" has been both more *and* less neglected than it deserves to be. One might wish that those biographers who found in it yet another instance of Hemingway's bad taste, callous contempt, and occasional stylistic infelicity had neglected the story altogether; one might also wish for a larger company of critics who thought of it as, possibly, a short story. Never a story to attract much critical notice, once the object of its satire was revealed, there was little more to say except to regret its triviality.[1]

Now, of course, everyone knows that it was originally titled "Mr. and Mrs. Smith," that Hemingway had Chard Powers Smith in his sights, and that the two exchanged angry and characteristic letters in 1927, two years after the story's publication. Smith called Hemingway "a worm who attempted a cad's trick, [and] a contemptible shadow"; Hemingway, of course, threatened to knock him down.[2]

Most biographers have followed Carlos Baker in dismissing the satire as a "malicious gossip-story" ridiculing the Smiths' "alleged sexual ineptitudes."[3] We are not told who, other than Hemingway, made that allegation, or with what evidence if it was not common knowledge. But for Hemingway, Chard Powers Smith was an easy mark and natural enemy, several times over: he was independently wealthy; he had degrees from both Harvard and Yale; he lingered in Latin Quarter cafés, rented chateaux along the Loire, and wrote poetry in perfect classical meters with perfect Petrarchan emotions; and Yale published his first volume in 1925.

By the spring of 1924 Hemingway was writing at an astounding pace, nearly half his titles had been published and *re*published—six poems, six *in our time* chapters, and "My Old Man"—and he turned again to Edward O'Brien. He wrote that he had "quit newspaper work," was "about broke," and needed an agent to "peddle" the ten stories he had written. He enclosed three, one of which he was sure would not sell but which O'Brien could keep "as a souvenir." This story was titled "Mr. and Mrs. Smith."[4]

I suspect that Hemingway sent the story partly as an appreciative memento to the publisher who first accepted "My Old Man" and partly to pass on literary gossip—but not to be published, for soon after that he sent a typescript of the same story to Jane Heap for publication in the *Little Review's* winter issue of 1924–25 with the name Smith crossed out and Elliot inserted.

Hemingway's motive for changing the name from Smith to Elliot might have arisen from his inordinate fear of a libel suit. Or perhaps, sometime in the late spring of 1924, his original satiric intent was deflected by the news that Mr. and Mrs. Smith's "alleged sexual ineptitudes" had been overcome, tragically, for Mrs. Smith died in childbirth in Naples on 11 March 1924, a month before Hemingway wrote his story and sent it to O'Brien as a souvenir. Perhaps, finally, submitting the story to the very literary *Little Review*, Hemingway decided to direct his satire against another poet, one with more fame than Chard Powers Smith: T. S. Eliot, who had been published in that journal since 1917 and was by Hemingway's lights even more deserving of contempt.

Why Eliot? Consider the ways in which Hubert Elliot's career in the story is similar to the poet Hemingway most envied and whose success he could not abide. Like Hubie—in the annals of history or gossip—T. S. Eliot came from Boston, was a graduate student at Harvard, wrote long poems, was a virgin, was enticed (in the polite phrase) by his wife on the dance floor, and by all biographers' accounts, suffered through a loveless marriage of "sexual ineptitude."[5]

Hemingway was always and in several ways one step behind Eliot. He arrived in Paris in December 1921 at about the time that Eliot returned from his six-week stay in a sanatorium above Vevey in Switzerland, retrieved his wife from another sanatorium near Paris, gave Ezra Pound some 1,000 lines of the draft of *The Waste Land*, and returned to London. In their month in Paris the Hemingways set up digs on the rue Cardinal Lemoine and then departed for two weeks of skiing at Chamby, above Montreux, only a few miles from the sanatorium Eliot had left.[6]

When Hemingway returned to Paris and belatedly presented his letter of introduction to Ezra Pound, the poet might well have shown him "The Waste Land" manuscripts he was editing, if only to impress this young, arriviste writer with his editorial authority. And Pound, as given to gossip as Hemingway, must have passed on the tales of the Eliots' troubled marriage of which, by several accounts, "everyone within miles of it was aware."[7] Vivien Eliot's marginal note on the typescript of the "Game of Chess" section of the poem—she wrote "Wonderful"—may be no more than innocent literary praise,[8] but rumor overcame that benign notion to whisper that, of course, she recognized herself as the harried and neurotic woman in those lines. So did Hemingway when he crossed out Smith's name, wrote first "Eliot," then "Elliott," then finally dropped the last *t*—leaving, as in all his occasional satires, a clue to identify his victim.

So one returns to the now-delightful exchange of letters between Chard Powers Smith and Hemingway in January 1927. Smith noted, with good reason, that the story "suggests my wife at no point" and delicately implied that neither he nor his wife was sterile. But he went on to charge that Hemingway still had to learn the difference between writing like a "reporter" from motives of "petty malice" and writing like a true artist. That must have stung Hemingway to respond with his typical barroom invitation to step outside, but buried in his response are a backhanded apology and explanation. Hemingway wrote that he recalled the contempt he had for Smith, but he admitted that it was a "very cheap emotion and one very bad for literary production."[9] Hemingway did not contradict Smith's assertion that the story had nothing to do with his wife—by 1927 he could not—but he could, lamely, imply he had a larger literary object in mind, namely (as it were) T.S. Eliot.

One of the more persuasive arguments for Eliot as the object of this satire is Hemingway's deep indebtedness to the older and more famous poet—a paradox in any other writer than Hemingway. "Mr. and Mrs. Elliot" is one of Hemingway's three early responses to either the manuscripts of Eliot's poem he saw in Paris in March 1922 or the published version Pound showed him in Rapallo in February 1923. The two other stories completed before this one reflect the poem "Out of Season" of April 1923, with its setting by a turbid river by a dump heap and other testimony of sterility; and "Cat in the Rain" of March 1924, with its frenetic dialogue and the direct allusions to Sweeney and Mrs. Porter in its preliminary notes.[10]

Hubert and Cornelia Elliot of Hemingway's story are so like the deracinated figures of Eliot's poems that they would have been unnoticed along the shores of the Starnbergersee or chatting in the Hofgarten with those who "read, much of the night, and go south in the winter."[11] And, like the neurotic and sickly women and their indifferent companions in the poem, the Elliots' union is as barren and rootless as the landscape through which they aimlessly drift. These evident literary origins lift the story above the merely occasional: it is to Eliot's "Burial of the Dead" what "Cat in the Rain" is to Eliot's "Game of Chess."

There are inviting bits of biography that tempt us to return to the personal experiences behind the story. Nothing in the lives of the Smiths or the Eliots quite fully accounts for some of the story's details, and so we might add a third couple to this composite portrait: Mr. and Mrs. Hemingway. Like Hubert and Cornelia Elliot, the Hemingways sailed to Europe soon after their marriage (not so the Tom Eliots); for all Hemingway's claims of poverty, he was living well on Hadley's not insubstantial trust fund. Ernest, like Hubert, was 25 in 1924; and, although he was no virgin, he had married an older woman. And consider this passage on the Elliots' arrival in Paris, added to the 1925 version of the story: "Paris was quite disappointing and very rainy. . . . [E]ven though someone had pointed out Ezra Pound to them in a café and they had watched James Joyce eating in the Trianon and almost been introduced to Leo Stein . . . they decided to go to Dijon."[12] The Hemingways arrived in a rain-swept Paris, may have seen but did not meet Pound and Joyce, and left three weeks later. Or consider this passage on the Parisian cafés: "So they all sat around the Café du Dome, avoiding the Rotonde across the street because it is always so full of foreigners, . . . and then the Eliots rented a chateau in Touraine."[13] One of Hemingway's earliest *Toronto Star* articles of 1922 similarly condemns the Rotonde as a "showplace for tourists in search of atmosphere."[14] While the Elliots fled to a chateau on the Loire, the Hemingways left for a chalet in Chamby.

If the story reflected this much of the three years before it was written, it was uncannily prophetic of the next three. It was in the Loire valley of Touraine in the spring of 1926 that Hadley, motoring with Pauline and Jinny Pfeiffer, first recognized her competition. By June, Ernest and Hadley and Pauline were at a hotel in Juan-les-Pins, where, in Carlos Baker's nice phrase, "there were three of everything."[15] Hemingway's story had ended:

> Elliot had taken to drinking white wine and lived apart in his own room. He wrote a great deal of poetry during the night and in the morning looked very exhausted. Mrs. Elliot and the girl friend now slept together in the big mediaeval bed. They had many a good cry together. In the evening they all sat at dinner together in the garden under a plane tree and the hot evening wind blew and Elliot drank white wine and Mrs. Elliot and the girl friend made conversation and they were all three quite happy.[16]

David Bourne in *The Garden of Eden* did his writing in the mornings, of course, for he was otherwise engaged at night, although the regimen of his threesome was as exhausting as Hubert's. The dinner in the garden, the white wine, the hot evening wind, and the bisexual arrangement sketched in the story all find interminable variations in that late, bruised, and windfallen novel. Perhaps even the conflict between Catherine Bourne's jealousy and Marita's admiration of David's writing is suggested in Cornelia and her girl-friend's typing: with the touch system, Mrs. Elliot "found that while it increased her speed it made more mistakes. The girl friend was now typing practically all of the manuscripts. She was very neat and efficient and seemed to enjoy it."[17]

With the longer view of Hemingway's career and the literary history of his times, "Mr. and Mrs. Elliot" deserves another reading. I would argue that it is one of his best and most sophisticated satires, better than anything in *The Torrents of Spring*, as good as the satiric passages in *The Sun Also Rises*, and a satire that transcends its seminal gossip to reveal the social and literary pre-tensions among the elite expatriates who knew enough to frequent the Café du Dome rather than the Rotonde, but not much more.

Certainly the story should be read again for its importance in the Hemingway canon: it is his first portrait, if not a self-portrait, of the artist; it begins his long and sometimes querulous consideration of the relationship between the artist's sexual and creative impulses; and it should take its place, first with the "marriage tales" of the 1920s and then with the last, so far, of his posthumously published novels.

Finally, the story confirms the depth of Hemingway's indebtedness to T. S. Eliot. Sometime in late 1927 Hemingway listed on the back of an envelope his literary borrowings. The first was to "everybody" for his early imitations, and the second was to Elliot (note the spelling) with the phrase "watered the waste land and made it bloom like a rose."[18]

I am certain Hemingway recognized some similarity between the Chard Powers Smiths, the Eliots, and the figures in "The Waste Land." At least one other in that cast of the living and the literary did—Mrs. Smith. In a holo-graph dedication to the volume of poems Chard Powers Smith wrote as a memorial to his dead wife, he described her death: "Olive Cary Macdonald died in childbirth in Naples on March 11, 1924. 'Good-night, ladies, good-night, good-night,' she whispered."[19] To which one can only reply: "Goodnight Tom. Goodnight Chard. Goodnight Ernest. Ta ta. Goodnight, sweet ladies, good night, good night."

Notes

I am indebted to Professor Bruce Stark (University of Wisconsin/Milwaukee) and to Stanley I. Mallach and Allan S. Kovan of that university's library for a photocopy of the Hemingway typescript of "Mr. and Mrs. Elliot" published in the *Little Review* 10 (Autumn–Winter 1924–25): 9–12. I am also indebted to Professor Michael S. Reynolds (North Carolina State University) for sharing his discovery of the holograph "Dedication to OCM" at the Bancroft Library, University of California/Berkeley, intended for Chard Powers Smith's *Along the Wind*.

1. Carlos Baker and Charles A. Fenton are typical of those who dismiss the story; Joseph DeFalco is the only critic who has analyzed it at some length. See Baker, *Ernest Hemingway: A Life Story* (New York: Charles Scribner's Sons, 1969); Fenton, *The Apprenticeship of Ernest Hemingway* (New York: Farrar, Straus, Young, 1954) and DeFalco, *The Hero in Hemingway's Short Stories* (Pittsburgh: U of Pittsburgh P, 1963).
2. Chard Powers Smith to Ernest Hemingway, 2 January 1927, John F. Kennedy Library and Hemingway to Smith, ca. 21 January 1927, in *Ernest Hemingway: Selected Letters, 1917–1961*, ed. Carlos Baker (New York: Charles Scribner's Sons, 1981) 242.
3. Baker, *Life*, 133.
4. Hemingway to Edward O'Brien, 2 May 1924, *Letters*, 117.
5. See Eliot's biographers—Peter Ackroyd, *T. S. Eliot* (London: Hamish Hamilton, 1984); Caroline Behr, *T. S. Eliot: A Chronology of His Life and Works* (New York: St. Martin's P, 1983); Lyndall Gordon, *Eliot's Early Years* (Oxford: Oxford UP, 1977); and T. S. Matthews, *Great Tom: Notes Towards the Definition of T. S. Eliot* (New York: Harper, 1974).
6. Baker, *Life*, 84–85.
7. Matthews, 45.
8. Ackroyd, 115.
9. Hemingway to Smith, 21 January 1927, *Letters*, 242.
10. Items 670–74, John F. Kennedy Library.
11. T. S. Eliot, "The Waste Land," in *The Waste Land and Other Poems* (New York: Harcourt, 1934) 29.
12. Hemingway, "Mr. and Mrs. Elliot," *In Our Time* (New York: Boni & Liveright, 1925) 112.
13. Hemingway, "Mr. and Mrs. Elliot," in *The Short Stories of Ernest Hemingway* (New York: Charles Scribner's Sons, 1938) 163.
14. Hemingway, "American Bohemians in Paris," in *Dateline: Toronto, Hemingway's Complete* Toronto Star *Dispatches, 1920–1924*, ed. William White (New York: Charles Scribner's Sons, 1985) 114.

15. Baker, *Life*, 168, 171.
16. Hemingway, "Mr. and Mrs. Elliot," *In Our Time*, 115.
17. Hemingway, "Mr. and Mrs. Elliot," *Short Stories*, 164.
18. Item 489, John F. Kennedy Library.
19. Chard Powers Smith, holograph "Dedication to OCM," Bancroft Library, U California/Berkeley. Intended for *Along the Wind* (New Haven: Yale UP, 1925).

SCREAMING THROUGH SILENCE: THE VIOLENCE OF RACE IN "INDIAN CAMP" AND "THE DOCTOR AND THE DOCTOR'S WIFE"

Amy Lovell Strong

In her recent work of literary criticism, *Playing in the Dark*, Toni Morrison calls our attention to the way critics have ignored an abiding Africanist presence that weaves its way through the works of white American authors:

> There seems to be a more or less tacit agreement among literary schol-
> ars that, because American literature has been clearly the preserve of
> white male views, genius, and power, those views, genius, and power
> are without relationship to and removed from the overwhelming pres-
> ence of black people in the United States.... The contemplation of this
> black presence is central to any understanding of our national litera-
> ture and should not be permitted to hove at the margins of the literary
> imagination. (5)

Reprinted with permission from The Hemingway Review, *16 (Fall 1996), pp. 18–32. Copyright 1996, The Ernest Hemingway Foundation. All rights reserved.*

While my focus in this essay will be on the lack of an Indian (rather than Africanist) presence, I will explore the ways Hemingway negotiates the matter of "race" and racial difference in two short stories from *In Our Time*. Like recent readings of Hemingway's fiction which have begun to outline issues of "gender trouble,"[1] my work will center on two of his earliest short stories, "Indian Camp" and "The Doctor and the Doctor's Wife," to examine how Hemingway represents the instability of racial identity. In the first story, he presents race simply as a biological feature, but then in the second revises this model to create a complex, shifting depiction of race that anticipates the essentialist/constructionist debates waged today.[2] Secondarily, I hope this study might begin to uncover the ways his work has interrogated power relations built on racial identity, and even exposed the instability of power based on such a system of inequality.

Critics have long been aware of the Edenic and, more specifically, Adamic longings to be found in Hemingway's work, longings he shares with American writers such as Whitman, Hawthorne, and Melville. The Nick Adams stories, with their obvious gesture toward this tradition, have generated a number of comments on the symbolism of the name "Adams," but most critics seem to have internalized R. W. B. Lewis's formulation in *The American Adam* that to be Adamic is to efface racial history.[3] Quoting from an 1839 *Democratic Review*, Lewis defines the Adamic myth: "Our national birth was the beginning of a new history . . . which separates us from the past and connects us with the future only" (5). Traditionally, "Indian Camp" and "The Doctor and the Doctor's Wife" have been read as tales of initiation, focusing heavily on the final scene in "Indian Camp" and Nick's musing that "he felt quite sure that he would never die" (19), and/or on the unity between father and son in "The Doctor and the Doctor's Wife" when those choose to seek out black squirrels together.[4] To be sure, the Indians in these stories have been characterized, often as symbols of darkness and primitivism, but even this characterization functions primarily to offset Nick's character. My argument is not specifically with the way critics have characterized the Indians (although that racial subtext should be examined). It is rather that Hemingway's stories do, in fact, present an Adamic figure whose identity cannot be fully understood without historicizing his relation to these Indians—a relation based on racial domination. What takes place within these two stories is a male-male rivalry, white male against Indian male, where the endangered territory returns to eerily familiar historical subjects/catalysts for violence: the woman's body and the land. In the opening

scene of "Indian Camp," we find Nick, Dr. Adams, and Uncle George being
ferried across a lake through a gloomy, misty darkness. Joseph DeFalco
points out that "the classical parallel is too obvious to overlook, for the two
Indians function in a Charon-like fashion in transporting Nick, his father,
and his uncle from their own sophisticated and civilized world of the white
man into the dark and primitive world of the camp" (161). The Hades
metaphor not only seems "too obvious to overlook," but other details add
further support to his reading, such as the dogs "rushing out" at the men
once they reach the other side of the lake. "A dog came out barking. . . . More
dogs rushed out at them" (*IOT* 16). This seemingly gratuitous appearance
recalls Cerberus, the many-headed dog who challenged spirits trying to enter
or leave Hades. Furthermore, if a Charon-like figure ferries the men across
the lake, we may imagine the river Styx, but as the men return, now with Dr.
Adams at the oars, we may be reminded of another famous river in Hades.
Lethe, the river of forgetfulness, works well in this context for two reasons: it
helps illuminate Nick's final thoughts of immortality at the end of the story,
and it implicates both father and son in a larger historical pattern of forget-
ting. At the end of "Indian Camp," Nick and his father have a brief, but
pointed catechistic interchange about death, and because we have just witnessed Nick's "initiation" into the world of pain and death, his final thought
surprises some readers. Trailing his hand in the water as his father rowed
them back across, Nick "felt quite sure that he would never die" (19). Even if
we abandon the mythic elements here and simply see a boy being rowed
across the lake by his father, we must admit some element of willful forgetfulness and an enormous amount of psychical distancing from his experience at the Indian camp. The goal of this particular reading is not meant to
encourage discussion of Hemingway's familiarity with Orphic mythology, or
even to presume that he was referring to Greek myth in "Indian Camp."
Rather, it serves as a metaphor for the ways Hemingway's story has been
read; readers have also trailed their hands in the river of forgetfulness, over-
looking the Indians' role not only in this story, but in the making of
American identity. I believe we have not fully engaged with "Indian Camp"
or "The Doctor and the Doctor's Wife" unless we come to terms with the way
the identities of Nick and his father are constructed in relation to the
Indians' presence, and vice versa.

One of the most perplexing issues in "Indian Camp" springs from the
moment when Dr. Adams has successfully completed his crude operation on
the Indian woman and reaches up into the bunk to check on the father, only

to find—to his undisguised horror—that the Indian has slit his throat "from ear to ear" (18). We may simply wish to accept the explanation given by Dr. Adams: "He couldn't stand things, I guess" (19). It does seem true that the Indian "couldn't stand things," but does this simply mean he couldn't stand his wife's physical pain? However astounding the woman's pain, the doctor has arrived, and the two days of pain should be alleviated very soon. Which then raises a different question: is it the doctor's *presence* that drives the Indian husband to suicide? I believe "Indian Camp" tells a different kind of initiation story, one that, like the Orphic myth, shows how a purified and initiated identity cannot be constructed without the binary opposition of unpurified and fallen selves.

The imagery surrounding Dr. Adams, Uncle George, and Nick's entry into the opposing camp is permeated by structures of domination. Once across the lake, Uncle George's first action is to offer cigars to the Indians who have rowed them across. It is not clear why Uncle George gives the Indians two cigars; it would not be a form of payment for rowing them across, because the doctor is obviously doing the Indian family a favor. It must be a gift, either in the form of a traditional 'peace' offering, or as a congratulatory gesture for the newborn baby. We have no signs, however, that the Indians will give any gift in return. Gayle Rubin's work explains that "gifts were the threads of social discourse, the means by which . . . societies were held together in the absence of specialized governmental institutions" (172). She further suggests that "gift exchange may also be the idiom of competition and rivalry" (172), using the example of the "Big Man" who humiliates another by giving more than can be reciprocated. This first form of exchange between cultures establishes a subtle, unequal dynamic of dominator/dominated.

Jürgen C. Wolter's article, "Caesareans in an Indian Camp" describes the word *Caesarean* as "highly ambiguous; in addition to being a technical term in surgery, it connotes authority, imperialism, assumption of power, and even tyrannical dictatorship" (92). After introducing this formulation, however, Wolter reverts to the familiar theme of the father-son relationship: "through the unintentionally violent (Caesarean) initiation of his son, the pompous and omniscient Caesar-doctor is reborn as a responsible and humanly imperfect father" (93). Despite this gesture toward metaphoric imperialism, Wolter reiterates the same story of initiation, adding the Caesarean component to complicate our reading of Nick's father. But the "violent" Caesarean is not performed on the doctor's son; it is performed, without anesthetic, on a screaming Indian woman. And while the location of

this story may alleviate a severe condemnation of the doctor and his methods per se, because he saves the life of mother and child in an Indian camp
distant from "civilization" (where, for example, anesthetic would be available) it is precisely the story's location that highlights the racial inequality
between the two cultures with its insistent juxtaposition of light/dark, civi-
lization/wilderness, clean/dirty. Dr. Adams's "Caesarean" assumption of
power implicates both father and son in a violent history with relevance far
beyond the realm of familial bonds. As Hemingway draws the scene, the doctor appears to be the only person who can remain oblivious to the Indian
woman's screams. All others who do not have to assist in the operation have
moved up the road out of earshot. When Nick asks his father to quiet her
screams, he responds: "But her screams are not important. I don't hear them
because they are not important" (16). Some have read this as callousness,
others as professional distance; either way, Dr. Adams psychically distances
himself from the woman to the point that she loses her markers of humanity (this psychical distancing is repeated in Nick's belief that he will never
die). Dr. Adams chooses to envision her body as a territory without agency
or voice, a kind of uninhabited land he takes possession of and must get
under control (what Stephen Greenblatt, in *Marvelous Possessions*, refers to
as "*terrae nullius*"[60]). Once the doctor begins working on the Indian
woman, her pain is so great—"Uncle George and three Indian men held the
woman still" (17)—she bites Uncle George on the arm, resisting, fighting
back. This image echoes a scene from another Hemingway story, "A Way
You'll Never Be," which provides a visual and psychological analogue for the
Indian woman's experience at the hands of Dr. Adams:

> propaganda postcards showing a soldier in Austrian uniform bending
> a woman backward over a bed; the figures were impressionistically
> drawn; very attractively depicted and had nothing in common with
> actual rape in which the woman's skirts are pulled over her head to
> smother her, one comrade sometimes sitting upon the head. (SS
> 402–3)

A woman, reduced to nothing but screams and biting at the men who
held her down, must submit as they perform an act over which she has no
control. Certainly we cannot say that "Indian Camp" here depicts a rape; the
doctor and the men holding this woman down are attempting to deliver a
baby and save the mother's life. But what we can see, and perhaps more
importantly, what the Indian husband sees, is a woman's body as a territory

under complete control of white men.[5] The Indian husband, we must not forget, had endured the most painful part of his wife's suffering, when she had been attended by "all the old women in the camp" (16). His suicide comes later, when the Indian women mysteriously leave the birthing to be replaced by three Indian men, Uncle George, Nick, and Dr. Adams.[6]

When Dr. Adams finishes the operation, he feels "exalted and talkative as football players are in the dressing room after a game" (18).

> "That's one for the medical journal, George," he said. "Doing a Caesarian with a jack-knife and sewing it up with nine-foot, tapered gut leaders." (18)

Uncle George's sarcastic response, "Oh, you're a great man, all right" (18), not only reinforces the insidious connection between Dr. Adams and Caesar ("a great man"), but the doctor's immediate desire to have the operation written down in the medical journals recalls Stephen Greenblatt's research on ways explorers conquered the "new world." In *Marvelous Possessions*, Greenblatt explains that early settlers of the "new world" established themselves and gained property almost exclusively by means of speech acts: "For Columbus taking possession is principally the performance of a set of linguistic acts: declaring, witnessing, recording. The acts are public and official" (57). In addition to the verbal testimony, the speaker would take care that "everything would be written down and consequently have greater authority" (57). These documents would then provide both 'truth' and 'legality' for the procedure, "ensuring that the memory of the encounter is fixed, ensuring that there are not competing versions of what happened" (57). After the Caesarean, Dr. Adams feels "exalted," a word that not only means elated, but also connotes a rise in "status, dignity, power, honor, wealth" (*Webster's New World Dictionary*). He is "talkative," defining and declaring his accomplishment before witnesses. Dr. Adams feels like a "football player in the dressing room after a game," and when we consider football as a sanctioned form of violence between men, the dressing room represents a space where the winning team revels in a victory. Finally, there is Dr. Adams's wish to have this event written down in a medical journal. His medical journals represent an ultimate authority: a removed, consecrated sign of medical, legal, and institutional power, not unlike the proclamations sent back to the crown by Columbus as a form of institutional domination over the colonies.

Greenblatt further points out that Indians were unable to contradict the colonizers' proclamations, "because only linguistic competence, the ability to understand and to speak, would enable one to fill in the sign" (60). "Indian Camp" does not offer a single Indian voice, only the pregnant Indian woman's screams. Elaine Scarry's *The Body in Pain* explains the way extreme physical pain will "bring about an immediate reversion to a state anterior to language, to the sounds and cries a human being makes before language is learned" (4). The Indian woman loses her ability to make sense through language, and she is ultimately rendered altogether senseless: "She did not know what had become of the baby or anything" (18); moreover, when her screams are acknowledged in this story, we find that the men have purposefully devised ways to screen them out. First, we find that the Indian men "moved off up the road . . . out of range of the noise she made" (16), specifically removing to a place where they need not hear her screams. Second, when Nick asks his father to quiet her screams, Dr. Adams instructs his son outright that he does not hear them. Third, as suggested earlier, we cannot definitively assert that even the Indian husband is directly reacting to his wife's screams, because he must know that after enduring them for so much time, they will soon cease. Hemingway's juxtaposition of Dr. Adams's insistent discourse and the woman's pre-literate or illiterate state shows how her body becomes her only identity. Her body literally gets hollowed out in this story; the figurative metaphor of *terrae nullius* has become a reality in the hands of Dr. Adams, much like Greenblatt's description of early settlers and their official claims for territory in the "new world":

> [Y]ou shall make before a notary public and the greatest possible number of witnesses, and the best known ones, an act of possession in our name, cutting trees and boughs, and digging or making, if there be an opportunity, some small building. (56)

Dr. Adams has cut into the woman, like the early settlers leaving a gash in a tree, and her scar will serve as a marker (just as the scaler's mark of "White and McNally" signifies ownership of the logs in the second story). Because "Indian Camp" offers no anesthetic, offers a jack-knife rather than a scalpel, offers biting and screams of pain, the line between healing and violence becomes blurred. "The Doctor and the Doctor's Wife" also carries themes of gendered violence and bodily pain into a racially charged context. The opening scene hints at connections with "Indian Camp," both in the representation of landscape and similarity in themes:

> Dick Boulton came from the *Indian camp* to cut up logs for Nick's father. He brought *his son* Eddy and another Indian named Billy

Tabeshaw with him. They came in through the back gate *out of the woods*, Eddy carrying the long *cross-cut saw* . . . .

He turned and shut the gate. The others went on ahead of him down to *the lake* shore where the logs were buried in the sand. (italics mine, *IOT* 23)

The allusions to "Indian Camp" are impossible to overlook. Again, we have an Indian camp, a father and son pair, a cross-cutting saw, an entry-way, the woods, the lake. Paul Strong's article, "First Nick Adams Stories," offers a clear and startling summary of parallels between the two stories:

"Doc" arrives at the Indian camp with his jack-knife to deliver a baby trapped in its mother's womb; unless he is successful, it will probably die. "Dick" arrives at the Adamses' with cant-hooks to free up logs trapped in the sand; unless he does, the wood will probably rot. "Doc" heats water, washes his hands, delivers the baby and announces its identity—"it's a boy." Eddie and Billy Tabeshaw deliver a log, wash it, and "Dick" determines its identity—"It belongs to White and McNally." The Caesarean ends with "Doc" "sewing it up"; because of the set-to, "Dick" never does "saw it up." (86)

"The Doctor and the Doctor's Wife" almost serves as a reply to the doctor's Caesarean hubris in "Indian Camp," for here the roles between the white man and the Indian have reversed. In this story, the doctor now needs the Indian men to help him dislodge the logs and saw them up. Here one Indian speaks—has the last word, in fact—while the doctor is silenced, though the Indians "could see from his back how angry he was" (25). Dr. Adams's verbal threat, "If you call me Doc once again, I'll knock your eye teeth down your throat," is returned with "Oh, no, you won't, Doc" (25). Not only does Dick Boulton make the doctor back down, but he uses Ojibway, a language unfamiliar to Dr. Adams, to mock him. This scene presents an utter reversal of power relations, where the dominant language, or, the language of dominance, has lost its force. The threat of violence centers on the half-buried logs that lie along the lake's shore. One is reminded again of Kolodny's work, which shows a clear link between the land (virgin woods) and the female body as a primary site of contestation. Dick Boulton, described as a "half-breed," dares to accuse Dr. Adams of stealing the logs.

"Well, Doc," he said, "that's a nice lot of timber you've stolen."
"Don't talk that way, Dick," the doctor said. "It's driftwood." (24)

Dr. Adams chooses to re-name the wood, altering its status from "timber" which entails value and ownership, to "driftwood," implying a freedom from the rules of legal possession. Dick counters this with a kind of textual evidence, the ultimate source of "truth" and "legality."

> "Wash it off. Clean off the sand on account of the saw. I want to see who it belongs to," Dick said.
> The log was just awash in the lake. Eddy and Billy Tabeshaw leaned on their cant-hooks sweating in the sun. Dick kneeled down in the sand and looked at the mark of the scaler's hammer in the wood at the end of the log.
> "It belongs to White and McNally," he said, standing up and brushing off his trousers' knees.
> The doctor was very uncomfortable. (24)

Just as the doctor's mark was left on the Indian woman's body and could later be further consecrated in the medical journals, the log in this scene bears the mark of its possessor—White and McNally. The symbolic value of the name, White, should not be lost in our reading. Thomas Strychacz's article "Dramatizations of Manhood in Hemingway's *In Our Time* and *The Sun Also Rises*" offers a useful reading of the scene's significance:

> The mark of the scaler's hammer in the log shows that it belongs to "White" and McNally. In the same way, the fence around the white doctor's garden marks the extent of his domain in the forest, the Indian's traditional space, from which the three Indians appear and into which they disappear. The recognition that the land is stolen as well as the logs deepens the significance of the doctor's shame—it becomes his culture's shame too—and begins to explain why he fails to protect the integrity of his space. The doctor has no ground to stand on because the ground is, morally speaking, not his; the fence around the garden is as morally indefensible as stealing the logs. (250)

Thus Dick Boulton uses a "textual" reference, the institutional imprint of a company's legal right, to support his shaming attack on Dr. Adams, and if we think back to "Indian Camp," Dick's success should not take us by surprise. When Dr. Adams wished to applaud his achievement in performing the Caesarean section under such primitive conditions, he immediately exclaimed that the procedure would be "one for the medical journal" (18). So when Dick Boulton refers to the text for *his* authority, the doctor can only back down. This may also explain the doctor's subsequent irritation when he re-enters the cottage: "In the cottage the doctor, sitting on the bed in his room, saw a pile of medical journals on the floor by the bureau. They were still in their wrappers unopened. It irritated him" (25). These same journals had once been the textual representation and affirmation of his great power, but in this scene they lie on the floor, unread, impotent and useless to him.

The "Big Man" dynamic described earlier is also reversed here. In "Indian Camp," Uncle George distributes cigars, a gift that does not get reciprocated; but in "The Doctor and the Doctor's Wife," when the confrontation begins, we find that "Dick was a big man. He knew how big a man he was" (24). The previously sanctioned forms of competition and rivalry have at last given way to overt threats and potential violence. For if we read these two stories as a unit, then the progression of violence from "Indian Camp" to "The Doctor and the Doctor's Wife" moves from the obscured to the overt; "Doc" sits on his bed cleaning a shotgun: "he pushed the magazine full of the heavy yellow shells and pumped them out again. They were scattered on the bed" (26). Strychacz has pointed out that "the rifle . . . signifies the technological superiority that hastened the appropriation of the Indian lands" ("Trophy-Hunting" 36). More obviously, we can easily decode the sexual metaphor of shells pumped through a shaft and then left scattered on the bed, wasted and impotent. The scene where violent, sexual, and racial markers all coincide most completely is during the climactic confrontation between "Dick" and "Doc":

> "If you think the logs are stolen, leave them alone and take your tools back to the camp," the doctor said. His face was red.
> "Don't go off at half-cock, Doc," Dick said. (24)

This scene contains not only a sexual, but also a racial metaphor that finally dislodges the most stubborn racial marker of all—skin color. During the confrontation, the doctor's face, presumably because of his embarrassment and anger, has turned red. A fight, ostensibly between Dick, the Indian, and Doc, the white man, must also be read in reverse: as a confrontation between Dick, "many of the farmers around the lake really believed he was a *white* man," and Doc, whose "face was *red*" (italics mine, 24). A climactic scene between the "great man" and the "big man" forces social relations into the realm of violence, at once exposing and challenging the artificiality of power relations based on essentialist notions of racial difference, like those presented in "Indian Camp." Here, in the second story, the racial markers continually shift, and we in turn must shift our perceptions of race in Hemingway's stories.

Borrowing from Michael Omi and Howard Winant, I would suggest that Hemingway's stories represent race as an "unstable and 'decentered' complex of social meanings constantly being transformed by political struggle" (55). "Indian Camp" does present a biologically based view of racial difference and implies almost unwavering success for power relations that rely on white male dominance. The only crack in the veneer comes with Uncle George's sarcasm, which deflates Dr. Adams's self-aggrandizement, but George's remark loses its force in the wake of Nick's final musing that he will never die. Returning once again to Nick's final words in "Indian Camp," George Monteiro has suggested that the words reflect a belief he will never die "that way" (155), as the Indian has died. This reading again foregrounds Nick's extreme psychical distancing between self and other, a pattern of distancing he learned from his father, to whom the woman's screams are "not important." But "The Doctor and the Doctor's Wife" seriously complicates Nick's hyper-essentialist notion (that we are so different, even the ultimate leveler of humanity—death—divides the races). Dick defies racial categorization, co-opts forms of literacy valued by Dr. Adams, challenges him based on the law, and therefore reverses the power relations based in an authority ordinarily accessible only to whites. All of this simultaneously highlights the social constructedness of racial difference, undoing the hierarchy of power in "Indian Camp," and creating overt parallels between Dick/Doc, and to some extent between Dr. Adams and the Indian husband.

The brief interchange in the cottage between Dr. Adams and his nameless wife serves as yet another reference to the doctor's earlier authority in "Indian Camp":

> "Remember, that he who ruleth his spirit is greater than he that taketh a city," said his wife. She was a Christian Scientist. Her Bible, her copy of *Science and Health* and her *Quarterly* were on a table beside her bed in the darkened room. (25–26)

The depiction of the doctor's wife, in pain, lying in a room described twice as "darkened" and twice as "with the blinds drawn," may at first seem to present another helpless, colonized woman, whose nameless identity stems from her role as wife and mother. But her religion relies on divine law in times of

sickness, disregarding medical means of healing. Almost a direct attack on
the value of medical journals, her textual authority comes in the form of a
Bible, *Science and Health*, and the *Quarterly*, books entirely devoted to a faith
which "denies the necessity of [Dr. Adams's] professional function" (DeFalco
165). Furthermore, her quote from scripture draws a stark contrast between
the Caesar-doctor of "Indian Camp" ("he that taketh a city") and the
diminutive "Doc" who turns his back on a petty fight ("he who ruleth his
spirit"); the husband's power is productive here only when directed inward.
Of course, this form of power is the only kind afforded to the Indian husband as well.

As Dana Nelson has written, drawing on Foucault, "it is wrong to see
power as only oppressive. It can be productive and progressive—both by the
intentions of those who exercise it, and unintentionally, in the gaps left by its
constant failure to create a total, seamless system" (xii). For power to be total,
or invulnerable, the object of that power would have to remain static and
silent. While "Indian Camp" gives the impression of total domination, the
seams begin to show even within that story (Uncle George's sarcasm, the
Indian woman's biting back, Nick's tenuous immunity from death). In the
second story, "The Doctor and the Doctor's Wife," the forms of domination
in the first story come back to be co-opted and reinscribed by Dick, a man
whose racial markings will not hold. The non-speaking have become bilin-
gual; those without access to institutionalized literacy now rely on legal fine
print; the woman's body has been colonized by a higher power; the doctor
cannot control even the color of his skin. The conflict between Dick and Dr.
Adams becomes an almost entirely discursive one, implying yet again that
power relations depend on the social or cultural construction of "race," a
construction that must remain variable, in flux. But Hemingway's stories do
not allow such a simplified resolution, and if we take up Joyce A. Joyce's
charge that to deconstruct race is to diminish or negate black identity (341),
we cut to the heart of my interest in these two stories as a unit, because
Hemingway does not deny the essentialist notion that some kind of inherent
racial identity remains lodged in the body. The jack-knife cuts a woman's
womb open, the razor slits a man's throat from ear to ear. These bodies are
real; pain has marked them.

Without denying the corporeal reality of lived racial experience, these stories also demonstrate that individuals can slide back and forth between the
larger categories of race. In the first story, racial essentialism comes from the
fact that characters are clearly defined as white or Indian, and their roles do

not shift or change in any way. White dominates and the Indian remains silent, passive, and under control of the whites. The only hint of role reversal comes when the Indian woman bites Uncle George's arm and the other Indian laughs at him, conscious of the incongruity and unexpectedness of her act. This laugh, however, is translated in the second story into outright mockery. The roles have been reversed, but in order to represent this, Hemingway actually has his characters' faces change color—to be humiliated is to be red and to be victor is to be white. In this scenario, then, the tag "race" remains stable, because "white" equates with power and "red" equates with submission, but the individuals move fluidly between these markers.

In an interview with George Plimpton in the *Paris Review*, Hemingway spoke of a writer's "unexplained knowledge which could come from *forgotten racial or family experience*" (italics mine, 85). His stories may have been spurred by an autobiographical "family experience," but we cannot ignore their relation to a larger "forgotten racial experience" in American history. What happens in the confrontation between Dick and Doc represents nothing less than a crisis of authority that betrays the unstable foundation upon which the white man has built his power. When relying on the institutional authority of the medical profession, Dr. Adams works on stable ground. But in the second story, his power rests on the speech act, a threat, and Dick derails its authority with the simple but devastating retort, "Oh, no, you won't." The beauty of this reply is that it not only offers an implicit counterthreat, but it exposes the creaky machinery behind the doctor's earlier dominance. Stripped of institutional authority, textual authority, or witnesses, the doctor's standard mechanisms of power are laid bare: without complicity, power cannot be effective. And this brings us full circle, because that, I believe, is the moral of Toni Morrison's story as well. The "more or less tacit agreement among literary scholars" (5) requires a complicity that, despite its hold on our literary imagination, can be controverted.

Notes

1. The term is taken from Judith Butler's *Gender Trouble: Feminism and the Subversion of Identity*. For readings that explore the instability of gender categories, see J. Gerald Kennedy, "Hemingway's Gender Trouble"; Debra Moddelmog, "Reconstructing Hemingway's Identity: Sexual Politics, the Author, and the Multicultural Classroom"; Mark Spilka, *Hemingway's Quarrel with Androgyny;* and Nancy R. Comley and Robert Scholes, *Hemingway's Genders: Rereading the Hemingway Text.*

2. Diana Fuss outlines the parameters of this debate in *Essentially Speaking: Feminism, Nature and Difference*. Chapter Six, "'Race' Under Erasure? Poststructuralist Afro-American Literary Theory," specifically focuses on the category of race, questioning whether racial identity can be seen as *either* a "question of morphology, of anatomical *or* genetic characteristics" or as a "psychological, historical, anthropological, sociological, legal" construct. Fuss argues that the essentialist/constructionist opposition is "largely artificial" because the two categories depend on each other for meaning, and we will see that Hemingway's stories sustain exactly this tension between the two categories in a way that destabilizes our grasp of racial identity.

3. See R. W. B. Lewis, *The American Adam*, for "the first tentative outlines of a native American mythology," covering the period between 1820 and 1860, where "Adamic imagery is altogether central and controlling." By "native American," Lewis does not refer to Indians; on the contrary, he refers to the "birth in America of a clear conscience unsullied by the past."

4. I am indebted to readings by Paul Smith, *A Reader's Guide to the Short Stories of Ernest Hemingway*, Joseph M. Flora's *Hemingway's Nick Adams*, Philip Young's *Ernest Hemingway: A Reconsideration*, and Joseph DeFalco's *The Hero in Hemingway's Short Stories*. Young highlights "Nick's initiation to pain, and to the violence of birth and death" in "Indian Camp," while "The Doctor and the Doctor's Wife" "teaches Nick something about the solidarity of the male sex"; Joseph DeFalco asserts that "the major focus of ['Indian Camp'] is Nick's reaction to these events," and "the central conflict that emerges [in "The Doctor and the Doctor's Wife"] reveals a further step in the learning process that Nick undergoes."

5. See Annette Kolodny's *The Lay of the Land: Metaphor as Experience and History in American Life and Letters*. Kolodny outlines the American metaphor of "the land as woman" and its attendant imagery of "eroticism, penetration, raping, embrace, enclosure, and nurture, to cite only a few."

6. Laurel Thatcher Ulrich's *A Midwife's Tale* explains that traditionally, childbirth had three distinct stages, "defined in social rather than biological terms, each marked by the summons and arrival of attendants—first, the midwife, then the neighborhood circle of women, finally the afternurse." Ulrich's work outlines how the growth of medical societies and "changing notions of womanhood" in the nineteenth century gradually allowed physicians, as a professionalized and exclusive group, to replace midwives. In this historical context, for all the women in "Indian Camp" to be replaced by the men (with the exception of the afternurse who should arrive the next day) offers an interesting symbolic representation of the way that a female-dominated craft lost its power to the more advanced, institutionalized (male-dominated) medical profession.

Works Cited

Butler, Judith. *Gender Trouble: Feminism and the Subversion of Identity.* New York: Routledge, 1990.

Comley, Nancy C., and Robert Scholes. *Hemingway's Genders: Rereading the Hemingway Text.* New Haven: Yale UP, 1994.

DeFalco, Joseph. *The Hero in Hemingway's Short Stories.* Pittsburgh: U of Pittsburgh P, 1963.

———. "Initiation ("Indian Camp" and "The Doctor and the Doctor's Wife")," *The Short Stories of Ernest Hemingway: Critical Essays.* Ed. Jackson J. Benson, Durham, NC: Duke UP, 1975. 159–67.

Flora, Joseph M. *Hemingway's Nick Adams.* Baton Rouge: Louisiana State UP, 1982.

Fuss, Diana. *Essentially Speaking: Feminism, Nature and Difference.* New York: Routledge, 1989.

Greenblatt, Stephen. *Marvelous Possessions: The Wonder of the New World.* Chicago: U of Chicago P, 1991.

Hemingway, Ernest. "The Art of Fiction XXI: Ernest Hemingway." *Paris Review* 18 (1958): 61–89.

———. "The Doctor and the Doctor's Wife." *In Our Time.* 1925, 1930. New York: Scribner's, 1958. 23–27.

———. "Indian Camp." *In Our Time.* 1925, 1930. New York: Scribner's, 1958. 15–19.

———. "A Way You'll Never Be." *The Short Stories of Ernest Hemingway.* 1938. New York: Scribner's, 1966. 402–14.

Joyce, Joyce A. "The Black Canon: Reconstructing Black American Literary Criticism." *New Literary History* 18 (1987): 335–44.

Kennedy, J. Gerald. "Hemingway's Gender Trouble." *American Literature* 63:2 (1991): 187–207.

Kolodny, Annette. *The Lay of the Land: Metaphor as Experience and History in American Life and Letters.* Chapel Hill: U of North Carolina P, 1975.

Lewis, R. W. B. *The American Adam: Innocence, Tragedy, and Tradition in the Nineteenth Century.* Chicago: U of Chicago P, 1955.

Moddelmog, Debra. "Reconstructing Hemingway's Identity: Sexual Politics, the Author, and the Multicultural Classroom." *Narrative* 1:3 (October 1993): 187–206.

Monteiro, George. "The Limits of Professionalism: A Sociological Approach to Faulkner, Fitzgerald and Hemingway." *Criticism* 15 (Spring 1973): 145–55.

Morrison, Toni. *Playing in the Dark: Whiteness and the Literary Imagination.* New York: Vintage, 1992.

Nelson, Dana. *The Word in Black and White: Reading 'Race' in American Literature, 1638–1867.* Oxford: Oxford UP, 1992.

Omi, Michael, and Howard Winant. *Racial Formation in the United States from the 1960s to the 1980s.* New York: Routledge, 1994.

Rubin, Gayle. "The Traffic in Women: Notes on the 'Political Economy' of Sex." *Toward an Anthropology of Women.* Ed. Rayna B. Reiter. New York: Monthly Review, 1975. 157–210.

Scarry, Elaine. *The Body in Pain: The Making and Unmaking of the World.* New York: Oxford UP, 1985.

Smith, Paul. *A Reader's Guide to the Short Stories of Ernest Hemingway.* Boston: G. K. Hall, 1989.

Spilka, Mark. *Hemingway's Quarrel with Androgyny.* Lincoln: U of Nebraska P, 1990.

Strong, Paul. "The First Nick Adams Stories." *Studies in Short Fiction* 28:1 (Winter 1991): 83–91.

Strychacz, Thomas. "Dramatizations of Manhood in Hemingway's *In Our Time* and *The Sun Also Rises.*" *American Literature* 61:2 (May 1989): 245–60.

———. "Trophy-Hunting as a Trope of Manhood in Ernest Hemingway's *Green Hills of Africa.*" *The Hemingway Review* 13:1 (Fall 1993): 36–47.

Tanselle, G. Thomas. "Hemingway's Indian Camp." *Explicator* 20 (February 1962): Item 53.

Thatcher Ulrich, Laurel. *A Midwife's Tale: The Life of Martha Ballard, Based on Her Diary, 1785–1812.* New York: Knopf, 1990.

Wolter, Jürgen C. "Caesareans in an Indian Camp." *The Hemingway Review* 13:1 (Fall 1993): 92–94.

Young, Philip. *Ernest Hemingway: A Reconsideration.* University Park: Pennsylvania State UP, 1966.

DRAMATIZATIONS OF MANHOOD IN HEMINGWAY'S *IN OUR TIME* AND *THE SUN ALSO RISES*

Thomas Strychacz

In the bullring, men are made or unmanned. The "kid," in the first bullfight vignette of Ernest Hemingway's *In Our Time*, submits to the code of the ring and, by killing five times, reaches his majority. Then, remarks the narrator, "He sat down in the sand and puked and they held a cape over him."[1] Such modest concealment does not satisfy the delighted crowd, which "hollered and threw things down into the bull ring," recognizing that this kid has "finally made it," in this moment, to manhood. Villalta, the matador at the height of his powers, plays to the crowd more deliberately. His killing becomes a test of intense watching as he "sighted" the bull along the sword blade and the bull "look[ed] at him straight in front, hating." With Villalta's life and manhood on the line, the crowd watches and roars with every pass of the muleta. The vignette refers repeatedly to the bullfight's quality of spectacle. "If it happened right down close in front of you, you could see Villalta

Reprinted with permission from American Literature *(May 1989), pp. 245–260.*

snarl at the bull and curse him," begins the narrator: the observer becomes "you" the reader, and Villalta the cynosure of all eyes. At the end, Villalta's "hand up at the crowd" announces the successful completion of this ritual of manhood—and acknowledges its essentially theatrical nature.

The physical characteristics of the ring shape the rituals enacted there, providing necessary boundaries within which potentially chaotic action may reveal a comprehensible structure. The presence of the audience, in particular, is crucial for the transformation of space into arena. Acting as an agent of legitimation for ritual gestures made in the ring, the audience assimilates all action to performance and invests performance with value. Part of the audience's function is to appraise rituals of manhood and bestow praise or condemnation on the protagonist. But such moments of evaluatory watching are not confined to bullrings: they pervade *In Our Time* and *The Sun Also Rises*. An audience may comprise only one other person, or even the protagonist watching himself. Many symbolic spaces in this early work—houses and hotels, bedrooms, camps and clearings—take on the characteristics of a ceremonial arena.[2] By the same token, the kid and Villalta are just two of many characters whose potency as men depends on their ability to transfigure space into spectacle.

Hemingway's biographers and critics have never doubted that his obsessions with male authority shaped both his writing career and life. An "incorrigible attention-getter and impresario of his need to be situated always centre-stage,"[3] Hemingway has been seen by defenders and detractors alike as the quintessential *macho* writer. Interestingly, feminist critics have accepted paradigms formulated decades ago by male critics, even though their conclusions differ radically. Earl Rovit, for instance, claimed that Hemingway "prized the adamant separateness" of the "isolate self," and Rovit's work on codes of masculine behavior, of which the bullfighter's heroism is part, has become standard in the field.[4] Feminist writers such as Judith Fetterley argue that Hemingway, locked into infantile and destructive male fantasies of the tough, autonomous male, succeeds only in creating an easily-parodied male posturing.[5] Few critics, though, have seen in Hemingway's early works the extent to which the act of performance before an audience constitutes male identity, and even fewer have considered the troubling implications of this. Arising out of an audience's empowering acts of watching, a protagonist's sense of self rests precariously upon the audience's decision to validate or reject his ritual gestures toward manhood. Mastery of the arena bestows power on him, failure invites humiliation: in either case the process implies a loss of authority to the audience. Performances of manhood imply a radical lack of self that must be constantly filled and refashioned "while the crowd hollered" (p. 83).

In stories like "Indian Camp," "The Doctor and the Doctor's Wife," and "The Battler," Hemingway explores the ways characters watch each other, exhibit their potency, and—more often—reveal their shame. "Big Two-Hearted River" becomes Hemingway's most remarkable effort in *In Our Time* to resolve his doubts about self-dramatization. The deliberate separation of action from ritual exhibition in the story contributes to its uniqueness—yet it becomes a dead-end for Hemingway. In *The Sun Also Rises*, the return to a near-obsession with the psychology of self-display and humiliation highlights the limitations of Nick Adams' solution in "Big Two-Hearted River." In none of these stories does Hemingway celebrate a set of merely stereotypical *macho* values. On the contrary, his exploration of male display challenges precisely the kind of formulations about his myth of the autonomous male that have become customary.

I

Images of doorways recur throughout "Indian Camp," linking the cabin metaphorically to the womb. But the entrance of Nick's father quickly transforms womb-space into a male arena and associates the baby's struggle to be born with other barely repressed racial and sexual conflicts. The cabin stages a series of cultural and sexual overthrows, in which male midwives (three whites and three Indians) supplant the traditional roles of the "old women" (p. 16) of the camp and in which the white doctor supplants the cultural and parental authority of the Indian father. "Indian Camp" concerns a struggle for male authority which Nick's father tries to achieve by directing the visual dynamics of a space transformed from shanty/womb to operating theater.

The three white characters transgress what has traditionally been an intimate female space. The doctor has been called only after customary procedures of birth, which tacitly preclude the presence of men, fail: "She had been trying to have her baby for two days. All the old women in the camp had been helping her." While this situation allows the doctor to demonstrate his skill, sharing his wife's experience of birth appears to have degraded the Indian father. After all, "The men" (not "the *other* men") of the camp have "moved off up the road to sit in the dark and smoke out of range of the noise she made." In a futile attempt to follow the appropriate male role, the Indian father is also smoking and will soon bury his head in blankets to summon his own darkness.

Already displaced from the authority of the other men's position "off up the road," the Indian father bears unwilling witness while the white doctor dramatizes his superior medical skills. Critics have defended Nick's father on the basis of his pragmatic handling of the operation, but the real point is that he constantly dramatizes his pragmatism, especially before the eyes of his son, whom he insistently invites to watch: "You see, Nick, babies are supposed to be born head first," "See it's a boy," "You can watch this or not, Nick," "Ought to have a look at the proud father" (pp. 17–18). The doctor plays out the fantasy of being both director and star actor in his own operating theater, to the point of imagining critical appraisals of his performance: "That's one for the medical journal." Clearly, the doctor's goal is less to initiate his son into the mysteries of birth than to draw attention to his skillful manipulation of those mysteries.

As if to underscore the doctor's transgressive role, Hemingway introduces the image of the football player to describe the doctor, who concludes the operation "feeling exalted and talkative as football players are in the dressing room after a game." The image of the football game is oddly appropriate for the conflicts in the cabin. Like the bullring, the football arena functions as a ceremonial space in which particular rules of conduct govern violent action; in both cases the importance of the display increases proportionately as it is watched. Throughout the operation, the doctor more or less consciously plays quarterback, controlling the field of play with his vision and expertise. Here, his son, the other "midwives," and (potentially) the reader of some future medical journal act as audience.

The Indian father, in contrast, actively shuns the audience that could witness his degradation; his vision is blocked by the wall he rolls over against and the blanket that covers his head. But this self-willed blindness has complex consequences. The refusal to be seen signifies his humiliation, but it is a refusal that also frees him from watching the doctor's performance. The doctor's subsequent move, as he "mounted on the edge of the lower bunk with the lamp in one hand and looked in" at the dead man, demonstrates the paradoxical efficacy of the Indian's action. In the context of the doctor's earlier self-display, holding the lamp suggests his attempt to force the "proud father" to acknowledge his own pride in his skill. Actually, the Indian father's ritual suicide forces the doctor into the role of observer and, even more telling, distracts Nick's attention from his father: Nick "had a good view of the upper bunk when his father, the lamp in one hand, tipped the Indian's head back." From Nick's point of view, his father has become the lamp-bearer to illuminate the Indian's final self-dramatization. Following this tableau, the doctor quickly loses his "post-operative exhilaration." On the doctor's arrival, after all, the role of watcher and lamp-bearer was played by an "old woman."

The doctor's authority, in other words, is not absolute; it grows—and diminishes—with his precarious ability to play to an audience. The next story in *In Our Time*, "The Doctor and the Doctor's Wife," essentially replays this drama of power and humiliation while reversing the dramatic structure of "Indian Camp": three Indians are invited into the doctor's garden. His garden, cleared from the surrounding forest and fenced-in (as the presence of gates attests), showcases the psychological battle between him and Dick Boulton. The garden becomes a highly charged symbolic space in which he and the three Indians enact a drama of great significance for their authority as men.

Like "Indian Camp," this story describes the wielding of personal power against a backdrop of cultural conflict. The quarrel over the stolen logs, to begin with, disguises the fact that the garden (like the logs) has been expropriated from the Indians in a centuries-old land-grab. The mark of the scaler's hammer in the log shows that it belongs to "White" and McNally. In the same way, the fence around the white doctor's garden marks the extent of his domain in the forest, the Indian's traditional space, from which the three Indians appear and into which they disappear. The recognition that the land is stolen as well as the logs deepens the significance of the doctor's shame—it becomes his culture's shame too—and begins to explain why he fails to protect the integrity of his space. The doctor has no ground to stand on because the ground is, morally speaking, not his; the fence around the garden is as morally indefensible as stealing the logs.

Playing quarterback/surgeon in "Indian Camp," the doctor transformed the Indian's cabin into a metaphoric arena; Boulton, conversely, threatens to turn the doctor's space into a real arena (a boxing ring) that will display physical strength rather than scientific knowledge. Appropriately, Hemingway emphasizes the relationship between audience and the (potential) protagonists: "Dick Boulton looked at the doctor," Eddy and Billy Tabeshaw "looked at the doctor," "They could see from his back how angry he was," "They all watched him walk up the hill and go inside the cottage." Although the doctor reciprocates in kind (he "looked at Dick Boulton"), he sees only Boulton's conviction of superiority: "He knew how big a man he was." The paradoxical nature of evaluatory observation is evident here, for whereas an audience empowered the doctor in the Indian's cabin, here it lays bare his inadequacy. Shamed by his ignominious retreat, the doctor withdraws (like the Indian father in "Indian Camp") from the gaze of spectators, leaving the garden/ring in their possession. Boulton, in fact, has re-appropriated the space for a drama of his own devising, in which he has convincingly upstaged the doctor and dispossessed him of his manhood.

These first two stories of *In Our Time* explore male authority in ways that seriously question its nature and value. The doctor's tendency toward almost pathological self-display, the Indian father's suicidal drama, even Boulton's tough assurance, all begin to dispel the myth of the autonomous male. Boulton above all should give us pause, for his identity is nothing but his role as "big man," fabricated out of his consummate acting before an audience. He differs from the doctor in his ability to play a tough male role, not because of any greater inner worth.

At the end of the first section of the Nick Adams stories, "The Battler," which features an avatar of Nick's father in Ad Francis, links together many of the functions of the symbolic arena registered so far and suggests new perspectives on the role of men within it. Before reaching the clearing where he will find Francis, Nick has already intimated that correlation between evaluatory watching and male identity. Touching his black eye, Nick, rather mysteriously, "wished he could see it," and then apparently tries to see his reflection: "Could not see it looking into the water, though" (p. 53). While berating himself for his immaturity, he nonetheless prizes his black eye as one sign of his initiation into manhood: "That was all he had gotten out of it. Cheap at the price." In lieu of the hollering crowd at the bull fight in chapter 9, Nick, another "kid," tries to become the audience to the spectacle of his own maturation.

The ensuing scene bears out that correspondence between manhood and performance. Nick enters the firelit clearing to find Francis using him as audience to Francis' exhibition of toughness. Francis constantly refers to the importance of visible wounds as an index of toughness, acknowledging, for instance, Nick's black eye with his first words ("Where did you get the shiner?") before going on to dramatize his own battered face: "Look here!" and "Ever see one like that?" The echoes of the doctor's comments to Nick in "Indian Camp" are telling, for both insistently draw attention to the iconography of their professions. The doctor's surgical skill warranted the attention of the other "midwives"; and Francis' "pain," manifesting his performances in the ring, signifies his indomitable courage: "I could take it," "They couldn't hurt me."

Francis' delight in displaying his battered face provides a key to his behavior during the rest of the story. For his failure to get Nick's knife destroys his self-image, carefully maintained before Nick, of the heroic prizefighter. Like the doctor, transformed from medical marvel to lamp-bearer in "Indian Camp," Francis becomes the frustrated but passive observer: "The little white man looked at Nick," "He was looking at Nick" (repeated twice), "Ad kept on looking at Nick," "He glared at Nick." Such manic staring suggests Francis' humiliation; it also suggests the root of his humiliation. For Francis, more than anyone else in the Nick Adams stories, has been battered in the public eye: first in the ring, where "he took too many beatings," and then in the papers, because his wife "Looked enough like him to be twins." Like the matador who admits "I am not really a good bull fighter" (p. 95), Francis' humiliation has grown because of the crowds that witness it. His compensatory solution in the clearing is to recall the scene of his most successful dramatizations of physical prowess: the boxing ring. Thus he does not swing wildly at Nick but adopts the stance of the trained boxer, stepping "flat-footed forward." But the battler's attempt at self-dramatization merely parodies his earlier ability to dominate arenas as he falls unconscious in the most dishonorable way possible—being hit from behind.

Nothing is easier than to see Francis as an archetypal Hemingway hero, beaten but never quite down. In fact, Hemingway confronts in "The Battler" a central dilemma about male identity, which is not Francis' failure but the fact that a successful shaping of manhood is predicated on being acknowledged by an audience. Male identity, this story suggests, is constituted by performance, and when performance no longer serves, identity suffers. Nick knows Francis "by name as a former champion fighter," and the narrator, at the moment when Nick refused him the knife, calls him the "prizefighter"; Francis has become commensurate with his role, existing as a name, a memory, a set of remembered movements enacted for others. Clubbed in an ugly parody of a boxing match, he fails to perform the expected role and falls unconscious—indicative of his profound absence of self.

The story of Nick's expedition to the Two-Hearted River is perhaps Hemingway's most remarkable attempt in *In Our Time* to attain a new vision of manhood. For the first time the protagonist stands alone, a strategy that divorces ritual gestures from their performance function. Indeed,

Hemingway flaunts the lack of a watching crowd as Nick arrives in Seney to find, unexpectedly, that "There was no town" (p. 133). And unlike the Nick of "The Battler," he does not attempt to play audience to his own posturing. At the beginning of "The Battler" Nick tries (unsuccessfully) to see his "shiner" in the water; at the beginning of "Big Two-Hearted River," Nick looks *through* the surface of the water to the trout beneath. Compared to Krebs, who "lost everything" (p. 70) because he was unable to stage his war experiences before other men, Nick's refusal to dramatize his injuries, even to himself, is astonishing.

"Big Two-Hearted River" constructs symbolic arenas in ways that recall earlier stories but recasts them in a different mode. The "good place" (p. 139) of Nick's tent, for instance, is the culmination of a series of references to symbolic arenas in *In Our Time*: the cabin of "Indian Camp" and, more distantly, his actual home (the cottage) in "The Doctor and the Doctor's Wife."[6] Yet this tent differs importantly from all of them in that it witnesses no exhibition of manhood. As Joseph M. Flora has remarked, the story is in one sense Nick's account of Genesis: nothing suggests that more than his Adamic ability to move into a space devoid of the audience that has, in the stories of *In Our Time*, customarily watched and celebrated tough male roles.[7] If anything, Hemingway emphasizes Nick's cultivation of a traditionally female role as he organizes and tends his "homelike" space.

Nick's distinction in "Big Two-Hearted River" is to act within a space of his own making. While Hemingway describes setting up camp and fishing realistically, the meticulous detailing of that process draws attention to the uniqueness of this space, lacking both prior structure and preexisting codes of behavior. Because this space never becomes an arena, "Big Two-Hearted River" at least postulates the existence of an autonomous male identity, fashioned without an empowering audience. In this respect, isolation appears to become a virtue. After all, "crowded streams" (p. 149) to Nick denote botched rituals: dead, furred trout in the rivers, the consequence of inexpert fishermen, whom Nick, alone, may refuse to emulate. And Nick's bitter coffee at the end of Part I evokes memories of the fishing trip to the Black River, where Hopkins' sudden wealth promotes invidious distinctions between the companions. What "broke up the trip" (p. 141) is not Hopkins' leaving but the conspicuous display of gift-giving that accompanies it.

When alone, Nick can evade the destructive competitiveness that characterizes these "crowded streams." But his isolation leads back, by a new route, to the same dilemma that haunted "The Battler." Francis' desperate attempts to dramatize himself disguised an empty self. The question arises in "Big Two-Hearted River" whether Nick's deliberate refusal to dramatize his ritual actions can be potent. Contextually, his actions do take on significance: cleaning the two trout recalls the Caesarian of "Indian Camp," yet the results of Nick's incisions, "clean and compact," are far removed from the blood and terror of the Indian's cabin. Dramatically and psychologically, however, the value of such restorative rituals is less obvious. The story records an odd displacement in which the act of seeing constantly effaces identity, a process that is not obvious until, at a moment of profound shock, the "I" irrupts into the text: "By God, he was the biggest one I ever heard of" (p. 151). At every other point Nick becomes little other than a recording consciousness, carefully choking off thoughts and memories that would force him to become aware of himself. The consequence is that Nick always stands center stage yet is never dramatically visible at all.

Critics have tended to view this displacement as a psychologically necessary strategy for healing Nick's war-fragmented self and have argued about whether his final promise to "fish the swamp" signifies the completion of that process. In the light of Hemingway's larger concern with evaluatory watching, it becomes clear that such analyses have inverted the meaning of Nick's actions. Significant as those actions are on an anagogical level, they cannot fashion a self because Nick constantly defers the self-awareness that would make them psychologically potent. Nick, as Peter Schwenger puts it, has "no way to deal with the emotion . . . except by the very strategies of detachment which threaten him."[8] While the absence of audience removes the need for the puerile self-display of "The Battler," that same absence makes impossible the completion of self. In story after story of *In Our Time*, Hemingway has demonstrated (however ironically) that manhood corresponds with being seen as a man, and "Big Two-Hearted River" does not essentially deny that thesis. In successfully avoiding "crowded streams," Nick also erases all opportunity for the self-dramatization that empowered characters like the "kid" and Villalta. Whatever therapeutic actions Nick generates from his experience on the river can only be partial gestures toward a manhood whose completion depends on the legitimating function of an audience.

II

The separation of ritual gesture from dramatization in "Big Two-Hearted River" resolves little for Hemingway. If Nick comports himself as a man at the sacred river, no one—scarcely even Nick himself—is there to acknowledge and validate his manhood. As another observer-figure at places of ritual, Jake Barnes shares with Nick the displacement of self into seeing. H. R. Stoneback has argued persuasively that in *The Sun Also Rises* "Hemingway is one of the great cartographers of the *deus loci*."[9] Yet if Jake's pilgrimage to sacred places wins spiritual peace, his psychological travail in the arenas where men demonstrate their potency is painful indeed. In particular, the key scenes where Pedro Romero performs in the bull ring before the eyes of Brett and Jake force a complete reconsideration of the usual claims about the moral, mythic, or spiritual significance of the ritual encounter, and about the psychic renewal Jake gains from it.

Watching Romero typifies Jake's role in this novel, which is firmly established as that of observer and sometimes seer. "I have a rotten habit of picturing the bedroom scenes of my friends," remarks Jake in the second chapter.[10] His impotence has transformed his friends' acts into theater and himself into director: his visionary ability appears to be at once a product of and compensation for his inability to participate in his own bedroom scenes.[11] In another sense, Jake's "rotten habit" corresponds to that passionate witnessing which is his afición. They "saw that I had afición" (p. 132), claims Jake of Montoya's friends, as if afición is a matter of seeing true rather than of interrogation. Several other characters comment on Jake's perceptiveness. Romero remarks: "I like it very much that you like my work. . . . But you haven't seen it yet. To-morrow, if I get a good bull, I will try and show it to you" (p. 174). And when Jake advises Montoya (to the hotel keeper's pleasure) not to give Romero the invitation from the American ambassador, Montoya asks Jake three times to "look" (pp. 171–72) for him. Cast as the archetypal observer by other men who accept his evaluations of their endeavors, Jake has managed to transform observation itself into a kind of powerful witnessing. The closing scenes at Pamplona, however, will show how flimsy his authority truly is.

Approved by the adoring crowd as well as by Jake's expert appraisal, Romero's victories in the bull ring after the beating by Cohn are not only the narrative conclusion of Book II; they become the focus of Jake's own attempts to redeem his impotence. Jake perceives Romero's painful trial in the ring as a testing and affirmation of the matador's spirit—and perhaps, since Jake is another survivor of Cohn's assaults, as a vicarious affirmation of his own spirit: "The fight with Cohn had not touched his spirit but his face had been smashed and his body hurt. He was wiping all that out now. Each thing that he did with this bull wiped that out a little cleaner" (p. 219).

Romero's process of recuperation, to Jake, depends upon a complex relationship between being watched and disavowing the watching audience (Brett in particular).

For *Sun*, and for Hemingway's early work in general, interpretation of this passage is crucial: "Everything of which he could control the locality he did in front of her all that afternoon. Never once did he look up. He made it stronger that way, and did it for himself, too, as well as for her. Because he did not look up to ask if it pleased he did it all for himself inside, and it strengthened him, and yet he did it for her, too. But he did not do it for her at any loss to himself. He gained by it all through the afternoon" (p. 216). Jake's conundrum of profit and loss (if Romero did it "all" for himself, what could be left for Brett?) involves, once again, the matador's intimate relationship with his audience. Unlike Villalta, who played to the crowd, Romero "did not look up" and thus, according to Jake, "did it all for himself inside." Even at the end of the fight, when the crowd tries to raise him in triumph, this most reticent of actors tries to resist: "He did not want to be carried on people's shoulders" (p. 225). Yet by defying the rules of performance in Hemingway's quintessential arena, Romero appears to Jake to increase the potency of his actions—a formulation that seems to contradict those many scenes in *In Our Time* where a man's prestige is seen to depend on the legitimating approval of an audience.

Most critics have concurred with Jake. Lawrence R. Broer speaks of the "self-contained Romero," Mark Spilka agrees that Romero's "manhood is a thing independent of women," and Allen Josephs has recently written in a similar vein that Romero is "an innocent."[12] Yet Romero's mode of asserting his manhood is far more self-consciously part of a "system of authority" (p. 185) than Jake (like the critics) perceives. All of Romero's actions, in fact, are unashamedly theatrical: he performs as close to Brett as possible; he follows the wishes of the audience when, with the second bull, "the crowd made him go on" (p. 219), and proceeds to give a complete exhibition of bullfighting. He also holds his posture as consciously as any actor: he "finished with a half-veronica that turned his back on the bull and came away toward the applause, his hand on his hip, his cape on his arm, and the bull watching his back going away" (p. 217).[13] Romero dispenses with the audience only because the audience is there. He never once looks up because the arena supplies an audience that looks down, celebrating his actions for him. At the dramatic climax of the fight, the presentation of the bull's ear to Brett takes on significance precisely because it happens before an audience. As Jake describes it, "He leaned up against the barrera and gave the ear to Brett. He nodded his head and smiled. The crowd were all about him. Brett held down the cape." The crowd here is not merely an element of the scene: it is "all about," the element that creates a scene, converting the act of giving into a ceremony and transforming these actors into celebrities.

Considering the subtle but insistent theatricality of Romero's performance, the motives behind Jake's assertion that he does it "all for himself inside" become more complex than critics have generally recognized. Christian Messenger is not unusual in claiming that Romero "provides Jake Barnes with a hero whom Jake can learn from and appreciate by spectatorial comprehension of the sporting rite."[14] Yet Jake's role at the ringside is actually far more than that of spectator, student, and teacher (for, as Messenger also notes, Jake constantly invites Brett to "watch how" [p. 167] Romero performs). Jake, in fact, represses the element of theatricality in Romero's actions because of his own failure, in crucial scenes, to control the way he displays himself. A complete characterization of Jake, then, must include the dramas of humiliation in which he plays the lead role.

The key scene where Jake tacitly pimps for Brett in the cafe quickly becomes, once more, a drama of evaluatory watching. Brett claims, "I can't look at him" (p. 184), but Romero (as his performance in the bull ring suggests) is eager to display himself, quickly inviting Brett to "look" and "see [the] bulls in my hand." As befits his active participation in bringing Romero and Brett together, however, it is Jake who finally stands center stage. On leaving the cafe, Jake notices that the "hard-eyed people at the bull-fighter table watched me go" and comments drily, "It was not pleasant." Several things are not pleasant for Jake here: the sense that Romero has usurped him sexually, the sense that he has betrayed his tough male role by pimping for Brett. Above all, it is not pleasant that his failures are played out before a crowd of aficionados that watches and judges him.

Jake's appreciation of Romero's disdain for the crowd takes on a richer significance in the context of his humiliating failure to dramatize himself successfully before the "hard-eyed people." In the cafe, for the first time in the novel, he inadvertently steps into the part hitherto enacted by characters like Romero and Dick Boulton: a man dramatizing his manhood before other men. Jake not only fails in this tough male role, he also betrays, before his co-aficionados, his compensatory ability to watch and evaluate others' masculine behavior. Every potent action of Romero's in the bullring thus recalls a double failure on Jake's part. It is telling that he prefaces his account of

Romero's victories in the ring with a long description of Belmonte, another man who has a "crowd . . . actively against him" (p. 214), and who also "watched" Romero perform. Belmonte's motives are Jake's: both men have suffered the contempt of the crowd, and both jealously watch Romero enact what they will never again possess.

In the two great works that begin his career, Hemingway returns almost obsessively to the arenas where, he suggests, men typically act out their dramas of power and shame. Some of these characters (Romero, Boulton, Villalta) demonstrate the authority accruing to the successful self-dramatist. More often, exposure to the watching crowd brings humiliation: in crucial scenes, Jake and Nick's father reach center stage only to display their inadequacy. Audiences may be disappointing, as Nick realizes in chapter 6 of *In Our Time*, but more importantly they function as legitimating agents for men's images of themselves. Nick's pilgrimage to the river in "Big Two-Hearted River" appears to deny this sense of male potency validated by the crowd; actually, the very strategy Nick uses to acquire wholeness contributes to the incompletion of self. Jake, witness *par excellence*, emulates Nick in cultivating an impression of the detached, potent observer. Yet Jake's valorization of Romero clearly disguises his own complex feelings about his failures to dramatize himself; seeing for Jake is not an antidote for his sexual impotency but rather another facet of it.

Taking their cue from the ostentatious swagger of Hemingway's life, critics have rarely credited him with a complex view of manhood. The evidence of *In Our Time* and *The Sun Also Rises*, however, suggests that his ambivalence about the way men fashion a powerful male identity has been little understood. Hemingway's work severely disables the myth of the autonomous male individual. Characters like Boulton and Romero are authoritative men; yet they derive their charisma from manipulating an audience which then participates in the establishment of their power. Though Nick's father, Ad Francis, and Jake look weak by contrast, the strategies by which they seek power are the same. Performance itself does not guarantee manhood; but manhood does require successful performance. Fashioning manhood "while the crowd hollers" and looks on is the crucial drama men undertake in Hemingway's early work: the moment when his characters undergo their most intense experiences of authority or humiliation.

Notes

1. *In Our Time* (New York: Scribner's, 1925), p. 83.
2. Many critics have done yeoman work on Hemingway's use of space. Carlos Baker, for instance, discusses Hemingway's "sense of place" in *Hemingway: The Writer as Artist* (Princeton: Princeton Univ. Press, 1952), p. 48. Robert W. Lewis treats the subject more fully in "Hemingway's Sense of Place," in *Hemingway in Our Time*, ed. Richard Astro and Jackson J. Benson (Corvallis: Oregon State Univ. Press, 1974), pp. 113–43. Much has been written about Hemingway's use of the sporting arena. See, in particular, John Griffith's "Rectitude in Hemingway's Fiction: How Rite Makes Right," which focuses on the moral and mythic significance of ritual encounters in "the bullfight, the boxing match, the hunting trip"—in *Hemingway in Our Time,* p. 166. And Christian K. Messenger writes most interestingly about sporting rites, though I shall later take issue with his claim for Jake's "heroic witnessing" of Romero's display—*Sport and the Spirit of Play in American Fiction: Hawthorne to Faulkner* (New York: Columbia Univ. Press, 1981), pp. 251–54.
3. A. Robert Lee, "Introduction," *Ernest Hemingway: New Critical Essays,* ed. A. Robert Lee (London: Vision Press, 1983), p. 8. Many studies have been devoted to Hemingway's notorious longing to be always "centre-stage." See John Raeburn, *Fame Became of Him: Hemingway as Public Writer* (Bloomington: Indiana Univ. Press, 1984); and Scott Donaldson, *By Force of Will: The Life and Art of Ernest Hemingway* (New York: Viking, 1977), pp. 1–9.
4. Earl Rovit and Gerry Brenner, *Ernest Hemingway,* rev. ed. (1963; rpt. Boston: Twayne, 1986), p. 37. See also Philip Young, *Ernest Hemingway* (New York: Rinehart, 1952), pp. 28–50.
5. See Fetterley, *The Resisting Reader: A Feminist Approach to American Fiction* (Bloomington: Indiana Univ. Press, 1978), pp. 46–71, and Faith Pullin, "Hemingway and the Secret Language of Hate," in *Hemingway: New Critical Essays,* pp. 172–92. And Leonard Kriegel bows far too readily to prevailing opinion when, speaking of Hemingway's life, he argues that "such manhood-posing explains the usual charges leveled against Hemingway . . . The man is adolescent. And the writer is, too." "Hemingway's Rites of Manhood," *Partisan Review,* 44 (1977), 418.
6. See also the all-male bedroom, open to the air, in "The Three-Day Blow," the "big hot bedroom" (p. 88) in "Mr. and Mrs. Elliot," and the claustrophobic room of "Cat in the Rain."
7. *Hemingway's Nick Adams* (Baton Rouge: Louisiana State Univ. Press, 1982), p. 157.
8. *Phallic Critiques* (London: Routledge and Kegan Paul, 1984), p. 46. The direct context of Schwenger's comment here is Hemingway's "A Way You'll Never Be."

9. "From the rue Saint-Jacques to the Pass of Roland to the 'Unfinished Church on the Edge of the Cliff,'" *Hemingway Review,* 6 (1986), 27.

10. *The Sun Also Rises* (New York: Scribner's, 1926), p. 13. Further citations of this edition are in the text.

11. Recently, there has been a swing back toward the idea of Jake as privileged observer. Allen Josephs, for instance, remarks that "Jake understands better than anyone because only Jake moves freely and knowingly in both the profane world of the Lost Generation and the sacred world of the toreo"—"*Toreo:* The Moral Axis of *The Sun Also Rises,*" *Hemingway Review,* 6 (1986), 93. See also Stoneback, p. 11.

12. Broer, *Hemingway's Spanish Tragedy* (University: Univ. of Alabama Press, 1973), p. 49; Spilka, "The Death of Love in *The Sun Also Rises,*" in *Twelve Original Essays on Great American Novels,* ed. Charles Shapiro (Detroit: Wayne State Univ. Press, 1958), p. 250; Josephs, p. 92. Earl Rovit (p. 39) also writes about the "self-containment" of the Hemingway tutor (code-hero).

13. Romero, as another scene shows, is an accomplished actor. In the cafe with Brett and Jake, he "tipped his hat down over his eyes and changed the angle of his cigar and the expression of his face. . . . He had mimicked exactly the expression of Nacional" (p. 186).

14. *Messenger,* p. 251.

LOVE AND FRIENDSHIP/MAN AND WOMAN IN *THE SUN ALSO RISES*

Sibbie O'Sullivan

It would be naive to say that *The Sun Also Rises* is a joyous book, or even a hopeful one; it is, of course, neither. Most often interpreted as a picture of post-war aimlessness and anomie, Hemingway's 1926 novel is usually said to be the bible of the Lost Generation, a modern-day courtesy book on how to behave in the waste land Europe had become after the Great War. However valid this interpretation may be, it is limiting and unduly pessimistic. It necessitates a particularly negative reading of the characters in the book and undervalues Hemingway's intuitive awareness of cultural and historical forces and the impact they have on personal relationships. Most damaging of all, the consensual interpretation fosters the harmful propagation of sexist stereotypes and ignores Hemingway's knowledge of and respect for the New Woman. Instead of reading *The Sun Also Rises* as the death of love,[1] we can read it as a story about the cautious belief in the survival of the two most basic components of any human relationship: love and friendship. Examined this way, the novel is a rather extraordinary document that unites the two separate sexual spheres of the nineteenth century and in so doing breaks

Reprinted with permission from Arizona Quarterly *(Summer 1988), pp. 76–97.*

away from the moral imperatives of the Victorian age while demonstrating
the possibility of love's survival in the more realistic but nihilist twentieth
century.

The coaxial themes of love and friendship inform this book in such subtle ways that they are easily overlooked even though they are the forces which
motivate the characters' behavior. In the case of Jake Barnes and Lady Brett
Ashley they form the basis of their relationship. Too often this relationship is
laid waste by stereotypical thinking. The cliché runs like this: Jake,
unmanned in the war, is not only physically but spiritually impotent and
allows himself to be debased by Brett, that "non-woman," that "purely
destructive force." Such critical abuse is understandable when we realize that
Brett is considered part of that long American tradition of the dark-haired,
bad woman. She must be termed "promiscuous" and a "nymphomaniac" if
her sexual behavior is to be explained at all. The mainspring of such a tradition is that "nice girls don't do it." But we've already seen in the short stories
that Hemingway refuses to bind his female characters to such strictures. His
women do "do it," and with relish.

Hemingway seems to take for granted that Brett is a sexually active
woman. And though he did not consciously set out to create the New
Woman, Hemingway's Brett is a fine example of one. Before examining
Brett's character in terms of the love/friendship theme of the novel let us
briefly examine the milieu from which she emerged.

The modern woman did not suddenly rise up from the rubble of 1918.
On both sides of the Atlantic Brett's predecessors had for some time rebelled
against personal circumstances and societal restrictions. Though it is agreed
that the so-called New Woman emerged as a type during the "naughty
nineties," as William Wasserstrom points out, "After 1860 Americans of even
the straightest gentility preferred girls with spunk."[2] It was well known in
Europe how independent and free-wheeling American girls were; Henry
James founded his literary career on such types. By European standards
American ladies had great freedom of movement. Frances Kemble remarked
on unescorted teenage girls "lounging about in the streets" of New York.[3]
Before 1860 chaperonage of unmarried women was neither enforced nor
required, and though this practice was reintroduced in 1880, it was popular
only with the upwardly mobile.[4]

In both America and England the rise of industry and business brought
men and women into close proximity. Though American women entered the
clerical occupations before their British sisters, by the end of the nineteenth

century the business office had been sexually integrated in both countries. The combination of more women leaving the home and women working closely with men moved to create a different mode of female behavior—women were perceived as beginning to "act like men." As K. G. Wells remarked in 1880, "Instead of grace, there has come in many women an affectation of mannishness as is shown in hats, jackets, long strides, and a healthful swinging of the arms in walking."[5] More radical behavior included smoking, drinking, living alone ("latch-key girls"), and sexual activity. The dissemination and use of birth control increased. Though such "liberated" activity was often frowned upon, it was alluring for many people, at least on an unconscious level. *Trilby*, George Du Maurier's 1894 novel, was wildly popular and took America by storm. Leading a bohemian existence, earning a living as an artist's model, dressing like a man when she felt like it, the title character defied the stupidity and insidiousness of Victorian propriety. Five years later in London, the 1889 premiere of Ibsen's *A Doll's House* ushered in the decade of the New Woman with a more somber but nonetheless resounding bang. The New Woman had entered the imagination of Western society.

Non-fictional modes of female behavior which had a liberating effect swept over America in the form of the British Blondes, a burlesque troupe which began its American tour in the 1870s. These British imports struck a new standard of feminine beauty. Even so proprietary a critic as William Dean Howells admired the "new buxom image of beauty they represented."[6] By the 1890s, this buxomness, a lower class trait, softened, elongated, and moved up to a more respectable rung of the social ladder and became the Gibson Girl. By 1913 the "hipless, waistless, boneless" (and, we must not forget, breastless) flapper appeared.[7] It seems, indeed, that women were becoming "mannish," as the de-emphasis of breasts implies.

But more important than how female these women looked was how they behaved. All three types of women, the British Blondes, the Gibson Girl, and the flapper, had the ability to be "pals" with men, to sustain friendships as opposed to courtships. This ability helped to break down long existing gender boundaries. Actresses and dancers, because they travelled with male actors and musicians, were not bound to conventional, sexually segregated behavior; their necessarily intimate living conditions worked against the Victorian fetish for modesty. Though such Broadway behavior earned actresses the reputation of being loose, it also promoted a free and easy exchange between male and female, a healthy demystification of "the opposite sex." In the case of the Gibson Girl, her behavior was more circumspect but still high-spirited and modern. She was more elegant than voluptuous, very athletic and healthy, progressive and college-educated. Though not overtly sexual, she was not without sensuality. The Gibson Girl was the representative woman for the novelists of the Progressive Era.[8] She was not dependent on men, yet valued their friendship; she would not hesitate to marry the "right one."

The flapper, by 1913 "the preeminent model of female appearance,"[9] not only looked but behaved like a man. She smoked, drank, drove, slept around, and earned a living. Her arrival coincided with "Sex o'clock in America."[10] Her behavior was "assertive, and independent, she experimented with intimate dancing, permissive favors, and casual courtships or affairs. She joined men as comrades, and the differences in behavior of the sexes were narrowed."[11] Her live-for-today attitude was announced in Owen Johnson's 1914 novel *The Salamander* and later immortalized by F. Scott Fitzgerald. She was destined to become part of Hemingway's lost generation.[12]

As expected, the push for female freedom, whether advanced by fashion, birth control or the vote, met with strong opposition. As women became more militant in their demands for equality, what were once only implications of female inferiority became flat pronouncements. While the British Blondes were showing their legs, male obstetricians virtually took over the birth process in America.[13] By pronouncing "the truth" about women's bodies men attempted to effect control over those bodies. In 1873, Anthony Comstock successfully lobbied Congress to prohibit the dissemination of birth control information. A year earlier Comstock founded the New York Society for the Suppression of Vice, an organization successful in shutting down Broadway productions and banning selected novels from the mails. The extent of Comstock's influence is best gauged by remembering that in 1915 then President Wilson appointed him as delegate to an International Purity Conference. It is a measure of how virulent and persistent the original Moral Majority was when we recognize that Comstock's campaign against vice spanned those same years in which women made the greatest strides in sexual and political freedom.

Of course, any loosening of the social strictures for women represented an assault on male omnipotence. The nineteenth-century demarcation of gender roles was fiercely guarded. The myth of the self-made man conspired with the Cinderella myth to make women hostages of the home and men absentee husbands and fathers pursuing the higher calling of business. A book such as *The Awakening* is a good index of how ignorant many men probably were of the inner lives of women.

This emotional segregation of women and men had obvious consequences. It accounts for the intense relationships between female friends as well as the sad and deplorable conditions of many Victorian marriages.[14] It burdened women with the preservation of all morals and manners, while it forced men to do homage to the unbending demands of progress. It safeguarded the male ego by denying that "nice" women had erotic drives, thereby insuring male sexual adequacy. It interpreted any change in female behavior as a threat to male dominance; the new mannish behavior was particularly threatening because it called into question heretofore supposedly self-evident gender distinctions. Fear of women was, as Peter Gay points out, an international preoccupation of the nineteenth century.[15]

But however fearful and discouraged at first, this mannish behavior of women had positive results. It helped to bring the two worlds of men and women closer together. And such bringing together had to be undertaken by women and actualized through a transformation of their behavior because it is less frightening for a woman to be masculinized than it is for a man to be feminized. Theron Ware discovered that the emergence of a man's sensual nature leaves him open to emotional and physical collapse, but Brett Ashley's deviant temperament gives her strength, determination, and resilience. The genius of Brett Ashley lies not in Hemingway's ability to create the Great American Bitch but in his ability to create woman as Friend.

The Sun Also Rises reflects the changing sex role patterns prevalent in Western society during the thirty years before its publication. In many ways this first novel is Hemingway's goodbye kiss to the Victorian ethos under which he was raised. As an expatriate, as a World War I veteran, as a young husband and father, and as an artist, Hemingway, since the age of eighteen, had lived an unconventional life. Living as he did in Europe he saw firsthand the shifting social structures that transformed the old order into the new. His sensibilities were equally attuned to both pre- and post-World War I mores. He was not so ignorant as to believe that 1918 had changed everything; it certainly had not changed Robert Cohn, the traditional, romantic, chivalric, and backward-looking character we meet when the book opens.

Cohn, of course, is a bridge figure. He lives in the waste land but does not adhere to its values. He represents the dual concepts of manly adventure and romantic love so important in the nineteenth century.[16] When we meet him he is engaged to Frances Clyne, a woman with "the absolute determination that he [Cohn] should marry her."[17] Though he wants to venture to South America and asks Jake Barnes, the book's narrator, to go with him, he physically silences Jake when Jake suggests in front of Frances that he and Cohn take a weekend trip to nearby Strasbourg. Frances, it seems, is the jealous type.

By focusing the first two chapters on Cohn and the dual concerns of romantic love and adventure, Hemingway establishes a backdrop against which the rest of the book is played. That backdrop becomes, as Cohn's daydream of South America fades, the conventional theme of courtship and marriage—in other words, the typical theme of the Victorian novel. Of course, conventional marriage does little to erode the rigid boundaries between men and women, and Robert and Frances act out scenes which accentuate, in a progressively negative manner, the worst attributes of both sexes. She becomes a nasty woman tremendously afraid of not being married, and he becomes a chump willing to take her verbal abuse lest he break into tears, as he habitually does whenever they "have a scene." The demise of this relationship is nothing less than a wicked parody of the engagement/marriage ritual itself. Fifty pages into the novel we see already that the old way offers nothing but anger and humiliation.

In Chapter II another Victorian ritual is enacted, but with a twist: Jake gets a prostitute but does not sexually use her. As he explains, "I had picked her up because of a vague sentimental idea that it would be nice to eat with some one" (16). Jake's motive is not sexual fulfillment or an escape from a dull marriage bed, but companionship. Prostitute or not, Georgette is recognized by Jake as a fellow human being, not as a mere commodity to buy and discard. But however kindly Jake treats Georgette his actions still reflect the rigid gender roles of the nineteenth century. The underbelly of the conventional Victorian marriage was, after all, prostitution; the erotic restrictions placed on wives encouraged husbands to use whores for sexual release, experimentation, and erotic delight. Coming as it does after the parody of Victorian marriage that Robert Cohn and Frances Clyne represent, this chapter enacts the inevitable decline of such a relationship were it to go on. When Jake introduces Georgette to some acquaintances as his "fiancée" the connection between marriage and prostitution becomes unmistakable.

So far the male-female relationships fall within the scope of the typical Victorian ethos of courtship/marriage, and customer/prostitute. With the entrance of Lady Brett Ashley the focus shifts. Brett's arrival in Chapter III trumpets a new set of relationships. Since Brett is neither a wife nor a prostitute, it is fitting that she emerge from an environment alien to these two opposites; hence she arrives with a group of homosexual men. Her mannishness is thus established through this group, but since she quickly leaves that group and bonds with Jake we learn that her inclinations are orthodox and acceptable. We know that she is not a lesbian, and that her association with male homosexuals, instead of being a detriment, enhances her attractiveness.

As soon as Brett and Jake begin talking we realize theirs is no conventional relationship. Their dialogue bristles with familiarity. Jake asks, "Why aren't you tight?" and Brett answers by ordering a drink. The jabs continue:

> "It's a fine crowd you're with Brett," I said.
> "Aren't they lovely? And you, my dear. Where did you get it?" (22)

The "it," of course, refers to Georgette. As this exchange indicates, Brett and Jake share a public language (remember that Cohn is with them) that includes mild insult and sarcasm. It is a language in which the indefinite pronouns need not be identified. The verbal volley continues on the dance floor and in the taxi, where, alone at last, Brett confesses to Jake, "Oh, darling, I've been so miserable."

What we know so far about Brett's and Jake's relationship is this. First, as the dialogue reveals, Jake and Brett are friends. No matter what else their relationship may be it has a solid base in friendship; such benign verbal ribbing only takes place between friends. Secondly, they share a history. Reference to Brett's drinking habits and how out of character it is for Jake to pick up a whore indicate a more than superficial knowledge of each other's habits. Thirdly, Brett has control. She neatly declines two dances with Cohn and instigates her and Jake's departure. And fourthly, there seem to be two languages operating for them: public and private. It is by the latter that the truth is revealed.

And the truth isn't pretty. They are in love with each other but because of Jake's wound that love cannot be sexually fulfilled. They have tried making love but failed: "I don't want to go through that hell again" (26). Love is "hell on earth," but they continue to see each other. There is a sense of things being out of control; at the end of the taxi ride Brett is shaky, and later when Jake returns alone to his apartment he cries himself to sleep. When Jake leaves Brett it is at another bar and in the company of another man.

This pattern of public/private behavior shapes Brett's and Jake's relationship in an important way. Jake accepts Brett's need for public display, her need to breeze around Paris with as many men as possible. He also accepts her need to tell him about it privately. After she interrupts his sleep to recap her night's adventure with the Count, Jake comments to himself, "This was Brett, that I had felt like crying about" (34). Though there is probably disgust in his voice at this point, there is also resignation, resignation that the woman he loves acts in such peculiar and unstable ways.

The ability to listen, the capacity to care, are not faculties belonging to Jake alone. Brett is also tender and solicitous in private moments. During her second visit to Jake with Count Mippipopolous, when she sees that Jake is a bit shaky, she sends the Count off to get champagne. As Jake lies face down on the bed Brett gently strokes his head. "Poor old darling. . . . Do you feel better, darling? . . . Lie quiet" (55). Though her actions are kind and genuine, Brett does not allow this moment to blunt the truth. When Jake, perhaps succumbing to her touch, to her motherly devotion, asks, "Couldn't we live together, Brett? Couldn't we just live together?" she answers the only way she knows how:

> "I don't think so. I'd just *tromper* you with everybody. You couldn't stand it."
> "I stand it now."
> "That would be different. It's my fault, Jake. It's the way I'm made." (55)

When the count returns with the champagne all three go out and Jake and Brett talk once more in their public manner until out on the dance floor. Brett, in the privacy of Jake's arms, recites again what is fast becoming her litany, thus closing Book I: "Oh, darling, . . . I'm so miserable" (64).

These two small scenes are interesting for what they tell us about how easily Brett and Jake merge the traditional sex roles. The two qualities of granting freedom and lending an ear that Jake exhibits in the first scene clash with the stereotypical image of the muscle-bound, closed-mouth husband/boyfriend who "doesn't want to hear about it." If Jake's attentiveness and meekness in the face of Brett's gallivanting seem in some ways feminine (Jake as the suffering wife?), then in the second scene Brett reenacts a particularly masculine ritual, characterized by the "line": "I love you babe, but I can't stay tied to one woman. I'm just that kind of man." Brett's version of this "line" is not delivered with any hint of bravado or cruelty as it has been delivered by men to countless women in books and movies, but as an assessment of, almost as an apology for her personality. What is striking about these role reversals is how easily and naturally they appear and reappear throughout the couple's interactions. Brett's behavior, especially, flows back and forth between being soft and caring, and hard and straight-forward. Jake has the ability to snap back after a painful relapse. Such flexibility is unthinkable in traditional relationships where sex roles are rigid. Robert Cohn and Frances Clyne do not have this kind of flexibility. One reason Brett leaves Romero at the end of the novel is that he demands that she conform to the rigid traditional female role.

If I over-emphasize that Jake's and Brett's departure from stereotypical male-female behavior is a positive dimension of their relationship, I do so because so many critics judge the couple's behavior in a negative way when measured against those stereotypes. Mark Spilka is one critic who is most ungenerous. In his essay "The Death of Love in *The Sun Also Rises*," Spilka sees Jake as emotionally impotent, as an emotional adolescent, and as a man of little integrity; according to Spilka, Jake has defaulted on his maleness. Brett fares no better. She is "the freewheeling equal of any man" who engages in the "male prerogatives of drink and promiscuity." She is a woman who allows her "natural warmth" to be replaced with "masculine freedom and mobility." Under such conditions, "there can be no serious love."[18] Obviously Spilka identifies "serious love" with traditional male-female gender roles. Though he acknowledges the general damage to love wrought by World War I, he points specifically to the damage done when woman "steps off the romantic pedestal [and] moves freely through the bars of Paris, and stands confidently there beside her newfound equals."[19] Such narrow-minded thinking not only oversimplifies a very complicated novel but blinds the reader to what demonstration of "serious love" there is in the book.[20]

Hemingway has a much broader definition of love than Spilka does, and he examines it in many types of relationships and under many different conditions. Such early stories as "The End of Something," "My Old Man," and "The Battler," indicate that Hemingway was less concerned with the outward form of a relationship and whether it conformed to the standard perception of a love relationship—heterosexual love that ends in marriage—than with the inner workings of such relationships. "The Battler" especially supports the suspicion that for some years before he wrote *The Sun Also Rises* Hemingway was interested in couples who deviated from the standard sex roles. Generally perceived as a story about homosexuality, as of course it is, "The Battler" is also a story about marriage roles, therefore a story about male-female behavior.

There is no reason why Brett's and Jake's behavior should be gauged by traditional gender roles since those roles have been modified to suit the couple's needs. Brett is, after all, the New Woman, and her claim to sexual freedom, though irksome to the critics, is both attractive and perplexing to her fellow characters. Jake cannot be the traditional man because he is impotent. Freed from the pressure to prove his worth through sexual intercourse, Jake must develop other means of asserting his personality.

Both Brett and Jake expect little of each other and have a relationship in which they agree to accept each other as they are. Early in the book Jake describes Brett's two worst habits to Robert Cohn: "She's a drunk" (38), and "She's done it twice" (39), referring to Brett's marrying men "she didn't love." Brett gives a clear self-assessment when she speaks of her intention to return to Mike: "He's so damned nice and he's so awful. He's my sort of thing" (243). Because Jake accepts Brett as she is he has been able to maintain their relationship for as long as he has. We should remember that Cohn and Pedro Romero do not accept Brett as she is and therefore lose her. Brett, too, accepts Jake as he is. They can never be completely, physically united, and for a woman as sexually alive as Brett this loss is deep and sad.

At the end of Book I the boundaries have been drawn. Brett and Jake, the New Woman and the shattered veteran, conduct a relationship based on the honest assessment of each other's failings. In any other arms Brett's lament of "darling I'm so miserable" could pass for a comment on the progress of a particular night's activities, but in Jake's arms it is properly received for what it is: a statement about Brett's soul. This kind of emotional shorthand conveyed in private moments through a private language is the backbone of Jake's and Brett's relationship and a testament to its strength. Though imperfect, their friendship is imbued with the survival mechanisms of honesty, shared histories, and serious love.

Book II begins by depicting male-male friendships, first in Paris and then in Spain. In many aspects Jake's friendship with Bill Gorton is similar to his with Brett. Though they are frequently separated, the two men can quickly restore intimacy. Bill's retelling of his experiences in Vienna is not only some of the best dialogue Hemingway ever wrote, but a wonderful example of that familiar speech we first heard between Jake and Brett. For instance, there is the shared knowledge of each other's drinking habits:

"How about Vienna?"
"Not so good, Jake. Not so good. It seemed better than it was."

> "How do you mean?" I was getting glasses and a siphon.
> "Tight Jake, I was tight."
> "That's strange. Better have a drink." (70)

Then there's the flippant talk about values: "'Simple exchange of values. You give them money. They give you a stuffed dog.' 'We'll get one on the way back'" (72); and the personal litany, in this case Bill's "Never be daunted. Secret of my success. Never been daunted. Never been daunted in public" (73).

Once Bill and Jake leave Paris they become more intimate; the pastoral Spanish setting invokes an even more private speech which allows them to discuss religion, literature, and personal problems such as Jake's impotency. (Though Jake's problems are not discussed at any length, and though his answers are frequently evasive or non-committal, the subject is mentioned often enough in a number of dialogues to warrant being designated a topic of conversation). Physical closeness is established by the freedom of movement between each other's rooms and by Jake watching Bill shave and dress. At one point, Bill even declares his love for Jake:

> "Listen. You're a hell of a good guy, and I'm fonder of you than any-body on earth. I couldn't tell you that in New York. It'd mean I was a faggot." (116)

Other examples of intense male interaction are the scenes with Wilson-Harris, the English angler Bill and Jake meet in Burguete, and with the aficionados in Pamplona. Wilson-Harris is very candid about how much he likes Bill and Jake. The sheer joy of buying his friends drinks almost overcomes him. At one point he says, "I say Barnes. You don't know what this all means to me" (129). When Jake and Bill leave to return to Pamplona, Wilson-Harris gives them each a present, a valentine of hand-tied fishing flies.

Not all male-male relationships are as successful as this. Once the characters are in Spain, Robert Cohn's presence grates on both Jake and Bill. Jake, of course, has reason to dislike Cohn because he recently vacationed with Brett. Jake is very forthright about his resentment:

> I was blind, unforgivingly jealous of what had happened to him. The fact that I took it as a matter of course did not alter that any. I certain-ly did hate him. (99)

Bills' dislike seems rooted in prejudice: "Well, let him not get superior and Jewish" (96). But even Jake and Bill cannot hold on to their hatred of Cohn for too long. Bill says to Jake:

> "The funny thing is he's nice, too. I like him. But he's just so awful."
> "He can be damn nice."
> "I know it. That's the terrible part." (101)

This assessment of Robert Cohn is so similar to Brett's assessment of Mike ("He's so damned nice and he's so awful") that the parallel should not be overlooked. Appearing when they do, these assessments frame the events at Pamplona. They remind us that friendship holds both the promise of betrayal as well as of forgiveness.

Carlos Baker[21] and others often divide the novel's characters into two groups: those who are solid, and those who are neurotic. Baker puts Jake, Bill, and Romero in the former category, and Cohn, Brett, and Mike in the latter. As fair as this division may seem on the surface, it belies the truth of human interaction and negates the web of friendship in which all the characters, at one time or another, are enmeshed. And what a complicated web it is. Throughout the fiesta the characters form new pairs or groups as they partake of the festivities. Everyone at one time or another shares the other's company. Of all the characters Brett seems most in control of choosing her companions. She maneuvers it so that, with one exception, she is never alone with Cohn. In contrast, she frequently asks Jake to go off with her alone, by now a rather predictable action.

Though Brett may behave consistently with Jake, she demonstrates new facets of her personality while interacting with others in the group. When we first see her in Pamplona she seems to have lost all patience with Cohn. "What rot . . . What rot . . . What rot" (134) she keeps repeating in response to his self-aggrandizement. She is sufficiently irked to put aside the charm that was so evident in Book I. A few pages later, however, she's protecting Cohn from Mike's drunken barbs. "Come off it, Michael. You're drunk . . . Shut up, Michael. Try and show a little breeding" (141). The next day at dinner Brett once again runs interference between Cohn and Mike; this time her refrain is, "Pipe down, Mike. . . . Oh, pipe down, Mike, for Christ's sake" (177)! But even Brett has her limits as, a few pages later, she purposely scorns Cohn in order to make him go away: "For God's sake, go off somewhere. Can't you see Jake and I want to talk? . . . If you're tight, go to bed. Go on to bed" (181).

Knowing that such an outburst is out of character, Brett checks with Jake to see if she's done the impolite, but necessary thing: "Was I rude enough to him? . . . My God! I'm so sick of him" (181)!

Jake says at one point to Brett, "Everybody behaves badly . . . Give them the proper chance" (181). Not only does this foreshadow Jake's own bad behavior when he arranges for Brett to meet Romero, but it explains everyone else's bad behavior as well. However, it does not excuse that behavior. When critics such as Baker define the moral norm of the novel as "the healthy and almost boyish innocence of spirit . . . carried by Jake Barnes, Bill Gorton, and Pedro Romero,"[22] he conveniently releases these three, already identified as the "solids," from responsibility for their actions. But if we look at the histories and current behavior of Jake, Bill, and Romero, we see that it is anything but boyish and innocent. There is nothing boyish about being in war and being wounded; nothing innocent about picking up whores, being blind drunk in Vienna, and defiling the code of the bullfighters by running off with an engaged woman. It is, however, boyish to think that one can get away with such things. But even boys discover there are consequences to such actions. Jake, for instance, suffers for pimping for Brett. Bill, who is good at bailing out strange boxers, is nowhere in sight when Cohn knocks out Mike and Jake. And it is doubtful that Pedro Romero can ever completely earn back Montoya's respect. Keeping these facts in mind, one reasonably concludes that the so-called "neurotics" behave in a better manner because they do not uphold false values and then act against them. Instead, they are consistent: Mike is consistently a drunk, so awful, so nice; Brett consistently exercises her right to sleep with whomever she wants and remains open and honest about it; and Cohn consistently acts like a "wounded steer," a sobriquet he earned early in the novel.

The separation of the group into two factions creates barriers if not as visible, surely, at least, as damaging as those erected between the sexes. Such barriers highlight how friends betray but not how they forgive one another. And in Brett's case, because she is grouped with the neurotics, she suffers under a double onus: she becomes the neurotic female, the "bitch," the "nymphomaniac." Clearly, it is the double standard and nothing else that permits the critics, both male and female, to criticize Brett for sleeping with Cohn and Romero while not criticizing Cohn and Romero for the same act. But Hemingway is not interested in erecting barriers but in destroying them. He does not see behavior as either male or female. Nor does he see passion as something solely inter-sexual. In *The Sun Also Rises*, bonding and passion occur in mysterious ways. There is no difference in the intensity of what Wilson-Harris feels for Jake and Bill and what Brett feels for Romero. Brett, however, is allowed the sexual expression of her intensity whereas Wilson-Harris would not be, even if his feelings were sexual. The bond that Jake establishes with Montoya is special because it is validated both by intensity and physical touch. Though this touch is not overtly sexual it certainly suggests sexuality because it is the symbol of a shared passion, just as the touching of sexual partners represents mutual passion.[23]

The above relationships, considering their brevity, their passion, and the intensity of mutual attraction between their participants, would be like one-night stands or casual affairs, were they to exist in the sexual dimension. I am not suggesting that we belittle the effects of sexual union, or that Brett's escapade with Romero is as inconsequential as Wilson-Harris's fishing trip. What I am suggesting is that there are parallels between male bonding and heterosexual bonding which should not be overlooked, and that both forms of bonding are as easily established as they are destroyed. By removing the sexual barriers which unduly place the burden of bad behavior on sexually active women (as Jake points out the woman pays and pays and pays), we see that Brett's transgression is no worse than Jake's; in fact, Brett's may have fewer repercussions. We can assume with good reason that Mike will take Brett back after her fling with Romero, but we are not as certain about a reconciliation between Jake and Montoya. True to form, Hemingway remains aloof in making clear any moral certainties. But one thing for certain is that Hemingway wants us to look at all the characters' behavior and not just Brett's. The structural parallels in the novel are too clear to ignore.

What seems to be more important than who does what to whom and why is the acceptance of the mysteries of behavior, and of bonding in particular. Those characters who survive the best are the ones who have cultivated a certain sense of negative capability. The ability to accept simultaneously two opposing ideas or modes of behavior becomes a means of survival. Those characters who do not have this capability end up exiled from the web of relationships established at Pamplona. Hence it is Cohn and Romero, those representatives of the traditional male role, who are ultimately excluded from any relationship with Brett, the object of their desires. Rigidity of values and, since these two men were Brett's lovers a corresponding rigidity of erectile tissue, are not what keeps Brett. Jake, it seems, wins again.

Book III opens with Jake's observation that "it was all over" (227). Ostensibly referring to the fiesta, Jake's statement is also an assessment of the condition of the web of relationships woven in the previous two hundred pages. It is in shreds. Brett has taken off with Romero. Cohn has left in disgrace, Jake is blind drunk for the first time in the novel, and Mike, as we presently discover, is penniless. Book III is, initially, a book of departures, but by the close of the book Jake and Brett have reunited, thus reconstructing the web. Jake and Brett have no parting scene; her departure with Romero, like Cohn's departure, takes place under cloak of night. We do see, however, the partings of Mike and Bill. Each has a different destination: Mike for Saint Jean de Luz, Bill for Paris and points west, and Jake for San Sebastian. We have no clue as to when these gentlemen will meet again, if at all.

Both Bill and Jake are visibly irritated at Mike for deceiving them into thinking he had money. When he learns that Mike is broke, "Bill's face sort of changed" (229). And after learning from Mike that Brett paid his hotel bill, Jake questions him repeatedly about Brett's financial well-being: "She hasn't any money with her . . . Hasn't she any at all with her" (230)? Clearly, Mike has become persona non grata. We're less sure on what terms Bill and Jake part. Their relationship has always been catch-as-catch-can, each going his separate way then reuniting in a burst of intimacy. Their parting words still exude that good-old-boy camaraderie first heard during their reunion at the beginning of Book II, but something is curiously missing from this final good bye. As they part in private, neither of them knowing when they will meet again, neither man mentions past events. Bill, who very consciously encourages Jake to get drunk at the end of Book II in order to "Get over your damn depression" (223), now has nothing to say. No words of encouragement, compassion, or advice, though he knows full well the extent of Jake's involvement with Brett and therefore the pain he must be suffering. Clearly, Bill makes no attempt at intimacy as a departing gesture. Unfortunately, Hemingway is predictably silent about how Bill's behavior impresses Jake. We are not told, either overtly or by facial expression, how Jake feels when Bill tells him "I have to sail on the 17th" and will not be in Paris when Jake returns. We are not told if Jake or Bill waves as the train pulls out, only that "Bill was at one of the windows" (231). We can not know if this scene represents the ordinary way two male friends say good bye, or if it represents a deeper rent in their friendship. What we do know, however, is that once Jake is alone his thoughts turn to friendship. He likes France because money will buy friends; in France "No one makes things complicated by becoming your friend for any obscure reason" (233).

But we also know by now that such thoughts are only partial truths. Jake, perhaps more than any other character, knows how obscure and unfathomable friendship can be. He knows that few situations and even fewer relationships offer up a fixed set of truths; as he states halfway through the book: "I did not care what it was all about. All I wanted to know was how to live in it" (148).

In San Sebastian Jake takes long, solitary swims, and hides behind irony and sarcasm in an attempt to recover from the events at Pamplona. We realize how damaged Jake has been by these events through his attitude towards others. Not only does he put friendship on a monetary basis by deciding which waiters he wants for "friends," but he discourages any form of bonding with men of his own station. He purposely snubs the bicycle team manager. This uncharacteristic but telling action is a good measure of Jake's suffering when we recall how easily and eagerly he bonded with Wilson-Harris and Montoya. Now, not even the purely masculine comradeship between fellow sportsmen appeals to Jake.

But the habit of loving is a most difficult one to break. Though Jake responds to Brett's telegram with his by now characteristic sarcasm, he nonetheless reserves a seat on the Sud Express and whisks off to Madrid. Their reunion exhibits all the tenderness and caring one wishes Bill had exhibited at his departure. Jake not only physically comforts Brett by holding and kissing her, but he solicits her words: "Tell me about it," he says. And when Brett rambles on with her story despite her refrain of "let's not talk about it," Jake is still attentive and caring. Though his answers are one word responses this does not necessarily indicate a lack of concern on Jake's part, but rather an instinct that less is more. When one friend is hurting, sometimes the best thing another friend can do is listen. Jake does exactly this. But not without a price.

Involvement, of course, means pain. Jake could have just as easily wired Brett some money; he knew already she was broke. But their friendship cannot be measured in monetary terms. Later at the bar and the restaurant, Jake begins to show the effects of his rescue mission. When Brett once more brings up the matter of Romero, he responds, "I thought you weren't going to ever talk about it" (245). The amount of food and alcohol he consumes seems to keep his mouth full so he won't have to talk, to speak what's on his mind. When Brett admonishes him that he doesn't have to get drunk, Jake replies, "How do you know" (246). She backs off, he finishes one more glass and they go for a taxi ride.

In effect they are back at the beginning when they took their first taxi ride together. But however similar the two scenes seem, something has changed. The web has begun to mend. Friendship is renewed. Jake, by rescuing Brett, reaffirms his love for her, and Brett, by recognizing her own faults and deciding not to be a bitch, recognizes the danger of passion for passion's sake. This realization, taking place as it does outside the narrator's scope of vision, can only be measured by its after effects. Brett's tears, her trembling, her sudden smallness, her hesitation in feeling proud for deciding not to be "one of these bitches that ruins children" (243), are completely believable, as is her heretofore uncharacteristic refusal of alcohol at dinner. Her concern at dinner that Jake not get drunk is genuine, almost motherly, what any good friend would do.

Hemingway has said that the more applicable epigraph for his novel is the one from Ecclesiastes and not the one attributed to Gertrude Stein. We must take the author's word on some things; the very title bears this out. If this novel exhibits traits of Stein's lost generation, it also exhibits the cyclical nature of friendship, its rhythm of disintegration and renewal. Brett's and Jake's relationship may have been dealt a cruel blow by fate or the First World War, but it is anything but lost, sadistic, and sick. It, and the bullfights, are the only lasting things in the book. Contrary to what many readers believe, Brett Ashley is a positive force, a determined yet vulnerable woman who makes an attempt to live honestly. Her struggle in choosing to marry one man while loving another strangely coincides with Hemingway's own dilemma. For a year before the novel's publication he wrestled with whether or not to divorce Hadley Richardson, his first wife, and marry Pauline Pfeiffer.

Hemingway broke with convention by creating a brilliant example of the New Woman and dismantled nineteenth century gender lines by uniting love with friendship. His masculine ego did not suffer one iota in the process. He, unlike many of his critics, believes as Jake Barnes does: "In the first place, you had to be in love with a woman to have a basis of friendship" (148).

Notes

1. Mark Spilka, "The Death of Love in *The Sun Also Rises*," in *Ernest Hemingway: Critiques of Four Major Novels*, ed. Carlos Baker (New York: Charles Scribner's Sons, 1962), pp. 18–25.
2. William Wasserstrom, *Heiress of All the Ages: Sex and Sentiment in the Genteel Tradition* (Minneapolis: University of Minnesota Press, 1959), p. 27.
3. Lois W. Banner, *American Beauty* (New York: Alfred A. Knopf, 1983), p. 79.
4. Banner, p. 132.
5. K. G. Wells, "Transitional American Woman," *Atlantic Monthly*, 278 (1880), 820–821.

6. Banner, p. 123.
7. Banner, p. 166.
8. Banner, p. 171.
9. Banner, p. 176.
10. James R. McGovern, "The American Woman's Pre-World War I Freedom in Manners and Morals," in *Women's Experience in America, An Historical Anthology*, eds. Esther Katz and Anita Rapone (New Brunswick: Transaction Books, 1980), p. 358n.
11. McGovern, p. 350.
12. In Ernest Earnest's *The American Eve Fact and Fiction, 1775–1914* (Urbana: University of Illinois Press, 1974), the author makes a nice argument that the novelists of the nineteenth century did not truthfully depict the American woman and therefore these novels have misrepresented what real women were like before World War I. "They were vastly more lively, able, full blooded, and interesting human beings than we have been led to suppose" (270). If this is the case, it is easy to understand how shocked the reading public must have been at the flapper's lifestyle, though in reality she was nothing unusual.
13. G. J. Barker-Benfield, *The Horrors of the Half-Known Life: Male Attitudes Toward Women and Sexuality in Nineteenth-Century America* (New York: Harper & Row, 1976). This is a well-documented history of nineteenth century gynophobia.
14. Carroll Rosenberg-Smith, "The Female World of Love and Ritual: Relations Between Women in Nineteenth-Century America," *Signs*, 1 (1975), 1–29.
15. Peter Gay, *Education of the Senses*, Vol. 1 of *The Bourgeois Experience: Victoria to Freud* (Oxford: Oxford University Press, 1984), p. 197.
16. Martin Green, *The Great American Adventure* (Boston: Beacon Press, 1984). According to Green the two main types of novels in the nineteenth century were the domestic novel, which focused on romantic love, and the adventure novel which justified imperialism and national expansion.
17. Ernest Hemingway, *The Sun Also Rises* (New York: Charles Scribner's Sons, 1970), p. 5. All quotations are from this edition and will be cited in the text.
18. Spilka, p. 20.
19. Spilka, p. 20.
20. Spilka, fortunately, has been challenged. Some of the critics who have given *The Sun Also Rises* a more positive reading include the following: Richard B. Hovey, "*The Sun Also Rises*: Hemingway's Inner Debate," *Forum* [Houston], 4 (1966), 4–10; Robert W. Lewis, Jr., *Hemingway On Love* (Austin: University of Texas Press, 1965); Linda Wagner, "*The Sun Also Rises:* One Debt to Imagism," *Journal of Narrative Technique*, 2 (1972), 88–98; Roger Whitlow, *Cassandra's Daughters: The Women in Hemingway* (Westport: Greenwood Press, 1984); and Delbert E. Wylder, "The Two Faces of Brett: The Role of the New Woman," *Kentucky Philogical Association Bulletin* (1980), 27–33.

21. Carlos Baker, *Hemingway, The Writer as Artist* (Princeton: Princeton UP, 1973).

22. Baker, p. 82.

23. "Men would come in from distant towns and before they left Pamplona stop and talk for a few minutes with Montoya about bulls. These men were aficionados . . . When they saw that I had aficion, and there was no password, no set questions that could bring it out, rather it was a sort of oral spiritual examination with the questions always a little on the defensive and never apparent, there was this same embarrassed putting the hand on the shoulder, or a 'Buen hombre.' But nearly always there was the actual touching. It seemed as though they wanted to touch you to make it certain" (*The Sun Also Rises*, 132).

GENDER–LINKED MISCOMMUNICATION IN "HILLS LIKE WHITE ELEPHANTS"

Pamela Smiley

Like a Gregorian chant in which simple musical phrases elucidate intricate poetic lyrics, so does "Hills Like White Elephants"'s straightforward simplicity of plot frame its subtle and dramatic dialogue. The dialogue contains the essence of the story's power; for to read Jig's and the American's conversation is to recognize the powerless frustration of parallel interchanges—in different words, in different places, and on different topics, but all somehow the same. It is to recognize both the circular noncommunication of strong gender-linked language differences and the consequent existential limitations and creative power of language.

The notion that men and women have difficulty communicating is not new. What is new is research, much of it from the 1970s, which indicates that men and women miscommunicate because they speak different languages (Key 124). If Hemingway's male and female characters are each clearly gender-marked—speaking as traditional American men and women would be expected to speak—then there are four distinct characters in the dyad of Jig and the American: Jig and the American as evaluated through the standard of traditional female gender-linked language patterns, Jig and the American as evaluated through the standard of traditional male gender-linked language patterns.

What is gender-marked language? Robin Lakoff has drawn a sketch of the typical male and female speaker. The male speaker's

> contribution is precise and to the point—utterly straightforward—and tells us as little as possible about the speaker's state of mind and his attitude toward the addressee. We expect . . . a low pitch, flat intonation, declarative sentence structure, no hedging or imprecision, and lexical items chosen for their pure cognitive content, not their emotional coloration. ("Stylistic" 66)

The female speaker's language is

> profoundly imprecise. There is a sense that the audience does not really know what she is talking about (nor does she), but that she is very concerned with whom she is talking to, concerned with whether he is interested in her and whether his needs are being met. . . . She uses interjections and hedges freely and her dialog is sprinkled with 'I guess' and 'kinda'. . . . ("Stylistic" 67)

When broken down into a more generalized paradigm, research indicates that there are three major areas of gender-linked differences in language: how, about what, and why men and women talk. This may seem all-encompassing, but as Tannen notes:

> male-female conversation is cross-cultural communication. Culture, after all, is simply a network of habits and patterns based on past experience—and women and men have very different past experiences. (22)

Conversational patterns differ and miscommunication results because of intolerance for the opposite gender-marked language. The tendency is for speakers to tenaciously hold on to the irrefutable logic of their own language and refuse to entertain the possibility that alternative translations exist.

> trouble develops when there is really no difference of opinion, when everyone is sincerely trying to get along . . . this is the type of miscommunication that drives people crazy. It is usually caused by differences in conversational styles. (Tannen 21)

Lakoff has pointed out that many of the descriptive differences between male and female language become evaluative judgements since men are the dominant cultural group and women are "Other" (Miller 4–12), everything that man is not: emotional rather than logical, yin rather than yang, passive rather than active, body rather than intellect. The effect of this otherness is that many feminine characteristics—language included—are devalued in comparison to their male counterparts. Because women's language in general, and Jig's in particular, focuses on emotions rather than facts and objects, it is judged more ambiguous, less direct and more trivial than masculine speech. If Jig is flighty, trivial, and deferential, then it must be remembered that all of those terms are judgements which depend on a foreign standard, maleness.

The qualification should be made that these gender-linked patterns are polarities, paradigms which are becoming less and less accurate as women attain positions of power and people become more sensitive to language patterns. Still, if such gender-marked traits in the dialogue are isolated and evaluated, first under the standards of the traditional male language patterns, then under the traditional female, four very different characters will emerge. Specific details from the story will make my hypothesis clearer.

The first conflict between Jig and the American is over the hills which she lightly compares to white elephants. Several characteristics of gender-marked speech are obvious from this interchange. The first is the content of language appropriate for each sex; the second is the implicit conversational objective of each.

The man insists on the "facts" and "proof" while Jig talks of fantasies, emotions, and impressions. Adelaide Haas writes:

> [Men] frequently refer to time, space, quantity, destructive action, perceptual attributes, physical movement and objects. [Women] use more words implying feeling, evaluation, interpretation and psychological state. (616)

Feminine language tends to be relationship-oriented while masculine is goal-oriented.

Jig's conversational objective is to establish intimacy through shared emotions and joke-telling. Tannen notes that intimacy for women is shared words, intimacy for men shared actions (22). In this context, Jig's initial remark becomes an invitation to join in the intimacy of shared banter. The American's reply, "I've never seen one," effectively ends that conversational tactic.

Humor is often described as a means of decreasing social distance. Cohesion is also a result in situations in which a witty remark is ostensibly directed against a target, but actually is intended to reaffirm the collectivity and the values held in common (Neitz 215). Therefore, refusal to laugh at someone's joke is a strong form of distancing and power (Neitz 222).

The American gives several very important gender-linked conversational clues. Shutting down Jig's attempt at intimacy with terse phrases and insistence on facts reveals the American's attempts to control the conversation and, by extension, the relationship. Since the topic itself is too innocuous for such negativity, the American must be rejecting Jig for some reason other than her quip about the hills like white elephants. At the end of round one, Jig looks at the beaded curtain and changes the subject. Her response to his rejection is, to use Lakoff's phrase, "classic female deference" ("Stylistic" 67).

All of the conclusions above evaluate the American through traditional female gender-linked language, however. If evaluated within a traditional male standard, speeches about hills like white elephants become irrelevant fluff and Jig's lightness and humor inappropriate in the context of a train ride to the Barcelona abortion clinic. The American, feeling victimized by Jig's pregnancy and mocked by her levity, insists on facts which protect him against her and reassert his control of his unstable world.

The differences in these translations of the American and Jig are important. Jig's superficiality and manipulativeness, for example, are judgemental labels linked to her language and contingent on an evaluation of her according to the foreign standard of a traditional male language. The American's sincerity in his love of Jig or his emotional manipulation of her depends on whether his rejection of Jig's attempts at intimacy is without justification or because of gender-linked presumptions. If the latter, then he makes a language, not a character, judgement which focuses and modifies his otherwise disproportionate cruelty.

Jig attempts reconciliation with her next question about the advertisement on the beaded curtain. Because the American can speak and read Spanish and Jig cannot, translation of her world is one of many things for which she is dependent upon him—permission to try new drinks, an audience to laugh at her jokes, entertainment, support, love are others. Such dependence can have several possible effects. One is that the man is flattered; ever since she could pick up *Seventeen*, a woman has been told to interest and soothe the ego of a man by asking lots of questions and allowing him to parade his knowledge. Jig's pattern of dependency on the American suggests that this tactic has proven successful before in their relationship. But this time, when Jig asks about the taste of Anis del Toro, the American answers politely but distantly, avoids even the most trivial personal disclosure—whether Anis del Toro tastes good with water—and follows Lakoff's paradigm of masculine language, to tell "as little as possible about the speaker's state of mind."

Another possible effect of dependence is that the man will sense entrapment and withdraw. At this awkward point in their relationship, Jig's dependency is probably not one of her most endearing qualities. Her questions remind him of his responsibility for her—a point he would rather forget.

Within the evaluative standard of traditional female speech patterns, the American's lack of disclosure is emotional withholding; he is not playing according to the rules. Within the evaluative standards of traditional male speech patterns, it is not the American's reaction, but Jig's action, which is at fault. Jig's dependence is smothering; because she is unable to make even the smallest decision on her own, the American's terseness becomes a kindness, giving her vital information to enable her to make her own decisions.

The conflict becomes more explicit in the next exchange, in which Jig voices her disappointment with the licorice taste of Anis del Toro and compares it to absinthe. Her reply, "like absinthe," must be an allusion to some disappointment in their shared past, which, since absinthe is an aphrodisiac, Johnston suggests is sexual. "Now he wished to be rid of the unwanted byproduct of that passion. He is not amused by such ironic references" (237). Whatever the allusion, her remark hits a nerve and she presses her advantage:

> "You started it," the girl said. "I was being amused. I was having a fine time."
> "Well, let's try and have a fine time."
> "All right. I was trying. I said the mountains look like white elephants. Wasn't that bright?"
> "That was bright."
> "I wanted to try this new drink. That's all we do, isn't it—look at things and try new drinks?"
> "I guess so."

Jig's series of questions are strongly gender-marked. She uses a proportionately large number of tag-end questions: "wasn't it?," "isn't it?" (Dietrich).

She also uses circular and vaguely generalized evaluations of their activities rather than direct statements—"that's all we do"—the goal of her conversation being consensus.

Tag-end questions are words tacked on to the end of a statement which turn it into a question. Women's language uses more tag-end questions than does men's. The advantages of tag-end questions are that a speaker can invite contributions, avoid commitment, and effect consensus. The disadvantage is that the speaker seems to lack self-confidence and authority (Dietrich). Robin Lakoff writes

> but the tag appears anyway as an apology for making an assertion at all ... women do it more [than men] ... hedges, like question intonation, give the impression that the speaker lacks authority or doesn't know what he's talking about. (Language 54)

Her use of vague generalizations and circular patterns is the opposite of the traditional male pattern of direct and objective statements. According to Lakoff, "a woman's discourse is necessarily indirect, repetitious, meandering, unclear, exaggerated ... while of course a man's speech is clear, direct, precise and to the point" (Language 23), because, as Scott states, these qualities "are effective ones for affiliative interactions in which warmth, co-operation, and self-expression are valued" (206). His achieves goals: hers facilitates consensus and builds relationships.

Evaluating Jig from the standard of women's language, it is clear that she is trying to do just those things: to lead the American into an admission that he is committed to her and desires a fuller life than they now lead. Evaluating Jig from the standard of male language, she is indirect and coercive and therefore superficial and manipulative.

The American's perfunctory replies are evasive. Since "to many women the relationship is working as long as they can talk things out," the traditional female standard would evaluate the American's weak replies as a warning sign of his insincerity (Tannen 23). While the traditional male standard might see the evasion as discomfort with emotional disclosure, since "Men, on the other hand, expect to do things together and don't feel anything is missing if they don't have heart-to-heart talks all the time" (Tannen 23).

There is no conversational intimacy in the American's echoes of her statements. Instead of effecting consensus, Jig's questions increase the distance between them.

If shared activities equal intimacy for a man, then Jig's reduction of their lifestyle to "trying new drinks" is a rejection of the American. That he resists retaliation is, therefore, at worst a gesture of apathy, but at best a gesture of affection. His reticence, instead of the withholding evaluated from the standard of feminine language, might be the kindest way of being gentle with Jig without compromising his own integrity.

His transition into the next conversational topic—that of the temperature of the beer—seems to support this softer view of the American. The American initiates small talk in which both he and Jig describe the beer, each remaining consistent in his or her use of gender-linked language. The American uses what Dietrich calls "neutral adjectives"—"nice and cool"; Jig uses an "empty adjective"—"lovely." Empty adjectives, characteristic of feminine speech, are words like "pretty," "adorable," "precious." Dietrich suggests women use these words to add impact linguistically they do not possess socially. Lakoff feels that their use dulls strong feeling and commitment (Language 11).

Their agreement on the beer is a momentary lull, a lead-in to direct conflict: the abortion.

> "It's really an awfully simple operation, Jig," the man said. "It's really not an operation at all."
> The girl looked at the ground the table legs rested on.
> "I know you wouldn't mind it, Jig. It's really not anything. It's just to let the air in."
> The girl did not say anything.
> "I'll go with you and I'll stay with you all the time. They just let the air in and then it's all perfectly natural."

With goal-oriented, objective, and precise language, the American distances the abortion by reducing it to an operation which lets the air in. If shared activity equals intimacy, then his offer to stay with Jig during the abortion is a gesture of love.

Unfortunately this does not translate well into feminine language. Since the American's facts do not fully describe Jig's experience, the abortion being "not anything," for example, she projects that neither could they fully describe his. Whether the distance between his language and his experience is due to self-deception, dishonesty or cowardice hardly seems important.

Both his reduction of the abortion to an operation and his offer to stay with Jig ignore the issue at the core of the conflict: emotional commitment and self-actualizing growth.

Ignoring the issue of the simplicity of the operation, Jig follows his appeal with a series of questions which keep bringing him back to the core issues: their relationship and their attitudes toward life. She asks him directly for the emotional commitment for which she previously only hinted. Jig's direct attack is uncharacteristic of feminine speech, and therefore very threatening (Lakoff, Language 41).

As the argument continues, Jig asks him whether he "wants" her to have the abortion: he translates his reply into what he "thinks," thereby denying his emotions. Directly contradicting his desire for the abortion, he twice repeats that he does not want Jig to do anything she doesn't want to do. Making several obviously impossible promises—to always be happy, to always love her, to never worry—he demonstrates flagrant bad faith. From the standard of male language these contradictions are the inevitable results of her unreasonable questions: abstract emotional responses to abstract emotional questions. From the standard of female language, they are inauthentic answers and betray trust. The differences stem from the gender-like premises that language does/does not deal with emotion and is/is not the basis of intimacy.

Jig's series of questions exposes both the American's and Jig's conversational double-binds. The double-bind, as described by Bateson, is a conversation with two objectives. To be true to one conversational objective, a speaker must be untrue to another (208).

Jig's direct insistence on the American's emotional commitment forces him into a double-bind. The American has two conversational objectives. The first, as Tanner phrases it, is to "maintain comaraderie, avoid imposing and give (or at least appear to give) the other person some choice in the matter" (22). For this reason he repeats six times within the forty-minute conversation: "I don't want you to [do anything you don't want to do]." The American's other objective is the abortion. Unfortunately it is impossible to maintain easy camaraderie while insisting on the abortion. Instead of choosing one or the other, he chooses both and ignores the contradiction. While a traditional masculine standard of the language might recognize the sincerity of the American's concern for Jig, the traditional feminine standard translates his contradiction as hypocrisy.

Jig is also caught in a double-bind. She wants both the American and the baby. Her series of questions establishes that she can accomplish at least one of her objectives, so she releases the other with her self-sacrificing statement "I don't care about me." While Jig may be totally sincere, not caring about herself and having only the American's interests at heart, such total devotion is highly unlikely; it is more likely that she is well-taught in the skills of social deference. But in this situation, where the American's interests equal lack of growth, eternal adolescence, and sterility, her deference is self-destructive.

Of course the unnaturalness of Jig's self-sacrifice and the artifice of her insincerity leave her vulnerable to the stereotype of "women as fickle, distrustworthy, and illogical" (Lakoff, "Stylistic" 71). Judged by traditional male language patterns, Jig is capricious and manipulative. Judged by traditional female language patterns, particularly within the context of the double-bind, the progression of Jig's conversation is logical and inevitable.

The American's reaction to Jig's acquiescence is immediate emotional withdrawal and disavowal of responsibility for her decision or for her problem. His distance contradicts all of the protestations of love he made minutes before. It also contains a thinly veiled threat of permanent withdrawal. His knee-jerk response shows that his desire for non-involvement and non-responsibility is much stronger than his desire to maintain a relationship with Jig. Of course, objectively, the abortion is Jig's problem: it is her body and the American has no right to interfere. However the objective facts do not take into account the emotional dimension of their shared reality: the body is hers; the relationship and baby is theirs.

Even though Jig agrees to the abortion, it is obvious that she is not emotionally reconciled to it. She moves away from the table and him, and, while staring at the fertile valley, continues the argument. Unwilling to give up her dream, she finds it impossible to believe he has deliberately chosen stagnation, sterility, and death. The American goes into shell-shock in this segment of the conflict. While she reveals her most intimate desires, he seems to be scarcely listening.

"And we could have all this," she said. [gesturing to the landscape] "And we could have everything and every day we make it more impossible." In traditional feminine language patterns, the goal of social facilitation leads to emphasis on politeness which, in turn, tends toward metaphors and indirect sentence patterns. Consistent with her gender-linked language, Jig speaks of the baby metaphorically, in terms of the land. This, Jig's most powerful argument, links the American's fertility to the obviously symbolic landscape. As

Mary Dell Fletcher writes:

> The life-giving landscape ("everything") is now associated in Jig's
> mind with . . . a fruitful life where natural relations culminate in new
> life and spiritual fulfillment, not barrenness and sterility, as represent-
> ed by the dry hills. (17)

The possibility of change and self-actualization, the fertility of the land,
and the continuation of life affirmed through Jig's pregnancy are evidence
that sterility and stagnation are the American's choice, not his fate. As she
stands next to the tracks, the crossroad of their choice, Jig turns her back on
the sterile, burnt hills and the American and looks out onto the fertile fields.
He calls her back into the shadows with him where there is both the anes-
thesia and sterility of his choice: "'Come on back in the shade,' he said. 'You
mustn't feel that way.'"

The American distances himself further by paying so little attention to
Jig's words that he must ask her to repeat herself. Assuming the truth of
Tanner's argument that for a woman intimacy is shared emotion and conversation, the American's "what did you say?" sets him apart from and above
her (22). Because she bases her argument on a series of factors which he does
not recognize as being important or true, the more she reveals her deepest
desires, the more he denies her reality and retreats from her. Feminist theorists argue that since women derive their language from a standard which is
men's, women's language is inadequate to express her experiential world. Jig's
stuttering and vague description of the world she sees slipping away from her
seems to illustrate this inadequacy; her slippery language describing "forces"
must frustrate his literal mind-set which does not deal in such intangibles
and insists on facts. The more she tries to establish intimacy, the less the con-
cord between them. As Tannen observes, the more problems she exposes, the
more incompetent and neurotic she knows she must appear in his eyes: the
more they both see her as problem-ridden (22). They end this section of the
conflict with this exchange:

> "Doesn't it mean anything to you? We could get along."
> "Of course it does. But I don't want anyone but you. I don't want
> anyone else. And I know it's perfectly simple."

Note how the American responds to the plural pronoun "we," with the singular pronouns "I" and "you." Tannen notes that the use of the singular pronoun

is the standard in male speech, the use of the plural pronoun in female. Women often feel hurt when their partners use "I" or "me" in a situation in which they would use "we" or "us." (23) In traditional female speech patterns, plural pronoun use indicates that the speaker feels he/she is half of a couple, singular pronouns an independent person. Jig, who is feeling vulnerable and looking for reassurance, would recognize the American's singular pronoun as a direct signal that no relationship existed. The American, for whom the singular pronoun is traditionally standard, would not find this switch meaningful. As Dietrich has noted, because women are relationship-oriented, they have higher social I.Q.s than men and are more sensitive to subtleties of words. This sensitivity can backfire, as this example of miscommunication pointedly illustrates.

In the next stage of the conflict there is simply more of the same. The repetition of key words and phrases and the circularity of issues has a tired predictability. As frustration from their miscommunication becomes more intense, each exhibits "more and more extreme forms of the behaviors which trigger in the other increasing manifestations of an incongruent behavior in an ever-worsening spiral." George Bateson calls this "conversational disorder" "complementary schismogenesis" (Stone 88).

The final conflict in the story leaves the issue of the abortion unresolved; the American states his intention of moving their bags to the other side of the track and Jig smiles. Politeness is a distinctive characteristic of women's speech, a facet of their role of making others feel at ease by decreasing distance and showing a lack of hostility. Unfortunately, Jig smiles at the American at a point when common sense indicates that she should have the most hostility toward him, leaving her again vulnerable to the charge of inauthenticity and manipulation.

In Jig's defense, it should be noted that she has used a variety of language skills in her confrontation with the American: she has been metaphorical, amusing, self-sacrificing, sarcastic, direct—and none has worked. No matter which tack she chooses, the American comes back at her with the same two sentences: "I think you should do it" and "I don't want you to do anything you don't want to do." According to Dietrich, even though traditional female language is generally more skillful and creative than traditional male language, because his is more authoritative, and powerful, the male's best effects submission. Since our society values authority and power, the inevitable result of the American's repetition is Jig's silent smile.

The final exchange between Jig and the American shows how far they are from understanding one another. When the American drinks a solitary anise at the bar he exposes the strain that this argument has had on his facade of reason and detachment. Johnston evaluates this gesture as the prelude to many other activities the American will do without Jig, since he is tired of her emotions and dependence (237).

The American's final question is the most powerful gender-linked language in the story. "Do you feel better?" assumes that Jig's pregnancy, her emotions, her desire to grow and change all are aberrations from which she must recover. As Lakoff writes, "women do not make the assumption that their ways are healthy and good ones, or the only ones . . . women do not, on the basis of their misunderstanding, construct stereotypes of men as irrational, untrustworthy or silly" ("Stylistics" 71). As the more powerful, the American is able to define what is healthy, even when that definition condemns him, Jig, and the land to stagnation and sterility.

In spite of the sparse details of plot, the subtle and dramatic dialogue in "Hills Like White Elephants" reveals a clear, sensitive portrait of two strong personalities caught in a pattern of miscommunication due to gender-linked language patterns. Jig's language covers a wide range of moods; but whether she is light, sarcastic, emotional, or deferential, her language is traditionally feminine. The American uses few words, speaks in direct sentences, effectively translates the world and achieves his goals, and is therefore traditionally masculine.

In short, Hemingway's accurate ear for speech patterns duplicates the gender-linked miscommunications which exist between men and women in the real world. As a result of these differences, there are two Jigs: the nurturing, creative, and affectionate Jig of female language, and the manipulative, shallow and hysterical Jig of male language. There are also two Americans: in the female language he is a cold, hypocritical and powerful oppressor; in the male language he is a stoic, sensitive and intelligent victim.

Recognizing the existence of four characters in the dyad of Jig and the American in "Hills Like White Elephants" shifts emphasis from affixing blame for conflicts of noncommunication to understanding the causes—a foregrounding of the function of language in the Modernist world. For example, nowhere is gender-linked language's inadequacy to express the range of experience more poignantly revealed than in the American's solitary drink of anise; through the chinks in his language of power and stoicism, the American's underlying emotion and sensitivity are betrayed. It is not that the

American perversely or stupidly chooses sterility and death, it is that he cannot imagine any escape. Jig's pregnancy, Family, Fatherhood, Love—all traditional solutions to his existential angst—are inadequate. What he does not recognize is that Jig does not represent tradition; she is "all this." Does this make him a victim of reality or a victim of his own definition of reality? The logical result of his definition of the world is his own victimization.

Even though the American's language is the language of power, it is also the language of limitation. The American is proof of Miller and Swift's thesis that masculine language's "inflexible demands . . . allow for neither variation nor for human frailty" (Lakoff, "Stylistics" 68). In contrast, one of the strengths of women's language, Irigaray argues, is that it is outside of traditional dualism and may creatively discover alternatives. Language does more than describe an objective reality; the relationship between the signifier and the signified is highly subjective—language does not describe as much as create reality.

Recognizing the subjective and creative potential of traditional gender-linked patterns at the comfortable distance afforded by "Hills Like White Elephants" verifies language's profound imaginative power to define and shape what has always been defined as objective reality, but what is, in fact, closer to the protean fluidity of Jig's "all this." It is only through an understanding of such linguistic functions that there is a possibility of harmonizing its frustrating circularity and actualizing its creative potential of breaking through the confining limitations of a language in which "all [is] so simple" is so sterile and so hopeless.

Works Cited

Bateson, George. *Steps to an Ecology of the Mind.* New York: Ballantine, 1972.

Dietrich, Dan. "Men, Women, and the Language of Power." Madison, Wi.: Women's Studies Program Lecture, 7 March 1986.

Fletcher, Mary Dell. "Hemingway's 'Hills Like White Elephants.'" *Explicator,* 38.4 (19): 16–18.

Goldsmith, Andrea. "Notes on the Tyranny of Language Usage." In *The Voices of Men and Women.* Ed. Cheris Kramarae. Oxford: Pergamon Press, 1980: 179–191.

Haas, Adelaide. "Male and Female Spoken Language Differences." *Psychological Bulletin,* 86.3 (1979): 616–626.

Hemingway, Ernest. "Hills Like White Elephants." *Men Without Women.* New York: Scribner's, 1927.

Irigaray, Luce. *This Sex Which Is Not One*. Ithaca: Cornell UP, 1985.

Johnston, Kenneth G. "Hills Like White Elephants: *Lean, Vintage Hemingway.*" *Studies in American Fiction*, 10.2 (1982): 233–238.

———. "Hemingway and Freud: the Tip of the Iceberg." *The Journal of Narrative Technique*, 14.1 (1984): 68–71.

Jones, Deborah. "Gossip: Notes on Women's Oral Culture." *The Voices and Words of Men and Women*. Ed. Cheris Kramarae. Oxford: Pergamon Press, 1980: 193–197.

Kennedy, Carol Wylie. "Patterns of Verbal Interruptions Among Men and Women in Groups." *Dissertation Abstracts International*, 40.10 (1980): 5425.

Kramarae, Cheris. "Sex-Related Differences in Address Systems." *Anthropological Linguistics*, 17 (1975): 198–210.

Key, Mary Ritchie. "Male and Female Linguistic Behavior: Review of Words and Men by Casey Miller and Kate Swift." *American Speech: A* 124–129.

Lakoff, Robin. *Language and Woman's Place*. New York: Harper and Row, 1975.

———. "Stylistic Strategies Within a Grammar of Style." *Language, Sex, and Gender: Does La Difference Make a Difference?* Eds. Judith Grasanu, Mariam K. Slater, and Lenore Loeb Adler. New York: Annals of the New York Academy of Science, Vol. 327, 1979: 53–80.

Miller, Jean Baker. *Toward a New Psychology of Women*. Boston: Beacon Press, 1976.

Neitz, Mary Jo. "Humor, Hierarchy and the Changing Status of Women." *Psychiatry*, 43 (1980): 211–222.

Organ, Dennis. "Hemingway's 'Hills Like White Elephants.'" *Explicator*, 37.4 (1979): 11.

Presley, John. "Hawks Never Share: Women and Tragedy in Hemingway." *Hemingway Notes* (Spring, 1973): 10.

Salem, Christine. "On Naming the Oppressor: What Woolf Avoids Saying in A Room of One's Own." In *The Voices and Words of Men and Women*. Ed. Cheris Kramarae. Oxford: Pergamon Press, 1980: 209–217.

Scott, Kathryn P. "The Perceptions of Communication Competence: What's Good for the Goose is not Good for the Gander." *The Voices and Words of Men and Women*. Ed. Cheris Kramarae. Oxford: Pergamon Press, 1980: 199–207.

Stein, Gertrude. *Autobiography of Alice B. Toklas*. New York: Harcourt Brace, 1933.

Stone, Elizabeth. "Are You a Talking Hog, a Shouter, or a Mumbler?" *McCalls* (1986): 24ff.

Tannen, Deborah. "Why Can't He Hear What I'm Saying?" *McCalls* (1986): 20–24ff.

PART II

The Inevitable Consideration of Hemingway's Style

ERNEST HEMINGWAY

Wright Morris

We passed through a town and stopped in front of the posada, and the driver took on several packages. Then we started on again, and outside the town the road commenced to mount. We were going through farming country with rocky hills that sloped down into the fields. The grain-fields went up the hillsides. Now as we went higher there was a wind blowing the grain. The road was white and dusty, and the dust rose under the wheels and hung in the air behind us. The road climbed up into the hills and left the rich grain-fields below. Now there were only patches of grain on the bare hillsides and on each side of the water-courses.

The impersonal tone of this narration is a highly personal glimpse into the narrator. His reserve has *style*. The use of "now" evokes presence and immediacy. The language is simple enough, but in the word repetitions, in the pacing of the phrases, the contrast of the long and short sentences, the writer deliberately appeals to the senses, both to what is seen and how it sounds to the ear. Only talent will explain why this style of narration captivated and

---

Reprinted with permission from Wright Morris, Earthly Delights, Unearthly Adornments, American Writers as Image-Makers *(NY: Harper & Row, 1978), pp. 141–146.*

enthralled a generation of writers and readers. We can assume they all coveted the posture of the cool, capable but secretly vulnerable exile. The music of the style owes much to Gertrude Stein, which it was part of his talent to recognize and purloin, thereby inhibiting by his example, her own experiments with language. Nor would style alone have captured the literate public. The deeper, irresistible appeal is the presence in the writing of what is most personal to the writer.

> If I could have made this enough of a book it would have had everything in it. The Prado, looking like some big American college building, with sprinklers watering the grass early in the bright Madrid summer morning; the bare white mud hills looking across toward Carabanchel; days on the train in August with the blinds pulled down on the side against the sun and the wind blowing them; the chaff blown against the car in the wind from the hard earthen threshing floors; the odor of grain and the stone windmills.

This is Hemingway in Spain (*Death in the Afternoon*). It is not fiction but the style is the same, and projects the same persona. The eye of memory he casts back on his experience burns and glances off the sun-baked surface, like that of a scanning camera, yet it captures the emotion invisible to the camera. This is the art of it, the secret to the style, the siren voice that lures the reader to possess the experience and write about it *in this manner*. The manner is crucial. The author believes this, and is always at pains to talk, write and live in this style. The reader believes this, and is at pains, through absorbing this style, to possess the experience. When applied to a place, an event or a woman, the style simulates possession.

> . . . I know things change now and I do not care. It's all been changed for me. Let it all change. We'll all be gone before it's changed too much and if no deluge comes when we are gone it will still rain in summer in the north and hawks will nest in the Cathedral at Santiago and in La Granja, where we practiced with the cape on the long gravelled paths between the shadows, it makes no difference if the fountains play or not. We never will ride back from Toledo in the dark, washing the dust out with Fundador, nor will there be that week of what happened in the night in that July in Madrid. We've seen it all go and we'll watch it go again. The great thing is to last and to get your work done and see and hear and learn and understand; and write when there is something that you know; and not before; and not too damned much after.

Both Fitzgerald and Hemingway, in their contrasting voices, chronicle the same downward path to wisdom, the resignation of the American man-child turning thirty, the dark fields of the republic, the dun-colored mountains of Spain, forever and ever receding behind them. The soliloquy of Hemingway is more manly in its resignation, but no longer conceals, as it once seemed to, the prodigal saying goodbye to his youth. The sentiments are heightened, the emotions are swayed by the musical play of light and shadow, of hawks and fountains, of dust, Fundador and whatever happened that night in Madrid, better left unmentioned now that it is gone. Readers who had little notion of work to be done, and writers who had little talent for lasting, were never quite the same after reading this passage, or free of its romantic and haunting renunciation. We'll to the woods no more: *les lauriers sont coupés.*

Hemingway has few equals in the emotion he is able to evoke from the surface of an image. It is often in passing, before the mind's eye of memory, or from the window of a train or a moving car, a *series of images* being important, each one reduced to the power of a symbol—light and shadow, hawk and fountain, rain in summer—which he orchestrates for the desired effect.

What about the ranch and the silvered gray of the sage brush, the quick, clear water in the irrigation ditches, and the heavy green of the alfalfa. The trail went up into the hills and the cattle in the summer were shy as deer. The bawling and the steady noise and slow moving mass raising a dust as you brought them down in the fall. And behind the mountains, the clear sharpness of the peak in the evening light and, riding down along the trail in the moonlight, bright across the valley. Now he remembered coming through the timber in the dark holding the horse's tail when you could not see and all the stories that he meant to write.

Not France, not Spain, but the range in the West evoked in the same hypnotic rhythms a similar flow of impressions, the use of "now" to enhance immediacy, suggesting a moving panorama, as if these scenes were painted on a canvas that unrolled before him, cinematic in quality. The stream-of-consciousness technique has been adapted to the fluency of narration. Without apparent strain, as if it came naturally, the writer incorporates the innovations of the decade into an artlessly flowing vernacular style. The flow of this style calls for a dialogue that is in sharp contrast, cryptic and laconic.

"How do you feel?" she said. She had come out from the tent now after her bath.
"All right."

"Could you eat now?" He saw Molo behind her with the folding
table and the other boy with the dishes.
"I want to write," he said.
"You ought to take some broth to keep your strength up."
"I'm going to die tonight," he said. "I don't need my strength up."
"Don't be melodramatic, Harry, please," she said.

Lyrically flowing, poetically sensitive narration contrasts perfectly with
the hard-boiled dialogue. Hemingway sensed and provided the formula for
the public-private sectors of American life, the tough exteriors, the sensitive,
brooding interiors, spawning the macho-tough fiction and the Bogart
movies.

When the tautness of the Hemingway line slackens, the words in the line
lose their charge of emotion, hang like limp sails. The cinematic flow of
images is displaced with a series of static stills, connected by "then" and
"and."

They went under the white bridge and under the unfinished wood
bridge. Then they left the red bridge on the right and passed under the
first high-flying white bridge. Then there was the black iron fret-work
bridge on the canal leading into the Rio Nuovo and they passed the two
stakes chained together but not touching: like us the Colonel thought.

The formula is operative here: we recognize the hand of the potter, but
without the usual charge of emotion it seems a retarded impression, like that
of Faulkner's Benjy in *The Sound and the Fury*. The images are inert, the repetitions horizontal rather than flowing, the words drained of the energy that
once made them vibrant. They are now *signs*, and please only the reader who
remembers them as symbols and treasures the style for its nostalgia as the
Colonel treasures Venice.

Christ, I love it, he said, and I'm so happy I helped defend it when I
was a punk kid, and with an insufficient command of the language and
I never even saw her until that clear day in the winter when I went back
to have that small wound dressed, and saw her rising from the sea.

This is self-parody, pitiless as the scorn Hemingway so freely applied to
those who displeased him. *Across the River and into the Trees* is a writer's
manual of the treacheries of a great "style." The music that once held the

reader now captivates the author. He can hear nothing else. The author's first mistake was to return to the scene of an early, image-making triumph. Time has not displaced that experience. The tremors of emotion felt by the Colonel are not communicated to the reader. An old lover, in a gondola, warming himself with his own clichés. About Spain he had written:

> ... Pamplona is changed, of course, but not as much as we are older. I found that if you took a drink that it got very much the same as it was always.

For the drinker, perhaps, but not for the reader. If this writer is to escape from his own fiction, he must find new objects of affection, of attachment. *Islands in the Stream*, published posthumously, finds him at ease with sentiment, indulgent with humor and admitting of binding ties with a cat named Boise.

> One time on the Central Highway he had seen a cat that had been hit by a car and the cat, fresh hit and dead, looked exactly like Boy [his own cat].... He knew it couldn't be Boy ... but it had made him feel sick inside and he had stopped the car and gone back and lifted the cat and made sure it was not Boy and then laid him by the side of the road so nothing else would run over him.
> That evening, coming back to the farm, the body of the cat was gone from where he had left him so he thought that his people must have found him. That night, when he had sat in the big chair reading, with Boise by his side in the chair, he had thought that he did not know what he would do if Boise should be killed. He thought, from his actions and his desperations, that the cat felt the same way about the man.

There is neither sarcasm nor manly detachment in this admission of sentiment, of vulnerability. The truly binding ties are merely there to be acknowledged, rather than challenged, mocked or explained.

In Thomas Hudson, the central figure of the novel, we have a self-portrait that contradicts the familiar, long-standing representation, the hunter, the warrior, the public figure and self-approving, if tormented, creator. For a brief moment, in the shelter of the sun and sea at his home in Cuba, he seemed free of the destructive obsessions, the increasing paranoia, that determined his public image. Although *The Old Man and the Sea* is in the mannered and celebrated style that inhibits more than it releases, it provides the parable for Hemingway's vision of life as a losing battle, over which style, courage and tenacity triumph.

As the gifts of age crowned his lifetime's effort, the last losing battle of his life found him in the role of both the hunter and the hunted, a theme that would have challenged him more profoundly than the bullrings of Spain, or the green hills of Africa. How well he had come to know each protagonist! Romantically ready, predictably disenchanted, the postwar writers were committed to heroics that excluded the possibility of growing old. They shared the expectations that made them vulnerable and unmistakably American. The old man of the sea, of Pamplona, of Kilimanjaro, whom we see bearded and brooding in Karsh's portrait, is still the youth cleaning his trout on the banks of the Big Two-hearted River. He had found that if you took a drink it had got very much as it was always. The way alcohol has fueled and prematurely depleted the gifts Americans reserve for the highest calling suggests that the brook between youth and age has long been too broad for leaping. Falling into it had become the heroic way of life.

HEMINGWAY'S STYLE AND JAKE'S NARRATION

Terrence Doody

In the morning it was raining. A fog had come over the mountains from the sea. You could not see the tops of the mountains. The plateau was dull and gloomy, and the shapes of the trees and houses were changed. I walked out beyond the town to look at the weather. The bad weather was coming in over the mountains from the sea.[1]

With its insistent observation, simplicity, and repetitions this paragraph, which opens Chapter XVI of *The Sun Also Rises*, is a quintessential example of Hemingway's style, which we have honored because it has worked so well to recover for us (in Merleau-Ponty's phrase) "a naive contact with the world."[2] Despite its naiveté, however, Hemingway's style is not simply simple. And this paragraph of description is also a paragraph defining character. For it proceeds from the mouth of Jake Barnes, the novel's narrator, who makes it not because he is interested in giving a weather bulletin; but because at this point in the chaos of the fiesta at Pamplona, the weather is a certainty and getting it exactly gives Jake something, however incidental, to hold on to. It is an arresting paragraph because, as Edwin Muir says,

---

Reprinted with permission from The Journal of Narrative Technique *(1974), pp. 212–225.*

Hemingway's power of "observation is so exact that it has the effect of imagination."[3] For Hemingway, observation is an imaginative act, the issue of his style; but for Jake, who does not have "a style," it is something else. And this discrepancy is what raises problems about Jake's act of narration.

Other critics have seen certain difficulties in Jake's characterization. Earl Rovit, for instance, calls Jake a "particularly opaque first person narrator." Richard B. Hovey finds in Jake a psychological unreliability that makes his relation to Hemingway more ambiguous and revealing than we usually suppose it to be. Yet Rovit and Hovey, like most other critics, eventually affirm the formal success of Jake's narrative and, with E. M. Halliday, praise Hemingway's solution to the problem of preserving a convincing immediacy in a retrospective narration. Halliday's very cogent argument has become the orthodox formal reading of *The Sun Also Rises* in much the same way that Mark Spilka's "The Death of Love in *The Sun Also Rises*" has become the orthodox reading of the novel's principal theme. Epitomizing Halliday's argument, Sheldon Norman Grebstein says: ". . . certainly the remarkable technical feature of the novel is the consistency and control of its narrative perspective and narrative voice." Grebstein goes on to say that one of the reasons Hemingway succeeds as well as he does is that "he deliberately avoids identifying the narrator at a precise point in time and space and thus minimizes the artificiality that sometimes attaches to the I-narratives of James and Conrad."[4]

Grebstein's praise seems to beg the essential problem, however. The fundamental questions we ask about first person narrators deal with irony, reliability and distance. These are rhetorical categories, but their real concern is epistemological: what does the narrator know, how does he know, how fully do these constitute the meaning of the novel? Beneath these, there is another question, equally serious and moral as well as technical: how free is the narrator? By asking this question, we reverse the equation of distance in order to ask: how far away does the author allow his narrator to get? how specifically does he dramatize his narrator's autonomous capacity to make the narrative he makes? Successfully realized narrators who are placed "at a precise point in time and space," like James and Conrad's, have an autonomy that always makes them at least slightly "unreliable" simply because they are not the author of themselves nor the entirety of the fiction they inhabit. Now, we can all agree that Jake is not Hemingway himself, nor is he problematically unreliable in the way that, say, Gulliver is, and what Jake knows is certainly central to the meaning of *The Sun Also Rises*. Yet Jake remains a problem precisely because he has not been located in space and time, so he is never as far away from Hemingway as he should be and, therefore, never free enough to substantiate his own agency as the narrator. In *The Sun Also Rises*, Jake is more a function of the style than its source, and he finally gives to the style more than he gets from it because his voice and character are used to justify a vision of the world that Jake is never allowed to possess as his own.

What Jake does for the style is probably best exemplified in the variety of effects his voice can educe from the device of polysyndeton Hemingway uses so frequently.[5] This polysyndeton Hemingway generally directs against the habits and assumptions of perception that organize experience into hierarchies of abstraction, value and time. For polysyndeton democratizes sensations and impressions; and in giving them all their equality, it preserves the primitive fullness and immediacy that is the hallmark of Hemingway's prose. In *The Sun Also Rises*, this democratizing effect is most patent in the landscape passages where the repeated use of *and* suggests peaceful slow time and an undiscriminating passivity, as the details of the scene accumulate themselves and compose Jake's mind while he travels from Paris into Spain or up to the Irati fishing ground. To the arrival scene in Pamplona, however, these same *and*'s are spoken in a more active voice that imparts a rush of enthusiasm to Jake's happy first impressions.

> The driver helped us down with the bags. There was a crowd of kids watching the car, and the square was hot, and the trees were green, and the flags hung on their staffs, and it was good to get out of the sun and under the shade of the arcade that runs all the way round the square. Montoya was glad to see us, and shook hands and gave us good rooms looking out on the square, and then we washed and cleaned up and went down-stairs in the dining room for lunch. The driver stayed for lunch, too, and afterwards we paid him and he started back to Bayonne. (94)

A few pages later in the same chapter, and is "utilized" (as Jake would say) to conduct Jake's stream-of-consciousness as he tries to pray in the Pamplona cathedral. Though this next passage would never be mistaken for one of Joyce's, in 1926 Hemingway's style is still fresh enough to be more effective than embarrassing.

I went inside. It was dim and dark and the pillars went high up, and there were people praying, and it smelt of incense, and there were some wonderful big windows. I knelt and started to pray and prayed for everybody I thought of, Brett and Mike and Bill and Robert Cohn and myself, and all the bull-fighters, separately for the ones I liked, and lumping all the rest, then I prayed for myself again, and while I was praying for myself I found I was getting sleepy, so I prayed that the bull-fights would be good, and that it would be a fine fiesta, and that we would get some fishing. I wondered if there was anything else I might pray for, and I thought I would like to have some money, so I prayed that I would make a lot of money, and then I started to think how I would make it, and thinking of making money reminded me of the count, and I started wondering about where he was, and regretting I hadn't seen him since that night in Montmartre, and about something funny Brett told me about him and as all the time I was kneeling with my forehead on the wood in front of me, and was thinking of myself as praying. I was a little ashamed, and regretted that I was such a rotten Catholic, but realized there was nothing I could do about it, at least for a while, and maybe never, but that anyway it was a grand religion, and I only wished I felt religious and maybe I would the next time; and then I was out in the hot sun on the steps of the cathedral, and the forefingers and thumb of my right hand were still damp, and I felt them dry in the sun. The sunlight was hot and hard, and I crossed over beside some buildings, and walked back along side-streets to the hotel. (96–97)

In mixing Jake's memory and desire, this passage could have used some variety of tense and perhaps a more elliptical method for the transitions that are so earnestly consecutive. Nonetheless, the crudeness of the polysyndeton itself suggests very clearly the difficulty that self-consciousness causes in Hemingway's characters when they try to think. And the momentum the prose gathers enacts the motive, hidden in the passage's one ellipsis, that drives Jake from the church. When he discovers the holy water he has used to bless himself still on his hand, he begins to regain the control he has lost in thought by cataloguing the sensations that are always more certain.

Jake's voice also has an effect on Hemingway's style of conversation, which in *The Sun Also Rises* is characteristically laconic and very smart, and which is the least expressive literary technique ever to exert so great an influence on expression. What we tend to forget, unless we read Hemingway aloud, is that his conversation can also be very funny, as it is in the fishing episodes. But Jake is even capable of deliberate self-parody. In a passage he speaks to himself as he tries unsuccessfully to fall to sleep, not only does he comment on his own "hard-boiled" honesty, he even counters the flaccidity of the earlier stream-of-consciousness.

> What a lot of bilge I could think up at night. What rot, I could hear Brett say it. What Rot! When you are with English you got into the habit of using English expressions in your thinking. The English spoken language—the upper classes, anyway—must have fewer words than the Eskimo. Of course, I didn't know anything about the Eskimo. Maybe the Eskimo was a fine language. Say the Cherokee. I didn't know anything about the Cherokee either. The English talked with inflected phrases. One phrase to mean everything. I liked them, though. I liked the way they talked. Take Harris. Still Harris was not the upper classes. (149)

Hemingway does not often laugh at himself like this. Think of the preposterously dignified idiom he creates for the Spanish peasants in *For Whom The Bell Tolls*. And Hemingway's own conversation in *Green Hills of Africa* is so seriously sincere that it betrays him into one of his silliest pronunciamentos: "All modern American literature comes from one book by Mark Twain called *Huckleberry Finn*."[6] Whatever this amounts to as literary history, it is a sentence rich with pomposity. Yet because Jake Barnes is usually prevented from taking himself so seriously, he almost never succumbs to the portentousness that can inflate Hemingway's "simplicity."

When Jake does succumb, however, as he does in a paragraph in Chapter XVII, the fall is obvious and revealing.

> The bull who killed Vicente Girones was named Bocanegra, was Number 118 of the bull-breeding establishment of Sanchez Taberno, and was killed by Pedro Romero as the third bull of that same afternoon. His ear was cut by popular acclamation and given to Pedro Romero, who, in turn, gave it to Brett, who wrapped it in a handkerchief belonging to myself, and left both ear and handkerchief, along with a number of Muratti cigarette-stubs, shoved far back in the drawer of the bed-table that stood beside her bed in the Hotel Montoya, in Pamplona. (199)

This passage is the most explicit statement of the absurdity Hemingway sees in a world where the sun does not seem to rise for anyone. The prose feels highly organized, with its hard turns, rapid accretion of detail, and sharp grade of declination, but the facts the first sentence juxtaposes so tightly have no causal connection at all. The bull that accidentally kills Vicente Girones is not for that reason then killed by Pedro Romero; the bull's name, number, and owner are pointedly irrelevant. On the other hand, the connections in the second sentence that are consequential are destructive. Brett's thought-lessness reduces what is both a ritual trophy and a gift of love to the value of the random cigarette butts; and her use of Jake's handkerchief emphasizes his collusion in what he himself recognizes as Brett's corruption of Romero.

This paragraph sounds very different from the weather report, the arrival scene, the stream-of-consciousness; and for all its "significance," it sounds wrong. "A handkerchief belonging to myself" (which could have been "my handkerchief" without upsetting the rhythm of the line) is clumsier, more precious than it has to be; "in the Hotel Montoya, in Pamplona" is the kind of phrase that creates the invisible italics of a mannerism. These phrases heighten the effect, but cheapen the absurdity toward cynicism, and nowhere else in the novel is Jake so merely cynical. Moreover, nowhere else in the novel does he violate the chronology of the original events for the sake of such an effect. Jake could not have known about the bull's ear in the drawer until much later, until after Brett has left Pamplona with Romero.[7] So while this paragraph may or may not be bad Hemingway, depending on your own taste, it is uncharacteristic of Jake Barnes, the narrator. And though Hemingway's intrusion here is slight, it points to the novel's central problem. Jake is most convincing when he is least self-conscious; yet because he is so unself-conscious about the whole of his narrative, he is hard to accept as the authoritative and autonomous source of the fiction his own voice delivers. As the paragraph about Bocanegra, which is so deliberately *written*, inadver-tently hints, Jake is possessed by a style that will finally not allow him any possession of himself.

All first person narratives require of the reader a certain suspension of disbelief, the willingness to overlook such matters as the narrator's perfect total recall and contentions like Conrad's that Marlow actually could have told the long story of Lord Jim in those few hours after dinner with the men on the verandah. But the reader can legitimately ask for some indication that the narrator knows what he is doing and why he is doing it. If Jake were sim-ply a passive behavioralistic register, there would be no problem; for then we could resign ourselves to seeing him as the medium through which events are made manifest and read *The Sun Also Rises* as something other than the novel of education that it is. Or if Jake were more completely dramatized in time, there would be no problem with the conclusions he draws in the paragraph about Bocanegra. But Hemingway wants it both ways. In order to preserve the famous immediacy, Hemingway cannot acknowledge that Jake's different perceptions have different styles of expression, which originate in Jake and for which he should have the authority. In other words, the prose changes, but Jake is not allowed to change it himself or see himself as changing. Time is denied, in effect, and with that denial Hemingway deprives Jake of both his freedom and his autonomy.

Jake seems to be at his most behavioralistic when he describes the Spanish street dancers in Chapter XV.

> In front of us on a clear part of the street a company of boys were dancing. The steps were very intricate and their faces were intent and concentrated. They all looked down while they danced. Their rope-soled shoes tapped and spatted on the pavement. The toes touched. The heels touched. The balls of the feet touched. Then the music broke wildly and the step was finished and they were all dancing up the street. (165)

The dancers' gaze directs Jake's; responding to them first, he then sees and appropriates their dance, the music that orders it, and their career up the street. Though Jake does not give meaning to this dance in the way he gives meaning to the weather, his response is not simply determined by it. No one else in the novel has the intensity of perception that allows Jake to see this dance so clearly; and in fact, his description of the dance comes in answer to Bill Gorton's unsatisfying generalization that "They dance differently to all the different tunes."

Jake's ability to see into the nature of things and to inform these things with his own values becomes even more apparent during the bullfights, which are at the center of the novel's meaning. Though he is no longer an able Catholic, Jake is an *aficionado* who has been confirmed by a laying on of hands, and he can see in the bullfights what most of the native Spanish spectators cannot: Belmonte's arrogant, classical integrity and Romero's act of romantic transformation. When he comes to describe Belmonte, Jake's paragraphs grow noticeably longer, and his narration is more fluent than it is anywhere else in the story. This next paragraph could not be more different than it is from the earlier stream-of-consciousness paragraph when Jake tries to pray in the Pamplona cathedral. The two paragraphs are exact thematic counterparts: Jake has difficulty praying, but no trouble at all in seeing the ritual that Belmonte both enacts and defies.[8]

Also Belmonte imposed conditions and insisted that his bulls should not be too large, nor too dangerously armed with horns, and so the element that was necessary to give the sensation of tragedy was not there, and the public, who wanted three times as much from Belmonte, who was sick with a fistula, as Belmonte had ever been able to give, felt defrauded and cheated, and Belmonte's jaw came further out in contempt, and his face turned yellower, and he moved with greater difficulty as his pain increased, and finally the crowd were actively against him, and he was utterly contemptuous and indifferent. He had meant to have a great afternoon, and instead it was an afternoon of sneers, shouted insults, and finally a volley of cushions and pieces of bread and vegetables, thrown down at him in the plaza where he had had his greatest triumphs. His jaw only went further out. Sometimes he turned to smile that toothed, long-jawed, lipless smile when he was called something particularly insulting, and always the pain that any movement produced grew stronger and stronger, until finally his yellow face was parchment color, and after his second bull was dead and the throwing of bread and cushions was over, after he had saluted the President with the same wolf-jawed smile and contemptuous eyes, and handed his sword over the barrera to be wiped, and put back in its case, he passed through into the callejon and leaned on the barrera below us, his head on his arms, not seeing, not hearing anything, only going through his pain. When he looked up, finally, he asked for a drink of water. He swallowed a little, rinsed his mouth, spat the water, took his cape, and went back into the ring. (214–215)

The long sustained lines of this paragraph are Jake's tribute to Belmonte's endurance and as firm in their expression as Belmonte is in his. But because Romero is doing something quite different in converting his bullfight into an act of tribute to Brett, Jake's description of him is appropriately different.

Pedro Romero had the greatness. He loved bull-fighting, and I think he loved the bulls, and I think he loved Brett. Everything of which he could control the locality he did in front of her all that afternoon.

Never once did he look up. He made it stronger that way, and did it for himself, too, as well as for her. Because he did not look up to ask if it pleased he did it all for himself inside, and it strengthened him, and yet he did it for her, too. But he did not do it for her at any loss to himself. He gained by it all through the afternoon. (216)

Jake is both uncertain and insistent here. The hesitancy and repetition of these sentences, the parallels of contrast, express and enforce the tension between Romero's discipline and his aspiration, between what he is doing in conformity with the rite and what he is doing beyond that as an offering to Brett. And we can feel Jake working as hard as Romero does to understand exactly what Romero is doing. Although he loves Brett desperately, Jake re-creates Romero's gift and makes its creation understood with a generosity even more impressive than his ability to see it in the first place.

Watching the bullfights forces Jake to face again the sad inadequacies of his situation and all the things Romero can do, for himself and for Brett, that Jake cannot. Still Jake loves the bullfights because they offer him an authentic, historic ritual—more meaningful than the Church, more permanent and communal than the fishing trip—that is the only mode he has to satisfy his need for order and control. When he describes Romero, he comes as close as he is allowed to describing himself and his own activity; for he too works within the discipline of an imposed style, without looking up, and gains from that fidelity a private strength. Jake's description re-enacts Romero's deed and gives it its personally expressive form—without which it would have meant something else and less, as it does to the native spectators. But it is impossible to tell whether Jake knows exactly what he is doing. For all his clarity of vision, he is opaque; but he is too old to be a Huckleberry Finn. He is, in fact, much closer to Nick Carraway, and he does for Romero what Nick does for Gatsby: he sees in Romero more than anyone else does and makes of that insight the definition of a hero, which entails a correlative definition of himself. But unlike Nick, Jake is finally deprived of that insight's ultimate personal advantage.

At the end of *The Great Gatsby*'s third chapter, Nick says that in re-reading his manuscript he has discovered a false emphasis, which he immediately corrects by explaining what else he did when he was not Gatsby-watching. In Chapter VI, at a time when Gatsby "caught his breath" with Daisy, Nick fills us in with what he learned much later of Gatsby's background. In re-arranging the experience's real chronology, Nick himself is making Gatsby's greatness: for he shows us Gatsby at the height of his romantic potency before we have to watch Gatsby being defeated and destroyed. The self-conscious manipulation Fitzgerald devises for Nick is not an exceptional formal maneuver, but it does make Gatsby's meaning the clear result of Nick's participation, his understanding, and his disposition of the narrative. Nick, therefore, is justified in achieving the apotheosis he works up to in the narrative's final moment. He may not possess Gatsby's intuitive power of self-conception, but he does have a personal empathy and historical vision that save Gatsby from being only an "elegant young roughneck" and Nick himself from being an otherwise feckless bond salesman.

Jake, however, does not have Nick's freedom or distance. For Jake is only self-conscious enough to be suspicious of "all frank and simple people, especially when their stories hold together" (4) and to be worried about how fair he is being to Cohn, whom he initially likes in spite of everything (45). These signs—and there are others like them—are fairly unexceptional notations of Jake's credibility, and they all come early in the novel, in Paris, long before Jake is required to face the bullfights. Moreover, Cohn is much less important as the test of Jake's honesty than he is as Jake's antagonist and anti-type. In *The Sun Also Rises*, Cohn absorbs much of the self-indulgence and sentimentality that later afflicts, and consecrates, so many of Hemingway's leading men. And what is most damning about Cohn is that he is a bad novelist, who profiteers on his popularity and who is described by Bill as a "great little confider" (101). Jake, of course, is no confider at all. Only Brett knows his real pain, and only the unspecified reader has any access to Jake's thought. For though he is a writer by profession, Jake neither writes nor tells his narrative to anyone in particular, not even to himself. There is in *The Sun Also Rises* no formal recognition of the motive or the occasion of Jake's retrospect, nor beyond that is there any indication of his imaginative agency in producing the narrative, if even only for the purpose of his own self-discovery. So, we are asked to suspend our disbelief to the extent that we can accept the perfect paragraphs about Belmonte and Romero as coming from right off the top of Jake's head. And we are therefore led to conclude that Jake cannot be self-conscious without violating Hemingway's code. For if he were to solicit an audience, or commit his perceptual experience and moral education to a formal mode, Jake would apparently relinquish the integrity and self-control, with all their noble helplessness, that Cohn relinquishes all the time by being so helpless in public. Art and morality are therefore at odds in *The Sun Also Rises*, and Jake's narrative is left formally suspended in the caesura between the many things Jake is supposed to be and the very few things he is allowed to do. Jake himself is left with only the bullfights and his "good behavior" because he does not have the novel he narrates. The only thing we see Jake write is a telegram.

Beyond all the familiar questions about Hemingway's indifference to history, culture and the mind, there is still the question of his personal *involvement* in his own art and how this affects the nature of his characters. In the case of Jake Barnes, the first answer to suggest itself is that Jake, despite his general reliability and clear virtue, is a profoundly ironic characterization: a portrait of the artist as an early middle-aged loser. For he has been given formidable powers of perception and a fine sense of language, but is left holding them in a situation that suggests they are insufficient and effete. Though this may be the case in fact, it does not seem to be the novel's intention, and there is nothing else in Hemingway's work or career to support such a reading. For all his other interests in the sporting life, Hemingway speaks of the artist's vocation always with the utmost seriousness; and no one in the twentieth century fashioned a more public and romantic career *as a writer* than Hemingway did.

The second answer is that Hemingway does not realize what he is doing to Jake because he has not thought out the first person novel and its demands with enough care. This reading seems more defensible. Hemingway's most frequent mode of narration is the kind of omniscience he uses to tell the story of Nick Adams in "Big Two-Hearted River." In time and characterization, Nick Adams is close to Jake. Nick's retreat to a pastoral fishing ground and his need for personalized rituals are, like Jake's, the method of his postwar education in the discipline necessary to "live in it" (Jake's phrase, p. 148). Nick, however, is not the narrator of his story. All of his experience and responses are presented through the intimately omniscient third person that Hemingway uses so well to close the distance between subject and object, reader and character. Nick need not be conscious of all the implications of his experience, nor its shape, because the style—Hemingway's style—does all the work of focus and exclusion necessary to convey the pressure Nick works through and against to achieve his self-possession. The power of "Big Two-Hearted River" results from our awareness that Nick endures his need to not-think with such resolution, and our necessarily distant perspective on his enforced unconsciousness is essential to the poignancy we are made to feel in Nick's self-control.

Because Jake Barnes is the narrator, however, the style of *The Sun Also Rises* is supposedly his style. So, our experience of Jake and, therefore, our expectations of him are different. And immersed in his consciousness, we come to see that Jake's value and significance results precisely from his ability to understand the experience he undergoes. Unlike Nick Adams, Jake is not simply holding on and watching; for during the bullfights, he gives himself away to an experience that fosters in him not only a moral selflessness (which is why he pimps for Brett), but also the aesthetic impersonality that is the fundamental imperative of modernist literature. This impersonality is an ideal Hemingway honors in his definition of "the real thing, the sequence of motion and fact which made the emotion and which would be as valid in a year or in ten years or, with luck and if you stated it purely enough, always. . . . "[9] Now, Carlos Baker has compared this "real thing" to Eliot's objective correlative, but Baker overlooks a crucial difference between them.[10] Eliot does not define the objective correlative as an experiential source—"the sequence of motion and fact which *made* the emotion"—but as a metaphor—"a set of objects, a situation, as chain of events *which shall be the formula* of that particular emotion" (my emphasis). In all of his statements about writing, Hemingway is not long on theory, nor nearly as influential as Eliot has been. But Hemingway is brilliant with practical advice and with descriptions of what it feels like to sit down and write, especially in *A Moveable Feast.* He is so, I think, precisely because he is so personally involved in his writing that he never achieves the "continual self-sacrifice," "the continual extinction of personality" that Eliot calls for in "Tradition and the Individual Talent."[11]

Malcolm Cowley has said that "Hemingway himself sometimes seems to regard writing as an exhausting ceremony of exorcism"; and Philip Young has argued at length that Hemingway's stylistic austerity is his method of self-control. More recently, Alfred Kazin has concluded that for Hemingway the sovereignty of the storyteller himself is the "*matter of* fiction."[12] The ultimate implication of these insights is that whatever integrity results from this way of writing is, first, the property of the artist himself and only secondarily the property of the artifact. Yet for Hemingway's most important contemporaries—Joyce, Faulkner, and Lawrence—the integrity of the artifact is what establishes the artist's sovereignty; and for them, style is not at all an exorcism, but the continual project of discovery, self-extension, and even transcendence. Consequently, Joyce, Faulkner and Lawrence have changed The Novel, while Hemingway's real and most enduring effect has been on the construction of the sentence.

Hemingway does not transcend himself in Jake Barnes because Jake is never free enough to move away and establish an autonomy that could rival

Hemingway's own. Jake is held close and kept down as though Hemingway were competing with him. And it is this "competitive" need that Reynolds Price defines in his essay of homage, "For Ernest Hemingway," when he says:

> His early strategy is always, at its most calculated, an oral strategy. If we hear it read, it seems the convincing speaking-voice of this sensibility. Only on the silent page do we discover that it is an unidiomatic, as ruthlessly intentional as any *tirade* of Racine's. For behind and beneath all the voices of the actors (themselves as few in number as in Sophocles) rides the one real voice—"This is what I see with my clean keen equipment. Work to see it after me." What it does not say but implies is more important—"For you I have narrowed and filtered my gaze. I am screening my vision so you will not see all. Why?—because you must enact this story for yourself; cast it, dress it, set it. Notice the chances I've left for you: no noun or verb is colored by me. I require your senses." What is most important of all—and what I think is the central motive—is this, which is concealed and of which the voice itself may be unconscious: "I tell you this, in this voice, because you must share—*must* because I require your presence, your company in my vision. I beg you to certify my knowledge and experience, my goodness and worthiness. I mostly speak as *I*. What I need from you is not empathy, identity, but patient approving witness—loving. License my life. Believe me."[13]

Price's insight has more drama and intensity than a critic usually allows himself. Yet it is, I think, absolutely right. "I mostly speak as *I*." Although Hemingway's name cannot be easily corrupted into an adjective, his style is always his, unmistakably. And Hemingway's need for the reader's belief and confirmation is both his principal strength and his greatest weakness. His need gives his prose its lucidity and weight, but this same need has kept him in *The Sun Also Rises* from giving to Jake Barnes the free authority that would make the novel Jake's fiction. His courage, his honesty, and his generosity make Jake a convincingly good man—the hardest kind of character to do. But if Jake is to be pitied, it is because Hemingway cannot give to him as much as Jake himself gives to Romero. Jake is so good, perhaps, that Hemingway cannot allow him to be quite true, lest we forget Hemingway himself is in charge of Jake and the author of the book.

Perhaps the final irony is, that of all Hemingway's imitators, Faulkner has used the Hemingway style with the most command. Yet the character who sounds most like a Hemingway narrator, limited to the immediate immutable present and unpossessed of himself, is Benjy Compson in the opening paragraphs of *The Sound and the Fury*. Without an explicit authority like Nick Carraway's, Jake remains, like Benjy, a brilliant observer but helpless. If Hemingway had known what he was doing to Jake and had done it on purpose, he would, perhaps, not have lost the reputation he has been losing, decade by decade, as we have come to understand the exigencies of the modernist novel and to shift our allegiances to Faulkner and Fitzgerald. A naive contact with the world does not provide us with "world enough and time."

Notes

1. *The Sun Also Rises*, The Scribner Library (New York: Charles Scribner's Sons, 1954), p. 170. All further citations will be made in the text.
2. "What is Phenomenology," *The Worlds of Existentialism*, ed. Maurice Friedman (New York: Random House, 1964), p. 83.
3. "Fiction [*Fiesta*, by Ernest Hemingway]," *Studies in The Sun Also Rises*, ed. William White, Charles E. Merrill Studies (Columbus, Ohio: Charles E. Merrill Publishing Company, 1969), p. 15.
4. *Hemingway: The Inward Terrain* (Seattle and London: University of Washington Press, 1968), pp. 62 ff. Halliday, "Hemingway's Narrative Perspective," *The Sewanee Review*, Vol. LX, 1952, pp. 202–218. Spilka, "The Death of Love in *The Sun Also Rises*," *Twelve Original Essays on Great Novels*, ed. Charles Shapiro (Detroit: The Wayne State University Press, 1958), pp. 238–256. Reprinted in *Hemingway: A Collection of Critical Essays*, ed. Robert Weeks, Twentieth Century Views (Englewood Cliffs, N.J.: Prentice Hall, Inc., 1962), pp. 72–85. Grebstein, *Hemingway's Craft* (Carbondale and Edwardsville: Southern Illinois University Press, 1973), pp. 67 and 68–69.
5. See also Harry Levin, "Observations on the Style of Ernest Hemingway," *Contexts of Criticism* (Cambridge: Harvard University Press, 1957), pp. 140–167. Reprinted in Weeks, pp. 72–85. A contrasting analysis is John Graham's "Ernest Hemingway: The Meaning of a Style," *Modern Fiction Studies*, Vol. 6, 1960–1961, pp. 288–313. Reprinted in *Ernest Hemingway: A Collection of Criticism*, ed. Arthur Waldhorn, Contemporary Studies in Literature (New York: McGraw-Hill Book Company, 1973), pp. 18–34.
6. *Green Hills of Africa* (New York: Charles Scribner's Sons, 1953), p. 32.
7. Grebstein maintains: "We can discover no instance in which what Jake Barnes says to us exceeds what his vantage point in time, place, and experience allows him to know." See p. 67.

8. Hovey's claim that Jake makes more of Romero's purity than Hemingway does seems to overlook the fact that Jake sees Romero in clear contrast to Belmonte. See p. 66.
9. *Death in the Afternoon* (New York: Charles Scribner's Sons, 1953), p. 2.
10. *Hemingway: The Writer as Artist* (Princeton, N.J.: Princeton University Press, 1963), p. 56.
11. *Selected Essays* (New York: Harcourt, Brace and World, Inc., 1964), p. 7.
12. Cowley, Introduction, *The Portable Hemingway* (New York: The Viking Press, 1944), p. xii. Reprinted in Weeks as "Nightmare and Ritual in Hemingway," p. 43. Young, *Ernest Hemingway: A Reconsideration* (New York: Harcourt, Brace and World, Inc., 1966). Kazin, *Bright Book of Life* (Boston-Toronto: Little, Brown and Company, 1973), p. 10.
13. *Things Themselves* (New York: Atheneum, 1972), p. 203.

ERNEST HEMINGWAY, PSALMIST

George Montiero

The subject of Ernest Hemingway and the Bible has been touched on here and there in Hemingway scholarship and occasionally acknowledged by the critics, yet the matter continues to call for extended treatment. It is clearly the subject for a book. Here, however, it may be worthwhile to sketch out one small segment of such a study: Hemingway's reading of one well-known piece of Scripture and its effect on his writings in the late twenties and early thirties. The Biblical text is King David's "Twenty-Third Psalm," and the Hemingway texts are "Neothomist Poem," published by Ezra Pound in *The Exile* in 1927, *A Farewell to Arms* (1929), and "A Clean, Well-Lighted Place" (1933). By examining, in some detail, Hemingway materials—in manuscript and typescript—at the John F. Kennedy Library, we can trace the genesis of an idea and relate it to Hemingway's vision.

I

Among the Hemingway papers at the Kennedy there are five texts included in four numbered documents that are relevant: documents 597a, 597b, 597c, and 658a. Two of these are typescripts (597a and 658a), the other two (597b and 597c) are penciled manuscripts in Hemingway's hand. Of the typescripts,

Reprinted with permission from Journal of Modern Literature, *14 (Summer 1987), pp. 83–95.*

658a presents Hemingway's "Neothomist Poem" as we know it from publication in *The Exile*. The only one of these five texts that carries the poem's title, it now rests as part of a sheaf of Hemingway's poems, eighteen in all, including the seventeen poems that appear in the several unauthorized editions in which Hemingway's poetry has circulated for decades. The eighteenth poem entitled "They All Made Peace—What Is Peace?" does not appear in those pirated chapbooks. The second typescript (597a), untitled, is a single sheet of ten lines. A clean copy of the longer version of Hemingway's poem, this text is reproduced in facsimile on page 82 of Nicholas Gerogiannis' edition of *Ernest Hemingway: 88 Poems.*[1] The manuscripts survive in two notebooks. Item 597b, the flyleaf of which contains the signature and address "Ernest Hemingway/Note Book/113 Rue Notre Dame des Champs/Paris VI,"[2] offers two tries—the earliest of those at Kennedy—at the longer version of the poem. The second half of the first of these two (on the second manuscript page) is reproduced in facsimile in *88 Poems* (also page 82), along with the complete second attempt at the longer version on the third page. These versions are untitled. Item 597c is also an untitled manuscript in pencil in Hemingway's hand. It appears in a lined notebook with writing on the first five leaves. The front flyleaf is signed "Ernest Hemingway/69 Rue Froidevaux/155, Bould Saint-Germain/Paris G." At the Kennedy this item is described, in part,

> 597c   Manuscript. Untitled pencil manuscript beginning "The Lord
>   is My Shepherd I shall not want. . . " 1 p.
>   Also one page of sentences on the dust and dew in the dark in
>   Italy.

This manuscript offers, in some ways, the most intriguing of the five versions available at Kennedy. The description of it, as I shall argue later on, is misleading—as is, I think, the numbering. For reasons that I hope to establish, I now list the five texts contained in these manuscripts and typescripts in their order of composition and/or recording:

Version 1, 597b (first and second pages);
Version 2, 597b (third page);
Version 3, 597a (typescript of ten lines);
Version 4, 597c; and
Version 5, 658a ("Neothomist Poem").

To begin at the beginning as we can best know it from the extant materials, here is Version 1, before Hemingway's cancellations:

>   The wind blows in the fall
>   and it is all over
>   The wind blows the leaves
>   from the trees
>   and it is all over
>   They do not come back
>   And if they do
>   are
>   We're gone.
>   You can start it any time
>   But you in ———
>   It will flush its self.
>   When it goes it takes
>   everything with it
>   The Lord is my shepherd
>   I shall not want him long.
>   He maketh me to lie down in
>   green pastures
>   And lo there are no green pastures
>   He leadeth me beside still waters
>   And still waters run deep.
>   Surely goodness and mercy shall
>   follow me all the days of
>   my life   And I shall
>   never escape them
>   Though I walk through the
>   vale
>   shadow of the shadow
>   of death I shall return
>   to do evil.
>   For thou art with me

> In the morning and the evening
> Especially in the evening
> The wind blows in the fall
> And it is all over
> When I walk through the valley
> of the shadow of death
> I shall (feel) fear all evil
> For thou art with me.

In revising this version, Hemingway crossed out the first thirteen lines, as well as lines 21–29. He also rearranged lines 30–33 so that they would come at the end of the poem:

The temporarily final poem that emerges from these revisions reads:

> The Lord is my shepherd
> I shall not want him long.
> He maketh me to lie down in
> green pastures
> And lo there are no green pastures
> He leadeth me beside still waters
> And still waters run deep.
> When I walk through the valley
> of the shadow of death
> I shall fear all evil
> For thou art with me.
> In the morning and the evening
> Especially in the evening
> The wind blows in the fall
> And it is all over.

My first observation is that the poem appears not to have been conceived, if the opening thirteen lines constitute its true beginning, as a parody of the "Twenty-Third Psalm." Yet when, with line fourteen, the poet moves in that direction, he remains on target for the remainder of the poem with the single exception of lines 29–33, which return the poem to its opening motif— the blowing wind. These four lines would remain in the poem, in some form or other, through the ten-line typed version (597a). Purged of its first thirteen lines, the poem reads as a rather straightforward if a trifle lachrymose rewriting of David's "Twenty-Third Psalm":

> The Lord *is* my shepherd; I shall not
>   want.
> He maketh me to lie down in green pastures: he leadeth me
>   beside the still waters.
> He restoreth my soul: he leadeth me in the paths of
>   righteousness for his name's sake.
> Yea, though I walk through the valley of the shadow of death,
>   I will fear no evil: for thou *art* with me; thy rod and
>   thy staff they comfort me.
> Thou preparest a table before me in the presence of mine
>   enemies: thou anointest my head with oil; my cup
>   runneth over.
> Surely goodness and mercy shall follow me all the days of my
>   life: and I will dwell in the house of the Lord for ever.

This version of Hemingway's poem parodies the "Psalm" only at certain points, namely verses one and two, and only the first three quarters of verse four. It does not touch verses three, five, and six. In the next version of the poem Hemingway makes several changes in wording and phrasing, adds lines (later canceled), and inserts a treatment of verse six of the "Psalm" (also largely canceled). Some of the changes and additions are significant:

(1) In the line "And still waters run deep" he crosses out "run deep," replacing it with "reflect thy face."
(2) As an alternative to the line "For thou art with me" he writes, "you are not with me," only to cross it out.
(3) He writes and then crosses out "In the morning and in the evening." He then adds the line, "In the morning nor in the evening," which he changes, by adding "Neither" and crossing out "nor," to "Neither In the morning and in the evening"; and then he crosses out "Neither." (There may be a step here that I have left out.)
(4) He writes and then crosses out the line, "Nor in the valley of the shadow of death." (It will not reappear in later versions.)

(5) He writes "And," crosses it out, and then begins again, "In the night the wind blows and you are not with me," only to change, first, "you" to "thou" and "are" to "art," then interpolating the clause, "I did not hear it for" so that the line reads: "In the night the wind blows and I did not hear it for thou art not with me," and finally, puzzlingly, he crosses out "thou" and "not."

(6) He writes, "You have gone and it is all gone with you," only to cross it out.

(7) He writes, "Surely goodness and mercy shall follow me all the days of my life and I shall never escape them. For thou art with me"—all of which he cancels.

Here is what is left, the second extant version of the poem:

> The Lord is my shepherd
> I shall not want him long
> He maketh me to lie down in
> green pastures
> And there are no green pastures.
> He leadeth me beside still
> waters
> And still waters reflect thy face.
> For thou art with me
> In the morning and in the evening
> In the night the wind
> blows and I did not hear it for [thou] art
> [not] with me.
> The wind blows in the fall
> and it is all over

The next version of the poem is the ten-line version in typed clean copy. My hunch is that the poem went through additional intermediate stages, but at this late date we can only speculate idly as to the nature and the number of steps by which Hemingway arrived at the shape of the last four lines.

> The Lord is my shepherd
> I shall not want him for long
> He maketh me to lie down in green pastures

> and there are no green pastures
> He leadeth me beside still waters
>   and still waters run deep
> the wind blows and the bark of the trees is wet from the rain
> the leaves fall and the trees are bare in the wind
> Leaves float on the still waters
> There are wet dead leaves in the basin of the fountain

(In the eighth line, incidentally, Hemingway had first written "bare in the rain," crossed out "rain" and written in "fall," and then crossed out "fall" in favor of "wind."[3])

Between the final revisions of the second manuscript version and the typing of this version Hemingway reinstated some of the first version's cancellations. Hence the second version's "And still waters reflect thy face" becomes here (once again) "and still waters run deep," while the second-version lines "In the night the wind blows" and "The wind blows in the fall" are replaced (with a specific echo of the first version's reference to "leaves") by "the wind blows and the bark of the trees is wet from the rain / the leaves fall and the trees are bare in the wind / Leaves float on the still waters / There are wet dead leaves in the basin of the fountain."

The poem, too, is wet and dead. Fortunately, Hemingway did not publish it in this form, although it is possible that it was this version that was first offered to Pound for *The Exile*. If so, it might well have been Pound, famous for his editorial blue pencil, who cut the poem down to its published form and who made the crucial decision on how to arrange the words of the poem on the page:

> The Lord is my shepherd, I shall not
>   want him for long.[4]

It is of course in this "truncated" form that the poem appears in typescript (658a) in the sheaf of eighteen poems that constitutes, chronologically, the final text of this poem at Kennedy, a text the preparation of which, I suspect, came after the publication of the poem in *The Exile* and was undertaken for the possible purpose of an authorized collection of Hemingway's verse that never materialized.

II

In this chronological consideration of the extant texts of "Neothomist Poem," I have so far skipped document 597c, even though I would place its date of composition somewhere between that of the ten-line typescript (597a) and that of the published version in *The Exile* in 1927. I consider it now, seemingly out of order, mainly because in manuscript 597c this "text" is squeezed in at the top of the first page of Hemingway's notebook in this form: "The Lord Is My Shepherd I Shall Not Want / him / for / long," with the last three words written down the right margin horizontally, one word to the line. Crammed in as it is, with each word in the top full line showing an initial capital, it is obvious to me that this is not the text of a poem but the title for the piece of fragmentary writing that follows it. And what is that piece of fragmentary writing? Whatever it is, it is not a parody of the "Twenty-Third Psalm," one might be surprised to learn, but an entirely different text unmistakably in prose:

> Now that I know that I
> am going to die none of it
> seems to make much difference
> there are a few things that
> I would like to think about.
> When you have them you can
> not keep them y but maybe
> after you have gone away they
> are still there. You can not
> keep them but if you try but
> later, when they have gone, they
> return
> come
> come again and sometimes
> *they will stay.*
> You can not keep them but
> after you are gone they are
> still there. In the fall the leaves
> fell from the trees, and we walked

It was very dusty
 Toward evening it was not
so hot but it was still
dusty and the dust
rose from the road

 When it was dark the
dew came and settled the
dust on the road that
we marched on.
 In Italy when it was
dark the dew came settled the
dust on the roadw and
the men that the troops
marched on in the dark
and beside the road there
were poplar trees in the
dark
 In Oak Park Illinois

Hemingway would cross out all but two of the first thirteen lines, expunge
the whole of lines eighteen, thirty, thirty-one, and thirty-five, and cancel
individual words and phrases in lines seventeen, twenty-eight, and twenty-
nine, thereby leaving this residual text:

The Lord Is My Shepherd I Shall Not Want
 him for long.
When you have them you can
not keep them y
You can not keep them but
after you are gone they are
still there.   In the fall the leaves
fell from the trees
 Toward evening it was not
so hot but it was still

> dusty and the dust
> rose from the road
>   When it was dark the
> dew came and settled the
> dust on the road that
> we marched on.
> In Italy when it was
> dark the dew settled the
> dust on the road
> and beside the road there
> were poplar trees in the
> dark

To Hemingway's attentive readers there will be something undoubtedly familiar about this unpublished text, crude as it is, with multiple starts. Dating from 1926, it is the forerunner (quite possibly the very first version), I would propose, of that famous text with its memorable opening lines:

> In the late summer of that year we lived in a house in a village that looked across the river and the plain to the mountains. In the bed of the river there were pebbles and boulders, dry and white in the sun, and the water was clear and swiftly moving and blue in the channels. Troops went by the house and down the road and the dust they raised powdered the leaves of the trees. The trunks of the trees too were dusty and the leaves fell early that year and we saw the troops marching along the road and the dust rising and leaves, stirred by the breeze, falling and the soldiers marching and afterward the road bare and white except for the leaves.[5]

Here, with its evocative references to falling leaves and dust rising from the road (there are three attempts at getting the imagery right in the manuscript numbered 597c), we have the ur-text for the opening of *A Farewell to Arms* (as well as the opening of Chapter 25, with its echoing imagery of "bare trees" and "wet dead leaves"), one that can be dated considerably earlier than any so far suggested.[6] In any case, if I am right in seeing this as the ur-text for the novel, we would do well to mull over the fact that Hemingway had originally begun his book with the clear indication that the narrator (and hero) is convinced that his death (suicide, perhaps) is imminent. Taken in combination with the sardonic title (crammed in at the top after, as I have already suggested, the author had sat down the prose text), this rejected text suggests even more strongly that the context in which ex-Lieutenant Frederic Henry sets down his own retrospective narrative of his losses in war and love is one of personal despair and acedia.[7] As such, then, the line, "The Lord Is My Shepherd I Shall Not Want Him For Long" should not merely be acknowledged as another of the titles, considered and rejected, for the novel that would eventually be called *A Farewell to Arms* but recognized as the very first of that string of titles (at least the earliest one so far uncovered) to be set down.[8] In this case, I suspect that the author would have rejected the title soon after crossing out the opening six lines about the narrator's impending death as sounding too orthodox a religious note. But having considered the opening lines of his poem parodying the "Twenty-Third Psalm" as a title for a work of fiction he proposed to write and isolating them for that purpose, he may well have discovered, I would venture, the poem he (or Pound) would later entitle "Neothomist Poem."[9]

III

Echoes of the "Twenty-Third Psalm" and Hemingway's parodies of that Old Testament poem would resurface still again. And they would reappear creatively in combination with the dual themes of death and suicide in what would turn out to be one of Hemingway's finest stories: "A Clean, Well-Lighted Place."

Consider that in this dark parable there are not only nihilistic parodies of "The Lord's Prayer" and the Catholic prayer to the Virgin recited by the so-called older waiter, but also a context for those culminating prayers, the conversation between the two waiters about an old man (a "client") and his unsuccessful attempt at suicide: his failure to commit, in short, the unpardonable sin against the Holy Ghost, an act undertaken in the first place because, as the older waiter explains, the old man was in the state of despair. "He was in despair," the waiter says wryly (in what is, after all, a privately grim joke), about "Nothing."[10] Three times on the opening pages of this story we are told that the old man, in a deliberate echoing of the shadow image of the "Twenty-Third Psalm" ("though I walk through the valley of the shadow of death"), is sitting there in the "shadow" made by the leaves of the tree (17–18). (But note as well the even closer echo of Luke 1:79 on the purpose of John the Baptist: "To give light to them that sit in darkness and *in* the shadow of death.") The old man, deaf and alone, orders another drink of brandy. The younger waiter pours him one, filling up his glass. But then, in a remarkable literalization into action of one of the most familiar metaphors employed in the "Twenty-Third Psalm"—"my cup runneth over"— Hemingway writes, "The old man motioned with his finger. 'A little more,' he said. The waiter poured on into the glass so that the brandy slopped over and ran down the stem into the top saucer of the pile" (19).

If the talk of suicide and the imagery of shadows caused by the leaves of trees recall the discarded opening for *A Farewell to Arms* the second sentence of the story echoes closely the opening of the novel as published. Here is *A Farewell to Arms*: "the dust they (the troops) raised powdered the leaves of the trees. The trunks of the trees too were dusty and the leaves fell early that year and we saw the troops marching along the road and the dust rising . . . " (17).

At one point in "A Clean, Well-Lighted Place," the older waiter tries to spell out just how his situation differs from that of his fellow-waiter. When the latter asserts, "'I have confidence. I am all confidence,'" he replies, "'you have youth, confidence, and a job'" (22). As for himself, he is no longer young, he acknowledges, and he has never had "confidence." Even as it was for Herman Melville, "confidence" is a key term here. If it can mean something like self-assurance (as it does, undoubtedly, for the younger waiter), it also means "faith"—the Spanish term *confidencia*. Indeed, if the older waiter has never had such *confidencia*, such "faith," then I am even more certain that his expressions of nihilism are a form of displaying his acedia. The consolations to the believers—to men of faith—that are the "Lord's Prayer" and the prayer to the Virgin Mary are not available to those who lack "confidence," even as the "Twenty-Third Psalm"—sometimes described as *"David's confidence in the grace of God"*—serves only as a repository of sentiments and images that can only be taken ironically by the author who not only constructed parodies of the "Twenty-Third Psalm," but also wrote *A Farewell to Arms* and "A Clean, Well-Lighted Place." To the expansive pastoral consolations of the "Twenty-Third Psalm"—its "still waters," "paths of righteousness," the "table" prepared "in the presence of mine enemies," and the promise of anointment—man can only counter with the narrow virtues of a localized cleanliness and man-made light. For the "house of the Lord" in which the psalmist, confident in the grace of God, shall "dwell . . . for ever," Hemingway's older waiter offers only the café, "clean, well-lighted," which, though he would "stay late," will perforce close each night while the night is still dark and will remain so long, ostensibly, after the first glimmer of "day-light." "It is probably only insomnia," the waiter says to himself; "Many must have it" (24). And indeed they must in Hemingway's peopled world, from the rattled Nick Adams of "Now I Lay Me" (with its ironic titular reference to still another prayer) to the author who himself compulsively parodied the "Twenty-Third Psalm" in the late 1920s, both in his poem and in his frag-mentary first try at writing his novel about the loss of confidence in war, love, and self.

Yet the story is not a simpler retreatment of the implosive matter of the novel. Although the themes of faith and *confidencia* appear and reappear the-matically in the novel, the emphasis there is more secular than in the story. In fact, the novel and story differ in this matter nowhere more distinctly than in the way each of the texts handles the shared matter of empty high-mind-edness, bankrupt idealism, and the words and beliefs attending both. Although it is not common to relate the two passages, I shall juxtapose here two of the best known excerpts in all of Hemingway. I have in mind the pas-sage from *A Farewell to Arms* in which Lt. Henry identifies the words that embarrass him, along with those that do not, and the sentences from "A Clean, Well-Lighted Place," in which the older waiter utters his prayer to "*nada*." The first quotation comes from the novel:

> I was always embarrassed by the words sacred, glorious, and sacri-fice and the expression in vain. We had heard them, sometimes stand-ing in the rain almost out of earshot, so that only the shouted words came through, and had read them, on proclamations that were slapped up by billposters over other proclamations, now for a long time, and I had seen nothing sacred, and the things that were glorious had no glory and the sacrifices were like the stockyards at Chicago if nothing was done with the meat except to bury it. There were many words that you could not stand to hear and finally only the names of places had digni-ty. Certain numbers were the same way and certain dates and these with the names of the places were all you could say and have them mean anything. Abstract words such as glory, honor, courage, or hallow were obscene beside the concrete names of villages, the numbers of roads, the names of rivers, the numbers of regiments and the dates. (184–85)

In "A Clean, Well-Lighted Place," it should be noted, there are no words that seem to convey "dignity." Indeed, the first time the word "dignity" appears in the story, it is used to describe the old man, who, as the waiter watched him, "walk[ed] unsteadily" down the street "but with dignity," while later the word is used to indicate not its existence but its absence: "Nor can you stand before a bar with dignity." As for the reality behind "words," here is the older waiter's utterance of the "Lord's Prayer":

> Our *nada* who art in *nada*, *nada* be thy name thy kingdom *nada* thy will be *nada* in *nada* as it is in *nada*. Give us this *nada* our daily *nada* and *nada* us our *nada* as we *nada* our *nadas* and *nada* us not into *nada* but deliver us from *nada*; *pues nada*. (23–24)

To make clear just what is at stake in this prayerful blasphemy of a prayer, we need only recall the Catholic prayer itself. I have underlined the words the older waiter has replaced by his *nadas* to bring to the fore just what he is denying:

> Our Father who art in heaven, hallowed be Thy name; Thy Kingdom come; Thy will be done on earth as it is in heaven. Give us this day our daily bread: and forgive us our trespasses as we forgive those who trespass against us; and lead us not into temptation, but deliver us from evil. Amen.[11]

Denied here—not just their value but their very existence—are not the abstract words of *A Farewell to Arms*—such as sacred, glorious, and sacrifice, along with the virtues encoded in the expression in vain—but words such as *Father, heaven, hallowed* ("hallow" does appear in Lt. Henry's litany), *earth, day, bread, trespasses, forgive[ness], temptation,* and *evil.* Father, heaven and hell, in this context, might well be considered conceptualized abstractions, but surely earth, day, and bread would be considered by most to be at least as real as those proper names and nominative numbers that still carry meaning for Frederic Henry. If it can be said that the strongest subtext of *A Farewell to Arms* is religious, it is equally clear that in "A Clean, Well-Lighted Place" Hemingway makes that theme fully explicit. In the story he again succeeded in drawing on the same emotional pressure and spiritual capital that had energized his novel about a young soldier's acedic experience of war and love.

Notes

1. *Ernest Hemingway: 88 Poems*, ed. Nicholas Gerogiannis (Harcourt Brace Jovanovich/Bruccoli-Clark, 1979).
2. This and all quotations from Hemingway's manuscripts and typescripts at the John F. Kennedy Library, Boston, Massachusetts, have been permitted by Mary Hemingway with the consent of the Library.
3. The aesthetic/biographical function of the echoes here of two other texts— although of sufficient significance to call for close investigation—cannot be taken up at this time. I refer to (1) the anonymous sixteenth-century poem beginning: "O Western wind, when wilt thou blow / That the small rain down can rain?" (for an analysis of the way allusions to this text—already present in this discarded opening—work at certain points in *A Farewell to Arms*, see Charles R. Anderson's "Hemingway's Other Style," *Modern Language Notes*, LXXVI [May 1961], 434–42); and (2) Ezra Pound's "In a Station of the Metro"— "The apparition of these faces in the crowd; / Petals on a wet, black bough"—a poem which, suffice it to say here, also resulted (as in Hemingway's case) from its author's success, to quote Hugh Kenner, "after several decreasingly wordy attempts, over a period of months . . . in boiling away the contingent distractions of the original experience" (*The Poetry of Ezra Pound* [New Directions, n.d.], p. 73).
4. *The Exile*, I (Spring 1927), 21. If the layout of the poem cannot be definitively attributed to either the author or his editor, we can nevertheless find the precedent for so breaking the opening line of the "Twenty-Third Psalm." The line is so broken, of course, in the King James Version of the Old Testament: "The Lord is my shepherd; I shall not / want." This traditional line-break is maintained even in the New International Version of the *Holy Bible*: "The Lord is my shepherd, I shall lack / nothing."
5. Ernest Hemingway, *A Farewell to Arms* (Scribner's, 1929), p. 3. All further references to the novel will be to this edition and will be indicated in the text by page number.
6. See Michael S. Reynolds, *Hemingway's First War: The Making of "A Farewell to Arms"* (Princeton University Press, 1976), p. 285, who suggests that Hemingway began the novel in early March 1928.
7. Reynolds devotes an appendix to rejected titles (*Hemingway's First War*, pp. 295–97). To this list, Bernard Oldsey adds three other titles in his *Hemingway's Hidden Craft: The Writing of "A Farewell to Arms"* (Pennsylvania State University Press, 1979), pp. 21–22. Paul Smith presents a still longer list, one numbering forty-three titles in "Almost All Is Vanity: A Note on Nine Rejected Titles for *A Farewell to Arms*," *The Hemingway Review*, II (Fall 1982), 74–76.

    I wish to take this opportunity to thank Paul Smith for his advice regarding the manuscripts at the Kennedy Library.

8.   My reading of this discarded opening is not at all at odds, in my opinion, with
     Millicent Bell's telling interpretation of *A Farewell to Arms*. "The novel is about
     neither love nor war; it is about a state of mind, and that state of mind is the
     author's," asserts Bell. "Already on the opening page, in 1915, the voice that
     speaks to us exhibits that attitude psychoanalysts call 'blunting of affect,' the
     dryness of soul which underlies its exquisite attentiveness" ("*A Farewell to Arms:*
     Pseudobiography and Personal Metaphor," in James Nagel, ed., *Ernest
     Hemingway: The Writer in Context* [University of Wisconsin Press, 1984], pp.
     111 and 112).

9.   No one seems to have paid sufficient attention to the fact that it was Ezra Pound
     who explained in *The Exile* that "Mr. Hemingway's POEM refers to events in
     what remains of the French world of letters" (91–92). It's possible that Pound
     actually got this notion from Hemingway himself, but the early
     manuscripts/typescripts of the longer version of the poem indicate nothing of
     the sort. That these drafts are untitled as well suggests that it was not until 1927
     that either Hemingway or Pound thought up the title. When the poem
     appeared, its title was garbled: "Nothoemist Poem." Pound penciled in a correc-
     tion in every copy of *The Exile*, an act that perhaps indicated that he was the true
     author of the poem's title. (See Philip Young, *Ernest Hemingway* [Rinehart,
     1952], p. 236.) Later Hemingway would seemingly echo Pound's explanation in
     The Exile by insisting: (1) that this title referred to the "temporary embracing of
     church by literary gents" (Louis Henry Cohn, *A Bibliography of the Works of
     Ernest Hemingway* [Random House, 1931], p. 89); and (2) that (in a letter to
     Philip Young, June 23, 1952) "his poem was meant to 'kid' Jean Cocteau, who
     had then just switched from opium to Neo-Thomism. He added that the poem
     did not express his own personal beliefs." (Carlos Baker, *Ernest Hemingway: A
     Life Story* [Scribner's, 1969], p. 596.)

     Even before Hemingway sent in his poem, however, Pound had assured him
     that in his projected magazine "there shall be absolootly no neo-Thomism (will
     thot content you?)." In this letter dated 3 November 1926 (and only recently
     published: Jacqueline Tavernier-Courbin, "Ernest Hemingway and Ezra Pound,"
     Ernest Hemingway: The Writer in Context, p. 194), Pound goes on to describe the
     sort of contribution he would like from Hemingway: "Re yr own stuff . as I sez ,
     there is no use me paying a printer for to set up stuff you can sell to Scribner .
     What one wants fer this kind of show , is short stuff, so short that space rates
     cant make it worth while carrying to market ; and odd sizes , and unvendable
     matter ."

10. *Winner Take Nothing* (Scribner's, 1933), p. 17. All further references to the story
     will be to this edition and will be indicated in the text by page number.

11. *New Baltimore Catechism No. 1*, Official Revised Edition (Benziger Brothers,
     n.d.), p. 3.

IN OUR TIME AS SELF-BEGETTING FICTION

Elizabeth Dewberry Vaughn

In 1923, one year before Ernest Hemingway published the first *in our time*, T. S. Eliot proclaimed that the novel had "ended with Flaubert and with James" (482–483).[1] Any writer responding to the atrocities of World War One at that time could have complained, as Philip Roth did in 1961, that "The actuality is continually outdoing our talents, and culture tosses up figures almost daily that are the envy of any novelist" (224). Whereas conditions of crisis in the Sixties led many American writers to direct their creative energies into chronicling actual, rather than fictitious, events (new journalism, as Peter Hamill named it[2]), many writers in the early Twenties responded to the destructive horrors of their time by simultaneously transforming actual events into literature and exploring this creative process through metaliterature. E. E. Cummings' *The Enormous Room* (1922), for example, opens with an introduction comprised of a series of nonfictional letters and summaries of the responses they received. Written during World War One by Cummings' father asking U.S. government officials to arrange for his son's release from a French concentration camp, the letters establish a nonfictional premise for the book, which in turn uses allusions to John Bunyan's *Pilgrim's Progress*, illustrations, and typographical innovations to flaunt its status as invention. Thus, as Patricia Waugh claims all metafiction does, this

Reprinted with permission from Modern Fiction Studies *(Winter 1989), pp. 707–716.*

autobiographical novel "self-consciously and systematically draws attention to its status as an artefact in order to pose questions about the relationship between fiction and reality" (2). The elaborate system of literary allusions and notes explaining these allusions in T. S. Eliot's *The Waste Land* (1922) and William Carlos Williams' explicit incorporation of the idea of the great American novel into his 1923 work, *The Great American Novel*, function similarly.

Although Ernest Hemingway is usually labeled as a realist, his first full-length work, *In Our Time*, also exhibits many metafictional qualities. Ezra Pound suggested as much when he called the series in which Hemingway's first *in our time* was published an "Inquest into the state of contemporary English prose" (*in our time*, inside back cover). Yet although a few critics have noticed metafictional aspects in *In Our Time*, none to my knowledge has explored the metafictional ramifications of its announced inquisitional purposes. This essay approaches *In Our Time* as a work that uses realist and metafictional conventions to explore the relationship between fiction and reality and which therefore explores "a *theory* of fiction through the *practice* of writing fiction" as Waugh characterizes all metafiction (2).

Metafictional tendencies in "Big Two-Hearted River" were noted as early as 1959, yet surprisingly little critical thought has developed around this topic. In his essay "Hemingway's Two-Hearted River" Sheridan Baker observed, "Hemingway, indeed, consistently shows a kind of wilfulness in reporting fact with journalistic accuracy and then insisting that it is all fiction, that 'there are no real people in this volume.'" (157). Baker's discussion of metafictional tendencies in "Big Two-Hearted River" leads him to conclude that "what Hemingway himself counts as fiction seems to contain a very high saturation of actuality" (158). Nevertheless, his assertion that the narrator in the story suggests that "there are no real people in this volume" is significant in terms of what it implies about the narrator's own fictionality and the metafictional nature of *In Our Time*.

The deleted coda to "Big Two-Hearted River," first published in 1972 in *The Nick Adams Stories* under the title "On Writing," clarifies these implications by suggesting one way in which *In Our Time* is a metafiction. The coda provides evidence that Nick Adams is the writer of *In Our Time* and that the book therefore examines the relationship between art and reality by providing an account "of the development of a character to the point at which he is able to take up his pen and compose the novel we have just finished reading" (Kellman, "The Fiction of Self-Begetting" 1245). Susan F. Beegel has effectively demonstrated how an examination of the cuts Hemingway made in his manuscripts can illuminate "the thing left out" and therefore the meaning of the text, and this is certainly the case here:

> The only writing that was any good was what you made up, what you imagined. That made everything come true. Like when he [Nick] wrote "My Old Man" he'd never seen a jockey killed and the next week Georges Parfrement was killed at that very jump and that was the way it looked. . . .
>
> Nick in the stories was never himself. He made him up. Of course he'd never seen an Indian woman having a baby [as he does in "Indian Camp"]. That was what made it good. Nobody knew that. He'd seen a woman have a baby on the road to Karagatch and tried to help her. That was the way it was.
>
> He wished he could always write like that. He would sometime. He wanted to be a great writer. He was pretty sure he would be. (237–238)

This passage clearly indicates that Nick Adams wrote "My Old Man" and "Indian Camp," while the phrase "in the stories" implies that he has written others. Thus, when the last sentence of the coda states, "He was holding something in his head" (241), it is logical to ask whether this "something" is Nick's conception of *In Our Time*.

At the very least this information should lead to a determination of which stories Nick has written and an assessment of the significance of his authorship. I argue here that Nick is the sole narrator of *In Our Time* and that voices that identify themselves as someone other than Nick constitute Nick's experimentation with the convention of the narrator's status as a disembodied voice. These other voices contribute to the investigation conducted throughout *In Our Time* of the ramifications of language that creates and comprises identity, the ways in which the linguistic reality of fictional characters engenders that of fiction and vice versa, and the role of voice in determining and communicating the relationship between fictional and historical realities.

Conventional readings of *In Our Time* pay little attention to narrative voice. Joe, who identifies himself as the speaker in "My Old Man," is generally assumed to be a reliable narrator and tends to be discussed in terms of his characterization in the story rather than specifically as narrator of the story. In his only reference to Joe as narrator, Joseph DeFalco, for example, states: "By using this point of view, Hemingway is better able to exhibit the inner attitudes of the central character and reveal the pathos of the final learning situation" (56). Yet if Nick wants to be a fiction writer, he must "find his voice" by experimenting with voices other than his own, and in fact he announces in the coda that this is exactly what he does with Joe in "My Old Man."

The British voices heard in "On the Quai at Smyrna," Chapter Three ("We were in a garden at Mons"), Chapter Four ("It was a frightfully hot day"), and "L'Envoi" also tend to be dismissed, usually with a reference to possible sources among Hemingway's British acquaintances, but they, too, can be understood as significant attempts by Nick to develop a fictional voice. Carlos Baker suggests that Chapters Three and Four "aped the tight-lipped British style that Chink [E. E. Dorman-] Smith had used in telling [Hemingway] of the fighting around Mons" (108), and Robert O. Stephens identifies the story colorfully told by Shorty Wornall and reported by Hemingway in the 15 September 1923 *Toronto Star Weekly*, "King Business in Europe Isn't What It Used to Be," as the journalistic source that is echoed in "L'Envoi" (15). Yet the fact that the British speaker has more than one identifiable source raises questions that neither Baker nor Stephens addresses concerning whether these pieces are narrated by one or more than one speaker. These questions direct the reader's attention to the narrator and thus ultimately to Nick.

DeFalco convincingly argues that the clause "he said" in the opening sentence of "On the Quai at Smyrna" ("The strange thing was, he said, how they screamed every night at midnight") and in the first sentence of the fifth paragraph ("The worst, he said, were the women with dead babies") indicates that "the piece is being told second-hand by the narrator" (127). This distinction between narrator and story-teller affirms that the non-British narrator, who usually presents himself as an objective observer, is capable of speaking in other voices and thus establishes the possibility that all the British voices as well as the first-person speakers in "My Old Man" and "The Revolutionist" come from the same narrator. The presence of fictional narrators created by a fictional narrator "projects the illusion of art creating itself . . . like an infinite series of boxes within boxes" as Kellman says all self-begetting fiction does ("The Self-Begetting Novel" 119), and emphasizes the extent to which all the voices of *In Our Time* are realized only through language.

The four pieces with British speech mannerisms announce their concern with the role language plays in shaping the relationship between identity, fictionality, and reality in other ways as well. It is instructive, therefore, to observe the ways in which the linguistic voice that creates and is created by "On the Quai at Smyrna," Chapters Three and Four, and "L'Envoi" uses language both as a defense against his own (linguistic) reality and as a way of reaching toward it.

"On the Quai at Smyrna" graphically illustrates the language's inability to contain a reality that is inconceivably atrocious. In his account of a war-time evacuation the story-teller describes, among other things, screaming refugees, women who refuse to give up their dead babies, and mules whose forelegs are broken before they are dumped into the water to drown as "strange," "unimaginable," "the worst," "extraordinary," and "surprising." He closes the story, "It was all a pleasant business. My word yes a most pleasant business" (*In Our Time* 11–12).

Hemingway had learned from the *Kansas City Star* stylesheet to "avoid the use of adjectives, especially such extravagant ones as *splendid, gorgeous, grand, magnificent*, etc." (Rule 21), and in what Kenneth S. Lynn calls "the most celebrated passage in all of Hemingway's work" (385), he expresses his continuing belief in this idea through Frederic Henry: "I was always embarrassed by the words sacred, glorious, and sacrifice and the expression in vain" (*A Farewell to Arms* 184). Yet Hemingway's liberal use of adjectives here does not contradict these statements: where Frederic Henry and the editors of the *Kansas City Star* shun adjectives because they fail to communicate, the speaker in "On the Quai at Smyrna" uses them to demonstrate that they fail to communicate.

Critical commentary on this passage tends to emphasize the ways it uses inappropriate words to illustrate this inherent deficiency in language. Louis H. Leiter, for example, comments on the speaker's adjective choices, "This horror in order to be spoken of at all must be named for its opposite" (138), and S. P. Jain notes, "Obviously, the horror caused by the sight of dead bodies and their fragments has become too shattering for words: only the inversion of words, with its glinting ironic edges, comes closer to conveying it" (60).

Yet the "inversion of words" in this passage also testifies to the power of language. The horror of the scene is communicated, not despite the teller's apparent inability to express it through language, but through this inability, because an unspeakable horror is more horrifying than a spoken one. Furthermore, the British expressions such as "My word yes a most pleasant business" not only point to the vast chasm between what the language names and what it suggests but also contribute to the constitution of the voice's character as an Englishman and demonstrate a parallel between the composition of a story and the construction of reality. By contributing to the characterization of the story-teller as well as to the story, the British expressions demonstrate how the speaker's production of the text generates the text's production of the speaker. And by calling attention to themselves through their apparent incongruity while ostensibly calling attention to a reality that exists outside the language, they suggest a connection between language and reality. The speaker's inability to find terms that express the horrors he has seen bespeaks his inability to "come to terms" with that reality and therefore demonstrates that if language shapes thought, it dictates what can be perceived. The passage illustrates what Waugh calls "the most fundamental assumption" of metafictional writers, that "composing a novel is basically no different from composing or constructing one's 'reality'" (24). Events that are unspeakable are by definition inconceivable and vice versa.

Conflicts between language and reality that ultimately illustrate language's function in shaping reality are also present in Chapters Three and Four and in "L'Envoi." In Chapter Three the speaker describes a man he has just shot as "awfully surprised" (29), and in Chapter Four he describes a barricade as "perfect," "simply priceless," and "absolutely topping" (29). He uses the same expression, "frightfully," both to describe how hot a day it was and to explain how "put out" he and the people with him are when they have to retreat. Daniel Fuchs correctly notes that the narrator's word choices do not "blend well with the murderous activity in which the English are both agents and victims" and instead reveal "the inadequacies of a language not equipped to deal with the destructive realities" (42). Similarly, in "L'Envoi" the narrator speaks of a "very jolly" visit with the king and queen of Greece, who say, "Oh how do you do" and "Of course the great thing in this sort of an affair is not to be shot oneself!" (157). Again, as Fuchs points out, "A tension exists between the grim realities of revolutionary politics and the inanities of genteel conversation" (42). In both cases, however, the inadequacies or inanities of language and the tensions between language and the reality it names prompt larger questions about the relationship between language or linguistic reality and history or historical reality and demonstrate how narrator and text generate one another. By revealing the relationship between the speaker's inability to express and to understand the horrors he has seen, the language in the British speaker's pieces demonstrates the relationship between expressions of and perceptions of reality.

Although, as Robert Gibb observes, "There is nothing in 'Big Two-Hearted River' that is outside Nick's perceptions" (257), in the other stories and vignettes of *In Our Time* the narrator tends to take the conventional omniscient narrator's stance and tends to call attention neither to himself nor to his participation in the story. Indeed, except in "My Old Man" and of course the deleted coda, the narrative voices reveal so little about their identities through conventional channels of characterization that they can hardly be considered entities, "thing[s] which ha[ve] reality and distinctness of being either in fact or for thought" (*Webster's New Collegiate Dictionary*), because they have no "distinctness of being." It is instructive, therefore, to observe the ways in which the linguistic entity who creates and is created by *In Our Time* uses language to identify himself through the variety of narrative voices in the text.

What information can be pieced together about this narrator through a conventional reading of him comes from inferences that can be drawn about his interests through examination of the subject matters of his stories. For example, the topics about which he cares enough to write include war, bullfighting, human suffering, and Nick Adams. Indeed, Nick plays a central role in the book, which is commonly understood by critics as the "story" of Nick Adams' transition from childhood to adulthood. For example, Clinton S. Burhans traces Nick's "education in actuality" (95) through the stories to demonstrate that "For Nick Adams and others like him . . . the world 'in our time' turns out to be exactly what the vignettes suggests it is—a puzzling and disillusioning place" (97). Jackson J. Benson also argues that while he was writing "Big Two-Hearted River," "Hemingway must have decided to proceed roughly chronologically, filling in with stories from Nick's childhood, through his adolescence, to young manhood. This personal chronology [i.e., Nick's life] becomes . . . [a] major unifying force in *In Our Time*" (108). Yet closer examination of Nick's role in *In Our Time* and his thoughts and ambitions about writing that were cut from "Big Two-Hearted River" further suggests that Nick is a unifying force in *In Our Time* because Hemingway was using Nick to experiment with the idea of self-begetting fiction.

The text proper of *In Our Time* reveals that Nick has fought in a war, has experienced human suffering, and has fished for trout, all subjects with which the author must have been familiar, but the coda reveals that Nick also knew Maera, the bullfighter who is killed by a bull in Chapter Fourteen, and that Nick has had the intense, prolonged emotional involvement with his subject matter that often produces good writing. For example, it states that he had been "married" to fishing (234) and that "his whole inner life had been bullfights all one year" (236). Thus, the coda demonstrates that Nick has had more first-hand access to and more intense involvement with the components of *In Our Time* than the text proper reveals he has.

The coda also reveals Nick's ambition to write: "He wanted to be a great writer. He was pretty sure he would be. He knew it in lots of ways" (238). There is no question that the author is directly referring to Nick here rather than to himself, as some critics who quote fragments from this piece out of context imply. Carlos Baker, for example, does not even mention Nick in his discussion of the coda. He quotes from it and comments,

> Nothing that he [Hemingway] said afterwards on the subject of writing had quite the special poignancy of these fumbling attempts to describe his intention, his ambition, his developing esthetic bias, his consuming love both for writing and for the world. . . . Ernest wanted to be a great writer. He was pretty sure he would be. (132)[3]

Chaman Nahal also unselfconsciously substitutes Hemingway for Nick:

> Referring to his own work, he [Hemingway] asserts that the old man in his story "My Old Man" was totally made up; he had never seen a jockey killed in actual life. He also asserts that Nick Adams in his stories was never based on Hemingway himself. Nick was also made up. (194)

Similarly, Raymond S. Nelson dismisses Nick by asserting that the coda "is of interest for it speaks explicitly to Hemingway's purpose as a writer, articulated through the consciousness of his developing character, Nick Adams" (7). What the similarities between Nick and Hemingway suggest about Hemingway's life is a question for his biographers, but the fact that Hemingway writes the passage about Nick should lead to assessments of Nick's life as a writer. Given his body of experience and knowledge as well as his desire to write, and assuming that he has the talent he believes himself to have, Nick would almost certainly write something very close to *In Our Time*, if not *In Our Time* itself.

The coda states, furthermore, that Nick wants to "write like Cezanne painted" (239):

> He, Nick, wanted to write about country so it would be there like Cezanne had done it in painting. . . . He knew just how Cezanne would paint this stretch of river. . . . Nick seeing how Cezanne would do the stretch of river and the swamp, stood up and stepped down into the

stream. The water was cold and actual. He waded across the stream, moving in the picture. (240)

Many critics have pointed out that the narrator accomplished in "Big Two-Hearted River" exactly what Nick hopes to, although most assume that Hemingway was narrating here in his own voice.[4]

Thus although most critics view *In Our Time* as a more or less unified work about Nick Adams, they tend to avoid discussions of the implications of the coda's assertion that *In Our Time* is also by Nick Adams and therefore unified *by* Nick Adams in more than one way. They focus on what Hemingway reveals about his own views of writing in the coda at the cost of ignoring the implications of the fact that these opinions are specifically attributed to Nick. Robert Gibb acknowledges, "It is almost impossible not to see 'Big Two-Hearted River' as one of Nick's inventions" (256), but instead of exploring this idea, he states what Baker, Nahal, Nelson, and others imply, "It is not important whether Nick has written this story" (256).

Nevertheless, *In Our Time* exhibits many of the qualities that Kellman, who claims to have first coined the term "self-begetting fiction,"[5] identifies as characteristic of this subgenre. For example, Kellman points out the self-begetting novel's "heritage of French naturalism" ("The Fiction of Self-Begetting" 1246), while Hemingway wrote *In Our Time* when he lived in Paris, and he later named Flaubert and de Maupassant among those who influenced him.[6] Similarly, where Kellman argues that self-begetting novels' tendency "to make frequent and prolonged allusion to other literary works" ("The Fiction of Self-Begetting" 1250–1251), Hemingway scholars have traced in *In Our Time* echoes of works by T. S. Eliot, Ezra Pound, Gertrude Stein, Sherwood Anderson, James Joyce, and John Dos Passos, to name a few.[7]

Perhaps more importantly, *In Our Time* also treats several specific themes as self-begetting novels tend to treat them. For example, Kellman demonstrates that the "self-begetting novel begins with an urge toward immortality" ("The Fiction of Self-Begetting" 1255), and the narrator states at the end of "Indian Camp," the first full-length story in the collection, that "[Nick] felt quite sure that he would never die" (19). Furthermore, in light of Nick's admission in the coda that he wrote this story, the narrator's ironic tone in this statement illustrates the dialectic throughout *In Our Time* "between naive, questing hero and his narrator alter ego recollecting prior emotion in current tranquility" ("The Fiction of Self-Begetting" 1247). Kellman also stresses the prominence of birth imagery in self-begetting fiction: "'Self-begetting is not a merely fanciful critical label for these works, as is borne out by their own imagery. . . . The protagonist['s] . . . efforts are depicted as terminating in personal rebirth. And he conceives his projected novel through the explicit trope of gestation" ("The Fiction of Self-Begetting" 1252–1253). Hemingway employs explicit birth imagery in "On the Quai at Smyrna," "Indian Camp," and Chapter Two, as well as more subtle womb imagery throughout the collection.

Although Nick and many of the actions he performs in the book are based on real-life and journalistic prototypes,[8] the most obvious being Hemingway himself, Nick is clearly a fictional character. Nevertheless, *In Our Time*, some of which Nick explicitly claims to have written and the rest of which he implicitly claims to have written, is real, as its physical presence in the reader's hands affirms. The concreteness of the book nurtures the illusion of Nick's reality as it deflates it: because the book is real, its "author" must be real; and because the book is real, the fictional character's claims that he is its author must not be real, for if the idea that he wrote it is a fiction, he must be a fiction as well.

Waugh claims that the emphasis in self-begetting fiction "is on the development of the narrator, on the modernist concern of *consciousness* rather than the post-modernist one of *fictionality*" (14). Yet the emphasis in *In Our Time* is on consciousness (existence in the real world), fictionality (existence in the imaginal world), and the relationship between the two. Nick brings reality and fictionality together and blurs traditional distinctions between fact and fiction by forcing the reader, who reads the book a fictional character wrote, to participate in his fictional world.

The idea of *In Our Time* as self-begetting fiction may suggest a need for a reexamination of traditional assumptions both about the nature of this work and about Hemingway's place among the realists. Although many individual stories in the work seem to exhibit realist forms such as "the well-made plot, chronological sequence, the authoritative omniscient author, [and] the rational connection between what characters 'do' and what they 'are'" (Waugh 7), just underneath the surface of this realism is an implicit challenge to it and the assumptions about reality on which it is based. Thus while on one level *In Our Time* assumes the existence of an objective reality and attempts to create the illusion that it is representing that objective reality, on another it prompts questions about the validity of this assumption and attempts to destroy that illusion by creating "a structure within which its main character and his fiction come to life . . . [and thus which] begets both a *self* and *itself*" (Kellman "The Fiction of Self-Begetting" 1251), and, as Waugh says all metafiction does, examining "the fundamental structures of narrative fiction [and] . . . the possible fictionality of the world outside the literary fictional text" (2).

Notes

1. In his review of *Ulysses* T. S. Eliot argues that "the novel is a form which will no longer serve; . . . the novel, instead of being a form, was simply the expression of an age which had not sufficiently lost all form to feel the need of something stricter" (482) and that James Joyce is ahead of his time in feeling "a conscious or probably unconscious dissatisfaction with the form" ("*Ulysses*, Order and Myth" 483).
2. See Seymour Krim's letter to the editors of the *Village Voice*. My identification of Peter Hamill as the first to call new journalism by this name as well as the reference to Krim's letter is from Mas'ud Zavarzadeh's *The Mythopoeic Reality* (63 n18).
3. See also Jeffrey Meyers 591–592 n42.
4. Hemingway himself wrote to Gertrude Stein regarding "Big Two-Hearted River": "I'm trying to do the country like Cezanne and having a hell of a time and sometimes getting a little bit" (*Letters*, 122). See also William Adair's "Landscapes of the Mind: 'Big Two-Hearted River.'" Adair reviews critical commentary that tends to see the landscape in this story as "real and at the same time interior or symbolic" (260), which is also a rough way of summarizing what Paul Cézanne does with landscapes.
5. See "The Self-Begetting Novel" (119). All other quotations from Kellman in this chapter are from "The Fiction of Self-Begetting." Most of what Kellman says in "The Self-Begetting Novel" is repeated in "The Fiction of Self-Begetting," although his claim to have coined the term is not.
6. In a letter to William Faulkner, Hemingway refers to Gustave Flaubert as "our most respected, honored master" (*Letters*, 624), and in a letter to Charles Scribner he says that he "started out trying to beat dead writers and I knew how good they were" and specifically of Guy de Maupassant, "It took four of the best stories to beat him" (673).
7. See, for example, Jackson J. Benson, Linda W. Wagner, and Robert M. Slabey.

Works Cited

Adair, William. "Landscapes of the Mind: 'Big Two-Hearted River.'" Reynolds 260–267.

Baker, Carlos. *Ernest Hemingway: A Life Story.* New York: Scribner's, 1969.

Baker, Sheridan. "Hemingway's Two-Hearted River." Benson, *Short Stories* 150–158.

Beegel, Susan F. *Hemingway's Craft of Omission: Four Manuscript Examples.* Studies in Modern Literature, No. 74. Series ed. A. Walton Litz. Ann Arbor: UMI, 1988.

Benson, Jackson J. "Patterns of Connection and Their Development in Hemingway's *In Our Time.*" Reynolds 103–119.

———, ed. *The Short Stories of Ernest Hemingway: Critical Essays.* Durham: Duke UP, 1975.

Burhans, Clinton S., Jr. "The Complex Unity of *In Our Time.*" Reynolds 88–102.

Cummings, E. E. *The Enormous Room.* 1922. The Cummings Typescript Editions. New York: Liveright, 1978.

DeFalco, Joseph. *The Hero in Hemingway's Short Stories.* 1962: Philadelphia: West, 1983.

Eliot, T. S., "*Ulysses,* Order and Myth," *Dial* Nov. 1923: 480–483.

Fuchs, Daniel. "Ernest Hemingway: Literary Critic." Wagner, *Ernest Hemingway* 38–56.

Gibb, Robert. "He Made Him Up: 'Big Two-Hearted River' as Doppleganger." Reynolds 254–259.

Hemingway, Ernest. *A Farewell to Arms.* 1929. New York: Scribner's, 1975.

———. "King Business in Europe Isn't What It Used to Be." *Toronto Star Weekly* 15 Sept. 1923: 15. Rpt. in *Dateline: Toronto, The Complete "Toronto Star" Dispatches, 1920–24.* Ed. William White. New York: Scribner's, 1985. 295–300.

———. *In Our Time.* 1925. New York: Scribner's, 1930.

———. *in our time.* Paris: Three Mountains Press, 1924.

———. *The Nick Adams Stories.* New York: Scribner's, 1929.

———. *Selected Letters; 1917–1961.* Ed. Carlos Baker. New York: Scribner's, 1981.

Jain, S. P. *Hemingway: A Study of His Short Stories.* New Delhi: Heinemann, 1985.

Kellman, Steven G. "The Fiction of Self-Begetting." *MLN* 91 (1976): 1243–1256.

———. "The Self-Begetting Novel." *Western Humanities Review* 30.2 (1976): 119–128.

Krim, Seymour. Letter. *Village Voice* 25 May 1974: 4.

Leiter, Louis H. "Neural Projections in Hemingway's 'On the Quai at Smyrna'" Reynolds 138–140.

Lynn, Kenneth S. *Hemingway.* New York: Simon, 1987.

Meyers, Jeffrey. *Hemingway: A Biography.* New York: Harper, 1985.

Nahal, Chaman Lal. *The Narrative Pattern in Ernest Hemingway's Fiction.* Rutherford: Fairleigh Dickinson UP, 1971.

Nelson, Raymond. *Hemingway: Expressionist Artist.* Ames: Iowa State UP, 1979.

Reynolds, Michael S., ed. *Critical Essays on Ernest Hemingway's "In Our Time."* Boston: Hall, 1983.

Roth, Philip. "Writing American Fiction." *Commentary* 31:3 (1961): 231–233.

Slabey, Robert M. "The Structure of *In Our Time.*" Reynolds 76–87.

Stephens, Robert O. *Hemingway's Nonfiction: The Public Voice.* Chapel Hill: U of North Carolina P, 1968.

Wagner, Linda Welshimer. "Juxtaposition in Hemingway's *In Our Time.*" Reynolds 120–129.

——, ed. *Ernest Hemingway: Five Decades of Criticism.* East Lansing: Michigan State UP, 1974.

Waugh, Patricia. *Metafiction: The Theory and Practice of Self-Conscious Fiction.* New York: Methuen, 1984.

Webster's New Collegiate Dictionary. 1956 ed.

Zavarzadeh, Mas'ud. *The Mythopoeic Reality: The Postwar American Nonfiction Novel.* Urbana: U of Illinois P, 1976.

PART III

The Response
to the Later Works

PASSION AND GRIEF IN
A FAREWELL TO ARMS:
ERNEST HEMINGWAY'S RETELLING
OF *WUTHERING HEIGHTS*

Lisa Tyler

In an *Esquire* article published in February 1935 (six years after *A Farewell to Arms*), Ernest Hemingway presented a list of books he "would rather read again for the first time ... than have an assured income of a million dollars a year." The fourth title on the list is *Wuthering Heights* ("Remembering" 21). The critical community has established the influence of several of the other authors listed (perhaps most obviously Mark Twain and Sherwood Anderson) on Hemingway's development as a writer.[1] Hemingway's inclusion of Brontë's novel in his list of important works suggests that, like the other works on the list, it may, in fact, have influenced his writings in ways we have yet to fully acknowledge.[2]

Certainly an appreciation of the importance of Hemingway's reading is vital to an understanding of his work.[3] Unlike, say, T. S. Eliot, Hemingway has not been known for his use of allusion—although he claimed to have learned the art of allusion from Eliot (*DIA* 139).[4] In *A Farewell to Arms* alone, however, Hemingway alludes to "The Waste Land," George Peele's poem "A Farewell to Arms," Shakespeare's sonnet 146, the Bible, the anonymous poem variously known as either "Western Wind" or "The Love in Winter Plainteth for the Spring," Alfred Lord Tennyson's "Sweet and Low"

Reprinted with permission from The Hemingway Review *(Spring 1995), pp. 79–96. Copyright 1995, The Ernest Hemingway Foundation. All rights reserved.*

from *The Princess*, "Now I Lay Me Down to Sleep," Christopher Marlowe's *Jew of Malta*, Rudyard Kipling's *Without Benefit of Clergy*, *Othello*, and folkloristic materials, specifically revenant ballads and second-sight motifs.[5] The author also deleted an allusion to Eliot's "The Hollow Men" (Reynolds 36). Clearly, as Edward Engelbert, Robert O. Stephens, and Michael S. Reynolds have convincingly demonstrated, *L'Education Sentimentale*, *The Charterhouse of Parma*, and *The Red Badge of Courage* were among Hemingway's sources for the book.

I want to argue that *Wuthering Heights* was also an important source for Hemingway's novel. *A Farewell to Arms* persistently echoes *Wuthering Heights* in its themes and symbols, sometimes even in its minutest details. The sheer number of such allusions, and the obviousness of many, suggest that they constitute deliberate signals to the reader of the underlying thrust of the book.

This relationship between *Wuthering Heights* and *A Farewell to Arms* has several ramifications. First, and most immediately, it makes Catherine sound less like a geisha girl and more like a Romantic heroine (or perhaps *hero* is the better term). She becomes a more comprehensible and better realized character, one with whom feminist readers can more comfortably sympathize, and her presence helps to disprove the claim that Hemingway could not portray "real" women in his fiction.

Second, Hemingway's use of Brontë places his novel squarely in the Romantic tradition. The allusions throughout *A Farewell to Arms* disprove the persistent myth that Hemingway was an unread "natural," as distinct from his more overtly literary contemporaries (like James Joyce, for example, or the somewhat older T. S. Eliot). He was, it is true, less learned than either Joyce or Eliot, but he was working within established traditions as much as they were. And he was hardly the "dumb ox" described by Wyndham Lewis. Hemingway's reading, as Michael Reynolds has so diligently demonstrated, was vitally important to his writing, as important as Eliot's reading was to his, and Hemingway's use of literary (as opposed to biographical and historical) sources deserves more attention than it has thus far received.

Third, the relationship I have documented in this essay further suggests that Hemingway was more open to the writing of women writers (and indeed feminist women writers) than might be expected. Perhaps the aggressively masculine image he so assiduously cultivated has obscured his literary debt to the brilliantly imaginative Yorkshire gentlewoman. Certainly the boxing analogy Hemingway uses to describe his relationship with previous writers (e.g., "I trained hard and beat Mr. de Maupassant," qtd. in Ross 23) obscures his relationship to *women* writers. True, he was primarily interested in the experiences of men (and often specifically *gendered* experiences, like hunting, fishing, prizefighting, and combat, that women of his generation would have been unlikely to share), and most of his literary models were male. Nonetheless, as his informal apprenticeship with Gertrude Stein confirms, Hemingway both appreciated and learned from at least some women writers.

Many of the arguments developed in this essay rest on what is still a fairly unusual reading of *A Farewell to Arms*. According to this interpretation, most fully developed by Ernest Lockridge,[6] Catherine Barkley, as a character, is *not* an artistic failure on Hemingway's part. In spite of her apparent submissiveness and self-abnegation, she is not the adolescent male fantasy that so many critics have found her to be. Lockridge elaborates:

> . . . Hemingway does not have Catherine abnegate herself to Frederic Henry; rather, she abnegates herself, when she does so, to an idea in her head. Motivated by the agonizing grief and loss that she still feels after a year of mourning, Catherine Barkley is acting out through the narrator a one-sided, therapeutic game of "pretend." . . . Through willed, deliberate projection upon the narrator, Frederic Henry, Catherine has temporarily resurrected her fiancé of eight years, blown "all to bits" on the Somme. (173–74)

This interpretation of the novel is confirmed by an allusion not mentioned in the list given earlier. Twice Hemingway alludes in this novel to Andrew Marvell's poem "To His Coy Mistress." At one point, Frederic himself quotes two lines from the poem:

> But at my back, I always hear
> Time's winged chariot hurrying near. (*FTA* 154)

Later, Frederic seems to be referring to these same lines more obliquely (Anderson 435): "We knew the baby was very close now and it gave us both a feeling as though something were hurrying us and we could not lose any time together" (*FTA* 311). Furthermore, Hemingway considered titling his novel either *World Enough and Time* or *In Praise of His Mistress* (Reynolds 297). These various allusions are generally interpreted as a foreshadowing of Catherine's death, which of course they are. Leo Gurko, for example, observes, "The lovers are acutely conscious of time passing and wish to make the most of what they have" (109). But at the same time, Marvell's words have an even more literal significance. When the novel opens, Catherine has already committed the "crime" the poem's speaker describes: she refused to marry her fiance, refused to give herself to him sexually, until it was too late, and he was dead (*FTA* 19). She perhaps a little naively assumed that they had "world enough and time," and because of the war, they did not. Her coyness with her fiance became a "crime"—in her eyes, at least—when he was killed. It is her perfectly understandable but grievous error which haunts Catherine when the novel begins: "He could have had anything he wanted if I would have known. I would have married him or anything. I know all about it now. But then he wanted to go to war and I didn't know" (*FTA* 19).

Catherine is grief-stricken and traumatized by her loss, and it is her grief which launches the love story, as another of Hemingway's allusions suggests. One of the titles in Hemingway's list of possible titles for the novel was *Disorder and Early Sorrow*, the title of a short story by Thomas Mann (Reynolds 296). In that story, a little girl cries inconsolably because she has had to go upstairs to bed and leave a man she has become attached to at her parents' party; she weeps hysterically until he comes up to her room to comfort her. Catherine, like the child in Mann's story, has also lost a man she loved, and she, too, mourns her loss and longs inconsolably for his return.[7]

As Lockridge concludes, in his penultimate paragraph: "It is Catherine's effort to resurrect her lost love . . . that is the whole novel's primary mover" (177). This admittedly unusual reading establishes a profound thematic parallel with *Wuthering Heights*, in which it is Heathcliff's effort to resurrect a lost love that is the whole novel's primary mover. The correspondences between these two novels are not between characters, but between emotions and themes. I am not arguing that Frederic is Heathcliff or that Catherine is Heathcliff; I am arguing that the lovers in Hemingway's novel experience the same passion and grief as do those in Brontë's and that readers can better understand *A Farewell to Arms* if they recognize that parallel.

The most obvious and most superficial similarity between the novels lies in the name: both heroines are called Catherine, and both give birth to a child named Catherine. Catherine Barkley's child is only given that name *in utero* (*FTA* 157, 293, 294, 304, 306), of course, and eventually turns out to be a stillborn son; nonetheless, Hemingway has perhaps acknowledged a debt rather pointedly here. When Frederic Henry first meets Catherine Barkley, she carries "a thin rattan stick like a toy riding crop, bound in leather" (*FTA*

608 Catherine as 2nd Catherine

18)—an article reminiscent of the ship that Catherine Earnshaw asks her father to bring her in her first (non-ghostly) appearance in *Wuthering Heights* (38).[8] Both Catherines are Englishwomen, and both are said to have "beautiful hair" (Brontë 50; *FTA* 19, 114). Catherine Barkley, in telling Frederic Henry of her first love, says, "We grew up together" (*FTA* 19)—not unlike Catherine Earnshaw and her first love. Just as Heathcliff returns to Catherine at dusk (Brontë 82), Catherine envisions her first lover's return one evening, when she tells Frederic to say, "I've come back to Catherine in the night" (*FTA* 28, 30).

Catherine Earnshaw makes Heathcliff promise not to shoot any more lapwings (Brontë 105); Catherine Barkley asks Frederic, "You don't shoot larks, do you, darling, in America?" (*FTA* 149). Frederic says to a dream-vision of Catherine, "You wouldn't go away in the night, would you?" (*FTA* 197); both Catherines do precisely that, dying at night and leaving their lovers alone (*FTA* 331–32, Brontë 137).

In both works, too, rain functions as a poignant and pointed symbol of separation and death. A thunderstorm marks Heathcliff's departure (Brontë 76), and he dies sitting before a window, letting the rain drive in upon him (Brontë 264). In *A Farewell to Arms*, Catherine Barkley expresses her apparently irrational but ultimately prescient fear of the rain (*FTA* 126). Lieutenant Henry leaves her on a rainy night to return to active duty (*FTA* 158), and she dies on a rainy night (*FTA* 332).

More fundamentally, each of these women experiences an intensely passionate love affair (or, in Catherine Barkley's case, at least *pretends* to) with a more or less nameless man: Catherine Barkley never refers to her fiance by name at all; she instead refers to him as "a very nice boy," "he," and eventually just "someone" (*FTA* 18, 20, 115). Frederic Henry remains nameless through much of the first half of the novel, and Catherine invariably calls him "darling" (Lockridge 171). Heathcliff is given someone else's name, that of a son who had died, and "it has served him ever since, both for Christian and surname" (Brontë 39); Nelly later calls him a "nameless man" (Brontë 88).

None of these characters subscribes to conventional religious beliefs, although both Catherines mention the possibility of a ghostly existence after death. "I'll not lie there by myself; they may bury me twelve feet deep, and throw the church down over me, but I won't rest till you are with me. I never will!" Catherine Earnshaw tells Heathcliff in her delirious ravings (Brontë 108). Catherine Barkley, as usual, is more circumspect: "I'll come stay with you nights," she quietly warns Frederic (*FTA* 331). Both women experience what Catherine Earnshaw calls "temporary derangement" (Brontë 107): both die young, in childbirth, after losing consciousness (Brontë 137, 139; *FTA* 331). Finally, both are grievously misunderstood and misrepresented by those who surround them and by the narrators of their stories in particular.

The declarations of love that Catherine and Heathcliff express in *Wuthering Heights* are terrifying in their intensity: "Nelly, I *am* Heathcliff—he's always, always in my mind—not as a pleasure, any more than I *am* always a pleasure to myself—but as my own being . . . " (Brontë 74). Catherine had earlier told Nelly, ". . . he's more myself than I am. Whatever our souls are made of, his and mine are the same . . . " (Brontë 72); years later, during her last hours of madness, she tells Nelly again, "he's in my soul" (Brontë 134). Heathcliff experiences the same passion: "Oh, Cathy! Oh, my life!" he cried (Brontë 132); the two are clearly, for him, indistinguishable. When he has her body exhumed, Heathcliff bribes the sexton to open the sides of his coffin and hers, after he dies, so that "by the time Linton gets to us, he'll not know which is which!" (Brontë 228–29). He speaks longingly "of dissolving with her, and being more happy still" (Brontë 229).

Catherine Barkley's expressions (whether genuine or feigned) sound suspiciously similar: "There isn't any me any more. Just what you want," she tells Frederic Henry (*FTA* 106). Later, she elaborates further: "There isn't any me. I'm you. Don't make up a separate me" (*FTA* 115). "We really are the same one," she insists (*FTA* 139). When she learns that Frederic has had gonorrhea, she says, "I wish I'd had it to be like you"; shortly thereafter, she asks him to let his hair grow:

> ". . . Then we'd both be alike. Oh, darling, I want you so much I want to be you too."
> "You are. We're the same one." (*FTA* 229)

A moment later she adds, "I want us to be all mixed up" (*FTA* 229).

This association of love with life, and the consequent indissolubility and self-sufficiency of the relationship, crops up in both novels. Catherine Earnshaw expresses this concept eloquently: "If all else perished, and *he* remained, I should still continue to be; and, if all else remained, and he were annihilated, the Universe would turn to a mighty stranger. I should not seem a part of it" (Brontë 74). Nelly Dean relates of Heathcliff and Catherine that, as children, "it was one of their chief amusements to run away to the moors in the morning and remain there all day" (Brontë 46); clearly, they need no one else. Even in her final hours, Catherine tells Heathcliff, "I only wish us never to be parted" (Brontë 133).

The lovers of *A Farewell to Arms* echo these sentiments. "Now if you aren't with me I haven't a thing in the world," Frederic tells Catherine, later adding, "I'm just so in love with you that there isn't anything else" (*FTA* 257). Catherine says, later in the novel, "I don't live at all when I'm not with you," to which Frederic in turn responds, "I'm no good when you're not there. I haven't any life at all anymore" (*FTA* 300). They repeatedly rejoice that they don't see (and don't need to see) other people (*FTA* 132, 297, 303); Frederic asserts, ". . . we were never lonely and never afraid when we were together" (*FTA* 249) and "We always feel good when we're together" (*FTA* 150). Catherine responds "We always will be together" (*FTA* 150), though she knows when she says it that it isn't true, at least not in a literal, physical sense.

Both of these doomed couples recognize that they can themselves destroy the relationship. As Catherine Barkley tells Frederic, "there's only us two and in the world there's all the rest of them. If anything comes between us we're gone and then they have us" (*FTA* 139). She tells him, too, that they "mustn't misunderstand on purpose" as other people do: "They love each other and they misunderstand on purpose and they fight and then suddenly they aren't the same one" (*FTA* 139). She could be describing the parallel relationship in *Wuthering Heights*; as Heathcliff tells Catherine, "Because misery, and degradation, and death, and nothing that God or Satan could inflict would have parted us, *you*, of your own will, did it. I have not broken your heart—*you* have broken it—and in breaking it, you have broken mine" (Brontë 135). Clearly, they embody each other's destruction; Heathcliff calls Catherine both his murderer and her own (Brontë 135). Frederic and Catherine Barkley repeat the idea, but lightly:

> "Hell," I said, "I love you enough now. What do you want to do? Ruin me?"
> "Yes. I want to ruin you."
> "Good," I said, "that's what I want, too." (*FTA* 305)

The novel ends with Catherine's death in childbirth and (at least implicitly) Frederic's devastating grief; certainly their words here hold more truth than they know. Catherine's friend, the pragmatic hospital nurse nicknamed Fergy, offers the most accurate assessment of the relationships in these novels: "You'll die then. Fight or die. That's what people do. They don't marry" (*FTA* 108).[9]

These mutual destructions become even more painful given the characters' complete lack of faith in conventional religion. Catherine Earnshaw doesn't want to go to heaven if it means separation from Heathcliff (Brontë 72). She tells Heathcliff, "I shall not be at peace" (Brontë 133), and Lockwood's encounter with her early in the novel certainly bears out this statement. Nelly describes Heathcliff as "unchristian" and pleads unsuccessfully to be allowed to send for a minister to prepare him for death; he, too, rejects heaven, preferring reunion with his lost love (Brontë 262–63).

Such rejections become even more explicit in *A Farewell to Arms*. In telling Frederic of her lost love, Catherine specifically and emphatically denies the possibility of immortality:

> "... and then of course he was killed and that was the end of it."
> "I don't know."
> "Oh, yes," she said. "That's the end of it." (*FTA* 19)

She tells the hospital clerk she has no religion (*FTA* 313), and Frederic later tells himself the same thing (*FTA* 327). Catherine explains to Frederic, "... I haven't any religion," adding later, "You're my religion" (*FTA* 116). Similarly, when Frederic asks her, on her deathbed, if she wants him "to get a priest or anyone" to come and see her, she responds, "Just you" (*FTA* 330). With his references to "Your lovely cool goddess. English goddess" that Frederic Henry can only "worship," Rinaldi suggests that Frederic experiences a corresponding displacement of devotion from a religious deity to a human one (*FTA* 66); Rinaldi later calls the relationship a "sacred subject" (*FTA* 169). Love is a religious feeling, according to the oracular Count Greffi (*FTA* 263); the statement illuminates both novels.

The intensity of such loves, coupled with the lack of faith in a conventional afterlife, virtually guarantees that any separation, let alone death, will create grief so intense that it threatens sanity. When Heathcliff runs away, Catherine Earnshaw comes down with a dangerous fever and the doctor worries that in her delirium she may become suicidal—partly as a result of her exposure to the rain, and partly, surely, as a result of her lover's departure (Brontë 77–78). Tormented by her love for Heathcliff, she later becomes literally mad, hallucinating and regressing to childlike behavior (Brontë 106–07).

Heathcliff, confronted with news of Catherine's death, refused this abandonment: "You said I killed you—haunt me, then! . . . Be with me always, take any form—drive me mad! only *do* not leave me in this abyss, where I *cannot* find you! . . . I *cannot* live without my life! I *cannot* live without my soul!" (Brontë 229). He tells Nelly, ". . . it seemed that on going out, I should meet her; when I walked on the moors I should meet her coming in. When I went from home, I hastened to return; she *must* be somewhere at Heights, I was certain!" (Brontë 230). He is unable to escape her presence:

> I cannot look down to this floor, but her features are shaped on the flags! In every cloud, in every tree—filling the air at night, and caught by glimpses in every object by day, I am surrounded with her image! The most ordinary faces of men and women—my own features— mock me with a resemblance. The entire world is a dreadful collection of memoranda that she did exist, and that I have lost her! (Brontë 255)

As the prosaic Nelly observes, "He might have had a monomania on the subject of his departed idol; but on every other point his wits were as sound as mine" (Brontë 256).

Nelly Dean's diagnosis of Heathcliff's condition is a strikingly apt one for Catherine Barkley's condition as well, given Lockridge's explication. As Catherine herself acknowledges, "I was a little crazy. But I wasn't crazy in any complicated manner" (*FTA* 154). Perhaps, like Heathcliff, she sees her dead lover in all that surrounds her; certainly she sees him in the "most ordinary" face of the young, unformed Frederic Henry. Driven by devastating, even pathological grief, Heathcliff tries brutally to work his will on the descendants of three families; Catherine Barkley limits herself to one impressionable American soldier who "seems, at best, an amiable, presentable-looking blank" (Lockridge 173). Catherine Barkley seems to be a somewhat tougher Catherine Earnshaw whose Heathcliff has predeceased her.

Each woman betrays her first love in a spectacular way while simultaneously maintaining her own faithfulness. Nelly Dean reports of Catherine Earnshaw: "She had a wondrous constancy to old attachments" (Brontë 61). Catherine in fact proposes to support Heathcliff *by means of* her marriage to another: "He'll be as much to me as he has been all his lifetime," she insists (Brontë 73). Heathcliff, infuriated by news of her peaceful death, cries, "Why, she's a liar to the end!" (Brontë 139). Again, the words could conceivably be applied to Catherine Barkley as well—although Sandra Whipple Spanier contends, and I agree, that during the course of the story, "both [Catherine] and Frederic . . . grow into their parts until they're no longer acting" ("Catherine" 135).[10] As Catherine in turn fervently protests to Frederic, "I'm not unfaithful, darling. I've plenty of faults but I'm very faithful. You'll be sick of me I'll be so faithful" (*FTA* 116). Lockridge neatly tempers Catherine's assertions, paraphrasing Ernest Dowson's "Cynara" to describe Catherine Barkley as "faithful in her fashion" (175).

Both women, then, construct models of constancy that differ markedly from conventional ideals, and both must maintain a pretense, wear a mask, in order to uphold their models of constancy. The mask drops occasionally for each, however. During Catherine's final illness, Nelly notes, "The flash of her eyes had been succeeded by a dreamy and melancholy softness; they no longer gave the impression of looking at the objects around her; they appeared always to gaze beyond, and far beyond—you would have said out of this world" (Brontë 131). Long before her madness began to manifest itself in this "vague, distant look" (Brontë 131), however, "Catherine had seasons of gloom and silence, now and then" (Brontë 81).

Catherine Barkley has similar moments of retreat into the self—or perhaps, given Nelly Dean's interpretation, of retreat into a world beyond—as when Frederic responds less than ideally to the news of her pregnancy: "She went away a long way without stirring or removing her hand" (*FTA* 139). Similarly, on one of their first encounters, after she stops playing her "rotten game" of pretend, "She came back from wherever she had been" (*FTA* 31).

Both women are, moreover, lamentably misread and misunderstood by those who surround them. Their stories are told only after they die, and even then by someone who in retrospect still fails to realize the story's true import. Nelly Dean clearly does not understand Catherine Earnshaw's motives and dismisses her passionate declarations of love as "nonsense" (Brontë 74). Given Lockridge's reading, Frederic Henry is equally unacquainted with Catherine Barkley's motives and dismisses her emotional declarations of terror as "nonsense" (*FTA* 126). The uncomprehending narrators who describe these women emphasize their enigmatic, perplexing, even perverse qualities, and utterly fail to recognize, let alone empathize with, the terrible grief occasioned by the loss of an all-encompassing love.[11]

Hemingway's apparent borrowings from *Wuthering Heights* suggest that the novel's themes of separation, loss of love, and the terrible egoism of the bereaved may be equally important in *A Farewell to Arms*. Such a supposition tends to confirm Lockridge's argument, since both novels then depict a grieving individual who in anguish tries to re-enact the past. What is Heathcliff doing, after all, when he compels Catherine Linton and Linton

Heathcliff to marry, but re-enacting *his* Catherine's marriage to Edgar Linton? And what is he doing by ruining Hareton, but trying to recreate Hindley's attempted destruction of Heathcliff himself? Catherine Barkley's parallel act seems rather meager, in comparison, but invites the reader's sympathy rather more.

William A. Madden has argued that Heathcliff, in his obsession with recreating the past, is responding to what Freud termed a repetition compulsion: "The psyche, disturbed by a shock which it cannot absorb and surmount, is unable to achieve psychic wholeness until the subject relives and retrospectively binds the excess of emotion that is the cause of his illness" (Madden 148–49; see also Bercovitch). Hemingway's allusions to *Wuthering Heights* suggest that Catherine, too, has sustained such a psychic wound,[12] and that she is trying to relive her trauma in order "to achieve psychic wholeness." Thus, his use of allusion helps to confirm the positive readings of Catherine's character that Joyce Wexler and Sandra Whipple Spanier present. Catherine could have wrought on others the pain she herself had suffered; she could have become another Heathcliff, perpetuating her loss by inflicting it upon those around her. Instead, she chose, while reliving her trauma, to relive it *constructively*, rather than *destructively*: to try to give Frederic what she had denied her fiance, rather than to try to inflict on him the pain that she had suffered.[13] *Is Frederick also purging her death by writing the novel?*

Arguing that Catherine's choice of self-sacrifice in an all-encompassing love is a positive, *healthy* choice may initially seem sexist, but in *The Sun Also Rises*, Jake Barnes, who is traumatized by his combat experience and his injury, does precisely the same thing, albeit platonically because of his presumed impotence. Jake Barnes is as much a Romantic hero as Catherine, and Frederic Henry's friend the priest espouses a similar philosophy when he tells Frederic, "When you love you wish to do things for. You wish to sacrifice for. You wish to serve" (*FTA* 72). Catherine merely puts this belief into practice (Spanier, "Catherine" 140).

Catherine's choice of love may have to do with the options available to her, as well. She can hardly throw herself into her work (as Rinaldi does) when patients are scarce, and the fishing that works for Nick Adams in "Big Two-Hearted River" seems unlikely to appeal to a woman of Catherine's era. According to Sandra Whipple Spanier:

> [G]iven the treacherousness of Hemingway's world, the consequences of structuring one's existence within the confines of a love relationship seem hardly less "healthy" than living by the rituals that other code

heroes have chosen in order to structure their lives—the bullfight, the prizefight, the hunt. ("Catherine" 137)

But what, finally, does all this have to do with Frederic, who is after all the narrator of *A Farewell to Arms*? What about *his* passion and grief? When the novel ends, he is as bereaved as Catherine was at the novel's beginning—more so, since he has lost a child as well as a lover. Frederic, I would argue, has learned from Catherine how to cope with trauma with courage and grace. Spanier has proposed a reading of *A Farewell to Arms* that I want to endorse and extend. She argues that Catherine is the "code hero" of *A Farewell to Arms*:

> As much a victim of the war as her boy who was killed, her ideals shattered and her psyche scarred in confrontation with a chaotic and hostile universe, Catherine refuses to be helpless. She pulls herself together with dignity and grace, defines the limits of her own existence, and scrupulously acts her part, preferring romance to the theater of the absurd. By imposing an order on experience, she gains a limited autonomy, as much control over her own destiny as a human being in Hemingway's world can hope to have. From her example, Frederic Henry learns how to live in it too. ("Catherine" 147–48)

Acting as her own therapist, Catherine overcomes her pain through her role-playing with Frederic Henry. Through transference, she is able to master her trauma, much as she might have through formal psychoanalysis.

Frederic has had an advantage in that, unlike Catherine, who had only her own resources to fall back on, he has had her as his "mentor in matters of psychological survival" (Spanier, "Catherine" 139). She recognizes the danger that Frederic might try to overcome his trauma by reliving it, as she did, and even on her deathbed she tries to warn him against a psychologically precarious solution, saying, "You won't do our things with another girl, or say the same things, will you?" (*FTA* 331). Frederic immediately responds, "Never" (*FTA* 331). He will have no need to re-enact their relationship the way she re-enacted her relationship with her fiance with him, as the existence of *A Farewell to Arms* makes clear.

To understand why, it is necessary for a moment to consider the psychological role that narrative serves. Peter Brooks, in *Reading for the Plot*, proposes a model of narrative that has its basis in psychoanalysis; he suggests that narrative is a way of first provoking and then binding emotional energies, much as the repetition compulsion does: "Analysis works toward the more precise and orderly recollection of the past, no longer compulsively repeated, insistently reproduced in the present, but ordered as a retrospective narrative" (227). Frederic's narrative, then, is a way of working through his grief in an even healthier way than Catherine was able to manage. Frederic has mastered his trauma by making of it an ordered narrative, much as Nick Adams claims to have done in "Fathers and Sons": "If he wrote it he could get rid of it. He had gotten rid of many things by writing them" (491). The novel itself becomes a kind of testament to Frederic's recovery.

It is interesting to note here how first Catherine's and then Frederic's willed triumphs over trauma parallel their creator's. In his highly influential early study of Hemingway, Philip Young argued that the author had sustained psychic wounds of his own and dealt with them by "returning compulsively to the scenes of his injuries" again and again in his writings (166). Young concludes, "It is not the trauma but the use to which he put it that counts; he harnessed it, and transformed it to art" (171). Like Catherine, Hemingway chose to become his own therapist.[14] Unlike Heathcliff, who seems to be trapped forever in a vicious cycle of unending pain, both Hemingway's characters and Hemingway himself overcame their grief through the healing "make-believe" of fiction. *A Farewell to Arms* testifies to the way in which the art of literature can give meaning to human suffering.

Notes

1.   The entire quotation lists works by Leo Tolstoy, W. H. Hudson, Thomas Mann, Emily Brontë, Gustave Flaubert, Ivan Turgenev, Fyodor Dostoevsky, George Moore, Mark Twain, Sherwood Anderson, Alexandre Dumas, Guy de Maupassant, Frederic Stendhal, James Joyce, and W. B. Yeats.

   See Bordinat for a comparison of Tolstoy and Hemingway. See McIlvaine for a discussion of W. H. Hudson and Hemingway. For Thomas Mann's influence on Hemingway, see Adair; see also the less convincing case presented by Mertens. For Flaubert's influence on Hemingway, see Engelberg. See Chapple, Coltrane, and Wilkinson for Turgenev's influence on Hemingway. See Chapter 6 in Young (211–41, but especially pages 230–41) for the influence of *Adventures of Huckleberry Finn* on Hemingway's writing, especially his Nick Adams stories. See also Wyatt and Baker.

   Hemingway himself acknowledged his debts to Turgenev and Anderson in "Fathers and Sons" and *Torrents of Spring*, respectively; the latter, a parody of

Anderson's *Dark Laughter*, is perhaps a backhanded compliment, but it does indicate Hemingway's interest in Anderson's work. For discussions of Anderson's influence on Hemingway, see Flanagan, Somers, and Schorer. For Stendhal's influence on *A Farewell to Arms*, see Lawson, Stephens, and Reynolds (134, 154–58). For a brief discussion of the influence of de Maupassant's "La Maisson Tellier" on "The Light of the World," see Martine; Jobst and Williamson explore the subject further. For Joyce's influence on Hemingway, see Gajdusek and O'Connor (especially 156–69).

2. Mark Spilka is the only critic to have considered *Wuthering Heights* as an influence on Hemingway's work (although Joseph M. Flora has noted the similarity briefly (271). I agree fully with Spilka's argument that Emily Brontë's vision of androgyny must have held both appeal and terror for Hemingway, and I see my argument as complementing rather than contradicting Spilka's, especially since he focuses more closely on the relationship between *Wuthering Heights* and Hemingway's posthumously published short story, "The Last Good Country." For Spilka's brief discussion of Brontë's influence on *A Farewell to Arms*, see Chapter 5 of *Hemingway's Quarrel with Androgyny*, especially pages 139, 211, and 215–22, as well as 333.

3. Reynolds maintains that "Hemingway's reading is as important to his art as that of Coleridge" (283). Young, too, insists on the importance of Hemingway's reading (160–61).

4. Bernard Oldsey contends that what Hemingway specifically learned from Eliot was how to use allusion "not simply as decoration, but as a means of achieving resonance, depth, layers of sometimes contradictory meaning" (26). Hemingway seems, in fact, to have taken some of his allusions from Eliot rather than from a primary source, perhaps including allusions to Marlowe (Bartlett, Oldsey 19, Lynn 246) and Marvell (Gerstenberger).

5. See Gerstenberger and Adams for further discussion of Hemingway's debt to Eliot. On Peele's poem, see Keeler, Mazzaro, Anderson and Fleming. Stoneback discusses Shakespeare's sonnet 146; Reynolds discusses Biblical allusions (43–44). Anderson (437), Davison, Dekker and Harris (313), and Oldsey (23–24 and 32–33) all discuss "Western Wind." Anderson notes allusions to Tennyson (440) and "Now I Lay Me Down to Sleep" (438). On Marlowe's influence, see Young (59), Oldsey (25–26), and Bartlett. Wilson proposes Kipling as an influence (239n1). The allusion to *Othello* is direct (*FTA* 257). Dekker and Harris analyze the folkloric motifs in the novel. For other possible allusions in *A Farewell to Arms*, see Davis and McIlvaine ("Literary").

6. Although unusual, Lockridge's reading is not unique. His essay develops more fully a thesis posited in John Stubbs' "Love and Role Playing in *A Farewell to Arms*." Other critics who subscribe to this view include Roger Whitlow (20), George Dekker and Joseph Harris (311–12), Robert W. Lewis (75), Sandra Whipple Spanier (see especially "Hemingway's" 86 and "Catherine" 134–35), and Wexler (see especially 114–18 and 122).

7. Two other titles from the list published in Reynolds' book (295–97) would seem to confirm this interpretation. Reynolds suggests that the title *Sorrow for Pleasure* may have been taken from the anonymous poem "Icarus": "Blinded they into folly run and grief for pleasure take" (Reynolds 296). That is, of course, precisely what I am arguing that Frederic Henry does: mistake Catherine's grief for pleasure. Another title, *If You Must Love*, Reynolds identifies as an allusion to one of Elizabeth Barrett Browning's *Sonnets from the Portuguese* which begins: "If thou must love me, let it be for naught/ Except for love's sake only" (Reynolds 297). Catherine "loves" Frederic—but not, certainly, for love's sake only, at least not at the beginning of their relationship.

8. It is interesting to note, here, that when Catherine Earnshaw asks for a whip, her father brings home Heathcliff instead, almost as if he were a substitute for what she requested (Gilbert and Gubar 264); for Catherine Barkley, the substitution is reversed, and the whip takes the place of her lover.

9. Hemingway appears to have subscribed to that view himself, as he echoed it in *Death in the Afternoon*:
   Madame, all stories, if continued far enough, end in death . . . Especially do all stories of monogamy end in death, and your man who is monogamous while he often lives most happily, dies in the most lonely fashion. There is no lonelier man in death, except the suicide, than that man who has lived many years with a good wife and then outlived her. If two people love each other there can be no happy end to it. (122)

10. Wexler shares this view: ". . . [T]he love she has willed becomes authentic" (118). Lockridge is less sanguine about the transformative powers of role-playing: ". . . [S]he never abandons the old love for the new, is never 'unfaithful'" (177).

11. Frederic learns to love Catherine during the course of their time together, but he does not genuinely understand and appreciate her until after she dies; it is only through the process of writing this narrative that he comes to understand her motives and appreciate what she, by her example, has taught him.

12. It is interesting to note that in his work outlining the nature of the "traumatic neurosis" which gives rise to the repetition compulsion. Freud wrote, in 1919, that "[t]he terrible war which has just ended gave rise to a great number of illnesses of this kind" (18:12).

13. It is only in the second generation that the characters of *Wuthering Heights* are able to respond constructively:
   . . . [T]he double drama of *Wuthering Heights* has provided the powerful experience of living twice through the same potentially traumatic circumstances, once ending in tragedy, but the second time with the energy bound and channeled into human wholeness and health through the transforming power of a love that both understands and forgives. (Madden 154)

14. Lockridge describes Catherine's behavior as "a serious and therapeutic game of 'pretend'" (177), and Wexler observes of Catherine, "She devises a kind of therapy for herself by pretending to love Frederic in place of her fiance" (114).

Whitlow suggests that Catherine is "using Frederic as an unwitting therapist" (20). Similarly, Young writes that the Hemingway hero was determined to be his own therapist (202), and John Portz has suggested that ". . . writing fiction was one of Hemingway's methods for controlling his painful memories and fears" (40). See Rose for a practicing psychiatrist's argument that art can act as therapy: "Both creative and clinical process follow the fundamental psychic principle of attempting to master passively experienced trauma by active repetition . . ." (44). Rose's description of the artist echoes Young's description of Hemingway: "Sensitized as a child, he learns to use his talent to create imagery to defend against loss" (Rose 127).

Works Cited

Adair, William. "*For Whom the Bell Tolls* and *The Magic Mountain*: Hemingway's Debt to Thomas Mann," *Twentieth-Century Literature* 35 (1989): 429–44.

Adams, Richard. "Sunrise out of the Waste Land." *Tulane Studies in English* 9 (1959): 119–31.

Anderson, Charles R. "Hemingway's Other Style." *Modern Language Notes* 76 (1961): 434–42.

Baker, Carlos. "Two Rivers: Mark Twain and Hemingway." *Mark Twain Journal* 11.4 (Summer 1962): 2.

Bartlett, Phyllis. "Other Countries, Other Wenches." *Modern Fiction Studies* 3 (1957–58): 345–59.

Bercovitch, Sacvan. "Literature and the Repetition Compulsion." *College English* 29 (1968): 607–15.

Bordinat, Philip. "Anatomy of Fear in Tolstoy and Hemingway." *Lost Generation Journal* 3.2 (Spring–Summer 1975): 15–17.

Brontë, Emily. *Wuthering Heights.* 1847. Ed. William M. Sale, Jr. 2nd ed. New York: Norton, 1963.

Brooks, Peter. *Reading for the Plot: Design and Intention in Narrative.* New York: Knopf, 1984.

Chapple, Richard. "Ivan Turgenev, Sherwood Anderson, and Ernest Hemingway: The Torrents of Spring All," *New Comparison: A Journal of Comparative and General Literary Studies* 5 (1988): 136–49.

Coltrane, Robert. "Hemingway and Turgenev: *The Torrents of Spring.*" *Hemingway's Neglected Short Fiction: New Perspectives.* Ed. Susan F. Beegel. 1989. Tuscaloosa: U of Alabama P, 1992. 149–61.

Davis, Judy W. "Three Novels Mentioned in *A Farewell to Arms.*" *Notes on Contemporary Literature* 19 (1989): 4–5.

Davison, Richard Allan. "Hemingway's *A Farewell to Arms.*" *Explicator* 29 (Feb. 1971): no. 46.

Dekker, George, and Joseph Harris. "Supernaturalism and the Vernacular Style in *A Farewell to Arms*." *PMLA* 34 (March 1979): 311–18.

Engelberg, Edward. "Hemingway's 'True Penelope': Flaubert's *L'Education Semtimentale* and *A Farewell to Arms*." *Comparative Literature Studies* 16 (1979): 189–206.

Flanagan, John T. "Hemingway's Debt to Sherwood Anderson," *Journal of English and Germanic Philology* 54 (1955): 507–20.

Fleming, Robert E. "Hemingway and Peele: Chapter 1 of *A Farewell to Arms*." *Studies in American Fiction* 11 (1983): 95–100.

Flora, Joseph M. *Hemingway's Nick Adams*. Baton Rouge: Louisiana State U P, 1982.

Freud, Sigmund. *The Standard Edition of the Complete Psychological Works of Sigmund Freud*. 24 vols. Ed. James Strachey. London: Hogarth, 1955.

Gajdusek, Robert E. "*Dubliners* in Michigan: Joyce's Presence in Hemingway's *In Our Time*." *Hemingway Review* 2 (1982): 48–61.

Gerstenberger, Donna. "*The Waste Land* in *A Farewell to Arms*." *Modern Language Notes* 76 (1961): 24–25.

Gilbert, Sandra M., and Susan Gubar. *The Madwoman in the Attic: The Woman Writer and the Nineteenth-Century Literary Imagination*. New Haven: Yale U P, 1979.

Gurko, Leo. *Ernest Hemingway and the Pursuit of Heroism*. New York: Crowell, 1968.

Hemingway, Ernest. *Death in the Afternoon*. New York: Scribner's, 1932.

———. *A Farewell to Arms*. New York: Scribner's. 1929.

———. "The Last Good Country." *The Nick Adams Stories*. New York: Scribner's, 1972. 70–132.

———. "Remembering Shooting-Flying: A Key West Letter." Esquire 3 (February 1935): 21. Rpt. in *Byline: Ernest Hemingway: Selected Articles and Dispatches of Four Decades*. Ed. William White. New York: Scribner's, 1967. 186–91.

———. *The Short Stories of Ernest Hemingway*. New York: Scribner's, 1938. 209–32.

Jobst, Jack W., and W. J. Williamson. "Hemingway and Maupassant: More Light on 'The Light of the World.'" *Hemingway Review* 13.2 (Spring 1994): 52–61.

Keeler, Clinton. "*A Farewell to Arms:* Hemingway and Peele." *Modern Language Notes* 76 (1961): 622–25.

Lawson, Carolina Donadio. "Hemingway, Stendhal and War." *Hemingway Review* 6 (1981): 28–33.

Lewis, Robert W. *A Farewell to Arms: The War of the Words*. New York: Twayne, 1992.

Lewis, Wyndham. "The Dumb Ox." *Men without Art*. 1934. New York: Russell & Russell, 1964. 17–41.

Lockridge, Ernest. "Faithful in Her Fashion: Catherine Barkley, the Invisible Hemingway Heroine." *Journal of Narrative Technique* 18 (1988): 170–78.

Lynn, Kenneth S. *Hemingway*. New York: Simon and Schuster, 1987.

Madden, William A. "*Wuthering Heights*: The Binding of Passion." *Nineteenth-Century Fiction* 27 (September 1972): 127–54.

Mann, Thomas. "Disorder and Early Sorrow." *Stories of Three Decades*. Trans. H. T. Lowe-Porter. New York: Knopf, 1979. 500–28.

Martine, James J. "A Little Light on Hemingway's 'The Light of the World.'" *Studies in Short Fiction* 7 (1970): 465–67.

Mazzaro, Jerome I. "George Peele and *A Farewell to Arms*: A Thematic Tie?" *Modern Language Notes* 75 (1960): 118–19.

McIlvaine, Robert M. "A Literary Source for the Caesarean Section in *A Farewell to Arms*." *American Literature* 43 (1971): 444–47.

———. "Robert Cohn and the Purple Land." *Notes on Modern American Literature* 5.2 (Spring 1981): Item 8.

Mertens, Gerald M. "Hemingway's *Old Man and the Sea* and Mann's *The Black Swan*." *Literature and Psychology* 6 (1956): 96–99.

O'Connor, Frank. *The Lonely Voice*. Cleveland: World, 1963.

Oldsey, Bernard. *Hemingway's Hidden Craft: The Writing of* A Farewell to Arms. University Park: Pennsylvania State U P, 1979.

Portz, John. "Allusion and Structure in Hemingway's 'A Natural History of the Dead.'" *Tennessee Studies in Literature* 10 (1965): 27–41.

Reynolds, Michael S. H*emingway's First War: The Making of* A Farewell to Arms. Princeton: Princeton U P, 1976.

Rose, Gilbert J. *Trauma and Mastery in Life and Art*. New Haven: Yale U P, 1987.

Ross, Lillian. "How Do You Like It Now, Gentlemen?" *New Yorker* 13 May 1950: 36–62. Rpt. in *Hemingway: A Collection of Critical Essays*. Ed. Robert P. Weeks. Englewood Cliffs, New Jersey: Prentice-Hall, 1962. 17–39.

Schorer, Mark. "Some Relationships: Gertrude Stein, Sherwood Anderson, F. Scott Fitzgerald, and Ernest Hemingway." *The World We Imagine: Selected Essays by Mark Schorer*. New York: Farrar, Straus, and Giroux, 1968. 299–382.

Somers, Paul, Jr. "The Mark of Sherwood Anderson on Hemingway: A Look at the Texts." *South Atlantic Quarterly* 71 (1974): 487–503.

Spanier, Sandra Whipple. "Catherine Barkley and the Hemingway Code: Ritual and Survival in *A Farewell to Arms*." *Ernest Hemingway's* A Farewell to Arms. Ed. Harold Bloom. New York: Chelsea, 1987. 131–48.

———. "Hemingway's Unknown Soldier: Catherine Barkley, the Critics, and the Great War." *New Essays on* A Farewell to Arms. Ed. Scott Donaldson. Cambridge: Cambridge U P, 1990. 75–108.

Spilka, Mark. *Hemingway's Quarrel with Androgyny*. Lincoln: U of Nebraska P, 1990.

———. "Original Sin in 'The Last Good Country': or, The Return of Catherine Barkley." *The Modernists: Studies in a Literary Phenomenon*. Ed. Lawrence B. Gamache and Ian S. MacNiven. Rutherford, New Jersey: Fairleigh Dickinson U P, 1987. 210–33.

Stephens, Robert O. "Hemingway and Stendhal: The Matrix of *A Farewell to Arms*." *PMLA* 88 (1973): 271–80.

Stoneback, H. R. "'Lovers' Sonnets Turn'd to Holy Psalms': The Soul's Song of Providence, the Scandal of Suffering, and Love in *A Farewell to Arms*." *Hemingway Review* 9.1 (Fall 1989): 33–76.

Stubbs, John. "Love and Role Playing in *A Farewell to Arms*." *Fitzgerald/Hemingway Annual* 1973. Ed. Matthew J. Bruccoli and C. E. Frazer Clark, Jr. Washington, D.C.: Microcard Editions Books, 1974. 271–84.

Wexler, Joyce. "E.R.A. for Hemingway: A Feminist Defense of *A Farewell to Arms*." *Georgia Review* 35 (1981): 111–23.

Whitlow, Roger. *Cassandra's Daughters: The Women in Hemingway*. Westport, CT: Greenwood P, 1984.

Wilkinson, Myer. *Hemingway and Turgenev: The Nature of Literary Influence*. Ann Arbor: UMI Research P, 1986.

Wilson, Edmund. "Hemingway: Gauge of Morale." *The Wound and the Bow: Seven Studies in Literature*. Cambridge, Massachusetts: Houghton Mifflin, 1941. 214–42.

Wyatt, Bryant N. "Huckleberry Finn and the Art of Ernest Hemingway." *Mark Twain Journal* 13.4 (Summer 1967): 1–8.

Young, Philip. *Ernest Hemingway: A Reconsideration*. University Park: Pennsylvania State U P, 1966.

RE-READING WOMEN: THE EXAMPLE OF CATHERINE BARKLEY

Jamie Barlowe-Kayes

I

In *Papa Hemingway* A. E. Hotchner narrates a story that he claims Ernest Hemingway told him. Apparently, once while out west, Hemingway learned that a black bear was blocking traffic on a particular road. Menaced by its size and attitude, people were afraid to use what had become the bear's personal road. Undaunted, though, Hemingway drove to the place, stepped from his car, strode up to the bear and began to harangue. Quoting Hotchner supposedly quoting Hemingway, the monologue goes something like this:

> Do you realize that you're nothing but a miserable, common black bear? . . . Why, you sad son-of-a-bitch, how can you be so cocky and stand there and block cars when you're nothing but a *miserable* bear and a black bear at that—not even a polar or a grizzly or anything worthwhile . . . (18).

Soon, the bear lowered his head, then dropped his front legs to the ground, and on all fours slinked off into the woods. To quote Hotchner again: "Ernest had destroyed him. From that time on he used to run behind a tree and hide whenever he saw a car coming and shake with fear that Ernest might be inside, ready to dress him down" (19).

If scholars attempt to understand something about Hemingway from such a story by examining only the story, they conduct one kind of inquiry and gain one kind of knowledge, making claims, in other words, about what happens in the story by focusing almost exclusively on what Papa said to the bear, how he said it, and what information that adds to the genre—in this case the tall-tale nature of the story—and perhaps even speculate about Hemingway's reasons for telling it. They might also point out that Hotchner's account is a re-telling, and focus on his relationship to Hemingway and his possible purposes for using this story. Such an analysis would yield other knowledge about Hemingway, and make yet another contribution to the critical context which surrounds this almost larger-than-life literary figure.

I open with this story because I see it as a metaphor for the relationship of traditional Hemingway scholarship to Hemingway's texts. This inextricably intertwined relationship has created a critical context, which is considered to be a stable body of knowledge—one as significant, essential, and influential as Hemingway's texts. His position as cultural icon and as claimed literary "forefather" of half the modern and postmodern authors of America is part of this critical context (e.g., Norman Mailer's keynote address in the Hemingway Society's International Conference, 1990).

In fact, in order to do a non-traditional reading of Hemingway and his work—for example, a feminist reading—the feminist critic/theorist must destabilize the traditional relationship between the reader and Hemingway's texts, as well as the relationship between Hemingway scholarship and Hemingway's texts. Moreover, she must often destabilize her relationship to that critical context, if it is one she has learned as part of her academic training. Although for Hemingway, the process of re-reading oneself or one's previous work did not necessarily destabilize it, he did such re-reading because it "places you at the point where it *has* to go on, knowing it is as good as you can get it up to there" (Interview with Plimpton, *Conversations with Ernest Hemingway* 113).

The kind of destabilizing re-reading discussed in this essay allows a re-examination of Hemingway and Hemingway scholarship not only in the light of feminist theory, but also other ideological, philosophical, cultural, linguistic, historical, and psychological theories. To complicate further the process of destabilization, some of these theoretical positions work to destabilize the traditional assumption that texts yield up their meanings—in other words, the assumption that there is a stable relationship between signifier (text) and signified (meaning). Others affirm the notion of "meaning," but destabilize its relationship to readers by exposing and questioning its implications. Still others consider the notion of textual meaning or textual affect to be irrelevant and apply the contextual signification of culture or history to literary texts. The consequence of inquiries based on such radical destabilizations revitalize—not ruin—Hemingway studies and should inform the Hemingway critical context, not merely be tolerated.

II

To put this process of re-reading less abstractly—but still relying on the Hemingway/Hotchner story as a metaphor for the relationship of Hemingway scholarship to Hemingway's texts, I want to re-tell the anecdote by *re-reading* it. I want to call attention to and question the absences and ambivalences related to the women in Hemingway's life and in his texts—as well as related to women reading Hemingway and Hemingway scholarship. My new version of the anecdote will in turn serve as a metaphor for a feminist perspective which is metonymically attached to Hemingway scholarship.

Here's my addition: as Hemingway advanced toward the bear, intent upon his task, he failed to notice that another car had stopped. A taller than average woman stepped out. Her hair was long, and her intensity equaled that of Papa. She walked quietly, remaining unnoticed, and watched. When Hemingway finished his dressing-down of the bear, he turned to walk back to his car. He saw her, then. He smiled the smile of success, proud of his shaming of the bear—yet unaware of the bear's shame as it slinked off into the nearby winter woods. She didn't return his smile; she only stared, surprised and appalled at his total lack of self-awareness—and at his failure of compassion. Papa seemed slightly disconcerted by her apparent refusal to join his self-congratulatory mood. But dismissing her reaction of silent condemnation, he turned to get into his car. As he turned the motor over, he forgot her. Continuing down the road toward the nearby town, his smile finally transformed itself into deep laughter and pleasure.

Later, she read Hotchner's account and found that she was not mentioned—once again outside the action, yet implicated in it. Hotchner missed the point, she felt. Sure, he had told the story well. Further, he had added to the Hemingway legend. His re-telling was, she had to admit, compelling and interesting—even funny—but it violated her memory and experience of the action. She noticed, too, that Hemingway had told Hotchner the story unproblematically, and then Hotchner re-told his reader unproblematically, neither aware of the implications of his narration. Later when other critics and scholars worked on the story, they failed to mention her presence, or they misread her dismay as desire, considering her a potential sexual interest.

If this woman—first as observer of Hemingway and then as a reader of Hemingway and of Hemingway scholarship—does not acknowledge the problematic nature of the narrations and of the context into which Hemingway scholars put those narrations and personal actions, then she is complicit in the narrowing of the context to avoid examining its implications and consequences in terms of gender, language, and power. She is, in other words, complicit in keeping alive the illusion of an unproblematic, stable, unquestioned, "pretty" Hemingway story. Moreover, if contemporary readers do not recognize the consequences of unproblematic, stable readings of both the primary writings and the secondary scholarship, they are complicit as well.

The woman I placed inside the story is also a metaphor for all those women who form the background—and the sexual interest—of Hemingway scholarship: Agnes, Hadley, Pauline, Adriana, Martha, Mary, and so forth— all those women who were there, but whose stories are retold without their agency and without acknowledging the implications of their involvement. These women have had to live as marginalized characters in the legend of this man.

My added female character represents as well female scholars such as Bernice Kert, Sandra Spanier, and Julia Edwards, whose work functions to destabilize Hemingway scholarship because it focuses on the women involved with Hemingway, re-reading and then re-telling the stories from their perspective. Hemingway's female characters who have their genesis in these real women have been examined by other scholars, for example, Millicent Bell, Mark Spilka, Kenneth Lynn, J. Gerald Kennedy, Nina Baym, Roger Whitlow, James Phelan, and Linda Wagner-Martin (see also Bardacke, Linderoth, Grant, Werlock and Shillinglaw, Wexler, Spanier). Some feminists—Judith Fetterley, for instance—have focused on the readers of Hemingway, inquiring into the consequences of ignoring the implications of Hemingway's representations of women, whether real or fictional. However, despite the inherent destabilizing potential of this scholarship, generally it has been tucked inside and absorbed by the traditional body of scholarly and critical work on Hemingway (and thus neutralized), ignored, or "proven" wrong.

Such responses to the destabilizing readings seem particularly disturbing, since much of the Hemingway critical context has complied with Hemingway's own marginalization and trivialization of women (even if it does not condone it) by not generally acknowledging or problematizing the cultural codes that allow a consistent focus on men as the only ones who have accomplished great things and/or as the ones whose perspective determines every aspect of life, real or fictional—what Nina Baym has called, "melodramas of beset manhood" (123–39). Robert Manning's description of Mary Hemingway is one of many descriptions of such a relationship to women: "A bright, generous, and energetic woman, Hemingway's fourth wife cared for him well, anticipated his moods and desires, enjoyed and played bountiful hostess to his friends, diplomatically turned aside some of the most taxing demands on his time and generosity" (*Conversations with Ernest Hemingway* 185). Women are inspiration, muses, sexual temptations and release from sexual tension; they serve as nurturers, solvers of domestic problems, and creators of conditions which allow men to go on accomplishing—and making decisions. Even Hemingway's ways of holding women in esteem marginalized them—kept them as objects, playthings, nurturers, allotting them the no-power of domestic power. Hemingway's highest praise for women was that they did not complain, although that did not keep him from abandoning them.

Those who were abandoned, but who did not complain, like Hadley, generated life-long guilt, but still they were better than outspoken women of power and ambition. Gertrude Stein, for example, was relegated eventually to the position of interloper and bitch—even to being too much like men. Hemingway trivialized Stein by focusing on her appearance after she had failed in his eyes, saying that she looked like "a Roman emperor and that was fine if you like your women to look like Roman emperors" (*MF* 119). Such comments rest on the cultural codes that a description of a woman's appearance is always relevant and essential and that while it is all right for men to pursue success (or argue critical positions) aggressively, it is not all right for women—and that has not changed much in our culture or in our profession.

Because Hemingway scholarship generally has continued to examine Hemingway inside the context he created and in terms of what he "intended" as an author, problematic codes, problematic language, and problematic relationships are perpetuated—perhaps not because anyone's overt intentions are to marginalize women, but because in not mentioning the problems and in not bringing a theoretical and ideological light to shine on them, their use seems to be familiar, accepted, and acceptable.

III

So far in this essay, the terms *ideology* and *ideological* have been used to describe particular political relationships to literary texts and to literary scholarship, specifically, feminist ideology as it has informed literary theories and critical methodologies. Feminists generally acknowledge the parameters, terms, foundational principles, and beliefs which underpin their reading and interpretive strategies. Their various strategies destabilize, as I have said, traditional reader-text-author relationships, exposing unacknowledged belief-systems and foundational principles of text, language, and culture. Another way to say this is that the literary theories based in feminist ideology function to reveal the ideologies of literary and critical texts. Thus, the concept of *ideology*, as used in this essay, encompasses the explicitly professed feminist political reading agenda and the literary representation of unacknowledged but deeply internalized cultural and linguistic codes and attitudes, as well as traditional Hemingway scholarship's alignment with and explanation of those codes and attitudes.

This complication of *ideology* is necessary in order to do a brief examination of Catherine Barkley in *A Farewell to Arms*, and the incomplete discussion of Barkley is meant to suggest the theoretical possibilities inherent in destabilized re-readings of her (and by implication, of actual women and other female characters). Not only is Barkley a partial representation of Agnes von Kurowsky, but also a metaphor, a literary character (see *SL* 21; Villard and Nagel 13). In other words, Hemingway is re-telling a personal story, although metaphorically through the characters of Frederic Henry and Catherine Barkley. This metaphoric distance allowed him the creative space to alter the events and the outcome of his personal experience (that Agnes rejected him), blurring finally the lines between fiction and non-fiction. Henry Villard reports that Agnes "thoroughly resented being taken for 'the alter ago of the complaisant Catherine Barkley' and thus indirectly the mistress of the man who wrote the book . . . 'Let's get it straight—please,' [von Kurowsky] insisted. 'I wasn't *that* kind of girl'" (41–2). Villard goes on to quote von Kurowsky as saying that Catherine was "'an arrant fantasy' created by the writer in the same way he had produced a 'macho' image of himself as the virile, resourceful ambulance driver, Frederic Henry . . . [H]e invented the myth years later—built out of his frustration in love. The liaison was all made up out of whole cloth, wishful thinking, if you will . . . " (42). Villard also notes that

Notwithstanding her attempt to play down the affair, there is no question in my mind that Agnes was strongly drawn to Hemingway . . . and that he thought . . . he was going to marry her after the war . . . Ernie took his dismissal very hard . . . Hemingway wrote bitterly that he had hoped Agnes would stumble and break all her front teeth when she stepped off the boat in New York. And when the first movie version of *Farewell* appeared in 1932, starring Helen Hayes and Gary Cooper in the saccharine Hollywood manner, an angered Hemingway was said to have told a reporter for the *Arkansas Democrat*: 'I did not intend a happy ending' . . . I had no doubt that the major contribution [to the characterization of Catherine] was that made by Agnes . . . Agnes might not have been her precise counterpoint, but without Agnes there would have been no Catherine (44).

Stephen Cooper describes as "one of the most significant [years] in [Hemingway's] life" the period of time from "May, 1918, when he left Oak Park to report for duty in New York with the Red Cross ambulance service," to March, 1919, "when he received a letter . . . from Agnes von Kurowsky, informing him that she was in love with someone else" (31). A re-reading of Hemingway could suggest that he was re-reading his own rather painful experience with von Kurowsky through the metaphoric re-telling and that the more he told the von Kurowsky story (as he also does in "A Very Short Story"), the more he repressed the pain of the original experience. Such pain is made particularly clear in his letter to Howell Jenkins in June, 1919: "I loved her once and then she gypped me. And I don't blame her. But I set out to cauterize out her memory and I burnt it out with a course of booze and other women and now it's gone" (*SL* 25). The ultimate repression of the painful experience comes, I would argue, in the death of Catherine Barkley and the romanticizing of Frederic Henry's reactions to that death. I would also argue that Hemingway's ambivalence toward von Kurowsky (toward women in general) is reflected in the particular metaphor called Catherine Barkley, an ambivalence which wavers not between love and loss—or even between immature and mature love—but between the more negative relationships of idealization and objectification.

Critics have often duplicated Hemingway's ambivalent metaphoric relationship to von Kurowsky/Barkley by disagreeing about whether Catherine is an example of a "code heroine," a passive male-fantasy, a neurotic bimbo, a "tough little partner," a paranoid romantic, an hysterical survivor, a self-hating cripple, a mature teacher, a threat, an "emotionally constricted and con-stricting woman," a brave sacrificer, or an emasculating spider-woman who separates Frederic from his work as war-hero (see Bell, Beversluis, Brenner, Fetterley, Friedman, Gajdusek, Gellens, Grant, Lewis, Linderoth, MacDonald, Nagel, Phelan, Pullin, Reynolds, Schneider, Solotaroff, Spanier, Waldhorn, Wexler, Whitlow, Young). Perhaps each particular critic has come to terms with Hemingway's problematic relationship to Barkley by re-read-ing it as a coherent representation, but as Gerry Brenner notes about the "irreconcilable" critical views of Robert Jordan, the body of scholarship of *A Farewell to Arms* reveals an incoherent picture of Barkley, and thus of Hemingway as her creator (23–4; see also Fetterley, 65–7).

In his essay on "The Inception and Reception of *A Farewell to Arms*" in the Special *FTA* issue of *The Hemingway Review*, Robert Lewis articulates what seems a similar response when he says that "[p]erhaps the only safe conclu-sions one may reach about Hemingway's depiction of women in general and of Catherine Barkley in particular is that it is complex and ambivalent." He also points out that there are "preconceptions of Hemingway's attitudes. . . ." These comments, however, problematize (and are problematized by) his conclusion that if such complicating and "impeding" circumstances were eliminated, there would be an "understanding of the work" accomplished through a "careful reading" (94). In other words, the recognition of the com-plexity, ambivalence, and preconceptions renders problematic the kind of coherent reading implied in his conclusion, *and* that kind of coherent read-ing renders problematic his insight about complexity and ambivalence.

Lewis's quotation illustrates the distinction between a stable, coherent reading and a destabilized reading of Catherine Barkley. His "understanding" of Hemingway's text rests on the assumption that "careful readings" yield truthful interpretations—ones which would claim to be "faithful" to the text's articulations of its ends and means. His comments about complexity, ambivalence, and preconception rest, however, on destabilized and destabi-lizing relationships between reader, criticism, and literary text/literary char-acter. It seems that the recognition of the presence of both readings (not only in Lewis's single sentence, but in the Hemingway critical context) is inevitably destabilizing, underscoring the tautological relationship between, in this case, Hemingway's representation of Catherine Barkley and literary scholarship on *A Farewell to Arms*—each profoundly influencing, perhaps even determining the other.

In this destabilized space, I want to re-read briefly some aspects of Hemingway's representation of Barkley, returning specifically to my claim that it reflects his ambivalent positions of idealization and objectification. Although for feminists idealization also implies objectification, for many critics idealization of a female character often obscures the consequent loss of subjectivity. Some critics argue that Hemingway created Barkley as an ideal character by arming her with the knowledge he personally privileged: awareness of the horrors of war—specifically its random malevolence in terms of individual deaths, the false sentimentality often associated with war-heroes, and the general inadequacy of human responses to death.

These critics support their arguments that Hemingway located such traditionally male knowledge in a female character by pointing out, for example, that Barkley conveys such information to Frederic Henry, who does not seem to know what she knows. He believes that the war cannot hurt him: "Well, I knew I would not be killed. Not in this war. It did not have anything to do with me. It seemed no more dangerous to me myself than war in the movies" (38). They note that within pages after his comment, his position is shelled, he is severely wounded, and one of his men is killed, illustrating and confirming her more cynical comments about war and the death of "the boy who was killed last year" (18). Those statements (and ones she makes later about war and war-heroes) are further illustrated when Henry jumps into the Tagliamento to avoid execution by his own army.

Yet, since Barkley is a woman—one whose own death is decided, not by war's random pointing finger, but by her own biological idiosyncracies (narrow hips and pelvis) and the inadequacies of contemporaneous medical treatment—her "knowledge" about war is not finally attachable to her experience, other than vicariously. She knows no more about dying in war (even as a nurse) than Frederic knows later about dying in childbirth. Thus, whatever subjectivity might seem to be implied in her articulation of the text's privileged information is instead undermined when she is re-read as Hemingway's version of an attractive puppet who speaks knowingly about what he does not allow her to know. There is no comparable loss of male subjectivity for Frederic Henry when he cannot share in the specifically female "knowledge" of childbirth. Moreover, Barkley's position as a female character who dies bearing an unwanted child further underscores the denial of female subjectivity in this text (see Fetterley).

The critical reading of Barkley as a subject, not an object, is further destabilized by re-reading her *willingness* to "educate" Frederic Henry and to subordinate herself to his desires—almost to the point of abandoning her responsibilities—as yet another screen behind which Barkley's objectification is hidden to Hemingway himself and to many Hemingway critics.

Behind that screen is the cultural/psychological context which has already decided her objectification when and if she makes such pre-determined, role-bound decisions—what Irigaray would call "ready-made grids" (29; see also Cixous, Kristeva). Thus, to see Barkley's supposedly "intentional" choice of self-sacrifice as an indicator of her subject-position is to deny a cultural history which gives her no other choice.

This re-reading of Barkley demonstrates that Hemingway's text, as a representation of the traditions of gender relations, repeats that tradition's inherent, unacknowledged objectification of women. As a metaphor, Barkley also iterates Hemingway's praise for acquiescent, self-sacrificing, fully supportive women (like Hadley and Mary). To bring this back to my earlier argument that Hemingway's *A Farewell to Arms* is at least in part his re-reading of von Kurowsky's rejection of him, Barkley's objectification functions to negate what might be seen as von Kurowsky's asserted female subjectivity: her initial rejection of Hemingway and her continuing desire to distance herself from association with Catherine Barkley.

IV

This essay has attempted to argue three main points. First, the space for destabilized and destabilizing re-readings already exists inside Hemingway scholarship because that body of thought is replete with conflicting critical readings. Such a destabilized space reveals that each reading which conflicts with a previous reading re-reads it rather than negating and replacing it, as traditional academic scholarship has believed. Generally, Hemingway studies has pursued a course based on the assumption that fully coherent, stable, replacement readings are not only possible, but desirable, and thus, has repressed what it has revealed. That repression repeats Hemingway's repression of the incoherent, problematic, unstable aspects of life into superficially coherent, stable fictional narratives.

Second, not acknowledging the already established space for destabilized re-readings has had particularly negative consequences for women scholars, especially for feminists, just as Hemingway's decision not to acknowledge or take seriously the women in his life or in his texts (beyond domestic idealization and sexual objectification and gratification) has had consequences for them and for his women readers. Despite the fact that women scholars and feminists have been working on Hemingway for more than two decades, their work has often been recontextualized inside the terms of traditional Hemingway scholarship and its goals, methods, and conclusions—and judged (and often consequently dismissed) by a set of text-based standards to which feminist readers do not necessarily adhere. The warrant for these feminist re-readings comes from feminist ideology and literary theories, not from Hemingway's texts. Application of such theories to Hemingway's texts and to Hemingway scholarship re-reads them. In that different light they signify differently.

Third, inside the destabilized space, feminist critical and theoretical re-readings of Hemingway's female characters expose cultural codes and attitudes about women which continue to haunt and limit their lives. The brief re-reading of Catherine Barkley in this essay has attempted to show some of the potential of such re-readings.

"Hemingway" is a more complex and valuable metaphor of our culture and history when his texts and their critical context are also re-read and destabilized than when he is only read and re-read in ways which re-explain his self-explanations. Thus, inside a shared, acknowledged, destabilized space our collective work as scholars and critics does not perpetuate the problematic implications of Hemingway's fictional and non-fictional work: that women are context, not text, and objects, not subjects.

Works Cited

Baker, Carlos. "Ernest Hemingway: *A Farewell to Arms.*" *The Merrill Studies in A Farewell to Arms.* Ed. John Graham. Columbus: Charles E. Merrill, 1971.

Bardacke, Theodore. "Hemingway's Women." *Ernest Hemingway: The Man and His Work.* Ed. John K. M. McCaffery. New York: World, 1950.

Barnes, Lois L. "The Helpless Hero of Ernest Hemingway." *Science and Society* 177 (1953): 1–25.

Baym, Nina. "Melodramas of Beset Manhood." *American Quarterly* 33 (1981).

Bell, Millicent. "*A Farewell to Arms*: Pseudoautobiography and Personal Metaphor." *Ernest Hemingway: The Writer in Context.* Ed. James Nagel. Madison: U of Wisconsin P, 1984.

Beversluis, John. "Dispelling the Romantic Myth: A Study of *A Farewell to Arms.*" *The Hemingway Review* 10.1 (1989): 18–25.

Brenner, Gerry. *Concealments in Hemingway's Fiction.* Columbus: Ohio State U P, 1983.

Bruccoli, Matthew J., ed. *Conversations with Ernest Hemingway.* Jackson: U P of Mississippi, 1986.

Cixous, Hélène. *Newly Born Woman.* Minneapolis: U of Minnesota P, 1986.

Cooper, Stephen. *The Politics of Ernest Hemingway.* Ann Arbor: UMI Research Press, 1987.

Edwards, Julia. "Asking for Trouble." *Women of the World: The Great Foreign Correspondents.* Boston: Houghton Mifflin, 1988.

Fetterley, Judith. *The Resisting Reader.* Bloomington: Indiana U P, 1978.

Friedman, Norman. "Small Hips, Not War." *Twentieth-Century Interpretations of* A Farewell to Arms. Ed. Jay Gellens. Englewood Cliffs, N. J.: Prentice-Hall, 1970.

Gajdusek, Robin. "*A Farewell to Arms:* The Psychodynamics of Integrity." *The Hemingway Review* 9.1 (1989): 26–32.

Gellens, Jay, ed. *Twentieth-Century Interpretations of* A Farewell to Arms. Englewood Cliffs, N.J.: Prentice-Hall, 1970.

Graham, John, ed. *The Merrill Studies in* A Farewell to Arms. Columbus: Charles E. Merrill, 1971.

Grant, Naomi M. "The Role of Women in the Fiction of Ernest Hemingway" (Ph.D. dissertation). University of Denver, 1968.

Hemingway, Ernest. *A Farewell to Arms.* New York: Scribner's, 1929.

———. *A Moveable Feast.* New York: Scribner's, 1964.

———. *Ernest Hemingway: Selected Letters, 1917–1961.* Ed. Carlos Baker. New York: Scribner's, 1981.

———. *The Short Stories of Ernest Hemingway.* New York: Scribner's, 1938.

Hotchner, A. E. *Papa Hemingway: A Personal Memoir.* New York: Random House, 1966.

Irigaray, Luce. *This Sex Which Is Not One.* Ithaca: Cornell U P, 1986.

Kennedy, J. Gerald. "Hemingway's Gender Trouble." *American Literature* 63.2 (June 1991): 187–207.

Kert, Bernice. *The Hemingway Women.* New York: W. W. Norton, 1983.

Kristeva, Julia. *Desire in Language: A Semiotic Approach to Literature and Art.* New York: Columbia U P, 1980.

———. *The Kristeva Reader.* New York: Columbia U P, 1986.

———. *Tale of Love.* New York: Columbia U P, 1987.

Lewis, Robert. *Hemingway on Love.* Austin: U of Texas P, 1965.

———. "The Tough Romance." *Twentieth-Century Interpretations of* A Farewell to Arms. Ed. Jay Gellens. Englewood Cliffs, N. J.: Prentice-Hall, 1970.

———. "The Inception and Reception of *A Farewell to Arms.*" *The Hemingway Review* 9.1 (Fall 1989): 91–95.

Linderoth, Leon Walter. "The Female Characters of Ernest Hemingway." (Ph.D. dissertation). Florida State University, 1966.

Lynn, Kenneth S. *Hemingway.* New York: Simon & Schuster, 1987.

Mailer, Norman. Keynote Address. "Ernest Hemingway at the Kennedy." Fourth International Hemingway Conference. Boston: 7 July 1990.

Nagel, James. "Catherine Barkley and Retrospective Narration in *A Farewell to Arms.*" *Ernest Hemingway: Six Decades of Criticism.* Ed. Linda Wagner. East Lansing: Michigan State U P, 1987.

Phelan, James. "The Concept of Voice, the Voices of Frederic Henry, and the Structure of *A Farewell to Arms.*" *Hemingway: Essays of Reassessment.* Ed. Frank Scafella. New York: Oxford U P, 1991.

———. "Distance, Voice, and Temporal Perspective in Frederic Henry's Narration: Powers, Problems, and Paradox." *New Essays on* A Farewell to Arms. Ed. Scott Donaldson. Cambridge: Cambridge U P, 1990.

———. *Reading People, Reading Plots: Character, Progression, and Interpretation of Narrative.* Chicago: U of Chicago P, 1989.

Pullin, Faith. "Hemingway and the Secret Language of Hate." *Ernest Hemingway: New Critical Essays.* Ed. A. Robert Lee. Totowa, N.J.: Barnes and Noble, 1983.

Reynolds, Michael. "Going Back." *Ernest Hemingway's* A Farewell to Arms. Ed. Harold Bloom. New York: Chelsea House Publishers, 1987.

———. *Hemingway's First War: The Making of* A Farewell to Arms. Princeton: Princeton U P, 1976.

———. *The Young Hemingway.* Oxford: Blackwell Publishers, 1989.

Rovit, Earl, and Gerry Brenner. *Ernest Hemingway.* New York: Twayne, 1986 (Twayne's United States Authors Series).

Rovit, Earl. "Learning to Care." *Twentieth-Century Interpretations of* A Farewell to Arms. Ed. Jay Gellens. Englewood Cliffs, N.J.: Prentice-Hall, 1970.

Schneider, Daniel J. "Hemingway's *A Farewell to Arms*: The Novel as Pure Poetry." *Modern Fiction Studies* 14 (1968): 283–92.

Solotaroff, Robert. "Sexual Identity in *A Farewell to Arms.*" *The Hemingway Review* 9.1 (Fall 1989): 2–17.

Spanier, Sandra Whipple. "Catherine Barkley and the Hemingway Code: Ritual and Survival in *A Farewell to Arms.*" *Ernest Hemingway's* A Farewell to Arms. Ed. Harold Bloom. New York: Chelsea House Publishers, 1987.

———. "Gender and War: The War Fiction of Hemingway and Martha Gelhorn." "Gender Issues in Hemingway's Fiction." Fourth International Hemingway Conference. Boston: 8 July 1990.

———. "Hemingway's Unknown Soldier: Catherine Barkley, the Critics, and the Great War." *New Essays on* A Farewell to Arms. Ed. Scott Donaldson. Cambridge: Cambridge U P, 1990.

Spilka, Mark. "The Death of Love in *The Sun Also Rises.*" *Ernest Hemingway: Critiques of Four Major Novels.* Ed. Carlos Baker. New York: Scribner's, 1962.

———. "Original Sin in 'The Last Good Country': or, 'The Return of Catherine Barkley.'" *The Modernist.* Eds. Lawrence B. Gamache and Ian S. MacNiven. Rutherford: Fairleigh Dickinson U P, 1987.

Villard, Henry Serrano and James Nagel. *Hemingway in Love and War: The Lost Diary of Agnes von Kurowsky, Her Letters, and Correspondence of Ernest Hemingway.* Boston: Northeastern U P, 1989.

Wagner, Linda W. "'Proud and Friendly and Gently': Women in Hemingway's Early Fiction." *College Literature* 7 (1980): 239–47.

————, ed. *Ernest Hemingway: Six Decades of Criticism*. East Lansing: Michigan State U P, 1987.

Wagner-Martin, Linda W. "Hemingway's Search for Heroes, Once Again." *Arizona Quarterly* 44.2 (1988): 58–68.

Waldhorn, Arthur, ed. *Ernest Hemingway: A Collection of Criticism*. New York: McGraw-Hill, 1973.

————. *A Reader's Guide to Ernest Hemingway*. New York: Farrar, Straus, and Giroux, 1972.

Werlock, Abby, and Susan Shillinglaw. "*For Whom the Bell Tolls:* The Rape of Maria." "Gender Issues in Hemingway's Fiction." Fourth International Hemingway Conference. Boston: 8 July 1990.

Wexler, Joyce. "E.R.A. for Hemingway: A Feminist Defense of *A Farewell to Arms*." *Georgia Review* 35 (1981): 111–23.

Whitlow, Roger. *Cassandra's Daughters: The Women in Hemingway*. Westport, Conn.: Greenwood Press, 1984.

Young, Philip. *Ernest Hemingway: A Reconsideration*. University Park: Penn. State U P, 1966.

TOWARD A POLITICALLY RESPONSIBLE ETHICAL CRITICISM: NARRATIVE IN *THE POLITICAL UNCONSCIOUS* AND *FOR WHOM THE BELL TOLLS*

James L. Kastely

Recent political criticism of literature has often felt the need to distinguish itself from ethical criticism, which it has seen as merely an ahistorical moralizing (Eagleton 194–217 and Jameson 234–35). The concern of political criticism has been to uncover the ideological and historical origins of past ethical criticism, and it has had little inclination to investigate whether ethical criticism need be either ahistorical or moralistic (Eagleton 17–53). It thus becomes the task of those practitioners of ethical criticism who wish to acquire a voice in the contemporary critical conversation to show that their mode of critical inquiry can do justice to the political and historical nature of discourse. However, as we shall see, the attempt to reach a rapprochement with political criticism expands into an exploration of how ethics, as a mode of inquiry that arises from a conflict of values, becomes a support for a plurality of interpretations.

Reprinted with permission from Style *(Winter 1988), pp. 535–558.*

I

Fredric Jameson's *The Political Unconscious* provides a good text against which to define a new ethical criticism, for Jameson argues that political criticism offers a methodology superior to other modes of criticism:

> This book [*The Political Unconscious*] will argue the priority of the political interpretation of literary texts. It conceives of the political perspective not as some supplementary method, not as an optional auxiliary to other interpretive methods current today—the psychoanalytic or the myth-critical, the stylistic, the ethical, the structural—but rather as the absolute horizon of all reading and interpretation. (17)

Grounding Jameson's inquiry are two key assumptions: first, that narrative is our fundamental mode of comprehending the world, and second, that the various particular modes of telling are ultimately reconcilable and placeable in a single political narrative that gives order to the human effort to be free. He combines these two assumptions and argues that there are finally no contending narratives to the political story; rather, there are only local attempts to narrate events that must be rewritten if we are to uncover their true content:

> Interpretation proper—what we have called "strong rewriting," in distinction from the weak rewriting of ethical codes, which all in one way or another project various notions of the unity and the coherence of consciousness—always presupposes, if not a conception of the unconscious itself, then at least some mechanism of mystification or repression in terms of which it would make sense to seek a latent meaning behind a manifest one, or to rewrite the surface categories of a text in the stronger language of a more fundamental interpretive code. (60)

There is consequently an interpretive hierarchy in which political criticism occupies a privileged place because it possesses the master code and thereby establishes the preconditions for knowledge.

Although Jameson is interested in placing all critical methods within his hierarchy, he is particularly concerned with undermining the autonomy of ethical criticism. For him, ethical criticism is not simply another mode to be placed, but rather it is a competing and antagonistic approach. Jameson sees ethical criticism as replacing a historical and political understanding of human beings as creatures embedded in and determined by modes of production with an essential and ahistorical understanding of human nature (59–60). Further, he is troubled by what he sees as the reduction by ethics of that which is other to that which is evil (114–16). Ethics seems to proceed by establishing a privileged set of definitions and then working out the manifold implications of these definitions. According to his understanding, ethics does not see itself as problematic and certainly not as historically determined; rather, it possesses a reductive certainty of an essentialist value system. Deconstructing ethics' privileged set of definitions and decentering the self are essential to Jameson's larger project of providing a way to interpret culture by making history available through rewritings of the text on three related but expanding horizons. These rewritings would allow history, which exists as an absent cause and is thus not available in itself, to be apprehended. Through a series of interpretive deconstructions, political critics would uncover the contradictions that shape and determine the particular texts and would make explicit the political unconscious that has been repressed in the production of these texts. As they pursued these critical investigations, critics would discover the "unity of a single great collective story," and they would demonstrate that the particular events of the literary past are "vital episodes in a single vast unfinished plot" (19–20).

Central to Jameson's enterprise of redefining the purposes and methods of political criticism is the relation of history and necessity. In Jameson's revision of Marxist historical explanation, we are no longer to make sense of history (to tell our story) through the mechanism of a base and superstructure that sees culture as determined by a more fundamental economic activity. For Jameson, reality is not an antecedent and independent existence outside of language that authorizes its claims; rather, reality is history. We are to see the history of our culture as the collection of the effects of the modes of production. And we are no longer to read "modes of production" as an exclusively economic activity. Instead, the modes of production do not exist apart from and prior to culture but are "an ultimate cause only visible in its effects or structural elements, of which linguistic practice is one" (46). They are the web of relationships that give a culture its identity or structure. This redefinition makes "causality" a term that marks a system of mutually implicating effects rather than one that explains these effects mechanically by a prior and privileged condition.

But to apprehend these causal relationships, a critic must be able to read them properly, and this means that a critic must have a way of reading the appearances before him or her. Criticism needs a method of interpretation that can deal with the deflections and repressions of language and that will ground its story not in the possibility of an imaginative free play but in a reality that cannot be reduced to an external and apprehensible referent. History is not itself a text, but "as an absent cause, it is inaccessible to us except in textual form, and . . . our approach to it and to the Real itself necessarily passes through its prior textualization, its narrativization in the political unconscious" (35). The mode of history's existence is its displacement and deflection in language, and interpretive efforts are attempts to uncover its traces as they are informed in culture. Such an existence is never available in itself but must always reach us as a form that mystifies reality. Consequently, any cultural text is a strategy of containment (52–53), and the critic must first deconstruct the strategy and then show how the text's form is a product of its management of our fundamental desire for freedom as it is lived in our history.

This need for a strong rewriting makes the interpretive process allegorical, and the notion of the unconscious becomes fundamental to a hermeneutics that sees culture as a process of management through deflection. Still this allegorical rewriting is different from the deconstruction of Paul de Man, for it does not open up an infinity of readings. What prevents this radical openness is the political nature of the unconscious. Jameson claims that the unconscious is political because all interpretive codes, except the political, are not fundamental sources of explanation but products of social development. These other codes are themselves historical texts whose ideologies must be reinterpreted to show how the codes are made possible by a historical development that they seek to contain. It is particularly important to show that the concept of the individual subject is not itself fundamental:

> the need to transcend individualistic categories and modes of interpretation is in many ways the fundamental issue for any doctrine of the political unconscious, of interpretation in terms of the collective or associative. (68)

The problem for Jameson with these categories is their conscious or unconscious ethical commitments that lead them to conceive of a transhistorical or essential human nature. They thus relegate the political to a surface phenomenon that can be explained in terms of a master code derived from human nature, and this, in effect, denies humanity's social and historical being.

To establish the methodological priority of a political interpretation, Jameson foregoes the apparent strategy of showing political criticism as more adequate or valid than a competing hermeneutics and instead argues that it is "something like an ultimate *semantic* precondition for the intelligibility of literary and cultural texts" (75). This argument is crucial but only partially successful. He does argue, quite convincingly, that his method of interpretation can account for both the individual text and culture in general, but this only proves that his version of Marxism can be one precondition for a text's intelligibility. What Jameson has shown, in effect, is that he can construct a comprehensive political account of literature; what he has not shown is that such an account is needed to ground critical intelligibility or that political criticism is the only way to construct such a critical architectonics. The hesitation in Jameson's phrasing, "something like an ultimate," suggests that he is aware of not having made a definitive case against other interpretive systems. Indeed, his use of the indefinite article, *an*, indicates that his solution is one among many. But this concession is fatal, for Jameson's theses are that there is a hierarchy and not a plurality of criticisms, and that political criticism is the architectonic criticism and not merely an acceptable alternative.

Jameson's problems with critical plurality emerge from his attempt to establish history as an absent cause. He begins his argument with the claim that "[h]istory itself becomes the ultimate ground as well as the untranscendable limit for our understanding in general and our textual interpretations in particular" (100). He then goes on to argue that only Marxism can explain the incompleteness and the essential unity of all historical events because its ultimate presupposition is that a socialist revolution must be one that is world-wide. With this premise, it can explain the contradictions that provoke a local revolution and the strategies which that revolution uses to contain those contradictions. Marxism thus sees necessity not as a content of events, but as the "inexorable form" in which events are finally intelligible. This necessity is then an essential narrative category, and in this way, Jameson's version of Marxism becomes a precondition for a knowledge based in narrative because this revision of Marxism is the source of the form of history. But such an understanding of history is itself problematic for three reasons. First, any narrative can be expanded to give an account of history that is complete and unified. Second, it is possible that history may be an irreducible multiplicity rather than an essential unity. If we must unify an event to comprehend it as an event, this does not mean that the absent cause that Jameson calls history need itself be unified. Finally, it could be argued that a fragmented apprehension of events may itself be more satisfactory than a unity which is too tidy.

In his justification for a theory of relational rather than deterministic causes as the precondition of narrative intelligibility, Jameson shows that he resembles the medieval allegorical critics more fully than he may know, for each system requires finally an act of faith. Each of these faiths is necessary to stop the inherent regress of the allegorical method. In the theologically based interpretation, there is, of course, the faith in his ultimate presupposition that all local revolutions are finally resolvable in the unity of an ultimate social revolution. But since this revolution would be a future event, it does not admit of proof, for it has not yet happened. It is thus not available to be apprehended historically as the form of the communal narrative.

Put in another way, the ultimate socialist revolution that guarantees an interpretive unity for Jameson's three critical horizons is a political fiction (in the good sense): that is, its necessity is a product of the human imagination's reworking of reality in terms of a more adequate form. Seen from this perspective, Jameson's political narrative of history would not be simply the emplotment of an absent cause but a political action. His narrative would become part of our history by becoming one of our modes of production. Also, this amending of Jameson allows us to capture a relation to history that he misses. In reading a political narrative of history, we are not merely concerned with ourselves as characters who have events happen to them or because of them; we are authors—writers and rewriters of texts—who contribute to ourselves as characters as we shape our narratives. We thus acquire responsibility in and for history.

Our responsibility for historical narratives points to the fundamental contradiction within Jameson's argument. It is not possible for narrative to be the fundamental instance of human understanding if there exists a single privileged interpretive code. Indeed, narrativity gives up its peculiar power for explanation and understanding when all stories are confined to one plot. If history is truly an absent cause known only in its effects and thus finally unrecoverable except in a narrative that is not a reflection or "vision" of history, then we cannot know this history completely. This impossibility follows logically from the nature of the unconscious, and Jameson's position becomes a support not for a critical hierarchy but for a critical pluralism. In fact, to borrow a thought from Marx, the task is not to know history, but to deal with it. The primary concern must be with action and not with knowledge. This must be so because by the nature of history, as Jameson has developed it, there are no marks to recognize structure independent of an interpretive code. Once there are marks, there is no longer an unconscious. This is what makes narrative both an essential form and a plural one, and it is what makes it impossible for there to be both an unconscious and a single privileged account of the unconscious.

There is a role for truth in narrative accounts of the unconscious (Kenneth Burke's term, "recalcitrance," comes the closest to catching this concern for truth that we bring to narrative [131]), but we will judge narratives by a set of standards that explain our engagement with narrative and the consequences of this engagement for ourselves. But because the unconscious can never be available except when figured in a text, we cannot have a single master code that uncovers the unconscious without destroying the conditions that make it possible for there to be an unconscious. Consequently, as a mode of understanding, narrative must be inherently plural, and our concern should be not to establish a critical hierarchy but to promote a dialectic between differing narratives.

This plurality, which is not capable of being given a final harmonious form, provides a new opening for ethical criticism. The human capacity for narrative brings with it an ethical openness, for it makes ethical choice not the discovery of the appropriate rule but the assumption of responsibility for calling a rule right. A critical ethical judgment cannot proceed deductively, for an ethical crisis is occasioned because there is no single appropriate rule that can be applied. Rather, we must proceed narratively and plot out futures, one of which we must finally assume responsibility for. For this reason, ethics inheres within the individual subject and becomes an irreducible component of human experience. It is irreducible not because humans have an essential nature but because they have an essential responsibility for their nature. No one can force a person to take this responsibility; rather, one acquires it individually as he or she chooses or avoids choosing among the competing narratives of history. Stuart Hampshire has argued recently that conflict is at the heart of ethical existence, for our key ethical choices are between competing narratives:

> It seems an unavoidable feature of moral experience that men should be torn between moral claims entailed by effectiveness in action, and particularly in politics, and the moral claims derived from the ideals of scrupulous honesty and integrity: between candor and kindness: between spontaneity and conscientious care: between open-mindedness, seeing both sides of a case, and loyalty to a cause. Such dispositions as these, and the contrary moral claims associated with them,

generate the more difficult moral problems, because morality originally appears in our experience as a conflict of claims and a division of
purpose. (117)

Since our stories project different fates for us, there is, as part of the enterprise of telling stories, the possibility of a conflict in valuing.

To see ethics as a creative imposing of order is to bring ethics very close
to Nietzsche's idea of a will to power. It is to view the world as indeterminate
prior to the operation of imagination and judgment. Ethics becomes a creative activity in the service of life rather than in the service of the repression
of life. As Nietzsche reminds us, his project was not to do away with ethics
but to do away with a particular ethics: he hoped to get beyond good and
evil, and that does not mean to get beyond good and bad (55). An ethics that
starts from the position that life involves conflicts in which we must choose
and in which our choices are not mere deductions from principles or legit-
imatizations of a power structure conceives of evaluation as projective.
Jameson's method of evaluation with its commitment to a three tier allego-
ry of cultural revolution is always retrospective. His concern is to discover
the ideologeme that embodies the social contradiction between old and new
values as they are structured into the ethical binary of good and evil (117).
His concern is not with the making of the judgment but with the made judgment. Since the made judgment is determinate, its structure can be discovered and a narrative of its necessity can be written after the fact. This is a fine
and proper critical inquiry. The only danger is that it can assume that the
principles of structure that allow a critic to analyze a judgment are equivalent to the implicit principles governing creation, that the retrospective evaluation adequately captures the projective impulse. But this equivalence cannot be the case because the necessary condition for a serious ethical conflict
is that there is no structure to a situation until an ethical agent creates one
through his or her choice.

There is an inherent link between ethics and history that follows from the
conflicts of value that provoke alternative narratives. In his commentary on
Aristotle, Hans-Georg Gadamer argues that an ethical judgment is neither an
empirical extension of past principles nor a deduction from first principles
but part of an ongoing process of delimiting the human under historical
conditions of constant change. This understanding of ethics is what distinguishes ethics from the other practical arts:

Moral knowledge can never be knowable in advance in the manner of knowledge that can be taught. The relation between means and ends here is not such that the knowledge of right means can be made available in advance, and that because the knowledge of the right end is not the mere object of knowledge either. There can be no anterior certainty concerning what the good life is directed towards as a whole. (286–87)

Instead, an ethical inquiry must imaginatively project and assess futures that might follow upon certain choices: that is, to make ethical judgments, a person must construct narratives.

The recognition of the radical openness of ethical choice is not Aristotle's alone; rather, ethical reasoning loses its point if the individual ethical decision is anything but problematic. Ethics is not concerned with abstract and legalistic correctness. Its interest as an enterprise arises, on the contrary, because of its concern with those moments at which we risk ourselves. Stanley Cavell conceives of this uncertainty as fundamental to the ethical enterprise, as making it a concern about our responsibility for ourselves and others:

What you do and fail to do are permanent facts of history, and the root of responsibility. But the trunk and branch of responsibility are what you are answerable for. And where your conduct raises a question, your answers will be elaboratives. I have described moral arguments as ones whose direct point is to determine the positions we are assuming or are able or willing to assume responsibility for; and discussion is necessary because our responsibilities, the extensions of our cares and commitments, and the implications of our conduct, are not obvious; because the self is not obvious to the self. To the extent that that responsibility is the subject of moral argument, what makes moral argument rational is not the assumption that there is in every situation one thing which ought to be done and that this may be known, nor the assumption that we can always come to agreement about what ought to be done on the basis of rational methods. Its rationality lies in following the methods which lead to a knowledge of our own position, of where we stand, in short, to a knowledge and definition of ourselves. (312)

Such an enterprise is inherently open and inescapably historical. If there is a permanent feature to this activity, it is that the question of the human is fated to be asked by those who are human. This question neither admits a single, final answer nor, given its historical development, can it accept just any answer. There is a necessity within ethics not because its categories are permanent but because human beings are fated as human beings to take responsibility for their history.

The role of the Other, then, in an ethical inquiry is not to be something evil but rather to be an origin for inquiry. Otherness becomes available to people as a consequence of being forced to account for their own humanity, for Otherness is not a fact of the world but a fate that humans make for the world and one for which they must assume responsibility. Contact with the Other is a dialectical requirement for people understanding who they are. Ethics, then, need not rest on a denial of the historical and political aspects of human nature but can focus, instead, on how and why the individual person must be held responsible for the acknowledgment or failure to acknowledge the humanity within a self or an Other. Ethics' concern is not with implementing a set of fixed rules or living up to an ideal and essential self but with inquiring into those situations in which the human is at risk. As a mode of inquiry, ethics asks how one can be a human being in a particular situation, and it answers this question by constructing a narrative that explores the necessities within, and the responsibilities that follow on, being a person.

Ethical inquiries inevitably flow into political inquiries as the question of what it means to be human becomes the question of with whom can I be human (of how this humanity is shared). Conversely, questions about the nature of community must, at some point, become questions about the kinds of personhood available in that community. Questions of persons and communities are interdependent. But to situate both kinds of questions in a hierarchy and make one of them more fundamental is to reduce and impoverish our ethical-political being. In contrast, to see both a separateness and an interdependence between the two kinds of inquiry is to hold open the possibility of irresolvable conflicts within a person and between a person and a community and to acknowledge a tension with which we must live. Such an understanding allows us to recover our situation as one of conflict that fates us to be creatures who choose and who by their choices assume responsibility for the world that their choices have defined.

Jameson cites tragedy as a genre in which the ethical opposition of good and evil is wholly absent (115–16). But one can also read a tragedy like *Antigone* as Luce Irigaray does as an essential tension between personal and communal loyalties, between ethical and political obligations. On such a reading, Jameson's attempt to rule out ethical considerations in favor of a new social understanding becomes a very Creonlike enterprise that seeks to reduce a complexity legislatively. As Martha C. Nussbaum has argued, in another reading of *Antigone* the desire to reduce complexity legislatively is an understandable response to indeterminacy and to the consequent vulnerability it opens up, but it is a response that is always unstable and finally in the service of impoverishing life (51–81).

II

The need for narrative arising from a crisis of value and the ethical task of assuming responsibility for narrative provide a new opening for ethical criticism. Rather than focusing on a privileged understanding of value or arguing for the emplotment of an essential and ahistorical set of values, a practical ethical criticism can read a narrative as a dramatization of an ethical crisis. The critic will read to see how value is problematic for the narrative and how the narrative either acknowledges or evades responsibility for itself. An ethical reading will not be primarily concerned with determining whether a narrative has the right allegiances but rather why and how the narrative puts value in question. This kind of reading can allow us to understand the achievement of certain narratives whose genuine merits have been obscured by readings that constitute those narratives not as inquiries into value but as articulations of particular ethical or political positions.

One work that has suffered from critics reading it as either a successful or flawed attempt to put forward a particular ethical or political position is Hemingway's *For Whom the Bell Tolls*. The critical history of the novel is itself a narrative of reduction in which the novel is read as denying either the political or the ethical dimension of action and never as affirming the legitimacy of both claims and acknowledging their essential conflict.[1] Certainly one consequence of this critical history is to prevent the novel from speaking with a serious voice about what would constitute an adequate ethical or political account of an individual's responsibility for and within a revolutionary action. The immediate need of the critics to conceive of the novel as endorsing either a particular political or ethical position has blinded them to the insight that *For Whom the Bell Tolls* emplots narrative as a mode of understanding. But this novel is obsessed with narrative as the means for comprehending the fundamental conflict between political duty and ethical responsibility. And Robert Jordan insists that the writer's task is not to give in to slogans, cynicism, or self-pity, but to "[k]eep it accurate" (466).

Part of the reason that *For Whom the Bell Tolls* is a difficult novel to place ethically and politically is a consequence of the peculiarity of its narration.

The novel's handling of the atrocities of the Spanish civil war creates what, at first, appears to be a paradox. The novel says little about the cruelties committed by the Fascists while it gives a detailed account of the Republican atrocities that marked the beginning of the civil war. Since Hemingway is unquestionably committed to the Republican cause, why did he choose a narrative strategy that seems to indict the Loyalists? The presentation of the Republican atrocities has led some critics like Jackson J. Benson to claim that the novel tries to undermine a political understanding, so that we come to question the validity of political positions and see only the human beings involved (159). But this reading must surely be wrong. First, Hemingway's political critics are right: there is no balance in his presentation of the atrocities. The rape of Maria, which is not as fully realized as the killing of the Fascists and which closes before showing the most important atrocity, the rape itself, is the only Fascist atrocity shown. The most heinous atrocity committed by the Fascists, when they retake Pablo's town, is pointedly not shown even though Pilar tells us that it was worse than that committed by the Republicans. Second, the recognition of the humanity of the enemy does not undercut the rightness in killing them. Anselmo's moral dilemma is occasioned precisely because killing is wrong, but killing the Fascists is necessary. Finally, a story that gave a balanced account of the atrocities on both sides would for Hemingway and any lover of freedom be a morally reprehensible story. Whatever political uncertainties Jordan may possess, he is firmly and unwaveringly anti-Fascist.

Clearly the episode is important; Hemingway is willing to interrupt his novel and, for thirty pages, tell a story within a story. I almost began to call these pages a digression but, of course, they are not, for the central event of the novel is not the blowing of the bridge but Robert Jordan's education as a potential writer. And Pilar's narrative of the Republic atrocities is essential to that education. Pilar's narrative is very much in keeping with Jameson's opposition to a naive empiricism, for what she gives Jordan through her narrative is a perceptual frame. She prefaces and justifies her story in terms of Jordan's incomplete understanding of the war:

> "No, Ingles, I am not joking. Didst thou see the start of the movement in any small town?"
> "No," Robert Jordan said.
> "Then thou has seen nothing. . . . "

Without benefit of this narrative, a character as intimately involved with the war as Jordan does not understand fully what is at issue. The story is intended to complicate Jordan's and the reader's understanding of the ethical responsibility inhering within any political action. The atrocities must be witnessed in detail so that they cannot be simply rationalized away as they could be if given only in a brief summary form. Pilar's story provides Jordan with no new information, for, in one sense, he already knows what Pilar is going to tell him. Rather the importance of Pilar's account lies in the fact that it is a narrative and thus gives the events an order that points up the forces at work in the event. And in ways that Jameson could appreciate, it does not locate the ethical issue by a simplistic portrayal of good and evil characters. Rather, the vividness and particularity of the account argue for a reality that acknowledges the full complexity of the individual actors who were involved, so that it becomes an origin for Jordan's questioning his own actions. The narrative contends as a historical account with the more abstract history of necessary sacrifices that Jordan has been telling himself to justify his actions. Significantly, it is this narrated event rather than any actual occurrence that begins Jordan's reassessment of his current political understanding.

Pilar's story never argues that the actions of Pablo and the other Republicans were wrong. Hers is not a tale claiming that the political situation should be transcended in favor of seeing the war only in terms of individuals. Rather than criticizing political activity, her story returns complexity to Jordan's understanding of the Spanish civil war, for Jordan needs a double perspective on the current struggle to allow him to see both the larger concerns and their impact on individual lives. If Jordan is to become a writer whose experiences can have an authority, then he must be able to place his actions in a narrative that is adequate to the Spanish struggle for freedom and dignity.

When the war is over, Jordan plans to write a book that explores the issue of responsibility:

> I wish I could write well enough to write that story, he thought. What we did. Not what others did to us. He knew enough about that. He knew plenty about that behind the lines. But you had to have known the people before. You had to know what had been in the village. (134–35)

Because of his mobility as a guerrilla fighter, Jordan has evaded this knowledge prior to his stay with Pablo's band, and this evasion has played a key role in the cynical narrative that he currently is telling himself. He has simply never been in one place long enough to see the consequences of his actions for individual human beings. Certainly Jordan is aware on an abstract level that his work is complex and corrupting, but his work requires that he limit his knowledge of the consequences of his actions. To keep at his work, he has composed a narrative without people, one in which all problems are only technical difficulties. However, for his actions not to contradict his political beliefs, he must come to terms with these consequences; for him to do otherwise is to lose the original sanction (his concern for the people of Spain) and to reduce his actions to mere instances of expediency. This is an especial temptation given the intrinsic appeal of action and the seduction of technical excellence. The sheer challenge of the difficulties and the adrenaline rush of action can provide sufficient motives for continuing as a guerrilla fighter even when the original political purpose becomes obscured or lost in the practical realities of fighting a war. The tension between the demands of action and the necessity for assuming responsibility for the consequences of this action is the novel's essential conflict. The ethical demands to acknowledge responsibility and political demands to act effectively are in fundamental contradiction, both exerting legitimate claims against Jordan. At the novel's opening, Jordan has made a decision to fight for the Republic and, as part of the decision, has suppressed further reflection about the inescapable corruption that follows upon his actions because it will hinder him as an actor. If Jordan is to act effectively, he cannot continually reexamine his fundamental decision to participate in the war, for then he could not act. Because of the demands of his work, he has allowed himself no interest in what happens to himself or others, and he has reduced the complexity of his situation to the one preeminent concern of doing his duty. He continually and consciously represses any thought or, indeed, the activity of thinking because of its potential for distracting him from doing his duty to the best of his ability:

> All the best ones, when you thought it over, were gay. It was much better to be gay and it was a sign of something too. It was like having immortality while you were still alive. That was a complicated one. There were not many of them left though. No, there were not many of the gay ones left. There were damned few of them left. And if you keep thinking like that, my boy, you won't be left either. Turn off the thinking now, old timer, old comrade. You're a bridge-blower now. Not a thinker. (17)

And since thinking necessarily returns him to the contradictions within reality, Jordan will not permit himself to reflect on the consequences of his
actions for himself and others. If at times, he takes comfort in a cold-mind-
ed pragmatism, we, however, should not let Jordan's strategy for survival
blind us to the assumed bravado of this attitude. Like most pragmatists, he is
engaged in an unstable dodge of an unpleasant skeptical insight. Jordan
knows that to pursue any course of action is to corrupt oneself; still, one
must act.

Certainly, Jordan's refusal to pursue his reflection precludes his seriously
acknowledging the demands of Others; but he is nonetheless right that if he
is to contribute effectively to a cause that he knows is true, he cannot allow
himself to reflect on his situation. Further, he is aware of the problems that
are entailed by his decision and does not deny the relevance of other considerations; rather, he assumes a position of intellectual suspension: "my mind
is in suspension until we win the war" (245). And he is not content to rest
even with this resolution but holds himself accountable to observing honestly all that happens:

> He would not think himself into any defeatism. The first thing was to
> win the war. If we did not win the war everything was lost. But he
> noticed, and listened to, and remembered everything. He was serving
> in a war and he gave absolute loyalty and as complete a performance as
> he could while he was serving. But nobody owned his mind, nor his
> faculties for seeing and hearing, and if he were going to form judg-
> ments he would form them afterwards. (136)

Jordan does not seek to deny responsibility or even to deny that the issue of
responsibility is appropriate for one pursuing a right end; he only seeks to
delay these concerns to a later date because raising them now could harm his
efforts to oppose what threatens to destroy the people he loves. In his future
narrative, Jordan will deal with the complexity, contradictions, and responsibilities that, as an actor, he must repress. It will be in the construction of the
narrative history of the war that Jordan will discover the ethical and political
reality that he has helped to create.

Jordan's internal debate and his continual reexamination of his positions,
despite his efforts to suppress his thinking, have caused some critics to question whether his values are finally realized (Young 106; Thorne 524; Trilling
78–81). These critics are right to suspect Jordan of attempting to bolster his
confidence in a new set of values. But this is not a failure of the novel to

assimilate material; rather, it is a presentation of the flux of Jordan's mind, and equally it is a register of the conflict within the ethical-political situation. Hemingway often shows Jordan's thoughts going where they will. And although Jordan tries to repress his thoughts, it is clear that his intelligence and honesty will not permit him to rest easy in such repression or to settle for a reduction of his situation's complexity. For Hemingway there is no single, unshakable truth: neither the vision that Creath Thorne wants of "the mystery of our being placed here in our consciousness to live our lives as the implicit tragedies they are" (535), which denies an essential political content to our lives; nor Jordan's exclusive commitment to his political work, which reduces him only to his political obligations. Nor can these positions be fully harmonized in this life; rather, they mark a tension between our ethical and political existences that cannot be resolved but must be lived.

For this reason Carlos Baker is only partly right when he sees the novel as "a study of the betrayal of the Spanish people—both by what lay within them and what had been thrust upon them" (241). Underlying this concern with betrayal is the deeper concern with evasion. Richard B. Hovey believes that "Hemingway expects us to admire his hero for exactly this tough-minded pragmatism—as, rightly, we do admire Jordan for the idealism he feels and articulates and finally proves with his life" (171), but, in this complex novel, our admiration for Jordan, at least at the beginning of the novel, must be mixed, especially because of his "toughminded pragmatism." This pragmatism is both an honorable choice and an evasion. If it is necessary for purposes of action to hold one's mind in suspension until the war is won (and it is necessary), it is also an evasion of responsibility for oneself and others. And Jordan knows and continually fights this truth:

> In all the work that they, the partizans did, they brought added danger and bad luck to the people that sheltered them and worked with them. For what? So that, eventually, there should be no more danger and so that the country should be a good place to live in. That was true no matter how trite it sounded. (162)

The recognition that the world one lives in is a consequence of the narratives that one composes means that one is responsible for that world and cannot simply leave a situation when it becomes absurd or inhuman, as Frederic Henry leaves the war in A Farewell to Arms.

The ethical-political situation in For Whom the Bell Tolls is thus inherently contradictory. Jordan's problems cannot be adequately dealt with only as some sort of metaphysical unfairness that besets each of us; for if the Fascists win, the world that Jordan and Hemingway value will be impossible and the people they love will suffer horribly. Fascism must be opposed—this is for Jordan an unshakable and fundamental political truth. But it is opposed by another equally fundamental truth:

> He [Jordan] was very happy with that sudden, rare happiness that can come to anyone with a command in a revolutionary army; the happiness of finding that one of your flanks holds. If both flanks ever held I suppose it would be too much to take, he thought. I don't know who is prepared to stand that. And if you extend along a flank, any flank, it eventually becomes one man. Yes, one man. This is not the axiom he wanted. (199–200)

Instead, Jordan tries to evade this axiom with its understanding that the individual human life functions as a value that limits political action.

The problem of evasion is highlighted by Jordan's knowledge that his mission is doomed from the start, and therefore his sacrifice of himself and the band cannot be justified on any pragmatic grounds. The mission's futility raises the question of the human cost and challenges the utilitarian reasoning behind Jordan's tough-minded pragmatism.[2] Indeed, the waste of human lives in the sacrifice almost makes the narrative's universe absurd. It seems to deny a purpose to action, and, as such, it could easily provoke despair and defeatism. But Jordan's decision not to question rescues him from substituting a personal interpretation in place of his political commitment.

Jordan's passage from a pure idealism to one maintained through cynicism is easy to understand. His experiences at Gaylord's educated Jordan about the compromises that are demanded in pursuit of a right action. And this education was founded on an important truth: it is necessary to see the world accurately. In fact, part of the emotional power of his cynicism is that it allows Jordan to continue to believe in his ideals while confronting the real world in which he must act. One benefit of the cynicism is that it permits him to act while he knows the compromises and contradictions that inhere within the action. Further, his cynicism is a necessary stage through which Jordan must pass if he is to be truly educated about the complexities of the civil war.

It would be an equal but opposite simplification and evasion of responsibility to insist on a moral purity for political action, for such a position denies the complexity and the contradictions of the world.[3] Jordan's decision to put his mind in suspension until the end of the war and then to sort out his accountability is, despite his cynicism, an honorable solution to the problem of how to act. This choice, however, reveals the essential tension within the ethical-political situation, for Jordan's honorable choice corrupts him, reducing him from a person to an instrumentality and transforming all future choices into technical problems. This is the contradiction with which Jordan must deal: to aid the people he loves, Jordan must transform himself into a non-person, but such a transformation then calls into question the political sanction for his actions. This contradiction, however, is not an argument for the absurdity of Jordan's situation; rather, it reveals the need for a complex understanding that in some situations conflicts in value are not resolved through a hierarchical placing of values but by acknowledging an irreducible tension between them.

Jordan's attempt to keep his hierarchy of values and consequently to limit the problem of blowing the bridge to a technical difficulty fails because in his few days with the guerrilla band he is forced to recognize both his and their humanity. After two days with the guerrilla, he can say of this previous understanding of the war: "It was certainly a much simpler world" (228). And because of his education with the guerrillas, Jordan can no longer return to this world: "It was a long way from Gaylord's to the cave, though. No, that was not the long way. The long way was going to be from the cave to Gaylord's" (231). He has become fully aware of his conflicting responsibilities to the larger cause and to the members of the band in their particularity. This knowledge of the conflict allows him to regain his sense of himself as a person. The bridge still must be destroyed, but this act can now only be justified ethically if Jordan acknowledges that he is sacrificing the band and that a right action may bring suffering to innocent people.

His recognition of his humanity and the humanity of others then is not achieved at the cost of his political commitment. The ethical-political harmony at the end of the novel is clearly seen as momentary. Jordan's sense of completion is precarious, a product of luck and will, and he does not wish to undo it. His broken leg has created a special exemption for him. Because he can contribute no more to the larger political action, he is free to deal with the immediate consequences that his actions have raised for the guerrilla band. Jordan's parting with Maria reemphasizes the personal-communal conflict. He is forced to choose between allowing Maria to stay with him and pursuing the course that will best aid the band's escape. Jordan knows that he cannot keep Maria with him if he is to give himself wholly to this final stand against the Fascists. Without denying his love for Maria, he will subordinate it to his concern with helping the others escape. Even at the moment of death, all obligations cannot be reconciled. This recognition does not diminish the human consequences of the action or bring the world into a final harmony, but it does allow Jordan to recover his sense of personal responsibility and thus his humanity. When he dies, a human being perishes; his death is not simply the regrettable loss of a useful instrument. The novel ends with an act of responsibility shown in its full complexity: the Fascist that Jordan shoots must be Berendo, a decent human being, for any other Fascist's death would make the ending sentimental. This action aids the escape of the guerrilla band, which, however badly damaged, does endure.

The integrity that Jordan achieves before death is not a simple harmonizing of ethical and political purposes. Rather, it affords us a position both to see a successful life and, as Artistotle declares we must, to judge it in its completeness and to know that if that life continued it would be structured by an essential tension between political and ethical demands. Indeed, the novel's ending emphasizes the essential tension by focusing on Jordan's impatience for the Fascists to arrive. He is aware that his resolution not to commit suicide but to engage the Fascists in a final fight is subject to time and the intensity of his pain. His death embodies struggle. If, as Wirt Williams claims, the spiritual victory is unambiguous, it is only because Jordan's life is over (137). For life is finally ambiguity and conflict, and seeing it accurately is not a call to dispassionate observation but to ethical and political responsibility.

If *For Whom the Bell Tolls* is the story of a man in history coming to grips with reality through a concern with constructing a narrative adequate to the complexity of the ethical-political situation, then Jordan's death as an end gives a retrospective structure to the narrative of his life in the Spanish civil war. This retrospective structure is the opening for the political criticism of the narrative. The scene of Jordan's death is structured to highlight both his individuality and the social and historical nature of his situation, for his death parallels the death of El Sordo and his band, a major event in the narrative, which was witnessed by the reader and not by Jordan. The narrative's ending argues for a historical understanding of Jordan's death by displaying a pattern of heroism in the defiant deaths of the lovers of freedom who will continue to oppose Fascism even when their own deaths make such oppositions personally seem to be futile. The reality that the novel exposes through its narrative patterns is one of resistance to an overwhelming force. Because the pattern of the ending argues for a historical reality of continuing resistance, it calls into question the apparent Fascist victory.

Hemingway knew when he was working on *For Whom the Bell Tolls* that the Republic was doomed. It is thus possible to see the ending of his novel as challenging the interpretation of the war that events of the day seemed to make obvious. His narrative contends for a reading of the Spanish civil war as a historical event and offers an account of the history that places the Fascist victory as a local suppression of freedom in the context of a larger narrative of the human desire for freedom.

Further, the novel's concern with the necessity of narrative makes any claim for a literal understanding into a mystification of history. Pilar's education of Jordan through her narrative argues for the validity of Jameson's political unconscious. Jordan's ignorance arises not from a lack of information but because, with the aid of an act of repression, he has composed a narrative that places the civil war for himself. His narrative, however, cannot do justice to the complexity of his situation because it sees events only in terms of abstract causes, and it must therefore be rewritten. Pilar does not discredit Jordan's story; rather, she forces him to complicate it by acknowledging the legitimacy of both the political and the ethical interpretive horizons.

The novel itself becomes an instruction in political and ethical criticism. A political reading of the novel would follow Jameson's three-tier interpretation and move from the contradictions within Jordan's situation to an ultimate placing of Hemingway's contribution to the ongoing project of expanding human freedom (that is, the cultural revolution) by his effort at alternative history; an ethical reading of the novel would show that for a political interpretation to retain its validity, it needs to be complicated by a two-fold ethical inquiry. First, the reading needs to recover the crisis of value to which the narrative is responding. Second, it needs to explicate how the narrative assumes responsibility for its resolution of the crisis. It needs to remind the political interpreter of Camus's point that "[h]istory without a value to transfigure it, is controlled by the law of expediency" (287).

III

Rousseau's theory of the social contract explains the necessary conceptual link between ethics, politics, and history. But as Louis Althusser (125–34) and Andrew Levine (5–8) have shown, Rousseau's contractarian language obscures his insight into the historical nature of our ethical and political origin. The original convention cannot be a contract in any of our normal understandings of contracts, for there is no exchange between the parties to the contract. Rather, the social contract marks an act in which one party transforms itself into another party, in which a natural species becomes a conventional and hence human species. And as Cavell has pointed out in *The Claim of Reason*, Rousseau's use of the contract model makes clear both the role of consent in the way that we are implicated in a community and our responsibility for that community (23). And again as Cavell argues, Rousseau has not discovered a new knowledge but rather a new mode of knowledge and consequently a new mode of ignorance, one that we can call the unconscious (26). The consent that grounds the social contract is not the product of an active or conscious decision but the register of our responsibility for our choices. Thus the possibility of that mode of unconscious that we call political, which is marked by our being essentially creatures who have an identity because they are members in a community, depends upon our being creatures who can choose and who can be held accountable for their choices. When we move from our original, nonhuman condition in nature to form the state by the convention of mutually alienating all of our natural rights, we become a different species; for, however much we remain in nature, we have now created a set of possibilities that are radically new. With the convention of the social contract, humanity invents itself by transforming natural creatures into ethical beings:

> The passage from the state of nature to civil state produces a remarkable change in man, by substituting justice for instinct in his behavior and giving his actions the morality they previously lacked. Only then, when the voice of duty replaces the physical impulse and right replaces appetite, does man, who until that time only considered himself, find himself forced to act upon other principles and to consult reason before heeding his inclinations. (Rousseau 55–56; bk. 1, ch. 3)

The social contract explains the possibility of responsibility by arguing that we freely chose (that is, our original choice was emptied of any personal interest) to conceive of ourselves as bound to each other and that with this conception, we transcended our natural condition. There is, of course, a mystery at the heart of such freedom and responsibility as there is a discontinuity between ourselves and the rest of the natural world. This discontinuity is evident in the new possibilities for narrative. Causes must now contend with reasons as the narrative possibilities for the human condition become multiple and diverse.

When Rousseau argues that we cannot get from might to right, that power can never be the source of value, his point is a logical one. Might can

always externally compel obedience, but it can never require it. At most it
might be prudent to obey the powerful (48; bk. 1, ch 3). To be able to have a
political duty, we must be the kind of creature who can have an obligation.[4]
The question of how politics is possible is inextricably linked to the question
of how a person can be obligated. This is a question about the possibility of
ethical existence.

What then distinguishes politics, or any social science for that matter,
from biology as a natural science is that the creature it studies, the human
being, is no longer explainable completely in natural terms. Our self-inven-
tion through convention has altered our nature; it has made us fundamentally free creatures who are bound to each other by a set of duties. We have
constituted ourselves as political beings by becoming ethical creatures who
are responsible for their choices. Except for our transformation into ethical
beings, politics would lack a subject matter. For politics to be, ethics must be.

We can see the rightness of this conclusion by simply consulting the
Marxist enterprise. If human beings were not a special kind of creature capable of a unique dignity (a dignity derived from their responsibility for their
choices), why would we worry about the inadequacy, incompleteness, or
unfairness of economic, cultural, or political organization? Why are we not
simply content to describe this organization the way we would describe the
organization of any other species? Why are we compelled to pass judgment,
for it makes no sense to pass judgment on natural phenomenon? But it is
precisely because we conceive of human beings as ethical agents that we hold
them accountable for their actions.

It would be easy at this point for my argument to go astray and claim that
the ethical is the architectonic category of human experience. But it is not my
intention to replace Jameson's critical hierarchy with a competing one.
Rather, I want to establish that ethics is one of the constitutive aspects of a
human nature that is historical and that ethics is therefore an essential element in any attempt to interpret human experience. Its claim to authorizing
narratives with other than merely local integrity need not depend upon its
commitment to an essential and ahistorical human nature but can derive
from our being the kind of creature who can have a history precisely because
we make choices. Further, even if I wished to establish a new critical hierarchy, the ethical can no more exhaust or completely explain the political than
the political can exhaust or completely explain the ethical. My ethical reading of *For Whom the Bell Tolls* works against this kind of reduction and for a
continuing ethical-political tension. No community is simply a collection of
persons, and no person is reducible to being simply and wholly defined by

his or her obligations to a community, and this impossibility of reducing one to the other is logical. It is not my intention to reduce and contain Jameson or any other political critic, but rather to recover a purpose for ethical criticism so that it can meaningfully engage in a conversation with the political critic in which a condition of the conversation is not that the truth is the exclusive or final possession of either party. Such a possibility is what Jameson has denied.

The conflict whether ethical and political criticism should be placed hierarchically or should be conceived as existing in an essential tension raises the problem of determining the standards for human narrative. If, as Jameson contends, there is only one ultimate rewriting or textualization of history, then dialectic becomes uninteresting, for it is merely the rehearsal of a truth known in advance, at best, a clarification of details within an assured process. Such a view entails a projection of an end to our "single vast unfinished plot," and indeed, the nature of the end (because it is the guarantee that the unfinished plot is single) is what structures our understanding of the necessity within the plot. Such an understanding of interpretation vitiates Jameson's insight that narrativity is the central instance of the human, for underlying and structuring a diachronic surface would be a synchronous order that would make history beside the point.

By contrast, seeing the human as the product of conventions that create our ethical and political existences makes the narrative structuring of our experience one of human possibility rather than of natural or metaphysical necessity. Because we have created ourselves as a certain kind of creature through assuming responsibility for our choices, there are certain barriers we cannot cross and remain human. We are not infinitely malleable, and any law or necessity proposed for us must be capable of being reconciled with our understanding of ourselves as creatures who bear responsibility for being human. Our peculiar dignity as creatures who are fated to conflicts arising from our responsibility to acknowledge the humanity of ourselves and others is an irreducible component of our experience, as real as history or the material world. The community and the person imply each other and thereby limit each other. In this sense, personhood is not a category derived from history but one which is constitutive of a creature who is capable of having a history. Only such a condition makes us responsible to and for history. It does not, however, require us to have any particular history; rather, history will present us with choices from which we will define current possibilities for being human. One task of ethical criticism is to bring out the fundamental conflicts, the ethical crises, that are both the consequence and process of history. It is not the purpose of ethical criticism to claim that we will or even can resolve all conflicts; rather, its task is to insure that we do not evade them. Ethical criticism is thus essential to historical understanding; and instead of diminishing our responsibility for history, it highlights one strand that must be woven into the continuing tapestry of history.

IV

One of the ways to be responsible for history is to rewrite it so that it is available to us; and for this rewriting to be a true history, it must, as we have seen, be an interpretation. The openness of possibility and the constraint of limit find their resolution in a plurality of interpretations. And this plurality has consequences for our understanding the activity of interpretation, for we must finally address the question whether it makes sense to conceive of criticism as a system or as an art.

This question goes to the role of the interpreter. For Jameson, history has a determinate structure even if that structure is only available in a textual form. The interpreter always reads the text (rewrites the text) under the direction of a master code, a Marxist understanding of social revolution. The conflict and contradiction is always within the particular historical text, within the social classes, between the modes of production; and as these contradictions are contained into a textual form, they become the enactment of history. Curiously, there is no place in this paradigm for the critic in his or her historical and social dimension, at least if the critic is consciously political. In Jameson's approach a text cannot refute a critic. The critic's task is to dominate rather than to confront the experience of the text and other potentially conflicting readings. In such criticism, the text can never seriously take the role of the Other. As long as there is only one ultimate understanding of history, the interpretive task must be to make the materials conform to that understanding and criticism must be systematic because the universe is closed and finally knowable, for the text is an object to be known and not a force to be acknowledged. The critic tells only one story, even if he or she tells it in three different ways.

But, as I argued earlier, this is to make narrative as an intellectual function superfluous, for the act of telling ceases to be constitutive of understanding. If the master code embodies the true understanding of history, then narrativity is merely the possibility of the instantiation of that understanding. The condition that makes narrative essential to understanding is that history as a structure cannot be known apart from a particular story, and this must mean that all we have are stories. The activity of narrating is the activity of making sense of the world, of giving it form, and the standard for this activity is the satisfaction of the form. Since it is logically impossible on this understanding to invent a total form, the process of interpretation is inherently open and ongoing. There can finally be no master code but only master interpreters, critical artists. It becomes their work to acknowledge texts as human creations that implicate their readers in questions of value, so we can invent selves and communities that are adequate to our experience of the world. Critics, like artists, by their activity claim that their selves are representative. Criticism is essentially a placing of the self at risk, a using of personal experience to locate human limits and possibilities.

We can tell our story in political terms; but we can equally tell it in other terms, and one of these is the ethical. The task of ethical criticism as a critical art is to pursue the inquiries arising out of the conflicts that we cannot harmonize but on which we must act. This mode of ethical criticism is not committed to any particular theory of causality (certainly not to one of full rational explanation); rather, it attempts to uncover the possibilities that choices have opened and foreclosed, and it explores the commitments and costs that are embodied when a person must choose between narratives that cannot be reconciled. Such a conception of a person is neither ahistorical nor apolitical; just the opposite, such a conception must hold that a person is inherently social. If ethical criticism talks about reasons rather than causes, this is not primarily a commitment to theories of rationality but a register of the kind of responsibility that resides in a certain kind of creature. It is thus a way of characterizing action for certain purposes that cannot be addressed even through Jameson's sophisticated revision of causality. Ethical criticism sees some choices as crises that we understand through the projection of a future (to be sure, it is a future that must be consonant with our past) rather than seeing the situation through retrospection as the web of relationships that form around and from the resolved situation. This makes ethical criticism essentially narrative, for its goal is not knowledge but the recovery of humanly satisfying form. In this search for value, ethical criticism invents a human nature (a conventional understanding of ourselves) whose social, political, and historical forms become the special subject matter of those sciences that can rightly be called the human sciences. And if a political criticism must deconstruct a particular historical ethical understanding, we should not confuse this with debunking a category that is outside history. Rather, we should encourage the conversation between ethical and political criticism, so that our dialectic with ourselves and our texts will be adequate to the complexity of our existence.

Notes

1. That *For Whom the Bell Tolls* should be misread is not surprising, for Hemingway, the writer without politics, is writing about one of the major political events of the twentieth century. The immediacy of the subject matter, the Spanish civil war, makes readers ready to grapple with either Hemingway's political conversion or his universalizing of political concerns in the context of some larger human drama of personal existence. And although some readers have seen the novel as political (Beach 89), most readers have felt either that the novel was without politics (Benson 158; Broer 95; French 123; Hovey 170); or that Hemingway could not handle his political material (Sheridan Baker 109; Bessie 7–15; Geismar 79–80; Young 106); or that Hemingway could not make this material work in the literary form in which he shaped his tragic understanding (Thorne 535).

    Part of the reason that most critics have seen the novel in ethical rather than political terms is that its political understanding is not directed at the specific historical event which occupies its narrative. Hemingway was not arguing for the Republic cause. It is clear throughout the novel that the Republican cause stands in no need of justification. Rather Hemingway is investigating the very serious problem of the need for and the consequences of political commitment (Zehr 268–78).

2. Ivan Kashkeen has commented on Hemingway's fiction as a criticism of utilitarianism (174).

3. Bhim S. Dahiya is certainly right to complicate our appreciation of Anselmo and to argue that his kind of innocence cannot be a sufficient ethical standard for the novel (130).

4. Nietzsche, of course, offers an alternative history of our ethical and political obligations. In *On the Genealogy of Morals* he argues that might has made right, but even his account involves transforming a natural creature into a conventional one and recognizing that the change was momentous (85; essay 2/sec. 16).

Works Cited

Althusser, Louis. *Politics and History: Montesquieu, Rousseau, Hegel, and Marx*. Trans. Ben Brewer. London: NLB, 1972.

Baker, Carlos. *Hemingway: The Writer as Artist*. 4th ed. Princeton: Princeton UP, 1972.

Baker, Sheridan. *Ernest Hemingway: An Introduction and Interpretation*. New York: Holt, 1967.

Beach, Joseph Warren. *American Fiction: 1920–1940*. New York: Macmillan, 1941.

Benson, Jackson J. *Hemingway: The Writer's Art of Self-Defense*. Minneapolis: U of Minnesota P, 1969.

Bessie, Alvah C. "Review of *For Whom the Bell Tolls*." *New Masses* 37 (5 Nov. 1940): 25–29. Rpt. in *The Merrill Studies in* For Whom the Bell Tolls. Ed. Sheldon Norman Grebstein. Columbus: Merrill, 1971, 7–15.

Broer, Lawrence R. *Hemingway's Spanish Tragedy*. University: U of Alabama P, 1973.

Burke, Kenneth. *The Philosophy of Literary Form: Studies in Symbolic Action*. 3rd ed. Berkeley: U of California P, 1973.

Camus, Albert. *The Rebel: An Essay on Man in Revolt*. Trans. Anthony Bower. New York: Vintage, 1956.

Cavell, Stanley. *The Claim of Reason: Wittgenstein, Skepticism, Morality, and Tragedy*. New York: Oxford UP, 1979.

Dahiya, Bhim S. *The Hero in Hemingway: A Study in Development*. Chandigarh: Bahri Publications Private, 1978.

Eagleton, Terry. *Literary Theory: An Introduction*. Minneapolis: U of Minnesota P, 1983.

French, Warren. *The Social Novel at the End of an Era*. Carbondale: Southern Illinois UP, 1966.

Gadamer, Hans-Georg. *Truth and Method*. Trans. and ed. Garrett Barden and John Cummings. New York: Crossroad, 1982.

Geismar, Maxwell. *Writers in Crisis: The American Novel, 1925–1940*. Boston: Houghton, 1947.

Hampshire, Stuart. *Morality and Conflict*. Cambridge: Harvard UP, 1983.

Hemingway, Ernest. *For Whom the Bell Tolls*. New York: Scribner's, 1940.

Hovey, Richard B. *Hemingway: The Inward Terrain*. Seattle: U of Washington P, 1968.

Irigaray, Luce. *Speculum of the Other Woman*. Trans. Gillian C. Gill. Ithaca: Cornell UP, 1985

Jameson, Fredric. *The Political Unconscious: Narrative as Socially Symbolic Act*. Ithaca: Cornell UP, 1981.

Kashkeen, Ivan. "Alive in the Midst of Death: Ernest Hemingway." *Soviet Literature* 7 (1956): 160–72. Rpt. in *Hemingway and His Critics: An International Anthology*. Ed. Carlos Baker. New York: Hill and Wang, 1961. 162–79.

Levine, Andrew. *The Politics of Autonomy: A Kantian Reading of Rousseau's Social Contract*. Amherst: U of Massachusetts P, 1976.

Nietzsche, Friedrich. *On the Genealogy of Morals and Ecco Homo*. Trans. Walter Kaufmann. 1967. New York: Vintage, 1969.

Nussbaum, Martha C. T*he Fragility of Goodness: Luck and Ethics in Greek Tragedy and Philosophy*. Cambridge: Cambridge UP, 1986.

Rousseau, Jean-Jacques. *On the Social Contract with Geneva Manuscript and Political Economy*. Trans. Judith Masters. Ed. Roger D. Masters. New York: St. Martins, 1978.

Thorne, Creath S. "The Shape of Equivocation in Ernest Hemingway's *For Whom the Bell Tolls*." *American Literature* 51 (1980): 520–35.

Trilling, Lionel. "An American in Spain." *Partisan Reader*. Ed. William Philips and
    Philip Rahv. New York: Dial, 1946, 639–44. Rpt. in *Ernest Hemingway: Critiques
    of the Four Major Novels*. Ed. Carlos Baker. New York: Scribner's, 1962, 78–81.
Williams, Wirt. *The Tragic Art of Ernest Hemingway*. Baton Rouge: Louisiana State
    UP, 1981.
Young, Philip. *Ernest Hemingway: A Reconsideration*. University Park: Pennsylvania
    State UP, 1966.
Zehr, David E. "Bourgeois Politics: Hemingway's Case in *For Whom the Bell Tolls*."
    Midwest Quarterly 17 (1976): 268–78.

THE IMPORTANCE OF BEING ERNEST

Louis A. Renza

If you stand right fronting and face to face to a fact, you will see the sun glimmer on both its surfaces, as if it were a cimeter, and feel its sweet edge dividing you through the heart and marrow, and so you will happily conclude your mortal career.

—Henry David Thoreau, *Walden*

Like two bookends, Ernest Hemingway's *In Our Time* and *A Moveable Feast*, two collections of short prose, chronologically frame the official beginning and end of his literary career. Moreover, despite their generic dissimilarities, the two collections bear a certain topical relation to each other. *A Moveable Feast* comprises autobiographical sketches about the period in Paris when Hemingway actually wrote the stories and inter-chapters that would become *In Our Time*. *In Our Time* inaugurates a literary career that would endow these later sketches about his past life in Paris (and most notoriously, about his famous literary acquaintances there) with a virtually guaranteed public value—in other words, would justify and thus with hindsight motivate their very writing.

Beyond this loose symmetry of topic, the two collections also raise a persistent issue and perhaps even a continuing problem for Hemingway criticism in *our* time. The later collection reinforces the critical tendency to

Reprinted with permission from South Atlantic Quarterly, *88 (Summer 1989), pp. 661–689.*

regard Hemingway's fiction in "referential" terms. In the first place, "Hemingway" as established public persona mediates our apprehension of Nick Adams in *In Our Time* as pure fictive character, so that we tend to read this early collection as simultaneously tracing the reconstructed story of Hemingway's own education into the violence of nature, modern social relationships, and war stripped of romantic pretensions. In the second place, the stories and very title of *In Our Time* invite us to construe them as symbolic representations of violence endemic to "our time." One way or another, then, this collection attracts referential readings to which *A Moveable Feast* contributes, as when it reveals (and serves to corroborate a well-known critical interpretation) that a major story in *In Our Time*, "Big Two-Hearted River," "was about coming back from the war but there was no mention of the war in it."[1] Conversely, critical discussions of *A Moveable Feast* typically focus on the truth-value or distortions of Hemingway's often vengeful depictions of Stein, Fitzgerald, and other literary contemporaries, for this reason also deeming it a minor or uneven work in his literary canon.[2] Permeated by the sense of "outside" reference, the two works at the beginning and end of Hemingway's literary career remain vulnerable to post factum judgments about their metaphorical relevance, autobiographical accuracy, and, at least in our critical time, complicity with discredited ideologies such as a naive existential code, macho heroics, unresolved anxieties of literary influence, intentional fallacies or, as the following remarks illustrate, illusions about the power of writing to elicit self-present experiences: "Then I went back to writing and I entered far into the story and was lost in it. I was writing it now and it was not writing itself."[3]

Yet both works also evince at least minimal protests against their apparent referential frames. For example, Hemingway openly suggests in his preface to *A Moveable Feast* that the reader may prefer to regard "this book . . . as fiction." And in a passage from the omitted section of "Big Two-Hearted River," Nick Adams reflects that "The only writing that was any good was what you made up, what you imagined. That made everything come true."[4] To be sure, in light of much biographical evidence showing the correlation between his fictional materials and actual experiences (or vice versa, how he constructed a public persona along the lines of his fictional protagonists), such claims may seem misleading or even disingenuous. But at least in the case of *A Moveable Feast*, his referential writing indeed veers toward becoming fiction. The tenor of his memoirs, after all, suggests that he writes them to reassert his literary credentials as an original writer at the expense of former peers who, either then or in the intervening years, had threatened, at least to his way of thinking, the public's acceptance of these credentials.[5] As one could argue in the case of Wordsworth's *The Prelude*, more than *what* he writes about himself and these artistic acquaintances, Hemingway's *act* of vocational reassertion constitutes the primary subject of *A Moveable Feast*. If nothing else, his work unconsciously tracks his literary as well as physical and psychological decline, and expresses his nostalgic desire "to recollect how he learned to write" in "those first four years when he won the name of an original artist."[6] Moreover, the early text, the "original" writing of which he here recollects, necessarily leads him to adopt a fictional relation to writing about it now. For how can Hemingway recollect his learning to write the stories of *In Our Time* without trying to position himself as a writer willfully repressing the identity and literary self-consciousness he has accrued as a successful author since the writing of his inaugural collection of fiction?

One could also argue that *A Moveable Feast* uses autobiographical materials as pretexts for repeating what necessarily remains out of reach: the interior or private scene of writing *In Our Time*. In writing this later work, Hemingway projects writing as a project, both at the time of writing the stories of *In Our Time* and writing these sketches attempting to imagine that former scene of writing. First, *A Moveable Feast* not only thematically refers him back to the time when he wrote this former work, it structurally duplicates *In Our Time* as a collection of short, snapshot-like pieces of prose narrative. More important, in the past as he recollects it, he desired to write "'the truest sentence that you know,'" that is, to construe writing not as "about" but as virtually synonymous with the empirical consistency of the things to which it was referring at that particular moment. For Hemingway, writing "truly" comes to mean recovering the experience of his former desire to write truly. It means to recover his former *sense* of writing this earlier collection of stories as a series of representational events in which imagined perceptions—as he seeks to reimagine *them*—occurred with all the sensory force and particular thereness of actual perceptions:

> Some days [writing] went so well that you could make the country so that you could walk into it through the timber to come out into the clearing and work up onto the high ground and see the hills beyond the arm of the lake. A pencil-lead might break off in the conical nose of the pencil sharpener and you would use the small blade of the pen knife to clear it or else sharpen the pencil carefully with the sharp blade and then slip your arm through the sweat-salted leather of your pack strap

to lift the pack again, get the other arm through and feel the weight settle on your back and feel the pine needles under your moccasins as you
started down for the lake.[7]

Reference here gives way to the self-referential act of writing associated with
its materials ("pencil-lead"), which then returns to a referential sense of
physical, personal agency ("the sweat-salted leather of your pack strap" within the written scene) that in effect collapses or makes interchangeable the
perceptual immediacy of the referential scene disclosed through writing, the
material medium of this particular writing, and the psychological ambience
or scene of writing itself: "and you would . . . sharpen the pencil carefully
with the sharp blade and then slip your arm through the sweat-salted
leather."

Hemingway thus defines writing as a desirable and perpetually repro-
ducible concrete project in and for itself—as a metaphorical version of
hunger, which quite clearly constitutes the "central image" and dominant
trope of *A Moveable Feast* as a whole.[8] For this reason, he stops writing a section of "Big Two-Hearted River" at the point where a scene in the process of
representation continues to stimulate his imaginative appetite to write more:
"When I stopped writing I did not want to leave the river where I could see
the trout in the pool. . . . But in the morning the river would be there and I
must make it and the country and all that would happen. There were days
ahead to be doing that each day."[9] By focusing on the scene of writing *In Our
Time*, a completed work in the past, *A Moveable Feast* in effect purports to
convert both it and itself into projects still in process and interchangeably
infused with the ambience of physical hunger.

But certain kinds of "hunger" can also dilute this focus. Hemingway treats
his hunger as a trope replete with the torque of negative and positive consequences—"a *moveable* feast"—in relation to his no less tropological past
Parisian scene of writing *In Our Time*. On the one hand, hunger stimulates
the healthy desire *to* write truly, or, the same thing, to represent things in a
way that stimulates his desire to be with their concrete thereness. Thus he
learns "to understand Cézanne much better"—the painter whom he also
invoked in *In Our Time*'s omitted section of "Big Two-Hearted River" as his-
alias-Nick's artistic alter ego—"and to see truly how he made landscapes
when I was hungry."[10] Physical hunger here becomes synonymous with
hunger for and "in" his writing: "But [hunger] also sharpens all of your perceptions, and I found that many of the people I wrote about had very strong
appetites and a great taste and desire for food." On the other hand, hunger

also stimulates his desire to write according to public economic standards of success, thus frustrating the very possibility of writing "truly." Monetary pressures tempt him to write journalism or do easy writing; to gamble on horse races or not write at all; or to complain about his financial troubles ("I was disgusted with myself for having complained about things"), which can lead him to compromise his artistic dedication: "And the next thing you would be compromising on something else."[11]

Hemingway applies both aspects of hunger to his entire Parisian experiences. "Paris" serves as a metaphorical occasion or inscribed scene of writing for isolating *now*, as he writes *A Moveable Feast*, whatever interferes with his desire to construe writing as a physically appetitive or hungry act. In this sense, Hemingway takes care in choosing literal scenes for writing the stories of *In Our Time*. Bad cafés with "the smell of dirty bodies and the sour smell of drunkenness" evoke no imaginative hunger, but instead mark the hedonistic distractions of Paris that would reduce rather than conduce to the concentration of such desire. But Paris also proffers the "good" or "pleasant café, warm and clean and friendly," where he can begin writing, for example, "The Three-Day Blow."[12]

Moreover, he personifies this "good" scene of writing in the figure of Hadley, his first wife with whom he lived in Paris while he was in fact writing (and to whom he eventually dedicated) *In Our Time*. First, her notorious loss of his story manuscripts actually renews his vocational incentive ("I was going to start writing stories again") and leads him to formulate a new theory by which he can imagine his writing perpetually evoking the equivalent of hungry responses: "that you could omit anything if you knew that you omitted and the omitted part would strengthen the story and make people feel something more than they understood."[13] Second, in believing in his work as an original project before he becomes known, she not only protects his vocational dedication from sexual hedonistic distractions in Paris, she also signifies the possibility of an intimate versus impersonal audience for this work.[14] She frees him, that is, to write as if in terms of an *unknown* intimate audience—to experience writing as an imaginary, constantly unconsummated liaison with internalized muse-like figures, such as the woman he sees while actually writing in the "good café that I knew on the Place St.-Michel": "I've seen you, beauty, and you belong to me now, whoever you are waiting for and if I never see you again, I thought. You belong to me and all Paris belongs to me and I belong to this notebook and this pencil."[15]

Adopting the persona of a literary apprentice, Hemingway uses his recollections of Paris in *A Moveable Feast* primarily as imaginative space in which to encounter the "beauty" of his writing itself, which is to say writing understood as an act in process, coterminously sponsored by his imaginative internalization of its intimate audience. But the self-addressed "you" he uses throughout these sketches as a strategy to invoke such an audience willy-nilly turns into "people" or readers of his text who tempt him into thinking *about* his writing as he writes it—that is, as an abstract as opposed to bodily activity: "When I was writing, it was necessary for me to read after I had written. If you kept thinking about it, you would lose the thing that you were writing before you could go on with it the next day. It was necessary to get exercise, to be tired in the body."[16] In short, this readerly self-consciousness introduces the context of canonical comparison, the question of his writing's public value according to prevailing literary-marketplace standards, into his desired scene of writing. In one sense, the writers he portrays so reductively serve as figurative alter egos of *his* own potential relation to writing.[17] In another sense, they break into his scene of writing as "outside" influences. Indeed, Hemingway here regards his own literary career since *In Our Time* as exerting a public influence on his desired project of original writing. *A Moveable Feast*, after all, essentially tells the story of his fall from this original project largely as the result of his own ambition or surrender to the ideology of public literary fame, especially associated with the writing of novels. Thus, in writing his earlier collection of stories, he remains haunted by pressures to write the novel, the muse for which he will associate with "the other" woman who eventually takes him from the primary muse of *In Our Time*, his wife Hadley: "I knew I must write a novel. But it seemed an impossible thing to do when I had been trying to write paragraphs that would be the distillation of what made a novel. . . . I would put it off though until I could not help doing it."[18]

In literally pertaining to the issue of physical-sexual size, Hemingway's notorious portrayal of Fitzgerald's anxiety over "a matter of measurements" metaphorically pertains to Hemingway's own sense of writing a condensed "physical" prose ("paragraphs" in lieu of novels), not unlike the physically tactile art or statues in the Louvre he used to assuage Fitzgerald's anxiety. But Hemingway himself tends to measure his writing against the work of Russian novelists like Dostoyevski: "In Dostoyevski there were things believable and not to be believed, but some so true that they changed you as you read them." To resist this particular and generally unavoidable sense of textual or generic comparison, he uncritically cites Evan Shipman's unambitious but still hungry standard for writing: "'We need more true mystery in our lives, Hem,' he once said to me. 'The completely unambitious writer and the really good unpublished poem are the things we lack most at this time. There is, of course, the problem of sustenance.'"[19]

Hemingway, whose published comments elsewhere and even in *A Moveable Feast* tend to support critical assumptions about his virtually pathological literary ambition, turns out to harbor a latent wish at least to *write* without any sense of literary competition. He wishes, in other words, to write his works as "my own business," or as if in some private or secret scene of writing: "I was learning very much from [Cézanne] but I was not articulate enough to explain it to anyone. Besides it was a secret." At best, he shares his "secret" writing only in a post factum manner, and even then only with intimate doubles, those not associated with the public "literary" life. Until he meets Fitzgerald, who interrogates him directly about his writing, "I had felt that what a great writer I was had been carefully kept secret between myself and my wife and only those people we knew well enough to speak to."[20]

But despite his efforts to maintain a private scene of writing, Hemingway in the end cannot avoid simultaneously desiring the public fate of his activity. Like Fitzgerald but according to his own physically immediate criterion for writing the stories of *In Our Time*, Hemingway too succumbs to "the charm of [the] rich," namely to a view of his work endorsed by personifications of prevailing sociocultural powers. In reading aloud portions of his finished novel for "their" approbation, he surrenders his internal sense of its writing for "their" external relation to it. The publication of this novel marks the point in his career when he no longer becomes able to write without transforming private act into public product, in other words when his own writing becomes "a matter of measurements" or subject to the internalized surveillance of canonical expectations *as* he writes.

In short, like his sense of present-versus-past experiences of skiing in *A Moveable Feast*, Hemingway's experience of writing the stories collected in *In Our Time* "was not the way it is now": "the spiral fracture had not become common then, and no one could afford a broken leg. There were no ski patrols. Anything you ran down from, you had to climb up. That gave you legs that were fit to run down with." Imaginatively invoking "the way" it *was* to write these stories, he thus writes his memoirs to recover his present vocational "hunger": for his pre-patrol, pre-public, or private relation to writing construed as self-referential physical activity with potential physical consequences ("That gave you legs"); for a past paradisal scene of writing when "[t]here was no certainty" about the public value of *In Our Time*, but the writing "was as good and the happiness was greater" precisely because "no novel had been written."[21]

But in the first place, writing as a private psychophysical event remains an illusory goal—an unrealizable desire—because the linguistic medium precludes even as it engenders the possible perceptual coincidence between word and thing. In the second place, writing about one's past also forces one to encounter the abstract or self-alienated appearance of its facticity, its pastness per se. Even as it enables the possibility of recovering such hunger, then, Hemingway's *Feast* project constantly threatens to become sheer fantasy. How can he write now as if he were yet to write this earlier collection of short fiction? How can he reread its stories as if they were not yet completed—not yet existing signifiers precisely of a career responsible for his fall from writing "truly"?

Most interpretations of *In Our Time* construe it as an embryonic Bildungsroman, a collection of stories and interchapters teleologically unified around the theme of Nick Adams's evolving education from a boy averting his gaze from the violence or disorder of life, the tenor of the first story, "Indian Camp," to a young man who largely from his experience in World War I—the implicit experiential background of "Big Two-Hearted River"—comes to recognize violence or chaos as the primary condition of life "in our time."[22] Irony provides the narrative ligature for Hemingway's arrangement of stories and flash-forward interchapters. Taken separately or together, their very brevity and imagistic abruptness suggest photographic or prosthetic substitutions for life, the discontinuity or fragmentation of modern experience becoming shorn of socially sanctioned illusions about its ultimate coherence. For example, in "Indian Camp" Nick avoids looking at the Indian woman in labor: "Nick didn't look at it. . . . Nick did not watch. His curiosity had been gone for a long time." In the interchapter immediately following this story, the narrator cannot avoid witnessing the chaos implicit in a war evacuation scene where "a woman [was] having a baby with a young girl holding a blanket over her and crying. Scared sick of looking at it."[23]

Given its ironic formal and thematic cohesion, critics have reason to view *In Our Time* either as an embryonic novel or what Forrest Ingram would term a "short story cycle" comprised of "a set of stories linked to each other in such a way as to maintain a balance between the individuality of each of the stories and the necessities of the larger unity."[24] But to maintain this critical view, one must downplay the fact that barely half of the stories and only one of the interchapters literally concern Nick Adams. Second, the composition of *In Our Time* remains tentatively novelistic at best, and in this sense requests us to reflect on its status *as* a text. More important, certain of its stories effectively undercut its representational status as a (modern) novel by seeming to duplicate the way *A Moveable Feast* later frames this collection's scene of writing.

One could argue that the last story in this collection, the two parts of "Big Two-Hearted River," not to mention its omitted section "On Writing," inscribes the issue of writing per se—of writing literature "in our time" and Hemingway's particular writing of *In Our Time*. The traditional interpretation of this story, of course, argues that combined with the staccato simplicity of Hemingway's style, Nick's deliberate acts and focus on minute details serve to "banish [the] evil spirits" of Nick-alias-Hemingway's haunting war experiences.[25] But in "On Writing," Nick metaphorically equates his love of fishing and bullfighting with writing, and explicitly confesses his ambition "to be a great writer. He was pretty sure he would be."[26] According to one critic, then, "Big Two-Hearted River" contains a "metaphoric level" which casts "Nick's fishing trip as an attempt by Hemingway to write, perhaps for the first time, about the artist and the process of his art."[27] Catching small trout at first, then larger ones, "places a demand on all of Nick's fishing skills. The parallel to the artistic process is clear. Like the artist, Nick the fisherman has his limits"; thus Nick's refusal to fish the swamp where "the fishing would be tragic" metaphorically signifies Hemingway's own recognition at the time of writing *In Our Time* that he is not yet ready to meet "the ultimate test for the mature artist": namely, to write "tragedy."[28]

But the story also concerns something other than Nick's recognition of limits or his patient ambition to be "a great writer" along traditional aestheticist lines. Right from the beginning, Nick regards his fishing trip as an *escape* from the *demand* to write: "Nick felt happy. He felt he had left everything behind, the need for thinking, the need to write, other needs." Just as in *A Moveable Feast* where Hemingway associates his act of writing with its material ambience and "the sweat-salted leather of your pack strap," so "Big Two-Hearted River" concerns Nick's attempt to secure a private "camp," a private scene where the project of writing becomes interchangeable with the sense of hunger: "He was very tired. That was done. He had made his camp. He was settled. Nothing could touch him. It was a good place to camp. He was there, in the good place. He was in his home where he had made it. Now he was hungry."[29]

More than referring to itself, however, "Big Two-Hearted River" suggests that "Nick Adams" has authored the preceding stories and interchapters in the collection as well—its omitted section specifically informs us that he has written "My Old Man." Like a prefatory *A Moveable Feast*, this last story constitutes a retrospective, "self-referential" revision of *In Our Time* from a work readable as condensed representations of collective experience "in our time" to a work exercising Hemingway's private anxieties about becoming "a great writer." But the greatness these early stories strive to envisage has nothing to do with externally imposed criteria for literary success that would turn writing into competitive or "serious" work rather than an experience of private play: "[Writing] was really more fun than anything. That was really why you did it. . . . It wasn't conscience. It was simply that it was the greatest pleasure."[30]

As with his later autobiographical sketches, other stories in *In Our Time* variously reflect the obstacles to construing writing as private "fun." That is, "Big Two-Hearted River" allows us retroactively to regard each story as inscribing the desire for its writing to evince radically contingent acts of signification—of signifying percept-ridden imagined events exempt from the pressures of established if also heterogeneous literary formulations. In other words, each story paradoxically seeks to withdraw from its public identity as writing, by shedding, for example, the section "On Writing" itself from "Big Two-Hearted River." In *A Moveable Feast*, Hemingway represents himself as having read "after-work books" so as not to think about the story (or its potential literary value) he was still in the process of writing.[31] In "The Three-Day Blow," Nick and Bill's discussion of minor writers (Walpole, Hudson, and Chesterton) as if they wrote "classic" works at once ironically exposes the arbitrary aspect of personal literary standards, and also inscribes Hemingway's desire to regard literature as a noncompetitive activity, as writing altogether free from the context of official literary evaluation. In this overdetermined scene (of writing), Nick and Bill at first juxtapose discussing writers with discussing baseball, a "fun" game but nevertheless a competitive sport; then they turn to fishing, a noncompetitive activity and, as endorsed by "Big Two-Hearted River" later, a metaphor for Hemingway's ideal writing: "'There isn't any comparison,' said Nick. 'How did we ever get talking about baseball?'"[32]

The relationship between Nick and Bill exists in marked contrast to Nick's later hermeticism. Personal intimacy, especially between vocational peers, can puncture the writer's sense of private literary space. In short, Nick's intimate relationships mark the point of Hemingway's testing his own vocational dedication to writing "truly." In "The End of Something," Marjorie, Nick's girlfriend, "loved to fish. She loved to fish with Nick," which dependence indicates her failure to understand the writer's or Nick's need to exclude all sense of others while writing. When Nick and Marjorie set up and leave behind their "fishing" lines to eat together (thus sharing a metaphorical hunger), the situation prevents Nick from a direct physical experience of fishing, that of feeling a trout "taking line out of the reel in a rush and making the reel sing with the click on"—experiencing the act of *writing* about this scene as no less a radically particular perceptual event. In the same allegorical vein, their fishing where "there was nothing of the [old lumber] mill left except the broken white limestone of its foundations" possibly alludes to the modernist literary situation in which past values of writing (or an inherited literary tradition) clearly no longer apply or are "broken." Of vocational necessity, then, Nick, here a surrogate for the modern apprentice writer, rejects Marjorie's desire to romanticize this place in the manner of Victorian novelists: "'[The ruin of the old mill] seems more like a castle,' Marjorie said. Nick said nothing."[33]

Yet even as it inscribes Hemingway's attempt to reject intimately familiar, hence imminently influential criteria synonymous with past modes of writing, criteria that would deny the sense of writing as personal "fun" ("'It isn't fun any more,'" Nick tells Marjorie in the "end"), *In Our Time* also tracks his rejection of alternative literary models available in the modern world. To fish or write in his own private camp or scene of writing, Hemingway's Nick Adams, his surrogate Adamic (or original) writer in "Big Two-Hearted River," moves beyond "the burned-over country" around the abandoned town of Seney—beyond T. S. Eliot's modernist literary topos of "The Waste Land."[34] Suggested by its very title ("Elliot"), its allusion to the couple's sexual infertility, and the formal manner ("Mr. and Mrs.") by which the narrator refers to the poet husband and his wife who painstakingly types his "very long poems," "Mr. and Mrs. Elliot" satirizes the Eliotic writer's aesthetic quest for a pure "formalist" writing: Mr. Elliot "wanted to keep himself pure so that he could bring to his wife the same purity of mind and body that he expected of her." In other words, the story represents the modern "abstract" artist— potentially Hemingway himself in this "self-referential" work—whose all-consuming project for a self-contained art results in a referentially frustrated muse and thus lacks any physical connection to life. Like the picador and his bull-maimed, bleeding horse awaiting the action of the vital bull in the following interchapter, Mr. Elliot produces an art that at best remains uncertainly related to life: "The bull could not make up his mind to charge."[35]

Conversely, modern realistic art, art that purports to represent the chaotic realities of modern life, tends to traffic in sociopolitical agendas that make it no less abstract, no less subject to publicly authored ideals rather than private perceptions. Like the boy in "The Revolutionist" who ends up "in jail near Sion," metaphorically near yet so far from the utopian community or Zion promised by his revolutionary activities, so the politicized modern writer remains trapped within social ideals that prevent him—the boy prefers artistic "reproductions" to originals, painters of benign religious subjects to Mantegna's more graphically violent ones—from recognizing the presocial or "original" force defining Hemingway's desired experience of writing.

Yet neither does *In Our Time*'s ironic exposé of such idealisms as egregiously unrepresentative of one's brute experience of modern life automatically result in his realizing this vocational desideratum, for *In Our Time* also immediately calls to mind an autobiographical precedent that threatens to make Hemingway construe his own writing of these stories in the context of "reproductions." In representing the education of Nick Adams, *In Our Time*, whether taken as a whole or metaphorically focused in one story, "The Doctor and the Doctor's Wife," allusively doubles as the fictional counterpart to *The Education of Henry Adams*. Just as by the end of Hemingway's text Nick learns that past notions of order no longer work in the chaos of modern life, *The Education* tracks Henry Adams's uneasy surrender of past notions of ordered existence, for him especially symbolized by the medieval Virgin, to a realization of modern chaos, the release of new "supersensual" forces symbolized by the technological dynamo. Condensed and disguised so as to seem utterly farfetched—Hemingway cannot allow writing to become an explicit issue in his writing lest it also become subject to canonical demands—this internalized inscription nevertheless also applies to Hemingway's story. In "The Doctor and the Doctor's Wife," Nick's doctor father, who happens to be named Henry, backs down from a physical confrontation with Dick Boulton, an American Indian half-breed. So too, Henry Adams backs down from—admits failure in the face of—the chaos synonymous with brute nature in *The Education*.[36] Yet where Adams's narrative ambivalently betrays its nostalgia for the spontaneous order inspired by the Virgin as opposed to the reactionary modes of order proposed by modern patriarchal science in the face of (and also ironically contributing to) the forces unleashed by the Dynamo, Hemingway's Henry Adams receives no such inspiration from his "Virgin," the Christian Scientist wife whose fundamentalist

Christianity instead drives him to masculine solitude (hunting alone) and even intimations of a solitary suicide: "'Remember that he who ruleth his spirit is greater than he that taketh a city,' said his wife. . . . Her husband did not answer. He was sitting on his bed now, cleaning a shotgun."[37]

In Our Time continues this internalized disaffiliation from modernist writing by outlining a return to an albeit equally revised tradition of American regionalist writing.[38] On the one hand, for example, Nick abandons his reading in nature, "sitting with his back against a tree," and goes off with his father to hunt "black squirrels" in a place Nick knows they reside, rather than return to his mother. With this move, Hemingway metaphorically abandons American writing associated with Thoreau ("sitting" in nature) and affiliates his project with that of the modern American Adams: "'All right,' said his father. 'Let's go there.'" But this affiliation also remains equivocal, for in having Nick and his father leave together only to hunt "black squirrels," the story indicates its resistance to the desire of Adams's text to evoke as well as disclose the chaos of modern life *as a whole*. Hemingway, that is, resists the universalistic claims of modernist literary writing, just as *In Our Time* ultimately resists the internationalist ideology of modernism when it has Nick return not only to America but to the region-specific Michigan woods in the last story.

With Nick's return, moreover, Hemingway reverses the direction and in effect positions himself before the rural-to-cosmopolitan movement defining the latent Bildungsroman of Sherwood Anderson's collection of stories, *Winesburg, Ohio*. In particular, "My Old Man," a story clearly beholden to Anderson's "I Want to Know," constitutes an extended narrative pun through which Hemingway inscribes Anderson himself as "my old man" or immediate literary father within the act of writing *In Our Time*.[39] In this story, he places Anderson in Europe because of his modernist expatriate position, or the way Anderson's *Winesburg* collection exhibits nostalgia for yet final rejection of rural American society: "He'd tell me about . . . the old days in the States before everything went on the bum there." But in alluding to Anderson's subsequent failure as a full-fledged modernist writer (alias European jockey), Hemingway reinterprets this older writer's project not as blocking but as opening up American literary space yet to be explored.[40] At the very least, like the potential literary rivals he treats as his own vocational options in *A Moveable Feast*, Hemingway here regards Anderson as staking out the danger zones facing any would-be American writer in the modernist era who strives to determine his own relation to writing: "And he'd say, 'Joe, when we've got a decent stake, you're going back there to the States and go to school."[41]

By having his protagonist go back to Michigan, Hemingway indeed goes back to the American school or tradition of writing, the exemplary figure of which for him was—precisely under the influence of Anderson—Mark Twain.[42] Many critics, of course, have frequently remarked on Hemingway's stylistic and thematic indebtedness to Twain's *Huckleberry Finn*. Couldn't one regard Nick's uncanny encounter with Ad and Bugs in "The Battler" as Hemingway's revised, ironic reading of Huck and Jim's escape from all forms of social slavery to the American mythic territories of personal freedom?[43] In this sense, "The Battler" traces Hemingway's encounter with Twain as former American *literary* "champion." In depicting Nick's hungry repast with the two men and his ultimate expulsion from their firelit camp, the site of a still influential but distanced literary past, Hemingway seems to clear a space for the "mounting" significance of his own text: "Looking back from the mounting grade before the track curved into the hills [Nick] could see the firelight [of the two men's camp] in the clearing."[44]

But here again, just as with Adams, Thoreau, and Anderson in the aforementioned stories, so Hemingway links his collection not primarily with Twain's major work of fiction but with his literarily lesser though still canonical work written around the same time, the autobiographical *Life on the Mississippi*.[45] Not only "The Battler" but both the first and last stories in *In Our Time* redound to "camps" or, as we have seen, metaphorical scenes of writing. More specifically, "Indian Camp" and "Big Two-Hearted River" strategically allude to Twain's depictions of the Mississippi River region "before and after" the Civil War in *Life:* from the apprentice writer-alias-pilot's former antebellum relation to an endlessly original or Emersonian American nature, the metaphorical significance of the river in part 1 of his work, to the established writer's postbellum loss and recovery of such nature in part 2. In Twain's work, the frontier aspect of American nature endows his very act of writing with frontier or original status, hence his transformation of Chicago, synecdoche of a postbellum industrialized American society, into an endless "novelty"; hence the way he ends his revisitation to the Mississippi region "on the upper river" in Minnesota where, while "modern" boats are manned "with not a suggestion of romance about them anywhere," he can still experience scenes such as "a black night" when he encounters "dense walls of foliage that almost touched our bows on both sides; and here every individual leaf, and every individual ripple stood out in its natural color, and flooded with a glare as of noonday intensified. The effect was strange, and fine, and very striking."[46]

Referentially ending in a yet unsettled or "strange" American nature, Twain's *Life* textually ends on a recapitulation of Indian legends; in other words, it entertains the dream of an American or "Indian" mode of writing indissociable from this original nature. Once framed in the revisionary context of "Big Two-Hearted River," Hemingway's "Indian Camp," the beginning of *In Our Time*, marks the termination of precisely this dream. In this Michigan "camp" or misprision of Twain's metaphorical (Minnesota) scene of writing *Life*, Hemingway finds an American nature irreversibly permeated with the superior urban indifference about its value manifested in Anderson's *Winesburg*, and with the modernist scientific perspective of nature's "supersensual" status expressed in Henry Adams's *Education*. When first rowing to the Indian camp over a lake in Twain-like darkness, Nick's "Uncle George [Willard?] was smoking a cigar in the dark. . . . [He] gave both the Indians cigars." Lacking an available "anaesthetic" with which to operate, Henry the doctor seeks to repress registering the Indian woman's labor pain: "'her screams are not important. I don't hear them because they are not important.'" The doctor's "Caesarian" incision and the jackknife (or *pen*knife) instrument he uses to perform it metaphorically adumbrate the modern American writer's scientific or realistic—hence alienated—relation to nature, here represented in a scene wherein the latter rêproduces itself in human form through the act of childbirth. This disengaged relation to nature also redounds to the event of writing itself. For the modern writer, the value of writing no longer resides in one's apprehension of its referent about to become a new, all but sensory event in the particular moment of its occurrence within the *act* of writing (the Indian woman's labor), but rather in its abstract, separable quality as a *socially* original performance (the doctor's Caesarian operation). Its value "in our time," in other words, accrues from its status only as a written, public, and therefore publishable *product*, perforce bypassing the private experience of writing per se, and which Hemingway here again associates with the activity of fishing: "'That's one for the medical journal, George,' [Nick's father] said. 'Doing a Caesarian with a jack-knife and sewing it up with nine-foot, tapered gut leaders.'"[47]

No one "in our time" can escape this abstract and public contamination of American nature, especially not the Indian husband who represents the lost and so now self-destructive illusion of living an aboriginal relation to nature: "He had cut his foot very badly with an ax three days before. He was smoking a pipe. The room smelled very bad." If his suicide, like Nick's averted gaze, thematically indicates an inability to face the stark, socially disorientating (and in his case, deracinated) implications of modern life ("'He couldn't stand things, I guess'"), in our present context it reversibly suggests his unwillingness to surrender the Twain-like ideal of an unmediated relation to nature. By itself, this ideal cannot result in Hemingway's recovery of Twain's "river" position in writing *Life*, not even in his own "river" story of vocational declaration, "Big Two-Hearted River." But in exposing it as an ideal at the very beginning of *In Our Time*, Hemingway can imagine recovering, if not an original American nature as metaphor of writing, at least an original relation to writing as metaphor of such nature.

But his misprision of Twain does not mitigate the extent to which other kinds of influence also haunt his project to write an American prose as if for the first time. For example, "Soldier's Home" concerns the deleterious effect actual American society "in our time" has on Hemingway's desire to return "home," or to write in a radical American grain. The American social ethos, in this story made experientially imminent through Krebs's relation to his parents and especially his mother, leads him to question the very value of his vocation in terms of social definitions of work, ambition, success; it also tempts the apprentice writer. Krebs's main pleasure is to read "about all the engagements he had been in," "really learning about the war," and "to lie" about "everything that had happened to him," or to translate it into attractive conventional terms ("Now he would have liked a girl if she had come to him and not wanted to talk. But here at home it was all too complicated"), hence to destroy its private originality to himself: "Krebs acquired the nausea in regard to experience that is the result of untruth or exaggeration. . . . In this way he lost everything."[48]

Potential invasions of Hemingway's American scene of writing lurk everywhere. Like Krebs, he can try passively to resist them, simply declare them *non*influential: "He had tried so to keep his life from being complicated. Still, none of it touched him." But "Soldier's Home" ironically discloses how this strategy leaves Krebs in a negative or spectatorial relation to life, which is to say that it subliminally frames the act of writing as impotent inactivity unrelated to "real" experience: "He would go over to the schoolyard and watch Helen [Krebs's younger sister] play indoor baseball."[49] Writing, that is, becomes a mere self-referential or private ("indoor") game that he can only fantasize doing through Helen, a childish muse.

But if "Soldier's Home" inscribes Hemingway's self-imposed test for vocational integrity in the face of antithetical cultural odds, other stories in *In*

Our Time exercise the consequences of his vocational dedication as itself a potentially disruptive influence on his scene of writing. Both "Out of Season," if only in an allusive sense, and "Cross Country Snow" suggestively concern a male character's ambivalent dissatisfaction and resignation at the prospect of his spouse's pregnancy. In the first story, the man manifests guilt for such feelings: "'I'm sorry I talked the way I did at lunch. We were both getting at the same thing from different angles.'" Whatever its allusions to Hemingway's actual relation to Hadley at the time of writing *In Our Time*, the story plainly concerns the man's guilty flirtation with and second thoughts about fishing "out of season": "'We're probably being followed by the game police by now. I wish we weren't in on this damn thing.'"[50] As metaphor of writing, this potential fishing violation unconsciously traces the writer, here in the guise of the young husband, musing about violating social norms (for example, writing what Stein would term "inaccrochable" stories[51]), or even allowing his vocational dedication to take priority over—by using as materials for writing—his intimate relations to others.

But the man's sense of guilt in "Out of Season" also devolves on the violation of social norms *endemic* to the act of writing. For as we have seen in the case of *A Moveable Feast* and in certain stories from *In Our Time*, vocational dedication for Hemingway is synonymous with determining a private scene of writing that requires the assiduous purgation of all public influences. First, to write "truly" is to incur the guilt of running counter to living or seeing life in conventional and/or "literary" terms. Second, such a project entails the potential guilt of using autobiographically intimate experiences with others for private vocational purposes. Moreover, having occurred in his past, these experiences could only introduce an "outside" source—the sense of *his own* influence—into his act of writing. Finally, insofar as it concerns the possibility of writing fiction that never quite gets written, such writing also abuses the conventional notion of fiction writing itself.

Such vocational issues permeate the themes of uneasy heterosexual relationships and ambivalence over female pregnancy that occur in Hemingway's inaugural collection of fiction. Marriage, that is, inscribes the demand for conventional projects of writing: writing as storytelling essentially projected for the judgment and participation of others rather than for the writer's experience alone. Pregnancy connotes the inevitable loss of this experience (the baby in term) to the world (upon its actual birth) at publication. Far from extolling the joys (or unconsciously revealing the patriarchal selfishness) of male camaraderie, "Cross Country Snow" shows Nick

Adams striving rigorously to forget the vocational implications of his wife's pregnancy and instead dwell on skiing, metaphor for writing *without* such implications, with his friend George, Nick's alter ego or the writer's internalized private audience *in* writing: "George and Nick were happy. They were fond of each other. They knew they had the run back home ahead of them." But the thought of his social obligation raised by his wife's pregnancy constantly intrudes: in the ski lodge, "Nick noticed that [the waitress's] apron covered swellingly her pregnancy." Except as fantasy, this surrogate writer's ideal scene of writing as pure play remains just that, a fiction of writing fiction free from public determinations. Nick gives an affirmative answer to George's question, "'don't you wish we could just bum together? Take our skis and go on the train to where there was good running . . . and not give a damn about school or anything'?" but then can't promise George that they will ever "'go skiing again'" together.[52]

What awaits Nick when he goes back to the States with Helen to have the baby are mountains too rocky for him to ski, too crowded with timber and too far apart.[53] What awaits Hemingway when he completes the stories of *In Our Time* with his muse are the relatively fixed, yet widely various and impersonal public criteria that will inevitably make it more difficult, if not impossible, for him to regard his future writing as emanating from a "good running" private scene such as he seeks to secure in writing these very stories. And so if he imagines the success of *In Our Time* as he writes *In Our Time*, he also tries to imagine ways of disarming his internalized demand for literary success ahead of time. For example, he projects the disastrous results of adopting a literary-competitive ethos in "The Battler," the last story Hemingway in fact wrote for this collection. The story tells of Ad Francis's fallen status as a professional fighter due to his scandalous romance with his manager "sister" who "'[l]ooked enough like him to be twins'"; but with boxing as metaphor of writing, it subliminally tells of the professional writer who, having already entered the competitive literary arena, surrenders his project entirely to the vocational self-image reflected by the ideology of public fame and fortune (the destructive attraction of the "sister")—precisely the fate Hemingway later tries to mitigate in *A Moveable Feast*.[54]

In a story like "Out of Season," he also senses that trying to avoid the competitive literary marketplace may possess no less vocationally disastrous consequences. If, as previously suggested, this story deploys the husband as Hemingway's surrogate writer, the variability of a text's unconscious displacements allows for another interpretation more in accord with the major exigency of Hemingway's particular allegorical project: his desire to write what he is writing "now" within a private scene of writing, the inscription of which desire he simultaneously needs to suppress as he writes. One could argue that in "Out of Season," not the husband but the unlikely drunken guide Peduzzi, the story's invested point of view, represents the writer who, the value of his talents perceived only by himself ("Nobody spoke or gave any sign to [Peduzzi's greetings] except the town beggar"), risks self-delusion for writing "out of season," that is, not in accord with publicly endorsed notions of writing. Wanting to alleviate the sense of isolation he experiences with his unconventional project, the Hemingway writer desires at least a limited sympathetic audience for it, here in the guise of the foreign couple Peduzzi wants to take fishing. But such an audience may not exist ("He had called the young gentleman caro several times and nothing had happened") except as self-evident illusory wish: "He was through with the hotel garden, breaking up frozen manure with a dung fork. Life was opening out." At best it remains a momentary illusion: in "Cat in the Rain," a woman, again the story's assumed point of view and self-disguised figure of the Hemingway writer, remains subject to her husband's indifference (the writer's public audience) and only receives sympathetic attention from the "padrone" of the hotel (the writer's private audience) who retrieves her desired "'poor kitty out in the rain'" (the vital yet, like the small cat subject to the elements, canonically pressured "minor" project of writing) and gives her "a momentary feeling of being of supreme importance."[55]

Either way, with an imagined or imaginary audience, *In Our Time* seems to track, as Hemingway himself suggests in *A Moveable Feast* when he informs us about the omitted fate of Peduzzi, a literally suicidal venture. This early work suspects its likely potential audience of introducing socially authored literary demands into its scene of writing, hence of working to deny its dream of becoming a series of radically original acts of writing. And so Hemingway seeks to occlude audience altogether, or, the same thing, to repress ahead of time his own literary ambition by writing the stories of *In Our Time* in a manner that defines them to himself as *preparatory* gestures *toward* writing them, that is, as if before becoming subject to public consumption, evaluation, influence. His compressed narrative praxis in these stories (in "Big Two-Hearted River," for example, where "nothing" happens[56]) foreshortens the occasions for registering their origins in his own past experience (or influence) and especially his sense of writing a "literature" that would be vulnerable to canonical scrutiny. The sense of omitted information in this story and others like "Out of Season" suggests their pre-narrative or only embryonic literary formulation. The interchapters amount to distillations of novels—of "major" literary writing.[57] Stories like "A Very Short Story" exhibit narrative impatience, or all but signify their wish to resist literary-generic identification altogether. Above all, *In Our Time* as a whole outlines a novel that from Hemingway's position—this is its phenomenological definition—never gets written, not even as a protonarrative portrait of the artist as a young man in the process of writing this very collection of stories.

These stories represent verbal photographs of "our time" largely through a central character named Nick Adams. Thanks to the revisionary function of the last story, "Big Two-Hearted River," they also retroactively reflect the (still referentially understood) autobiographical outlines of Hemingway-alias-Nick Adams's development as a literary artist. But for Hemingway this already muted artistic "autobiography" also entails a performative function: namely, to effect a particular relation to writing that would frame it as free from or as if occurring before the sense of its resulting in narrative cohesion, fictional or autobiographical. This function paradoxically requires him to disguise such a project from himself lest it become vulnerable to established narrative and/or public literary criteria—the reason for his unlikely identifications with *non*-Nick Adams figures such as the woman in "Cat in the Rain," Peduzzi in "Out of Season," or even more improbably, the Indian husband in "Indian Camp" whose omitted and narratively marginal presence nevertheless retroactively usurps the reader-alias-Nick's perceptual attention.

One could interpret each of the stories from *In Our Time* according to these three mutually exclusive levels of significance. For example, an early story like "A Very Short Story" formally enacts as well as thematically represents (1) an anonymous young man's experience of the pathetic anonymity or repeatability of modern love relationships, and (2) the young writer's temptation to abandon his career (turning it into "a very short story") after his first and failed relationship with the muse. But Hemingway's own rereading of *In Our Time* through *A Moveable Feast* allows us as well to regard this story as (3) part of a nonteleological sequence of stories attempting to expose and avert whatever threatens to make his act of writing them subject to public referential interpretations or literary comparisons. In this sense, "A Very Short Story" reflects *any* moment in the act of writing when Hemingway experiences the kind of vocational self-doubt about writing "truly" that he registers more directly in his later collection: "sometimes when I was starting a new story and [I] could not get it going ... I would stand and look out over the roofs of Paris and think, 'Do not worry. You have always written before and you will write now. All you have to do is write one true sentence.'"[58]

About "our time," *In Our Time* also struggles to be about itself. About its own writing, it resists becoming *mere* writing—desires to refer to life without the sense of its own textuality. And so it steers a course between representational reference and self-reference. As a collection of stories precisely in the process of resisting its literary associations and potential canonical ambitions, it particularly resists becoming a novel, which would drag it into the public domain or make its writing not seem "fun any more." Such writing paradoxically *works* to remain "fun." Thus, Hemingway's muted metaphorical connections between fishing and writing in "The End of Something," "The Three-Day Blow," "Out of Season" and "Big Two-Hearted River," even his repetitive and terse style which "make[s] us more conscious of the signifying function" or activity per se, indicate strategies to defer his writing's sense of meaning *to himself*.[59] Or rather, since language can never escape meaning, Hemingway's narrative and stylistic strategies help him focus on quasi-referential details of the world that one might experience as if prior to their accruing public meaning.

But to write about things as if only at the level of one's desire for physical interaction with them *here and now* requires the destruction of self as an established identity: that is, how one tends to present oneself or represent this experience to others in the act of writing. It is to become like the woman in "Cat in the Rain," separate from others like her husband who use literature to repress life ("'Oh, shut up and get something to read'") rather than seek to possess it originally: "'If I can't have long hair or any fun, I can have a cat'"—in other words, write "short" works as if in the process of eluding canonical demands of any kind, and therefore of disclosing privately determined experiences of life. But like Nick in the act of skiing to write this way is also to become wholly subsumed by the experience of one's own body: "The rush and the sudden swoop as he dropped down a steep undulation in the mountain side plucked Nick's mind out and left him only the wonderful flying, dropping sensation in his body."[60] It is, in short, by committing a kind of perceptual suicide through writing that one gets oneself into a radically original relation to things.

In the end, of course, Hemingway could not sustain the preconceptual vision of writing he desires to effect in *In Our Time* and desires to desire again in *A Moveable Feast*. After the public literary acclaim accorded *In Our*

Time and two subsequent novels, Hemingway adds "On the Quai at Smyrna" to this collection in 1930 and retroactively revises it as indeed a "novel" representative of experience "in our time." From that point on until *A Moveable Feast*, writing becomes wholly a matter of public literary performance. In this late collection, he realizes that Peduzzi's no longer omitted fate was his, or that vocational honesty always required that he obliterate public self-identity in a private "garden of Eden" or scene of writing. But even at the beginning of his career and first major collection of stories, Hemingway had inscribed the consequences of failing to do so in the barely discernible figure of the Indian husband: that trace of himself as a would-be aboriginal American writer who, committed to invoking the suddenly disclosed thereness of experience through razor-sharp writing, could not bear to see his conception born and borne into the world.

Notes

1. Ernest Hemingway, *A Moveable Feast* (New York, 1986), 76.
2. See, for example, Arthur Waldhorn, *A Reader's Guide to Ernest Hemingway* (New York, 1972), 212–13; and Kenneth S. Lynn, *Hemingway* (New York, 1987), 586, 278–80 (on Hemingway's self-serving distortions of Fitzgerald).
3. Hemingway, *Moveable Feast*, 6.
4. Ernest Hemingway, "On Writing," in *The Nick Adams Stories* (New York, 1972), 237.
5. Paul Smith, "Impressions of Ernest Hemingway," *Hemingway Review* 6 (Spring 1987): 4, suggests that one of the motives for Hemingway's *Feast* memoirs was to settle an old score with Gertrude Stein for her unflattering portrait of him in *The Autobiography of Alice B. Toklas*. Also see Lynn, *Hemingway*, 322, and Waldhorn, *Reader's Guide*, 216–19.
6. Paul Smith, "Impressions," 6.
7. Hemingway, *Moveable Feast*, 12, 91.
8. Waldhorn, *Reader's Guide*, 214.
9. Hemingway, *Moveable Feast*, 76–77.
10. Hemingway, *Nick Adams Stories*, 240; *Moveable Feast*, 69.
11. Hemingway, *Moveable Feast*, 100, 7, 61, 72.
12. Ibid., 3, 5.
13. Ibid., 74–75.
14. A letter from Hadley to Hemingway before they got married clearly suggests this belief and also the private intimacy with which she shared it with him. Quoted in Peter Griffin's biography, *Along with Youth: Hemingway, the Early Years* (New York, 1985), she comments on his (pre–*In Our Time*) "enormous power of living and how inside intuition stuff comes through to you very, very often and

gives you new food for tho't. . . . I have it too—not in the same degree—it's really the best gift I know of so don't tell anyone I said I had it. . . . But the great
beauty of it is ideas just appearing in your mind that make you understand the
way things are" (157–58).

15. Hemingway, *Moveable Feast*, 6. Paul Smith, "Impressions," notes that this
unknown woman "was his muse, exciting him to the creative act of writing" (7).

16. Hemingway, *Moveable Feast*, 25.

17. In *A Moveable Feast*, Hemingway criticizes Stein for needing "to have publication and official acceptance," for lacking vocational discipline or abjuring "the
obligation to make her writing intelligible" (17), for reducing literature to a
matter of personalities (28), and for all these reasons being unwilling to write or,
as in the case of his story "Up in Michigan," approve of "inaccrochable" stories
(15–16). But Hemingway represents himself as vulnerable to the same problems, as when he finds himself complaining about there being "no demand for"
his work (75), gets distracted from his work by his attraction to horse racing
(61–62), resists using conventional narrative practices, as with his "theory" of
omitting narrative information from readers, and of course effectively discusses
Stein as well as Ford Madox Ford, Eliot, and Fitzgerald, among others, in terms
of largely reductive anecdotes about their personalities in this very text.

18. Ibid., 75–76.

19. Ibid., 191, 133, 138, 146.

20. Ibid., 13, 150.

21. Ibid., 199, 208.

22. A number of critics have maintained this "unified" view of *In Our Time*: for
example, Philip Young, "Adventures of Nick Adams," in *Hemingway: A Collection
of Critical Essays*, ed. Robert P. Weeks (Englewood Cliffs, 1962), 97; Wirt
Williams, *The Tragic Art of Ernest Hemingway* (Baton Rouge, 1981), 30–31; and
David Seed, "'The Picture of the Whole': *In Our Time*," in *Ernest Hemingway:
New Critical Essays*, ed. A. Robert Lee (Totowa, 1983), 19–20. Robert E.
Gajdusek, "Dubliners in Michigan: Joyce's Presence in Hemingway's *In Our
Time*," *Hemingway Review* 2 (Fall 1982): 48–61, argues that the topical, themat-
ic, even teleological unity of Joyce's earlier collection of stories exerted a dis-
cernible influence on Hemingway's construction and arrangement of the stories
in *In Our Time*.

23. Ernest Hemingway, *In Our Time* (New York, 1958), 23, 19.

24. Forrest L. Ingram, *Representative Short Story Cycles of the Twentieth Century:
Studies in a Literary Genre* (The Hague, 1971), 15.

25. Malcolm Cowley, "Nightmare and Ritual in Hemingway," in Weeks, ed.,
Collection of Critical Essays, 48. Corroborated by Hemingway himself in
Moveable Feast, this "wound" or "war-trauma" theory of Hemingway's Nick
Adams stories, especially "Big Two-Hearted River," was extended by Young,

"Adventures of Nick Adams," 103–6, and has become a commonplace in Hemingway criticism, although it has recently become contested, especially by Lynn. See Frederick Crews's review of Lynn's biography in the *New York Review of Books*, 13 August 1987, 30–37.

26. Hemingway, *Nick Adams Stories*, 234–38.

27. B. J. Smith, "'Big Two-Hearted River': The Artist and the Art," *Studies in Short Fiction* 20 (Summer 1983): 130. For all his understanding of the story's "self-referential" implications, Smith still tends to construe its "metaphoric level" as *self-* referential or autobiographical in origin; that is, for him the story reflects Hemingway's attempt to come to terms with the "wound" he received not so much in the war but in Hadley's loss of his early manuscripts. See also Keith Carabine, "'Big Two-Hearted River': A Reinterpretation," *Hemingway Review* 1 (Spring 1982): 39–44.

28. B. J. Smith, "'Big Two-Hearted River,'" 131.

29. Hemingway, *In Our Time*, 179, 186–87.

30. Hemingway, *Nick Adams Stories*, 237–38.

31. Hemingway, *Moveable Feast*, 27, 25.

32. Hemingway, *In Our Time*, 51, 55.

33. Ibid., 36, 38.

34. Cowley makes this Eliotic connection in "Nightmare and Ritual," 49–59. Philip Young, *Ernest Hemingway: A Reconsideration* (University Park, Pa., 1966), 183, notes how Hemingway borrowed the Eliotic principle of the "objective correlative" in discussing his aesthetics of writing in *Death in the Afternoon*. In contrast to Lynn's biographical reduction of this story to Hemingway's thinly disguised satirization of Eliot's personal life (*Hemingway*, 246–47), I would contend that in both *A Moveable Feast* (111–12) and in *In Our Time*, Hemingway evokes in order to purge "Eliot" understood as synecdoche of modernist writing and/or the way it affects Hemingway's relation to his own acts of writing.

35. Hemingway, *In Our Time*, 113, 112, 110, 115.

36. See, for example, the chapter titled "Chaos" in Henry Adams, *The Education of Henry Adams* (Boston, 1973), especially 288–89.

37. Hemingway, *In Our Time*, 29.

38. James M. Cox, "Regionalism: A Diminished Thing," in *Columbia Literary History of the United States*, ed. Emory Elliott (New York, 1988), 776–77, provocatively suggests that in *In Our Time* "Hemingway moves to recover both realistic representation and naturalistic determinism," and does so by expanding the Nick Adams stories via interchapters or "very short stories, the hallmark of 'minor' [American] regional writing."

39. Although Hemingway publicly proclaimed that his story didn't derive from Anderson's, critics at the time and today all agree that it does. See Lynn, *Hemingway*, 140, 222, and 306.

40. Hemingway, *In Our Time*, 168. In *A Moveable Feast*, Hemingway praises Anderson's stories but "was prepared to tell Miss Stein how strangely poor his novels were, but this would have been bad too because it was criticizing one of her most loyal supporters"—Stein, of course, being for Hemingway a preeminent exemplar of modernist writing (28).

41. Hemingway, *In Our Time*, 168.

42. In *Hemingway*, Lynn maintains that Hemingway's early friendship with Anderson in Chicago "almost surely" resulted in a "heightening of [Hemingway's] consciousness about *Huckleberry Finn*," since Anderson admired Twain and thought this novel "a masterpiece . . . in a class by itself" (140).

43. Young makes this "ironic" connection between Ad/Bugs and Huck/Jim in "Adventures of Nick Adams," 101; also see his *Reconsideration*, 228–41. Young's observations, however, are mitigated by his literal and static—nonstrategic or nontropological—sense of literary influence.

44. Hemingway, *In Our Time*, 71–72, 79.

45. As far as I know, no extant biographical evidence exists to show that Hemingway ever read *Life on the Mississippi*, or for that matter Adams's *The Education of Henry Adams*. Neither work appears in his personal collection of books as compiled by Michael S. Reynolds, *Hemingway's Reading, 1910–1940: An Inventory* (Princeton, 1981). But it seems safe to assume that Hemingway was acquainted with both works by the time he wrote *In Our Time*. *The Education*, published posthumously in 1918, received the Pulitzer Prize in 1919, and exerted considerable influence on many American writers in the early twenties. See, for example, Sherwood Anderson, *A Story Teller's Story* (Cleveland, 1968), 275; and Louis Kronenberger, "The Education of Henry Adams," in *Books That Changed Our Minds*, ed. Malcolm Cowley and Bernard Smith (New York, 1939), 43–57. In 1944, Hemingway alluded to his acquaintance with Adams's less well-known companion volume to *The Education, Mont-Saint-Michel and Chartres* (Carlos Baker, *Ernest Hemingway: A Life Story* [New York, 1969], 405–6). Similarly, Hemingway's friendship during his early apprenticeship years with Anderson, a Twain devotee, not to mention with Stein, who in *Everybody's Autobiography* [New York, 1973], 257) extols *Life on the Mississippi*, surely indicates the probability of Hemingway's acquaintance with the Twain work. Ultimately, however, my discussion of his stories in dynamic relation to the specified works of Twain and Adams borrows from Harold Bloom's notion of poetry, which I here interpolate also to mean prose narratives: "the meaning of a [prose narrative] can only be . . . *another* [*prose narrative*] . . . *not itself*. And not a [narrative] chosen with total arbitrariness, but any central [narrative] by an indubitable precursor, even if the ephebe *never read* that [narrative]" (*The Anxiety of Influence* [New York, 1973], 70).

46. Mark Twain, *Life on the Mississippi*, ed. James M. Cox (New York, 1984), 416, 404. For a further discussion of Twain's "self-referential" concerns in *Life*, see my essay, "Killing Time with Mark Twain's Autobiographies," *ELH* 54 (Spring 1987): 157–82.

47. Hemingway, *In Our Time*, 15, 17, 19.

48. Ibid., 100, 99, 94–95, 90–91.

49. Ibid., 101.

50. Ibid., 129–30. Lynn, *Hemingway*, 200–204, reads the story's husband and wife "dispute" as reflecting Hemingway's "conflicted feelings" about Hadley's pregnancy around the time he was writing *In Our Time*.

51. Hemingway, *Moveable Feast*, 15–16.

52. Hemingway, *In Our Time*, 144, 143, 145–47.

53. Ibid., 146.

54. Ibid., 77. Lynn, *Hemingway*, 273, loosely suggests that "The Battler" refers to Hemingway's desire to gain "the literary championship of the world." Hemingway, of course, frequently indulged in this writing as boxing metaphor: see, for example, the quotation cited by Lynn regarding his competitive view of certain Continental writers (549).

55. Hemingway, *In Our Time*, 126, 134–35, 120.

56. Young, "Adventures of Nick Adams," claims that unless one sees Nick's "routine" as "desperately protecting his mind against whatever it is that he is escaping," then the story seems "pointless" (105–6).

57. Cox, "Regionalism," regards the compressed interchapters as "displacing the 'major' convention of the novel" (777)—a position I would maintain occurs in the "self-referential" undertow of the stories themselves.

58. Hemingway, *Moveable Feast*, 12.

59. Peter Schwenger, *Phallic Critiques: Masculinity and Twentieth-Century Literature* (London, 1984), 50.

60. Hemingway, *In Our Time*, 121, 139.

RECONSTRUCTING HEMINGWAY'S IDENTITY: SEXUAL POLITICS, THE AUTHOR, AND THE MULTICULTURAL CLASSROOM[1]

Debra A. Moddelmog

In 1977 Aaron Latham, having looked over the Hemingway papers that were to be kept in Boston's Kennedy Library, predicted that "hidden away" in these manuscripts was another Hemingway from the one we had known (99). In the past fifteen years, many of these manuscripts have been published or their contents described by scholars, and, judging from the critical reaction so far, one can certify that Latham's prediction is coming true. Even if one counts nothing else, the rash of biographies published in the 1980s and 1990s suggests that Hemingway's reputation and life—and, consequently, his fiction—are under extensive reevaluation, perhaps the most extensive ever undertaken in the world of literary scholarship.[2]

The information that has moved scholars the most concerns Hemingway's departures in his writing and his life from traditional codes of masculinity and heterosexuality, codes that he played no small part in fostering. Among the disclosures that have drawn the greatest scrutiny are Grace Hemingway's treating her son as the female twin of his older sister

Reprinted with permission from Narrative *(October 1993), pp. 187–206.*

and dressing him in girls' clothes, apparently for longer than was conventional for the time; Hemingway's attraction, both sexual and non-sexual, to lesbians; his fascination with the ménage à trois; and his engagement in role playing in bed, the man becoming the woman to the woman's man.

Not incidentally, much of this information has been available for some time. We have known, for example, since at least 1961 when Hemingway's older sister, Marcelline Hemingway Sanford, published *At the Hemingways: A Family Portrait* that their mother raised Hemingway and Marcelline as twins "even into [their] school life," encouraging them to share dolls and fishing alike (61–62). And we have known since 1976 when Hemingway's fourth wife, Mary, published *How It Was* that Hemingway played a role of female to his wife's male in bed (368–70). However, only with the release of Hemingway's "private" manuscripts, such as *The Garden of Eden*, and his personal letters has there been a widespread scholarly examination of this material. Perhaps, as Susan Beegel speculates, scholars have needed the weight of a novel (*The Garden of Eden*) to force them to confront "themes of homosexuality, perversion, and androgyny present throughout Hemingway's career in short stories like 'Mr. and Mrs. Elliot,' 'A Simple Enquiry,' 'The Sea Change,' and 'The Mother of a Queen' widely available for at least 50 years" (11).

Yet, considering the way in which many critics have been responding to and representing these "themes" in Hemingway's fiction and life, I would argue that at least part of the delay can be attributed to a fear that Hemingway's cultural image as a man's man might be damaged by the spread of this information. In other words, although a few critics (such as Cathy and Arnold Davidson, whose work I will discuss later) are undertaking a more thorough reconstruction of Hemingway, the majority of scholars who address this "new" information can be seen as attempting to ensure that the Hemingway "hidden away" in his manuscripts does not differ too greatly from the Hemingway we have always known.

Two major trends have developed within Hemingway criticism of the last decade, and both of them support this claim that many critics are doing image maintenance. On the one hand are those critics who regret that manuscripts like *The Garden of Eden* and "The Last Good Country" were published. Their ostensible objections are that publication controverts Hemingway's wishes, contradicts his reputation as a consummate artist who carefully controlled the publishing of his fiction, and confuses beyond usefulness (or is that used-to-ness?) the idea of intentionality.[3] However, given these critics' attitudes toward some of the subjects explored in these works (sexual role-playing, lesbianism, the ménage à trois, and suggestions of incest), their protests seem motivated by more than the desire to protect Hemingway's professional reputation.

Consider, for example, Earl Rovit's reasons for denouncing the publication of *The Garden of Eden*: "It's unfortunate it was commercially published because it's a rotten book. There are lovely things in it and the business of this unorthodox ménage à trois, and the haircuts, and what not. All struck me as personal material that a writer is getting rid of for his own therapy and is unable to universalize or make representative of anything other than his own peculiar warts and whims" (Brian 189). In this rejection of *The Garden of Eden*, Rovit presumes that Hemingway's portrayal of the ménage à trois and his characters' eroticization of hair *must* be the act of an author projecting and expelling the neuroses of his psyche, a private attempt to cure his own peculiar "tendencies." Even if one were to accept Rovit's assessment of Hemingway's subject matter as intimately personal to Hemingway—which surely it is not—this is an odd objection to bring to bear upon the work of a writer who constantly uses his experience in creating his fiction. Certainly Rovit would not wish to remove from critical scrutiny the many stories in which Hemingway draws upon his injury in World War I, his efforts to hunt big game, or his experience with his father's suicide.[4] This back-to-the-closet attitude discloses the huge personal and cultural investment that many readers have in retaining the image of Hemingway as a red-blooded, all-American, white, heterosexual male. As Mark Spilka puts it, there is a growing anxiety among Hemingway admirers that the Hemingway "who gave us male definitions of manhood to ponder, cherish, even perhaps to grow by" is about to be lost (327–28).

On the other hand are critics, like Spilka, who are working eagerly with materials from the Kennedy Library and with recently published Hemingway stories and letters to refashion our understanding of Hemingway and his fiction. But, despite their enthusiasm, the work of these critics promotes many of the attitudes held by those readers who want to return these materials to Hemingway's—or the Kennedy Library's—closet. Simply put, although these critics believe they are doing feminist service to Hemingway's reputation and fiction, their efforts reinstate that reputation and fiction within a sexist, heterosexist, and homophobic matrix. Occasionally a critic's language reveals that he is positioned within this matrix, as in Spilka's references to the Hemingway "who gave *us* male definitions of manhood . . . to grow by," "that one-eyed myth of mystical [male] camaraderie *we* have *all* more or less embraced" (328), and in his reference to Hemingway's ability to overcome "his own and *everyone else's* fear of female dominance" (213; emphasis added). More frequently, however, the sexism and heterosexism are ingrained in the paradigm chosen by these critics to explain the gender complexities in Hemingway's life and work: androgyny. Hence, one might say that the attitudes are institutional more than personal, although one could also argue that critics choose this paradigm because such attitudes are institutionalized within it.

In the following discussion, I will first briefly detail the ways in which Hemingway critics working with androgyny reassert and reflect sexist, heterosexist, and homophobic views. I will then present an alternative way to interpret the relations between gender and desire in Hemingway. Throughout this presentation, my principal example will be *The Sun Also Rises*, a text that has become known as "classic Hemingway," with its attention to male bonding and rituals such as fishing, drinking, and bullfighting, but that is, I believe, even more interested in exploring the conflict between cultural prescriptions for gender and sexual identity and the human desires and needs that refuse to be controlled by those dictates. Finally, I will consider how this recent work (mine included) on Hemingway's identity and its relationship to Hemingway's fiction might affect our understanding of the Author and our pedagogical/critical practice, especially as those practices are being reformed by the pressures of multiculturalism.

The Problem with Androgyny

Spilka's *Hemingway's Quarrel with Androgyny*, the most obvious example of the critical application of androgyny to Hemingway's life and work, is simply the most sustained representative of a widespread trend. For instance, Gerald Kennedy's "Hemingway's Gender Trouble" also draws upon the androgyny model to examine *A Moveable Feast* and *The Garden of Eden*, asserting that, "[q]uite apart from its biographical resonances," *The Garden of Eden* derives its interest from "Hemingway's blurring of gender roles and his exploration of androgyny" (188). Adopting a similar perspective, Robert Gajdusek's investigation of the thematic connections between *The Garden of Eden* and other Hemingway works also examines "androgeneity." And in *Hemingway and Nineteenth-Century Aestheticism*, John Gaggin looks at androgyny as one of many "decadent issues" that Hemingway explores (78).[5]

Even some recent biographers have adopted the paradigm of androgyny for analyzing Hemingway. Michael Reynolds, for example, claims that Hemingway learned in Paris that "To write, a man must cultivate that feminine side of himself, become both male and female." Reynolds then suggests that Hemingway began growing his hair to reach the bobbed length of Hadley's (Hemingway's first wife) so that they could be the same person: "man and woman blending to oneness in sexual union, one whole person at last: Plato's egg reunited" (1989, 98). The androgynous approach has thus been pervasive, and there is no sign that its influence is diminishing. The topic for the 1993 meeting of the South Atlantic Modern Language Association division of the Hemingway Society is "Androgyny: The New Key to Reading Hemingway."

At first glance, androgyny might seem the ideal way to conceptualize the self and the romantic union of a man and a woman in Hemingway's life and work. As a matter of fact, it is the word Mary Hemingway chose to describe her relationship with her husband. "[W]e were," she wrote, "smoothly interlocking parts of a single entity, the big cogwheel and the smaller cogwheel. . . . Maybe we were androgynous" (297).[6] However, as numerous gender theorists have pointed out, "androgyny" is a problematic word, especially when those who use it fail to challenge sexist and heterosexist definitions of masculinity and femininity. Adrienne Rich contends that, because critics rarely critique the sexual politics of "androgyny," it has become a "good" word, meaning many things to many people (76). Daniel Harris claims that "[f]or feminist men as well as for feminist women, the myth of androgyny has no positive value." According to him, "We cannot discuss the myth, in psychological terms, without resorting to sexist polarizations for the definition of identity. . . . [T]he myth, because it is a microcosm of heterosexual power relations within the dominant culture, can only perpetuate the habits of oppression we seek to reject" (171–72).

So, although androgyny seems to promise a way out of the masculine-feminine binarism, it simply moves that binarism from the external to the internal world. Such a move prevents—even prohibits—a truly political reading in which the critic exposes the binarisms that readers hold in place while they read. Instead, the critic becomes trapped into unwittingly embracing sexist polarizations. Hemingway critics working with the androgyny model constantly fall into this trap. Consider, for example, the assumptions that make possible a description of Frederic Henry, lying wounded in a hospital bed, as having "finally arrived at something like a woman's passive power" (Spilka 212) or those behind the suggestion that Robert Jordan learns from Maria the essentially feminine value of mystical knowledge (Crozier 6).[7] Or consider the way that stereotypes about masculinity and femininity are reproduced in Latham's conclusion about Hemingway's relationship to "the androgynous" *Garden of Eden*: "Perhaps Papa came to feel that he contained both Catherine and David inside himself" (96).

A term related to gender roles, androgyny also neutralizes, even removes, any sexual component of Hemingway's upbringing and role-playing, and of his characters' impulses. The concept of androgyny thus gives critics permission to avoid looking at Hemingway's explorations of sexual identity. This license to ignore seems to explain, in part, why androgyny has become so popular with Hemingway critics: it permits them to turn away from the continually returning rumor that Hemingway—or his male heroes—had homosexual "tendencies." The caveats that critics provide whenever their discussion comes close to confusing the androgyne for the homosexual support such a possibility, as in Spilka's assertion that he is not implying that Jake Barnes "would also like to make it with bullfighters and other males" (204). The homosexual, as Catharine Stimpson observes, is "a far more threatening figure than the androgyne," in part simply because the homosexual exists: "The androgyne is nothing more, or less, than an idea" (242).

When critics writing on Hemingway do deal with homosexual desire, it is almost always lesbian desire, but lesbian desire delineated along heterosexual lines. For example, both Kenneth Lynn, one of Hemingway's recent biographers, and Spilka suggest that Jake Barnes's war injury puts him into the position of a woman, more significantly that of a lesbian, whose dilemma is that she cannot penetrate her lover's body with her own (Lynn 323; Spilka 203). But this is a peculiarly phallic definition of lesbian lovemaking, assuming, as it does, that sex must involve penetration and that penetration must involve a penis. Further, this definition of Jake's situation ignores or refuses the additional possibility that his love for the "mannish" Brett—and hers for him—contains a dimension of male homosexuality. Such a refusal reconfirms my point that many critics are attempting to maintain Hemingway's identity as a heterosexual; under this ideology, it is safer to make Jake a lesbian because he can never really be one. Once we take seriously the idea that Jake has homosexual desires, it is a short step to taking seriously the idea that Hemingway's "attraction" to lesbians is an instance of the displacement of his own homosexual desires.

Clearly, looking through the bifocals of androgyny limits our understanding of Hemingway and his characters and prevents us from attempting to attain a more comprehensive vision, one that might see beyond conventional cultural codes. I am not, therefore, proposing that we simply reverse our viewpoint and identify Hemingway or his characters as repressed homosexuals or even as heterosexuals who occasionally act out homosexual desires by imaginatively recasting the sex of their partner or themselves. That approach would only continue our reliance on preconceived notions of homosexual and heterosexual as dichotomous identities. Nor am I arguing that we should view Hemingway or his characters as bisexual, for this designation also reinstates the binary system of sexuality.

I want to suggest, instead, that Hemingway's life and especially his fiction constantly call into question the validity of society's prescriptions for gender identification and sexual orientation. Ironically, in mapping out this territory of interrogation, I will have to draw upon the very concepts that I claim Hemingway's novel problematizes (masculinity/femininity, homosexuality/heterosexuality). As Gayatri Spivak notes, "There is no way that a deconstructive philosopher can say 'something is not something' when the word is being used as a concept to enable his discourse" (213). But by illustrating how Hemingway's text brings traditional significations of gender and sexuality into conflict, I hope to show that Hemingway's fiction and, ultimately, his life reveal the intellectual limitations that result when 'gender" and "sexuality" are read as innocent acts of nature and as fixed binaries.

Gender and Sexuality in *The Sun Also Rises*

To elucidate this thesis, let us look at an early scene in *The Sun Also Rises* that seems to establish the gender and sexual ideologies upon which the novel will turn: the occasion of Jake and Brett's meeting at the dancing club, Jake accompanied by a prostitute, Georgette Hobin, and Brett by a group of homosexual men. In a poststructuralist reading that provides the starting point for mine, Cathy and Arnold Davidson observe that, by switching dancing partners, these characters arrange themselves in different pairings: Jake and Georgette, Jake and Brett, the young men and Brett, the young men and Georgette. These partner exchanges initially suggest "the fundamental equivalence" of the women as well as of the men: Georgette and Brett are conjoined under the pairing of prostitution/promiscuity just as Jake and the young men are connected under the pairing of sexually maimed/homosexual. Consequently, this episode reveals the contradictions in Jake's own life. Jake relies upon the homosexuality of the young men to define his manhood (at least his desire is in the right place), but that definition is tested by the joint presence of Georgette and Brett (89–92). As the Davidsons conclude, "The terrifying ambiguity of [Jake's] own sexual limitations and gender preferences may well be one source of his anger (it usually is) with Brett's companions, and another reason why he articulates his anger and hatred for them before he reveals his love for her" (92).

But this perceptive reading illuminates only one of the "fundamental equivalences" set up in this scene; further, it fails to recognize that, as these equivalences multiply, the glue connecting the descriptive pairs loosens. In other words, through a series of interchanges, Jake and Brett are aligned with several equations; the units dissolve as they rearrange themselves into new pairs. What began as an inseparable unit (sexually maimed/homosexual) ends as free-floating signifiers (sexually maimed, homosexual), and the characters, particularly Jake and Brett, are revealed as bodies of contradictions. Ultimately these pairings challenge the validity of gender and sexuality binarisms: masculine/feminine, heterosexual/homosexual.

For instance, the pairing of Brett and Georgette, like the pairing of Jake and the homosexual men, is complex and multifaceted. The resemblance between the two women is underscored when Jake, half-asleep, thinks that Brett, who has come to visit him, is Georgette (32). Obviously such a correspondence reveals that both women sleep around, one because she believes it is the way she is made (55), the other because it is the way she makes a living. Yet this explanation of motives reminds us that women's outlets for their desires were closely intertwined with economic necessity in the years following World War I, even in the liberated Left Bank of Paris. As a white, heterosexual, upper-class woman, Brett still must depend, both financially and socially, on hooking up with some man or another. As Wendy Martin observes, "If Brett has gained a measure of freedom in leaving the traditional household, she is still very much dependent on men, who provide an arena in which she can be attractive and socially active as well as financially secure" (71).

Brett's self-destructive drinking and her attempts to distance herself from sexual role stereotyping—for example, her short hair is "brushed back like a boy's" (22) and she wears a "man's felt hat" (28)—indicate her resentment of this prescribed arrangement. Susan Gubar reminds us that many women artists of the modernist period escaped the strictures of societally defined femininity by appropriating male clothing, which they identified with freedom (478). For such women, cross-dressing became "a way of ad-dressing and re-dressing the inequities of culturally-defined categories of masculinity and femininity" (479). Brett Ashley fits within this category of women who were crossing gender lines by cross-dressing and behaving in "masculine ways." Indeed, although Brett's wool jersey sweater reveals her to be a woman, the exposure is not enough to counteract the effect of her masculine apparel and appearance on the men around her. Pedro Romero's desire to make her look more "womanly" (242) and to marry him might be explained as the response of a man raised in a culture that requires clear distinctions between the gender roles of men and women. But Mike Campbell's similar attempt to convince Brett to buy a new hat (79) and to marry him suggests that Brett is dangerously close to overturning the categories upon which male and female identity, and patriarchal power, depend. The "new woman" must not venture too far outside old boundaries.

Brett's cross-dressing conveys more than just a social statement about gender. It also evokes suggestions of the transvestism practiced by and associated with lesbians of the time (and since). Although sexologists such as Havelock Ellis, whose works Hemingway was recommending enthusiastically during the 1920s, recognized the Mannish Lesbian as only one kind of lesbian, wearing men's clothing was often viewed as sexual coding—and many lesbians chose to cross-dress in order to announce their sexual preference.[8] Significantly, the parallel to Georgette reinforces Brett's connection to lesbianism. When Jake introduces Georgette to a group seated in the restaurant, he identifies her as his fiancée, Georgette Leblanc. As scholars have noted, Georgette Leblanc was a contemporary singer and actress in Paris—and an acknowledged lesbian.[9] This association consequently deepens the symbolic relationship of Brett to Georgette, linking them in a new equation: independence/lesbian. Brett's transvestism crosses over from gender inversion to sexual sign: Brett desires the lesbian's economic, social, and sexual autonomy.

In fact, Brett's inability to sustain a relationship and her congruent alcoholism might be indications not of nymphomania, with which critics have often charged her, but of a dissatisfaction with the strictures of the male-female relationship. Brett's announcement, for example, that she can drink safely among homosexual men (22) can be taken to mean that she cannot control her own heterosexual desire, but it could also reveal an underlying anxiety toward the heterosexual desire of men. Such an anxiety might be related to her abusive marriage, but that experience need not be its only source. As Brett tells Jake after the break-up with Pedro Romero, "I can't even marry Mike" (242). Of course, soon after she says this, she declares, "I'm going back to Mike. . . . He's so damned nice and he's so awful. He's my sort of thing" (243). Yet, even in giving her reasons for returning to Mike, Brett reveals her inner turmoil and ambivalence. Like Mike, she is "nice" and "awful," and the book ends before this promised reunion takes place.

Brett's anxiety about male heterosexual desire should not be conflated with lesbian desire since, typically, the two emotions are not related causally. Brett's lesbianism manifests itself in other ways, however, most immediately through her association with her homosexual companions; as Jake states three times, she is "with them," she is "very much with them" (20). This homosexual identification helps to explain Brett's attraction to Jake who, according to Hemingway in a letter written in 1951, has lost his penis, but not his testicles and spermatic cord—and thus not his sexual desire (1981, 745).[10] If we accept this explanation, Jake lacks the feature that has traditionally been the most important in distinguishing sex as well as male sexual desire.[11] He is a sexual invalid and, as a consequence, sexually in-valid.[12] Jake's sex, gender, and sexuality, conflated as one under the law of compulsory heterosexuality,[13] are thereby separated and problematized. Like a woman, Jake has no penis to thrust into Brett. Instead, Brett ministers to him, rubbing his head as he lies on the bed (55), and recognizes that the absent male sex organ makes Jake different from other suitors.[14] In this context, Jake's notion that Brett "only wanted what she couldn't have" (31) takes on added meaning. Besides non-penile sex, she wants to find some way to accommodate the fluidity of sex and gender that characterizes her desire and her condition.

Brett's affiliation with the homosexual men and her gender-bending complicate, in turn, Jake's relationship with her. Jake calls Brett "damned good-looking" and describes her hair as being "brushed back like a boy's" (22), two attributions that dissolve into one in Jake's later identification of Pedro Romero as "a damned good-looking boy" (167). Jake's desire for Brett can thus be partially explained as homosexual, a desire that seems about to break through the surface of Jake's narrative at any time.[15] As the Davidsons point out and as I mention earlier, this desire can be seen in Jake's conflicted response to Brett's homosexual companions. It can also be seen in Jake's possession of afición, which must be confirmed by the touch of other men (132). To quote the Davidsons, there is something "suspect" in the aficionados vesting so much of their manhood in a boylike matador who woos a bull to death through "girlish flirtation and enticement." As a consequence, "the whole ethos of afición resembles a sublimation of sexual desire, and the aficionados—serving, guiding, surrounding the matador out of the ring and applauding him in it—seem all, in a sense, steers" (95).

Jake's descriptions of the meeting of the bull and bullfighter imply more than flirtation in the encounter; it is sexual foreplay and consummation. He states, "The bull wanted it again, and Romero's cape filled again, this time on the other side. Each time he let the bull pass so close that the man and the bull and the cape that filled and pivoted ahead of the bull were all one sharply etched mass" (217). Later Jake expresses the climax of the bullfight— the bull's death—in terms reminiscent of a sexual climax:

> [F]or just an instant [Romero] and the bull were one, Romero way out over the bull, the right arm extended high up to where the hilt of the sword had gone in between the bull's shoulders. Then the figure was broken. There was a little jolt as Romero came clear, and then he was standing, one hand up, facing the bull, his shirt ripped out from under his sleeve, the white blowing in the wind, and the bull, the red sword hilt tight between his shoulders, his head going down and his legs settling. (218–19)

Jake's relationships with Bill Gorton and Pedro Romero constitute two of the more important sources of sublimated homosexuality. During their fishing trip to the Irati River, Bill tells Jake, "Listen. You're a hell of a good guy, and I'm fonder of you than anybody on earth. I couldn't tell you that in New York. It'd mean I was a faggot" (116). In expressing his fondness for Jake, Bill realizes the risk he takes in declaring his strong feelings for another man: his words might be construed as an admission of homosexual love. To avoid being interpreted in that way, Bill must declare homosexual desire an impossibility. However, Bill's phrasing in this passage and his subsequent focus on homosexuality suggest that such desire is a possibility. For one, his statement "I'm fonder of you than anybody on earth" can be read as "I'm fonder of you than I am of anybody else on earth" or as "I'm fonder of you than anybody else is." Either reading elevates Bill and Jake's relationship to a primary position; it is a connection more binding and important than any other relationship Bill has formed.

In addition, Bill's view that disclosing his affection for Jake would, in New York, mean that he is "a faggot" indicates Bill's awareness of the permeability of the line separating homosocial and homosexual behavior and desire. Outside the geographic and psychological boundaries of America and its strict morality, Bill's feelings are platonic; inside those boundaries, they are homosexual. Bill's confusion about the boundaries for same-sex relationship suggests that he cannot be sure about the "purity" of his feelings for Jake or of Jake's for him. Having stated his fondness, Bill immediately moves the discussion away from their relationship, but he cannot drop the subject of homosexuality: "That [homosexual love] was what the Civil War was about. Abraham Lincoln was a faggot. He was in love with General Grant. So was Jefferson Davis. . . . Sex explains it all. The Colonel's Lady and Judy O'Grady are Lesbians under their skin" (116). By identifying homosexual desire as the cause of all private and public action, a supposedly absurd exaggeration, Bill defuses the tension that expressing his affection for Jake creates.[16] Yet homosexuality is still very much in the air—and "under their skin."

This homosexual current that flows throughout the text reaches its crisis at the same time that the heterosexuality of the text is also at its highest tension: during the liaison that Jake arranges between Brett and Pedro. As I observe, Jake describes Pedro in terms that repeat his descriptions of Brett; further, his first impression of the bullfighter is a physical one—"He was the best-looking boy I have ever seen" (163)—and his later observations continue this focus on Pedro's body. Jake tells Brett that Pedro is "nice to look at" (184), notices his clear, smooth, and very brown skin (185), and describes Pedro's hand as being "very fine" and his wrist as being "small" (185). Given the way Jake gazes upon Pedro's body, a body that, like Brett's, blends the masculine with the feminine, the moment when Jake brings together Pedro and Brett is also the moment when the text reveals its inability to separate heterosexual from homosexual desire within the desiring body.

This scene has typically been read as the tragic fulfillment of a traditional love triangle in which two men want the same woman and desire moves heterosexually: Jake wants Brett who wants Pedro who wants Brett. Or, as Robert Cohn puts it, Jake becomes Brett's pimp (190). Yet, given the similarity in the way Jake describes Brett and Pedro, given Jake's homoerotic descriptions of the bullfighter's meeting with the bull, and given the sexual ambiguities that Brett and Jake embody, it seems more accurate to view this relationship not as a triangle but as a web in which desire flows simultaneously in many directions. When Brett and Pedro consummate their desire for each other, Pedro also becomes Jake's surrogate, fulfilling his desire for Brett and hers for him, while Brett becomes Jake's "extension" for satisfying his infatuation with Pedro. Although Jake is physically/phallically absent from Pedro and Brett's "honeymoon" (190), his desire is multiply and symbolically present. Of course, the inadequacy of a figurative presence is disclosed when Brett persists in giving Jake the details about her relationship with

Pedro, a verbal reenactment that Jake cannot prevent hearing, even though it drives him to overeat and overdrink.

The final scene of the novel situates Jake between the raised baton of the policeman, an obvious phallic symbol, and the pressure of Brett's body. Such a situation suggests that the novel does not stop trying to bridge the multiple desires of its characters. However, Brett's wishful statement—"we could have had such a damned good time together"—and Jake's ironic question— "Isn't it pretty to think so?" (247)—reveal that at least part of the failure, part of the "lostness" conveyed is that such a bridge cannot be built. The prescriptions for masculinity and femininity and for heterosexuality and homosexuality are too strong to be destroyed or evaded, even in a time and place of sexual and gender experimentation.

The Canonized Author and the Multicultural Classroom

As this analysis suggests, to explore the fundamental equivalences implied during the dancing club scene and to follow their reverberations throughout *The Sun Also Rises* is to construct a network of ambiguities and contradictions pertaining to sexuality and gender. As I admitted above, in creating such a construction, I have had to draw upon the very concepts that I claim Hemingway's novel calls into question (masculinity/femininity, homosexuality/heterosexuality). But by refusing to qualify or resolve the contradictions surrounding these categories and focusing attention upon the points at which they conflict, I have tried to show how Hemingway's novel puts gender and sexuality into constant motion. Although our society attempts to stabilize conduct, appearance, and desire by encoding the first two as masculine or feminine and the latter as homosexual, heterosexual, or bisexual, desire and behavior are not that easily contained and categorized. Actions, appearance, and desire in *The Sun Also Rises* spill over the boundaries of these categories of identity and identification so that the categories become destabilized and collide with one another. The text asks us to suspect, and finally to reject, these systems of representation that are so insufficient and so disabling to efforts to understand human nature.

This is not to say that Brett and Jake have discarded society's scripts for femininity and masculinity, heterosexuality and homosexuality. Their actions, particularly Brett's flirtations and Jake's homophobia, show that they know these scripts well. Nevertheless, as we see by following the several parallels suggested in the club scene, both Jake and Brett continually stray from

252 Debra A. Moddelmog

the lines the scripts demand. That they lack a discourse by which the multiplicity and multifariousness of their desire and conduct can be understood—or understood as "normal"—is society's fault, not their own.[17] But as critics of that society, we must not make this fault of essentializing sexuality and gender our fault too. Toril Moi points out that an individual's experiences "cannot be understood other than through the study of their multiple determinants—determinants of which conscious thought is only one, and a potentially treacherous one at that." Moreover, Moi continues, "If a similar approach is taken to the literary text, it follows that the search for a unified individual self, or gender identity or indeed 'textual identity' [and here I would add sexual identity] in the literary work must be seen as drastically reductive" (10).

For too long it has been the business of Hemingway biographers and critics—and, consequently, of those of us who teach Hemingway, given the causal relationship between what goes on in the scholarship to what takes place in the classroom—to reduce both Hemingway and his characters to a unified self. Hemingway, of course, commanded this reduction; in his public life he, too, attempted to represent his various desires as a monolithic identity,[18] an attempt that most certainly resulted from his own understanding of the script for being a white, heterosexual male and that may have led to a confusion of self-understanding that he could not work his way out of.

We must not be similarly confused. And here is where my rereading of Hemingway interrelates with the ongoing investigation into the role of the author and the composition of the multicultural classroom. Although Gregory Jay correctly asserts that the "death of the author or of 'man' pronounced by commentators of poststructuralism was greatly exaggerated" (1990, x), Seán Burke also rightly claims that "radical anti-authorialism" has exerted a widespread impact, especially upon the Anglo-American tradition (162).[19] In particular, American literary critics of the past twenty-five years have been deeply involved in determining how, in the absence of the biographical author, the reader and/or the text announce their presence and produce meaning. In response to this anti-authorial stronghold, several lines of resistance have formed.

The strongest resistance to theories that posit the author's absence has come from historically marginalized groups, for whom, as bell hooks writes, "it has been an active gesture of political resistance to name one's identity as part of a struggle to challenge domination" (172–73). As a result of this demand by traditionally excluded groups to retain a notion of the writing subject, several critics have proposed various ways of defining the author.[20]

Cheryl Walker, for example, suggests that women critics must reanimate the author in terms of a politics of author recognition. What we need, she states, "instead of a theory of the death of the author, is a new concept of authorship that does not naively assert that the writer is an originating genius, creating aesthetic objects outside of history, but that also does not diminish the importance of difference and agency in the responses of women writers to historical formations" (560).

Although Walker restricts her salvaging of the author to women writers, surely the case of Hemingway reveals the importance of maintaining a working concept of the author for so-called canonized authors as well. Hemingway is, admittedly, one of the few authors of the United States whose life has been as thoroughly examined as his art. He has never been a subject who, as Roland Barthes puts it, slips away in his writing (142)—partly because readers have never allowed him to, all-too-often reading his fiction as autobiography. At most, one might argue that Hemingway critics have operated on Michel Foucault's principle of the author-function, whereby "Hemingway" becomes a signature, not a subjective presence, in which the author's name "serves to characterize a certain mode of being of discourse" (107).

But, if this is true, then Hemingway's history as a subject of literary study demonstrates how easily popular culture and scholarly enterprise collude. Foucault proposes that those aspects of an individual that we designate as "making him an author are only a projection, in more or less psychologizing terms, of the operations that we force texts to undergo, the connections that we make, the traits that we establish as pertinent, the continuities that we recognize, or the exclusions that we practice" (110). According to him, the functioning of the author's name can change, but only when we "discover" something that significantly affects the way we view that author, for example, that Shakespeare did not write those sonnets which pass for his (106). However, the case of Hemingway reveals what happens when discoveries coincide with "exclusions that we practice." The author-function ends up being as limiting as the traditional concept of the author that Foucault amends: it too becomes "the principle of thrift in the proliferation of meaning" (118).

I believe that, far from being unique, Hemingway's case is exemplary. It urges us to refuse any idea of the author's absence and push instead for its opposite: a recognition of the author's imperishability. Thanks to a ubiquitous media and the unending proliferation of literary scholarship, the author cannot die. The public and scholarly desire for information and the interpretive practices of literary critics and biographers assure the author's presence. From the moment we circulate the "facts" about an author's life—on book jackets, in headnotes within anthologies, in book reviews and criticism, in biographies, and in made-for-TV movies—the author lives. It is foolish, and foolhardy, for scholars to pretend that their reading or teaching of an author's work is unaffected by these biographical "facts."[21] Confronted with such facts, we must not then pretend they have no life within the text. We bring them there. Our critical readings evince their presence. If nothing else, the reassessment of Hemingway's identity that has taken place during the past few years demonstrates this point: as the life changes, so does the fiction. The relationship between the author and the work is interactive and interdependent.

In recognizing this interdependency, I am not advocating a return to pre-structuralist practices, to "a form of biographical criticism that would seem to be hopelessly naive in an era of poststructuralist suspicion of any equations between the maker and the text" (Mayne 115). Rather, I am suggesting that we follow through on the understanding that poststructuralism provides, namely, that, despite Latham's metaphor of a Hemingway "hidden away" in his manuscripts, an identity is constructed, not found. As Joan Scott observes, "the appearance of a new identity is not inevitable or determined, not something that was always there simply waiting to be expressed," but is rather "a discursive event" (792). The identity of an author, like the identity of a text or our own identity, is a process of becoming—or, more accurately, a process of articulating into being. It is based not only on the way in which the author performs and constructs that identity, but also on the way in which subsequent readers reinterpret that performance and construction.[22]

If, however, in constructing a new identity, we fail to interrogate the conventional cultural codes that enable identity construction, especially those codes related to gender, race, class, and sexuality, we will simply end up rehearsing what has already been culturally written. So far, this has been the failure of critics working on Hemingway, who have not been actually reconstructing Hemingway's identity so much as they have been giving the customary one a face lift. Only by moving beyond cosmetic surgery in our efforts to construct the identity of Hemingway can we improve our ability to comprehend Hemingway's life and, concurrently, his fiction. To put this another way, a proliferation of evidence that contradicts an identity-construction is not enough to overturn that construction since such evidence can be subsumed into the existing construction. Instead, we must shift the cultural paradigm used to interpret the evidence without losing sight of historical conditions that determine the kinds and boundaries of behavior influencing the subject.

In Hemingway's case, by employing a paradigm that enables the multiplicity of desire to come into full view and into full play, we see how Hemingway's life and fiction challenge cultural codes of the 1920s (and of today), even as they are still conditioned by these codes. Yet even as I make this statement, I acknowledge that such a model might itself be displaced in the future as our understanding of the world changes and as additional evidence about Hemingway's life comes to light. My point is that as critics and as readers we must conceive the author in such a way that encourages us to continually interrogate the identity that has been established for a particular author and to construct new identity-constructions based on our changing knowledge of historical formations, cultural imperatives, and the author's life.

As literary critics we must, therefore, work on the assumption that the author is a site, like the text and the reader, in which meaning is fluid and unstable rather than predetermined. Such an assumption implies that we still have a great deal to gain by continuing to study canonized authors, even those, like Ernest Hemingway, who have become more popularly known as Dead White Males. For many years Hemingway has typically been taught one way or not at all. In my classes I encounter students who either adulate or despise him and his work. Discussions with colleagues throughout the United States confirm this as a common experience. Thus, much of my time teaching Hemingway is spent dismantling the cultural and scholarly construction of Hemingway, or at least convincing students to recognize how that construction has shaped the way they read Hemingway's fiction. This essay will, I hope, open up that discussion even more and will simultaneously encourage members of our profession to engage in similar explorations as they ponder curricula revisions and the nature of the multicultural classroom.

As Gregory Jay asserts, "undoing the canon doesn't just mean adding on previously excluded figures; it requires a disturbance of the internal security of the classics themselves" (1991, 271). This essay reveals one way to "disturb" the classics, for it illustrates that Hemingway's fiction contains numerous instances of his struggle against acculturation into a homophobic patriarchy and, at the same time, provides extensive opportunities for dismantling binary oppositions of both gender and sexuality. To quote the female protagonist of Hemingway's short story "The Sea Change": "We're made up of all sorts of things. You've known that" (304).

Endnotes

1. I want to thank Ruth Ann Hendrickson, Rosaria Champagne, Paul Smith, Jim Phelan, Katie Dyer, and Linda Mizejewski for their help with this essay. Their perceptive comments have improved my thinking immensely. I also thank Mary Wehrle for her invaluable assistance with researching portions of this essay.

2. The biographies of the past 13 years include Michael Reynolds' *The Young Hemingway, Hemingway: The Paris Years,* and *Hemingway: The American Homecoming*; Peter Griffin's *Along With Youth* and *Less Than a Treason*; Kenneth Lynn's *Hemingway*; Jeffrey Meyers' *Hemingway*; Peter Hays's *Ernest Hemingway*; and James Mellow's *Hemingway: A Life Without Consequences.* One can also see the widespread interest in reevaluating Hemingway's life in such works as Bernice Kert's *The Hemingway Women*; Denis Brian's *The True Gen*; and Gioia Diliberto's *Hadley*, the second biography written on Hemingway's first wife.

3. I do agree, however, with those scholars who are displeased that *The Garden of Eden* was edited so drastically. We need an expanded version, one that provides the fuller manuscripts, enabling us to examine all of Hemingway's characters and themes.

4. Rovit and Gerry Brenner, who co-authored the revised edition of *Ernest Hemingway*, often approve of Hemingway's use of experience, stating, for instance, that "It was probably a fortuitous accident that Hemingway's personal wound and relationship of estrangement from the Booth Tarkington mores of Oak Park should result in the compelling symbolism of *The Sun Also Rises*, but such are the graces of literary history" (141). Further, Rovit and Brenner welcome the posthumous publication of other Hemingway material assembled by various editors, such as *Islands in the Stream* and *A Moveable Feast*, claiming that such work "richly supplements—albeit problematically—the Hemingway canon" (153). Since *The Garden of Eden* was published the same year as their book, Rovit and Brenner could not be expected to discuss it, yet one wonders why Rovit wouldn't later recommend that *Garden* be read according to the guidelines he and Brenner advance for other posthumously published Hemingway manuscripts: "we are happy to have [*Feast* and *Islands*] as additions to the shelf of Hemingway's works; however, to discuss them as works bearing upon any overview of his canon must be done only in the context of knowing that they have been edited in ways that Maxwell Perkins never dreamt of" (156).

5. Gajdusek and Gaggin do look at sexuality in Hemingway's works, but their approaches perpetuate the problems I focus on here. Gajdusek mentions that bisexuality and sexual inversion are, like androgyny, important concerns in Hemingway's fiction; however, he uses these terms to describe the desires and actions of Hemingway's women, not his men. Gaggin is more inclusive, looking at both lesbianism and male homosexuality, but his investigation is bound by his aim of showing Hemingway's links to nineteenth-century decadence. His

analysis of homosexuality is thus connected to the way that nineteenth-century decadent writers viewed androgyny; although such a view allows him to examine sexuality as well as gender, it limits his scope.

6. As far as I can determine, Hemingway's understanding of "androgyny" was ambiguous but included homosexual attraction. Apparently, Hemingway's son, Patrick Hemingway, recalled in 1982 that Hemingway had forbidden him to visit Grandmother Grace because she was androgynous. Such a restriction seems to have come about because of Grace Hemingway's relationship with Ruth Arnold, her live-in voice student, a relationship that was so close it caused Hemingway's father to "rant" about Ruth and ban her from their house (Reynolds 1986, 81).

7. Crozier does not use the term "androgyny," but does divide traits according to masculine and feminine.

8. George Chauncey observes that Ellis, like other contemporary sexologists, attempted to differentiate sexual object choice from sexual roles and gender characteristics, an attempt reflected in the distinguishing of the sexual invert from the homosexual. Chauncey also notes, however, that the sexologists were less willing to apply this separation to women. Hence, while Ellis could claim that male homosexuals were not necessarily effeminate or transvestites, he was less capable of distinguishing a woman's behavior in sexual relations from other aspects of her gender role (124–25). Although Ellis maintained that transvestism was unrelated to homosexuality, he still provided numerous examples of lesbian transvestites in *Sexual Inversion* and insisted that "even those lesbians who wore female attire usually showed 'some traits of masculine simplicity' in their dress" (Chauncey 120). Ellis even believed that a keen observer could detect "psychic abnormality" in a woman by watching her behavior: "The brusque energetic movements, the attitude of the arms, the direct speech, the inflexions of the voice, the masculine straight-forwardness and sense of honor, and especially the attitude towards men, free from any suggestion either of shyness or audacity will often suggest the underlying psychic abnormality" (qtd. in Smith-Rosenberg 280).

Ellis's observations reflect his belief in a heterosexual norm, assuming, as Shari Benstock remarks of many critics, that "all lesbian behavior has in common its *reaction* to the norm of compulsory heterosexuality and that all lesbians act out their sexual orientation in the same way—here, through cross-dressing." Benstock points out that different behavior patterns existed among members of the Parisian lesbian community of the 1920s (as they do among lesbian communities today) and suggests that many lesbians of the Left Bank based their choices on the sexuality of their audience (179–80).

9. Apparently, Hemingway's feelings for Georgette Leblanc were not kind. In a letter to Ezra Pound (c. 2 May 1924), Hemingway noted that Margaret Anderson was in Paris with "Georgette Mangeuse [man-eater] le Blanc" (1981, 115). But

whether he knew her personally is uncertain. According to Bertram Sarason, Margaret Anderson claimed that Leblanc had never met Hemingway and did not know that her name had been mentioned in the novel (81). Interestingly, Jake's identification of Georgette Hobin as Georgette Leblanc suggests a special kind of knowledge about prostitutes, who, according to Hemingway's contemporary, Havelock Ellis, were frequently homosexual. In *Sexual Inversion*, Ellis remarks that the frequency of homosexuality among prostitutes is very high, especially in Paris (210). He quotes a friend who states, "'From my experience of the Parisian prostitute, I gather that Lesbianism in Paris is extremely prevalent; indeed, one might almost say normal. In particular, most of the chahut-dancers of the Moulin-Rouge, Casino de Paris, and the other public balls are notorious for going in couples, and, for the most part, they prefer not to be separated, even in their most professional moments with the other sex'" (211).

10. Compare also Hemingway's description several years later during his interview with George Plimpton, in which he states that Jake's testicles "were intact and not damaged. Thus he was capable of all normal feelings as a *man* but incapable of consummating them. The important distinction is that his wound was physical and not psychological and that he was not emasculated" (230; Hemingway's italics).

11. Although this kind of statement does not need verifying, given the phallocentrism of our society, a quote from Ellis will possibly contextualize Jake's wound: "It is easy to understand why the penis should occupy this special place in man's thoughts as the supreme sexual organ. It is the one conspicuous and prominent portion of the sexual apparatus, while its aptitude for swelling and erecting itself involuntarily, under the influence of sexual emotion, gives it a peculiar and almost unique position in the body. At the same time it is the point at which, in the male body, all voluptuous sensation is concentrated, the only normal masculine center of sex" ("Erotic Symbolism" 123).

12. Peter Messent's essay suggested this play on words (see 92), although he does not state the matter as I have, and he seems to have borrowed this idea from Sandra Gilbert (409).

13. This conflation is examined by several scholars. For example, Holly Devor writes, "sex is seen as wholly determining gender and largely determining gender role. The practices of gender roles are thought to be biologically constrained by the demands of one's biological sex/gender and socially defined by one's particular rearing within their gender" (46). Similarly, drawing upon Adrienne Rich's notion of "compulsory heterosexuality" and Monique Wittig's idea of the "heterosexual contract," Judith Butler refers to the "heterosexual matrix," a term that characterizes "a hegemonic discursive/epistemic model of gender intelligibility that assumes that for bodies to cohere and make sense there must be a stable sex expressed through a stable gender (masculine expresses male, feminine expresses female) that is oppositionally and hierarchically defined through the compulsory practice of heterosexuality" (151, n.6).

14. Peter Messent has also recently explored gender fluidity in *The Sun Also Rises*, and his reading lends support to many of the suppositions I set forth here. Messent states, "In *The Sun Also Rises*, gender roles have lost all stability" (112), and as evidence he points to, among other things, Georgette's sexual forwardness with Jake, Brett's pre-dawn visit to Jake's room after he has retired there with a "headache," the count's bringing of roses to Jake, and Jake's crying (114).

15. As support for this argument, consider Susan Gubar's suggestion that seductive cross-dressers "can function as sex symbols for men, reflecting masculine attitudes that range from an attempt to eroticize (and thereby possess) the independent woman to only slightly submerged homosexual fantasies" (483). While I do not discount the first possibility (eroticism in the service of possession)— especially given my general argument that the characters of *The Sun Also Rises* are marked by multiple desires—here I am tracing the latter function.

16. In an early draft of the novel, Bill's obsession and confusion are even more apparent. Bill tells Jake that New York circles have marked him (Bill) as "crazy": "Also I'm supposed to be crazy to get married. Would marry anybody at any time. . . . Since Charley Gordon and I had an apartment together last winter, I suppose I'm a fairy. That probably explains everything." Bill also reinforces his awareness—and fear—of the instability of sexual identity when he attacks the literary world of New York by claiming that "every literary bastard" there "never goes to bed at night not knowing but that he'll wake up in the morning and find himself a fairy. There are plenty of real ones too" (qtd. in Mellow 312–13).

17. Michel Foucault insists that the nineteenth and twentieth centuries are the age of multiplication of sexuality: "a dispersion of sexualities, a strengthening of their disparate forms, a multiple implantation of 'perversions.' Our epoch has initiated sexual heterogeneities" (1980, 37). However, this multiplication has been controlled by medical and legal categorization that assumes monogamous heterosexuality as its norm; in other words, the proliferation of desire has been restricted to and regulated within the social body (there are pederasts, homosexuals, inverts, etc.) rather than articulated within the body itself. Any desire that deviates from the heterosexual norm is named an aberration, a perversion, an oddity, a pathological abatement, a morbid aggravation (Foucault 1980, 53), and the person harboring it is either cured or designated a deviant.

18. For a convincing analysis of Hemingway's part in constructing his identity, see John Raeburn's *Fame Became of Him*.

19. Despite the entrenchment of Anglo-American deconstruction in its anti-authorial position, Burke convincingly reviews the points at which Barthes, Foucault, and Derrida contest the notion of the author's absolute disappearance. Equally important, as Burke shows, their own work reveals an inability to let go of the idea of the author: "The death of the author emerges as a blind-spot in the work of Barthes, Foucault and Derrida, an absence they seek to create and explore, but one which is always already filled with the idea of the author" (154).

20. For other recent discussions of authorship in feminist and minority studies, see
    Nancy K. Miller, "Changing the Subject"; Richard Dyer, "Believing in Fairies";
    and Reina Lewis, "The Death of the Author and the Resurrection of the Dyke."
21. Gerald Graff makes a similar argument in regard to the way we respond to "pub-
    lished reviews, publicity, rumor, gossip, and advertising hype" that accompany a
    text (5). He suggests that such mass-communications material surrounds the
    text with a secondary text that affects our reading, whether we admit it or not.
    Graff proposes that, rather than fulminate against this "unofficial interpretive
    culture as a symptom of spiritual and cultural decline," we should try to under-
    stand it and "see what kind of useful adaptation can be made to it" (6).
22. The idea of the gendered body as performative comes from Judith Butler, who
    writes, "Gender ought not to be construed as a stable identity or locus of agency
    from which various acts follow; rather, gender is an identity tenuously consti-
    tuted in time, instituted in an exterior space through a *stylized repetition of acts*"
    (140; Butler's italics).

Works Cited

Barthes, Roland. "The Death of the Author." In *Image, Music, Text*, translated by
    Stephen Heath, 142–48. New York: Noonday Press, 1977.
Beegel, Susan F. Introduction to *Hemingway's Neglected Short Fiction: New
    Perspectives*, edited by Susan F. Beegel, 1–18. Ann Arbor: UMI Research Press,
    1989.
Benstock, Shari. *Women of the Left Bank: Paris, 1900–1940*. Austin: Univ. of Texas
    Press, 1986.
Brian, Denis. *The True Gen: An Intimate Portrait of Hemingway By Those Who Knew
    Him*. New York: Grove, 1988.
Burke, Seán. *The Death and Return of the Author: Criticism and Subjectivity in
    Barthes, Foucault and Derrida*. Edinburgh: Edinburgh Univ. Press, 1992.
Butler, Judith. *Gender Trouble: Feminism and the Subversion of Identity*. New York:
    Routledge, 1990.
Chauncey, George, Jr. "From Sexual Inversion to Homosexuality: Medicine and the
    Changing Conceptualization of Female Deviance." *Salmagundi* 58–59
    (1982–83): 114–46.
Crozier, Robert D. "The Mask of Death, The Face of Life: Hemingway's Feminique."
    The Hemingway Review 8:1 (1984): 2–13.
Davidson, Arnold, and Cathy N. Davidson. "Decoding the Hemingway Hero in *The
    Sun Also Rises*." In *New Essays on* The Sun Also Rises, edited by Linda Wagner-
    Martin, 83–107. Cambridge: Cambridge Univ. Press, 1987.
Devor, Holly. *Gender Blending: Confronting the Limits of Duality*. Bloomington:
    Indiana Univ. Press, 1989.

Diliberto, Gioia. *Hadley*. New York: Ticknor & Fields, 1992.

Dyer, Richard. "Believing in Fairies: The Author and the Homosexual." In *Inside/Out: Lesbian Theories, Gay Theories*, edited by Diana Fuss, 185–201. New York: Routledge, 1991.

Ellis, Havelock. "Erotic Symbolism." Vol. 3, *Studies in the Psychology of Sex*. New York: Random, 1936.

———. "Sexual Inversion." Vol. 1, *Studies in the Psychology of Sex*. New York: Random, 1936

Foucault, Michel. *The History of Sexuality: An Introduction* (1978). Translated by Robert Hurley. New York: Vintage, 1980.

———. "What Is an Author?" Translated by Josué V. Harari. In *The Foucault Reader*, edited by Paul Rabinow, 101–20. New York: Pantheon, 1984.

Gaggin, John. *Hemingway and Nineteenth-Century Aestheticism*. Ann Arbor: UMI Research Press, 1988.

Gajdusek, Robert. "Elephant Hunt in Eden: A Study of New and Old Myths and Other Strange Beasts in Hemingway's Garden." *The Hemingway Review* 7:1 (1987): 14–19.

Gilbert, Sandra M. "Costumes of the Mind: Transvestism as Metaphor in Modern Literature." *Critical Inquiry* 7 (1980): 391–417.

Graff, Gerald. "Narrative and the Unofficial Interpretive Culture." In *Reading Narrative: Form, Ethics, Ideology*, edited by James Phelan, 3–11. Columbus: Ohio State Univ. Press, 1989.

Griffin, Peter. *Along With Youth: Hemingway. The Early Years*. New York: Oxford Univ. Press, 1985.

———. *Less Than a Treason: Hemingway in Paris*. New York: Oxford Univ. Press, 1990.

Gubar, Susan. "Blessings in Disguise: Cross-Dressing as Re-Dressing for Female Modernists." *Massachusetts Review* 22 (1981): 477–598.

Harris, Daniel. "Androgyny: The Sexist Myth in Disguise." *Women's Studies: An Interdisciplinary Journal* 2 (1974): 171–84.

Hays, Peter L. *Ernest Hemingway*. New York: Continuum, 1990.

Hemingway, Ernest. *Ernest Hemingway: Selected Letters, 1917–1961*. Edited by Carlos Baker. New York: Scribner's, 1981.

———. Interview. *Writers at Work: The* Paris Review *Interviews*. 2d ser. Edited by George Plimpton, 215–39. New York: Penguin, 1977.

———. "The Sea Change." *The Complete Short Stories of Ernest Hemingway*. The Finca Vigia Edition, 302–05. New York: Scribner's, 1987.

———. *The Sun Also Rises* (1926). New York: Scribner's, 1970.

Hemingway, Mary. *How It Was*. New York: Knopf, 1976.

hooks, bell. "Essentialism and Experience." *American Literary History* 3:1 (1991): 172–83.

Jay, Gregory S. "The End of 'American' Literature: Toward a Multicultural Practice." *College English* 53:3 (1991): 264–81.

———. *America the Scrivener: Deconstruction and the Subject of Literary History.* Ithaca: Cornell Univ. Press, 1990.

Kennedy, Gerald. "Hemingway's Gender Trouble." *American Literature* 63 (1991): 187–207.

Kert, Bernice. *The Hemingway Women.* New York: Norton, 1983.

Latham, Aaron. "A Farewell to Machismo." *New York Times Magazine,* 16 October 1977.

Lewis, Reina. "The Death of the Author and the Resurrection of the Dyke." In *New Lesbian Criticism: Literary and Cultural Readings,* edited by Sally Munt, 17–32. New York: Columbia Univ. Press, 1992.

Lynn, Kenneth. *Hemingway.* New York: Simon, 1987.

Martin, Wendy. "Brett Ashley as New Woman in *The Sun Also Rises.*" In *New Essays on* The Sun Also Rises, edited by Linda Wagner-Martin, 65–82. Cambridge: Cambridge Univ. Press, 1987.

Mayne, Judith. "Lesbian Looks: Dorothy Arzner and Female Authorship." In *How Do I Look: Queer Film and Video,* edited by Bad Object-Choices, 103–43. Seattle: Bay Press, 1991.

Mellow, James. *Hemingway: A Life Without Consequences.* Boston: Houghton Mifflin, 1992.

Messent, Peter. *New Readings of the American Novel.* London: Macmillan Education, 1990.

Meyers, Jeffrey. *Hemingway: A Biography.* New York: Harper, 1985.

Miller, Nancy K. "Changing the Subject: Authorship, Writing, and the Reader." In *Feminist Studies/Critical Studies,* edited by Teresa de Lauretis, 102–20. Bloomington: Indiana Univ. Press, 1986.

Moi, Toril. *Sexual/Textual Politics: Feminist Literary Theory.* London: Methuen, 1985.

Raeburn, John. *Fame Became of Him: Hemingway as Public Writer.* Bloomington: Indiana Univ. Press, 1984.

Reynolds, Michael. *Hemingway: The American Homecoming.* Oxford: Blackwell, 1992.

———. *Hemingway: The Paris Years.* Oxford: Blackwell, 1989.

———. *The Young Hemingway.* Oxford, Blackwell, 1986.

Rich, Adrienne. *Of Woman Born: Motherhood as Experience and Institution.* New York: Norton, 1976.

Rovit, Earl, and Gerry Brenner. *Ernest Hemingway.* Rev. ed. Boston: Twayne, 1986.

Sanford, Marcelline Hemingway. *At the Hemingways: A Family Portrait.* Boston: Little, 1961.

Sarason, Bertram. *Hemingway and* The Sun Set. Washington, D.C.: Microcard Editions, 1972.

Scott, Joan. "The Evidence of Experience." *Critical Inquiry* 17 (1991): 773–97.

Smith-Rosenberg, Caroll. *Disorderly Conduct: Visions of Gender in Victorian America.* New York: Knopf, 1985.

Spilka, Mark. *Hemingway's Quarrel with Androgyny.* Lincoln: Univ. of Nebraska Press, 1990.

Spivak, Gayatri. "A Response to 'The Difference Within: Feminism and Critical Theory.'" In *The Difference Within: Feminism and Critical Theory,* edited by Elizabeth Meese and Alice Parker, 207–20. Philadelphia: John Benjamin, 1989.

Stimpson, Catharine. "The Androgyne and the Homosexual." *Women's Studies: An Interdisciplinary Journal* 2 (1974): 237–48.

Walker, Cheryl. "Feminist Literary Criticism and the Author." *Critical Inquiry* 16 (1990): 551–71.

PART IV

The Response to
The Garden of Eden

THE FUSION OF HISTORY AND IMMEDIACY: HEMINGWAY'S ARTIST-HERO IN *THE GARDEN OF EDEN*

Malcolm O. Magaw

In an essay in *Rolling Stone* in 1986, Lorian Hemingway, dismayed over Scribner's publication of *The Garden of Eden*, said about her grandfather, "I wonder what Hemingway, who created masterworks, would say about this unfortunate novel. He might say he wished he had burned his evidence, as did Catherine Bourne. Or he might just laugh at us all."[1] Earlier in the same essay she had declared, "The truth is that the novel is as dead as the man. It is not just bad, but god-awful" (42). As everyone knows, reviewers and critics have tended to take a more moderate position than this less-than-disinterested one on the right or wrong of Scribner's decision to publish the work, some even going so far as to compliment Tom Jenks on a job well-done in his editing of the cumbersome manuscript. In a piece in *The Boston Review* Allen Josephs says that Jenks "seems to have done a remarkable job."[2] And Wilfrid Sheed, in *The New York Review of Books*, says, "Warts (if that is word

Reprinted with permission from Clio *(Fall 1987), pp. 21–36.*

enough for certain cancerous blemishes) and all, *The Garden of Eden* is surely the novel Hemingway *should* have published after the war—supposing,
that is, that he still knew how to edit as sharply as Tom Jenks at Scribner's
which seems possible."[3] In the "Publisher's Note" prefacing the novel,
Scribner's itself asserts that, "In preparing the book for publication we have
made some cuts in the manuscript and some routine copy-editing corrections. Beyond a very small number of minor interpolations for clarity and
consistency, nothing has been added. In every significant respect the work is
all the author's."[4]

Hemingway began writing *The Garden of Eden* in 1946 and had finished
most of a first draft some time in 1947. But the job was never completed,
even though Hemingway worked on it intermittently until his death in 1961,
at which time the draft had reached 1500 pages.[5] Lorian Hemingway, commenting on Hemingway's decision not to tidy up the draft and publish it,
says, "He could gauge whether a work was good or bad, and so he chose not
to publish certain books" (42). She also speculates that "*The Garden of Eden*
might have been 'just personal'; perhaps a high exercise in self-analysis that
kept Hemingway's mind inviolate for a time" (72). Sheed, meanwhile, insisting that Hemingway's draft "isn't so much plain bad as what the kids would
call 'weird'" (5), argues that Hemingway decided not to publish for family
reasons on the one hand and for self-image reasons on the other. In reference
to the former, he says, "The first [reason] might be simple decency, or caution. The story is, superficially at least, a heavily mythological version of the
breakup of his first marriage, and both women involved, Hadley and Pauline,
were not only still alive, but attempting to mother his children" (5). In reference to the latter, referring to Bourne's response to his bride Catherine's
request for an androgynous relationship in which he will be her girl for just
one night, Sheed says, "Smitten with love, and riddled with manly confusion,
he complies to the fullest extent imaginable—which suggests another, possibly conclusive reason for not publishing. Hemingway might have a hard time
calling himself Papa after this fling at being the Little Woman—whose run
incidentally is extended over several days and nights *passim*" (5).

But no matter what may lie at the bottom of the mystery of Hemingway's
reticent posture regarding publication, the fact remains that, except for
Lorian Hemingway's essay, none that I have read denies the legitimate presence of the Hemingway genius in the book, although, of course, nearly everyone notes a stylistic unevenness in the text and an occasional glaring "god-
awful" (to borrow a phrase) passage now and then. Sheed, for example, says,
"It seems as if the boy wonder was making a last stand in this book against

the old rum-pot, winning a page here and losing three there. The result is wildly, almost zanily, uneven . . . " (6). But, as certainly was true in the posthumously published *Islands in the Stream* (1970), imperfect text notwithstanding, there is much to be appreciated and even learned from a thoughtful reading of *The Garden of Eden*.

The novel reflects the continuation of what was surely a lifelong preoccupation Hemingway had with the complexities of the creative process, particularly of writing fiction. That preoccupation is only indirectly addressed in his first novel's characterization of Jake Barnes two decades and more before he created his novelist protagonist David Bourne in *The Garden of Eden*, but it is nonetheless there. Barnes is *The Sun Also Rises'* journalist protagonist, and, it could be argued, something along the lines of a masked novelist too since the book is written in the first person with Barnes as narrator. Of course another character, Robert Cohn, *is* a novelist, though for my purposes this is more or less incidental since I will be concentrating on the kinship between the Barnes and Bourne characterizations. Cohn's role as an American novelist living in Paris in the 1920s does suggest, however, an early preoccupation with that profession and identity on the part of Hemingway.

In the early 1930s—by then long since preoccupied with his craft, not to mention under the exacting scrutiny of Gertrude Stein—Hemingway spoke out more definitively than he had before (although even then in what might be called the mask of analogy) about his concern for the novelist and his craft. As every reader of *Death in the Afternoon* (1932) knows and as John Reardon succinctly asserts, "Hemingway constantly sees a relationship between what happens to a bullfighter facing a bull and what happens to a man facing a blank page. . . . Repeatedly, a chapter of *Death in the Afternoon* begins by talking about bullfighting but ends in a discussion of writing. And though it is also an eminent manual of the *corrida* it is also the manual of a man learning how to write and how to evaluate his experience."[6] Three years later in *The Green Hills of Africa* (1935), the theme unsurprisingly appears again in a variety of turns and concerns, not the least of which are the writer's needs to work slowly and deliberately, with absolute concentration, and in utter isolation from other writers. On the latter point he says, "Writers should work alone. They should see each other only after their work is done, and not too often then."[7] These are opinions which Hemingway voiced again and again, indeed even as late as his Nobel Prize speech in 1954; moreover, they are all not only adopted but explicated and discussed by David Bourne two decades later.

One could go on and on. Any reasonably comprehensive bibliography of Hemingway scholarship will corroborate my point that Hemingway had a lot to say about the writer's creative imagination—its mysterious directions, indirections, and misdirections; its catalysts and potentialities, yet also its necessary restraints—and that critics in tune have also had a lot to say about Hemingway's views and reviews on the writer's imagination and the execution of his art. I myself would like now to join that discussion as I advance and elaborate the hypothesis that, in David Bourne, Hemingway is presenting, in mid-century and beyond, his final portrait of the artist as a young man and hero—a portrait that coalesces the early Jake Barnes/Pedro Romero hero in his *aficion*-imbued Eden before and outside time, on the one hand; with the post World War II man in tune with history, with time, and with memory on the other hand. When these two twentieth-century Adams merge, they form a mid-century Hemingway artist-hero, a new Adam in a new Garden of Eden.

In his early review of *The Garden of Eden*, Allen Josephs asserts "Writing itself is an integral part of the book. . . . David Bourne immerses himself in the childhood stories of his African youth, which we read as he writes them. For him, this is less a form of therapy than a method of survival. Nowhere else in Hemingway's work is the intricate relationship between reality and imagination, between self and art, so originally explored" (113). And, while not emphasizing their kinship as writers, Sheed does observe in the Barnes of the 1920s and the Bourne of mid-century a mirror image as it were: "The hero, David Bourne, is actually closer to Jake Barnes: to wit, he is passive, rueful, flawed, and much more dominated than dominating. Or so it seems at first" (5).

An analysis of the kinship between the two Adams and of the provocative fusion of what were originally their discrete identities into that unified new Adam that Bourne comes to represent must begin, of course, with the Barnes characterization, profile of a man numbed by history but recovering his identity and self-possession—at least once in a while—in the glow of *aficion*.[8]

When Hemingway prefaced *The Sun Also Rises* (1926) with the pair of familiar quotes from Gertrude Stein and Ecclesiastes, respectively, he was certainly suggesting that his novel would have something to do with modern man's perception of himself in history. Stein's stark pronouncement, "You are all a lost generation,"[9] is clearly historical in its context as it calls attention to what, in the 1920s, was viewed by her and many others as the legacy of history's latest war on its surviving younger adult generation. And unquestionably a part of what Hemingway set out to do in the book was both to validate and to generalize Stein's assertion. He would concur that the most devastating war in history had caused the lifegiving cultural/societal sun to set and to produce in its place a dark wasteland populated by noncitizens—"those hooded hordes swarming / Over endless plains, stumbling in cracked earth / Ringed by the flat horizon only," as T. S. Eliot describes them in *The Waste Land*—conditioned and/or resigned to societal displacement.

Ezra Pound, just a few years earlier in *Hugh Selwyn Mauberley*, was saying about that same "lost generation" that they had "come home, home to a lie, / Home to many deceits / Home to old lies and new infamy," while the "myriad" who had not survived the war had "died for an old bitch gone in the teeth, / For a botched civilization." In the mid-Twenties Hemingway simply protracts Pound's earlier vision and shows us a group of the more hardened and sophisticated survivors of the war drifting mindlessly, as it were, among the "two gross of broken statues" and the "few thousand battered books" that Pound's Mauberley declared were the only remnants of the war. Jake Barnes, Bill Gorton, and the others turned their back on history—on what Eliot's Gerontion was calling history's "reconsidered passions in memory only," not to mention her "many cunning passages, contrived corridors / and issues." Barnes and his group were not interested in the warmed-over passions of a past on which the sun had set.

By retreating from history as they did, Barnes and a few others of Hemingway's characters envisioned another sun, an asocietal sun, rising on something that was *not* lost and could never be lost—specifically, on nature and on certain art forms that imitate nature. Both nature and art transcend what Eliot's Gerontion perceived as the "cunning passages" and "contrived corridors" of history. The second quote in Hemingway's epigraph confirms the *un*lostness of these two resources of recovery for the lost citizens of a world betrayed by history. The quote from Ecclesiastes says, "One generation passeth away, and another generation cometh; but the earth abideth forever," an "earth" that for Hemingway translated into Nature and her grand imitator Art—Gardens of Eden, both of them, as it were.

Pedro Romero, the matador, is Hemingway's quintessential earthman *and* artist whose grand archetypal presence in the universe "abideth forever" along with the wind, the rivers, and the sea. He is an artist whose creative genius Hemingway views as coming from nature rather than from culture and history. As Keneth Kinnamon asserts, "The only completely admirable character in *The Sun Also Rises* is the young matador, Pedro Romero, whom Hemingway patterned after the contemporary Niño de la Palma and named for a great eighteenth-century matador. Thus the bullfighter had become a prototype of the Hemingway hero very early."[10] Barnes as a kind of novelist himself reveals the qualities of that prototype in a prose as simple, natural, and pure as the lines and movements he is attributing to Romero himself:

> The dampened, mud-weighted cape swung open and full as a sail fills, and Romero pivoted with it just ahead of the bull. At the end of the pass they were facing each other again. Romero smiled. The bull wanted it again, and Romero's cape filled again, this time on the other side. Each time he let the bull pass so close that the man and the bull and the cape that filled and pivoted ahead of the bull were all one sharply etched mass. It was all so slow and so controlled. It was as though he were rocking the bull to sleep. (217)

The flowing lines of this kinematic synthesis of man, nature, and art can be viewed as one of the symbolic "suns" that rise and shine on a Jake Barnes desensitized by (and removed from) a history without a sun. The Romero "sun" is subject, and Barnes is object. As Beongcheon Yu expresses it, "If one is not born to be a matador [himself], the next best thing, then, is to be an *aficionado* capable of appreciating the matador's art and putting in words the whole truth, the absolute truth about it."[11] Indeed, without a true a*ficionado* as object, Romero as subject would have neither a legitimate purpose nor a commitment to integrity in the execution of his art. Hemingway himself makes this point in *Death in the Afternoon*: "If a really good bullfighter is to come and remain honest, sincere, without tricks and mystifications, there must be a nucleus of spectators that he can play for when he comes," spectators indeed, Hemingway asserts in another passage, who realize "finally, [that] what they seek is honest and true, not tricked, emotion and always classicism and purity of execution."[12]

In the final analysis, the configuration of clean, rhythmic lines producing the etching of Romero and the bull, envisioned by Barnes as a synthesis of man, nature, and art, ultimately has the effect of calling Hemingway's epigraph from Stein into question. Jake is a vicarious participant in the Romero etching. Thus, rather than turning to one of Pound's broken statues or battered books from history as a predictably failing resource for recovery, Hemingway in the 1920s offers instead temporary but repeatable moments of passion to the historically "lost."

In summary, then, the point can be made that Barnes and the others in his group *are* a "lost generation" in one sense but *not* in another. They are lost in the sense that they neither intellectualize nor intuit any connections between themselves and history. But as individuals with *aficion* they are not all lost. Some of them merge with nature and/or with art outside history in the aesthetics of a Garden of Eden setting of landscapes and seascapes, bull-fights, big game hunting, swimming, fishing, and the like. In the indwelling dynamics of all of these aesthetic forms, the Romeros, Barneses, and Gortons of the world intuit and adopt vicariously a multiplicity of long-existing ritu-als, many of them seasonal and cyclic in their seemingly endless repetitions. A man of *aficion* himself, Hemingway suggests this cyclic pattern in a bril-liantly conceived spatial, directional, and geographical symbology in *The Sun Also Rises*. It works along these lines: Barnes and Gorton go south from Paris to the bullfights in Pamplona in June. Enroute they stop over in Burguete for a rendezvous with nature's frosty evenings and her peaceful afternoons when they walk through her beech woods and wild strawberry clearings to the cold brown waters of the Irati to fish for trout. Jake, immersed in *aficion*, says:

> I did not feel the first trout strike. When I started to pull up I felt that I had one and brought him, fighting and bending the rod almost dou-ble, out of the boiling water at the foot of the falls, and swung him up and onto the dam. He was a good trout, and I banged his head against the timber so that he quivered out straight, and then slipped him into my bag.
>
> ... In a little while I had six. They were all about the same size. I laid them out, side by side, all their heads pointing the same way, and looked at them. They were beautifully colored and firm and hard from the cold water. It was a hot day, so I slit them all and shucked out the insides, gills and all, and tossed them over across the river. I took the trout ashore, washed them in the cold, smoothly heavy water above the dam, and then picked some ferns and packed them all in the bag, three trout on a layer of ferns, then another layer of ferns, then three more trout, and then covered them with ferns. They looked nice in the ferns, and now the bag was bulky, and I put it in the shade of the tree. (119–20)

The seasonal rituals reach their climax a few days later in Pamplona in the pure art of the quintessential man of *aficion*, Pedro Romero the matador, in his *corrida* etching discussed above. After that we see Barnes enjoying a soli-tudinous reunion with nature and art at San Sebastian where his intricately described swimming rituals become a study in the aesthetics of another art form whose graceful rhythms and repetitions are modeled after those in

nature. It is Hemingway's portrait of a cynical and dissociated "lost-genera-
tion" man recovering his self-possession and his self-identity outside history
in the cyclical aesthetics of nature and art. This brief passage explains it all:

> . . . I swam out, trying to swim through the roller, but having to dive
> sometimes. Then in the quiet water I turned and floated. Floating I saw
> only the sky, and felt the drop and lift of the swells. I swam back to the
> surf and coasted in, face down, on a big roller, then turned and swam,
> trying to keep in the trough and not have a wave break over me. It
> made me feel tired, swimming in the trough, and I turned and swam
> out to the raft. The water was buoyant and cold. It felt as though you
> could never sink. I swam slowly, it seemed like a long swim with the
> high tide, and then pulled up on the raft and sat, dripping, on the
> boards that were becoming hot in the sun. . . .
>
> I sat in the sun and watched the bathers on the beach. They looked
> very small. After a while I stood up, gripped with my toes on the edge
> of the raft as it tipped with my weight, and dove cleanly and deeply, to
> come up through the lightening water, blew the salt water out of my
> head, and swam slowly and steadily in to shore. (237–38)

Soon after, Barnes takes the Sud Express to Madrid, summoned there by
Brett who is having a bad time. "The Norte station in Madrid is the end of
the line," says Barnes. "All trains finish there. They don't go on anywhere"
(239–40). The southward motion to periods of passion in the symbolic
Edenic sun of nature and art is over, for a while at least. Only the literal sun
shines now. Just before arriving at the Norte station, in the last thirty miles
of his journey from a passionate involvement with immediacy in San
Sebastian to this "end-of-the-line" rendezvous with Brett and bad memories,
Barnes says, "I saw the Escorial out of the window, gray and long and cold in
the sun, and did not give a damn about it. I saw Madrid come up over the
plain a compact white sky-line on the top of a little cliff away off across the
sun-hardened country" (239). Barnes's dispiriting stay in Madrid with Brett
is brief. He soon makes preparations to turn around, return northward to
Paris (the other end of the line), and thus to complete the seasonal and spatial run of the cycle for another year.

It will all happen again, more or less the same way, next year. There is no
sense of history repeating itself in this symbology of a man's roundtrip from
nowhere to a short but passionate "June" somewhere, then back to nowhere.
Jake Barnes is not a man who steps outside himself and then abstracts life

into a historical perspective. A journalist and therefore one who certainly has the capacity to do this, he has apparently elected not to do it because it would seem to have no bearing on what he views as the priorities of his existence. Whether man as a societal and historical being progresses, regresses, or remains static is of no concern to Barnes or anyone else in that so-called "lost generation" of his in the 1920s. They did not envision themselves as having come from some important societal "somewhere" that they had temporarily lost sight of and would find again. To historicize experience is to commit oneself to intellection and to social outwardness, not to an inward and passionate empathy with nature and the pure forms of art that imitate her. Barnes, both as man and as writer, was "lost" from history and its counterpart, an identity-providing memory. David Bourne, the much later Hemingway artist-hero of the 1950s and beyond, was not.

Like Barnes before him, Bourne is a war veteran and a writer. But unlike Barnes, Bourne's war experience has apparently not desensitized and dissociated him from a vital sense of history and its importance to his own and others' identities. He writes with a keen sensitivity to what was, what is, and what possibly will be. But Hemingway draws his portrait of Bourne with lines that are more distinct than those simply of a writer who is generally mindful of history as an indispensable and indisputable component in the working of his fictive vision of man. He goes to the extreme of making Bourne an actual historical novelist. After telling his wife Catherine that a manuscript of his that she is about to read is "a story about Africa back before the 1914 War in the time of the Maji-Maji war, the native rebellion of 1905 in Tanganyika," she says somewhat surprised, "I didn't know you wrote historical novels" (157). And David replies, "It's a story that happens in Africa when I was eight years old!" Meanwhile, it has been explained earlier that one of Bourne's published novels had to do with his experience as a flyer in the Second World War, which, though a subject of a more immediate past, was nonetheless history.

The fact is, the range of vision in Bourne's fictive imagination includes the events and myths of history and time on the one hand and the transcendent flights of an aesthete's passion on the other. And since all of Bourne's fiction, so far as we know, is autobiographical, it is as if Hemingway were saying that the Bourne sensibility can be viewed as a study in at least the collaboration if not the fusion of opposites. For it is a sensibility that balances the Jake Barnes passionate, aesthetic perspective of nature and art outside history on the one hand with the morning novel-writing Bourne's awareness that one's personal identity is inevitably and inextricably linked with history on the other.

In the 1920s Barnes was the 26-year-old Hemingway's tragic hero—"trag-ic" principally because he was the victim of a history that had betrayed him. Even this early, Hemingway perceived that a modern man who could find no link between himself and the supposed continuity of all the selves of time and history was a permanently wounded and less than whole man. But Barnes of course was nonetheless a hero in Hemingway's eyes, because, as has been explained above, he could partially compensate for history's betrayal of him by infusing his being with *aficion* and projecting himself into the ever-rising sun of imagination.

That was the early Hemingway. But the later Hemingway was envisioning in David Bourne a hero who did not view history as his betrayer and failed sponsor. Unlike Barnes—and indeed even the others in the Twenties group who had not been physically incapacitated by the war—he survived *his* war without cynicism and without dissociation, and accordingly he escapes Barnes's tragic alienation. Like Barnes, however, Bourne does have a vital capacity for *aficion*. He is, as it were, another Romero in the bullfight, anoth-er Barnes and Gorton fishing at Burguete, another Barnes diving and swim-ming at San Sebastian—indeed an offspring, like them, of Adam in the Garden of Eden untainted by history. But Bourne, unlike Barnes, also joins Adam as he steps out of Eden and takes his long walk into history. Bourne, however, unlike his prototype who was required to stay in history once expelled from Eden, *can* return from history to the Garden, and he does—again and again. There in afternoons of ecstasy he enjoys the sensual compa-ny of Catherine and Marita, his two Eves who, separated at times and togeth-er at times, join him in a series of passionate diving, swimming, and suntan-ning rituals reminiscent of Jake Barnes at San Sebastian. In short, Bourne can be seen balancing the two worlds—Eden, where imagination is infused with passion, and History, where intellection and design are infused with gravity—and doing so with relatively easy transition and self-possession.

Bourne is Hemingway's reasonably untroubled, early-morning writer of historical fiction in the mid-century, a rather different hero from the insom-niac journalist Barnes "having a bad time" at night in the 1920s. Bourne is as fulfilled when he is absorbed in memory and history while drafting his novel or story in the morning as he is when he is enjoying the company of a fellow fisherman named André (like a Bill Gorton) or a Catherine and Marita in the afternoon. He is a composite of the Adam before the Fall and the Adam after the Fall, and his world is a composite of the forms and rhythms of an Edenic nature and art on the one hand and the complex and perplexing doings of men in history outside Eden on the other.

The fact is, journeying into memory and history and perceiving their importance is a major commitment of Bourne the writer, and it involves a quest, moreover, that extends both into socio-political history (war) and personal history. Like Hemingway himself, Bourne writes of wars at the same time he writes of men's personal histories. But the images his journeying into the past evokes are of no interest to him simply as academic views of history, for ultimately he transforms them into fictive myth and therefore to a vision that is beyond history. More to the point of what goes on in Bourne's creatively activated consciousness and unconscious, however, is the fact that when imagination is strong—as it must be—it tunes out the present. It is like the wind sweeping in on the conscious mind and keeping it in a holding pattern in memory. Bourne himself describes it in this interesting way: "It was the third day of the wind. . . . He went on with the story, living in it and nowhere else, and when he heard the voices of the two girls outside he did not listen. . . . He was completely detached from everything except the story he was writing and he was living in it as he built it" (107). The passage shows the reader a David Bourne who has abandoned the present and entered history, but who has done so in the peculiar manner of a historical fictionist rather than in the conventional manner of a historian. That is, he has proceeded by joining will with imagination rather than by joining will with reason. And consequently he moves by intellection through history and then out of it into myth where he is in touch with universals.

Robert O. Stephens, probably unaware of a character named David Bourne hidden away in an unpublished manuscript when he, Stephens, was writing about Hemingway the writer not long after his death in the 1960s, comments pertinently as follows: "Hemingway's aim was imaginative rather than reportorial writing. . . . Created truth [he insisted] transcends facts or any logical inferences to be drawn from facts. What the exact nature of that truth is, he never said and apparently would not analyze it for fear he would dissipate it in the process. . . . If one accurately rendered an honest vision, [Hemingway] noted in *The Green Hills of Africa* [27], he could get 'a fourth and fifth dimension' in his created reality. Timelessness or permanence was one of these dimensions, and it would prevent the vision from dissipating."[13] And Hemingway himself comments in a 1935 essay, "Nobody knows a damned thing about [imagination] except that it is what we get for nothing.[14]

Bourne rather cryptically explains the process to Marita after she asks about his writing, "Was it difficult today?" He replies, "It is always difficult but it's easy too!" (140). The difficult part is the first part—that is, the forcing of his will upon the images he draws from memory in the attempt to order them into fictive design. The "easy" part is the second part—that is, letting his imagination somehow do the job for him in a kind of extrasensory step out of time and into spontaneous perception. Marita goes on to say, "I wish I could help," and Bourne the professional novelist says, "Nobody can help." This is the writer/visionary David Bourne who—outside the unhistoricized present where Marita his critic exists and also outside the unhistoricized *aficion* of his afternoons in Eden where Marita his Eve exists—ties into history and then transmutes his vision of it into myth. The process is conducted alone.

This exclusivity of the insulated writer at work is apprehended by Bourne when he comes out of its peculiar isolation, returns to the present, and observes in surprise that as he and Marita "held each other. . . . he had not known just how greatly he had been divided and separated because once he started to work he wrote from an inner core which could not be split nor even marked nor scratched. He knew about this and it was his strength since all the rest of him could be riven" (183), as indeed is now happening to him as he surrenders his concentration, his intellection, and his designing imagination to his Eve in the Garden. They take flight into *aficion* where the Edenic pleasures are immediate and thus have nothing to do with memory and history. Bourne acknowledges his dependence on his Eve to take him to the Garden. After having told Marita that "Nobody can help" a writer who is working out of his memory, Marita looks at her Adam and says, "But I can help in other things can't I?" And Bourne replies, "You have and you do." Eve can and she does take her Adam out of history and back into Eden where time stops for him as he shifts roles from writer to diver, swimmer, and lover in this one of several such scenes:

> . . . As she watched him and waded, the water came over her belly and touched her breasts and he straightened, rose on his toes, seemed to hang slowly without falling and then knifed out and down, making a boil in the water that a porpoise might have made reentering slickly into the hole that he had made in rising. She swam out toward the circle of milling water and then he rose beside her and held her up and close and then put his salty mouth against her own.
> "*Elle est bonne, la mer*," he said. "*Toi aussi.*"

> They swam out of the cove and beyond into the deep water past where the mountain dropped down into the sea, and lay on their backs and floated. . . . Her eyes were shut against the sun and David was

beside her in the water. His arm was under her head and then he kissed
the tip of her left breast and then the other breast. (241)

It is another one of Bourne's afternoon returns to the Garden of Eden, and it
refreshes him for his next morning's reentry into memory and imagination.

One unfamiliar with the book might mistakenly assume that this scene of
aficion, coming almost at the end of the novel as it does, is projected by
Hemingway as a culmination in the evolution of his hero's sensibility, that a
latent passion is now blossoming in Bourne and his journey into complexity is nearing completion. Of course that is not the point at all; the scene is
just one of many in which Bourne's seasoned involvement with *aficion* is
depicted. Indeed in the very first scene of the novel Hemingway gives an
elaborate four-page description of Bourne and a hotel waiter named André
combining their skills and sharing their passions in landing a giant sea bass,
"the biggest one I've ever seen," says André, "Oh what a wonderful fish!" The
ritual begins with Bourne getting a strike while pole-fishing from the edge of
a jetty; it continues with André's excited instruction that takes him and
Bourne and the fish all the way out to the end of the jetty, then down the full
length of its other side and around the perimeter of the jetty again. It ends
finally with Bourne and his guide exhausted and exhilarated at the completion of the grand ritual as Bourne lands the fish on the shore of the canal
with crowds of onlookers cheering and congratulating and embracing him.
The passage is Hemingway at his descriptive best and has the same high-spirited sense of the perfect forms of a performing art as he displayed in the
Romero bullfighting scenes in Pamplona.

What Hemingway has shown in Bourne so far, then, is something of a
dualist, a man with the capacity to live and enjoy the essences of two very different worlds—thus to operate from two different sensibilities—but to do so
separately, the one metaphorized as his "mornings," the other as his "afternoons." He can be what Jake Barnes could not be—a post-war hero who is not
of a "lost generation"—and he can be what Barnes and only a very few others
of his kind could (and can) be—a hero in the "sun" of *aficion*. Bourne's passage from one to the other is only rarely problematic, and it is never viewed
by Hemingway as hazardous. But that relative ease in going from morning to
afternoon and back to morning notwithstanding, Bourne as portrait of
Hemingway's emergent hero of mid-century and beyond is not complete until
he has moved from dualist to monist—until, that is, he has merged his morning and his afternoon sensibilities into a higher and more complex one that is
inclusive of, but no longer defined by, each of its component parts. Until that

fusion takes place, Bourne's mornings of memory and history can never share in any of his afternoons of *aficion* and immediacy. The two at best would merely be tangential. To give it its due, that dualist mode has had its appeal for Bourne, for neither sensibility has gotten in the way of the other. Bourne has not been trafficking in a frustrated ambivalence but rather in a pattern of mutual exchange. But approving of his mode as he apparently is, Hemingway is also envisioning in this book a new and more sophisticated landscape and seascape of imagination, one that becomes in effect a new Garden of Eden. Its unique hallmark is that each of the opposites surrenders its discreteness and allows itself to be assimilated into a higher, more refined and complex quality of sensitivity and perceptivity. Hemingway gives the careful reader the evidence necessary to perceive the emergence of this heightened state of mind.

In a conversation between Bourne and Marita concerning the state of Bourne's creative mind while he was drafting his historical (and autobiographical) novel about flying in the war, she says, "Now I've read it, but I don't understand about you. You never made clear what you believed." Bourne replies, "I didn't know until afterwards. So [at the time] I didn't try to act as though I did. I suspended thinking about it while it was happening. I only felt and saw. . . . I wasn't . . . intelligent [about it]" (184). Bourne's point is that, for a writer of historical fiction to go into memory and history with creative energy, he must experience a union of his two highest faculties: his imagination and his passion. Marita, tempering her criticism, says in the same conversation, "It is a very good book. The flying parts are wonderful and the feeling for the other people and for the planes themselves." And Bourne replies, "I'm good on other people. . . . But, Marita, nobody knows about himself when he is really involved. Yourself isn't worth considering. It would be shameful at the time." It would be shameful, Bourne realizes, because *aficion* is a phenomenon both of the unconscious and of feeling and therefore resists any process of self-translation at the time it is happening. And it is happening for Bourne in the mornings of his creative journeyings into history and memory. That precisely is his point: he doesn't save "passion" for his afternoons. Marita, obviously interested in this fusion of two creative faculties, adds, "But afterwards you know." "Sure. Sometimes," Bourne answers (184). This fusion of instinct, feeling, and intuition on the one hand, and a capacity for disciplined analysis on the other, is reflected in John Reardon's observation that, for Hemingway, a writer had to discover "what he truly felt rather than what he was supposed to feel, and what facts and actions produced that feeling, and how he might express it in a way that will not cheat it and will last" (15).

This process that requires that what is perceived is also felt is objectified and certified by Hemingway again as he takes the reader into the psychological center of another of Bourne's creative projects. On this occasion it is Bourne the man reentering his personal history as he writes a narrative about his boyhood when he was on an elephant hunt with his father and a native named Juma. Bourne says, "It was a very young boy's story, he knew, when he had finished it. He read it over and saw the gaps he must fill in to make it so that whoever read it would feel it was truly happening as it was read" (201). It may be inferred from this statement that Bourne senses that *most* of the story already has this quality of immediacy infused into it—that is, the reader's sense of being taken into the matrix of the author's emotional sensibility at the time he wrote the first draft. Bourne, a professional who writes with confidence, awareness of his craft and his creative temperament, most of the time, knows afterwards, while critiquing his own work, when he has and when he has not accomplished this fusion of a particular memory with its corresponding emotional intensity. The gaps, then, must be filled in where he has failed to dehistoricize memory through this complex fusing process. And in the very last paragraph of the novel Bourne apparently feels that he has filled in the gaps and can thus say with modest triumph about his story: "Not a sentence was missing and there were many that he put down as they were returned to him without changing them. . . . He wrote on a while longer now and there was no sign that any of it would ever cease returning to him intact" (247).

The morning mind trips into memory and the afternoon flights into passion have come together and taken him to a new Garden of Eden where imagination—"the third day of the wind"—has done its special kind of magic and achieved for him the highest goal of the mythmaker: the fusion of historical vision and memory with immediacy and passion.

Notes

1. Lorian Hemingway, "Ernest Hemingway's Farewell to Art," *Rolling Stone*, 5 June 1986, 72.
2. Allen Josephs. "In Papa's Garden," *The Boston Review* (June 1986), 20; rpt. *The Hemingway Review* 6 (1986): 113. Citations are from the reprint.
3. Wilfrid Sheed, "A Farewell to Hemingstein," *The New York Review of Books*, 12 June 1986, 6.
4. Ernest Hemingway, *The Garden of Eden* (New York: Scribner's, 1986). Subsequent citations are from this edition.

5. See Josephs, 112, and Lorian Hemingway, 42.
6. John Reardon, "Hemingway's Esthetic and Ethical Sportsmen," *The University Review* 34 (1967): 14.
7. Ernest Hemingway, *The Green Hills of Africa* (New York: Scribner's, 1935), 21.
8. In *The Sun Also Rises* Hemingway himself defines *aficion*: "Aficion means passion. An aficionado is one who is passionate about the bull-fights" (131). For an interesting discussion of the implications and nuances that are embedded in the concept of *aficion* as it relates to Hemingway's aesthetic and his perspective on the hero, see Earl Rovit and Gerry Brenner, *Ernest Hemingway* (Boston: Twayne, 1986), 136–38.
9. I have found quite interesting Joseph Epstein's suggestion that what Stein really said was "louche géneration" —that is, a dubious, slightly crooked generation: "Ephemeral Verities," *American Scholar* 49 (1979–80). Hemingway scholarship to my knowledge has not responded to the suggestion, either in terms of documenting or discrediting its authenticity or of speculating on its possible implications. Where my argument in this essay is concerned, I do not believe the difference between "lost" and "dubious" is significant, since a sense of dissociation is present in both. The difference could have some bearing on a number of other interpretations, however.
10. Keneth Kinnamon, "Hemingway, the Corrida, and Spain," *Texas Studies in Literature and Language* 1 (1959): 47.
11. Beongcheon Yu, "The Still Center of Hemingway's World," *Phoenix* (Korea) 12 (1968): 16.
12. Ernest Hemingway, *Death in the Afternoon* (New York: Scribner's, 1932), 163 and 12, respectively.
13. Robert O. Stephens, *Hemingway's Nonfiction: The Public Voice* (Chapel Hill: U of North Carolina P, 1968), 205.
14. Ernest Hemingway, "Monologue to the Maestro," *Esquire* (Oct. 1935), 21.

THE ENDINGS OF HEMINGWAY'S
GARDEN OF EDEN

Robert E. Fleming

B ibliographical purists may never be happy with the concept of a posthumous novel edited by someone other than the author. Nor are scholars the only ones who have such reservations. Even Jack Hemingway, who stands to gain financially from the posthumous publication of his father's works, has remarked, "Much of the posthumous work would have been rejected out of hand by [Hemingway's] own critical faculty without extensive rewriting—cutting and pruning he would have refused to have anyone do but himself."[1] Jack's brother Patrick, feeling ambivalent about the publication of the unfinished works, stresses the importance of readers' remembering that the posthumous works were never edited into final form by Hemingway himself.[2] Nevertheless, most readers are grateful to Tom Jenks, the Scribner editor who put the large manuscript into publishable shape so that all might see new facets of a standard American author.

An examination of the manuscript of *The Garden of Eden* suggests that Jenks probably performed his job as well as nearly anyone but Hemingway himself could have done. That job, like that of a novelist, was not to provide a definitive text with notes and tables of variant readings but to produce a

---

Reprinted with permission from American Literature *(May 1989), pp. 261–270.*

readable story in which the major themes come together to make a coherent statement about life. Jenks got most of the good material that was in the manuscript and cut out many distracting elements. Yet in handling the ending of the novel, Jenks departed radically from Hemingway's express intentions.

Anyone reading *The Garden of Eden* must be struck by the difference between the optimism of its final chapter and the endings of any other Hemingway novel. Jake Barnes's bitterly ironic reply to Brett Ashley in *The Sun Also Rises*, Frederic Henry's solitary walk back to his hotel in the rain in *A Farewell to Arms*, Robert Jordan's preparations for death in *For Whom the Bell Tolls*, and even Santiago's moral victory in the face of ostensible defeat in *The Old Man and the Sea*—all seem to have little in common with the optimism of chapter 30 of *The Garden of Eden*, in which David Bourne discovers that the sentences of his destroyed story "came to him complete and entire and he put them down, corrected them, and cut them as if he were going over proof. Not a sentence was missing and there were many that he put down as they were returned to him without changing them."[3] Some who know Hemingway's canon very well might have wondered whether Jenks had not concocted this optimistic ending on his own. Such is not the case, but neither is it true that Hemingway wrote the passage as the ending of the novel.

I

Before discussing a section of the manuscript that would have concluded the novel in a typically tragic Hemingway fashion or the parts of the manuscript which Hemingway labeled "Provisional Ending," it is necessary to sketch the dimensions of the manuscript novel and suggest the difficulties facing any editor, difficulties which so baffled the aging Hemingway that he was unable to complete the work.

The Garden of Eden manuscript contains three separate story lines concerning marital betrayal, sexual role-playing, and conflict between artistic commitment and human commitments; the most consistent and nearly complete of these was chosen by Jenks for publication.[4] In the Jenks edition, which might be termed the Bourne plot, David and Catherine Bourne's marriage is shattered by Catherine's approaching insanity, by David's obsessive devotion to his writing, and by the introduction of a new partner, Marita, into the relationship, creating a *ménage à trois*. But Hemingway actually wrote two variations on this marital triangle theme, and no definitive evidence in the manuscript suggests that he made a final decision to eliminate the two additional plots completely.

Alternate plot one can be called the Sheldon variant. In this version, the opening of Book Two introduces Nick Sheldon, a painter who knows the Bournes from Paris. He and his wife Barbara have played sexual reversal games much like those played by the Bournes in the published novel. For example, Barbara has persuaded Nick to let his thick black hair grow as long as hers—to shoulder length—although Nick complains that it makes him feel like a homosexual. Barbara, who has dabbled in painting, has no intellectual or artistic interest in life and displays the same sort of emotional instability that Catherine exhibits. David and Catherine meet Nick and Barbara in Biarritz. Catherine is fascinated by the bizarre appearance of the Sheldons, especially Barbara, and David is interested enough in the pair to begin a story about them. When David encounters Barbara at a cafe, she warns him that she is infatuated with Catherine, in whom she sees lesbian tendencies, and that if he loves Catherine, he'll get her out of town quickly. She also alludes to a character named Andy.

Andrew Murray is a central figure in what might be called the Murray variant. His plot appears intertwined with both the Bourne and Sheldon plots. In the former, Andy meets Catherine and David soon after they travel to Spain. Like David, he is a writer of integrity, interested in doing his best work whether or not it sells. Having inherited a small amount of money, Andy lives frugally in Europe while he attempts to become self-supporting through his art. Andy is something of a moralist, accusing David of "corrupting" Catherine by introducing her to Pernod and fast cars such as the Bugatti they drive (422a-7, pp. 1, 9). Catherine likes Andy at first but later dismisses him as too wholesome an influence (422a-8, p. 3). David assumes that Andy is in love with Barbara although she is not interested in him.

When the Sheldon plot meshes with the Murray plot, however, things take a tragic turn. Andy meets Nick and Barbara at Hendaye, and Barbara tries to persuade Andy to let his hair grow to match hers and Nick's. According to the symbolism throughout the novel, this is the opening ploy in a seduction. Barbara also shows signs of emotional instability: Andy views her paintings and finds them "very close to the edge" (422a.3, p. 19) while Barbara wonders if she is losing her mind. Like Catherine in the published novel, who encourages David to write an account of their life together, Barbara is eager for Andy to write the story of Nick, her, and himself, and she plans to take photographs to illustrate the book. One day when Nick is painting outside of town, Barbara comes to Andy's room and seduces him. Afterward she displays extreme remorse, drinking absinthe and denying that the sexual encounter took place. The next time Nick is away, however, she returns to

Andy's room and sleeps with him again. This time she feels less immediate remorse, but when two gendarmes come to report that Nick has been killed by a car, her latent guilt causes her to crack up completely. This is the background of a tragic draft ending for the novel which Jenks ignored in his editing.

None of these plot lines is as simple and distinct as the above synopses might suggest. Hemingway worked through a number of variations of the three plots and experimented with the characters in different roles. For example, in the Murray plot line just summarized, Nick's wife is first named Catherine, and that name is cancelled and replaced with Barbara. Later, when Barbara is talking to Andy, she mentions Catherine as a character in her own right and criticizes her destructive nature.

II

In one possible ending of the novel, Andy is writing the story of the aftermath of Nick's death. When the gendarmes questioned Barbara about Nick to complete their reports, she could not talk but was finally able to answer their questions in writing. At the funeral, she went to the graveyard but was unable to go to the gravesite with Andy. Afterward her depression was readily apparent to Andy:

> She did not talk for more than a week. She was in a nursing home with a good doctor and day and night nurses. She would hold my hand but would not look at me. After about two weeks her sister came over from America but she wouldn't see her. She saw her sister finally but asked her not to come back. The legal thing went on and on and she paid no attention to it. I did it all with the lawyers. She signed what I told her to sign. (422b.4, p. 46)

Andy attempted to help Barbara recover by taking her to Paris, then to Italy. Later he reflects that he should have taken her to Switzerland for treatment, "but she would not go. There was only one thing that she wanted and that was . . . not to go to a sanitarium or a hospital" (422b.4, p. 47). Andy vowed to take care of her while his money held out. In Italy they lived in adjoining rooms, eating together and going for walks. Finally Barbara seemed to emerge from her depression. She talked to Andy long into the night for two weeks. When they reached Venice, Andy was confident that she was recovering.

One night Andy left Barbara alone at the hotel. She had seemed to have a happy day and assured him that she was all right. When he returned, their rooms were empty, and Barbara had left him a note. Hemingway had a hard time composing the suicide note, writing three separate versions, and two variations exist even in the typescript. In one note, Barbara took an overdose of sleeping pills, while in another she drowned herself. The letter begins:

Dear Andy

Thank you very much. I know you'll write it very well. Not the marked down to $1.69 one. The short one. The monograph. I wish we had taken the snapshots though. . . . I was dead Andy of course. I know you will excuse it. People are so self-centered and it was kind of you to make me well so I could see what I should do. (422b.4, p. 49)

The first conclusion says that Barbara knew she was doing an "intelligent and proper" thing and hoped that the fact that she had saved up her legally pre-scribed sleeping pills for a month would keep the unpleasantness of the police investigation to a minimum. She urged Andy again to complete the book he was writing about the three of them and to look for any old snap-shots he could find to illustrate it. The second version suggests that she has drowned herself and emphasizes the cheerfulness of the day, its bright sun-shine and the cleanliness of the water that day when the tides were high in Venice; Barbara had not wanted to think of drowning herself in filthy water. She hoped her suicide would not cause Venice to have unpleasant associa-tions for Andy.

The segment on Barbara's suicide could not have served Jenks as an end-ing for *The Garden of Eden* if he followed the principle established by Mary Hemingway and Charles Scribner, Jr., to add nothing to the posthumous manuscripts in the course of editing them for publication.[5] It is probable, however, that at some point Hemingway considered Barbara's suicide as a possible ending. The holograph manuscript has the name Catherine signed to the suicide note; it is crossed out and Barbara is substituted. In the pub-lished novel Jenks retained the idea that Catherine might become suicidal. When she leaves David and Marita at the rural hotel, David insists that she take the train, not the Bugatti. The recklessness of her driving has convinced him that she may kill herself on the road either deliberately or in response to subconscious impulses. Like Catherine, Barbara is deeply committed to the idea of a written record of her love affair and to its illustrations. Catherine attempts to commission painters to illustrate the account David is writing, and Barbara is similarly obsessed with photographs. The two women are essentially versions of a single creation.

The passage depicting Barbara's suicide is in keeping with other Hemingway endings. Like Catherine Barkley at the end of *A Farewell to Arms*, Barbara dies and leaves Andy the sadder but wiser protagonist who must ponder the meaning of their love affair. Like Jake Barnes, Andy attempts to write the story to gain a better perspective. The importance of the suicide note, which Hemingway had to write three times, will not be lost on critics inclined to the biographical approach.

III

Hemingway's "Provisional Ending" would have concluded on an ironic note but with somber hints of tragedy to come. After Catherine has destroyed the manuscripts and left David and Marita alone, David acknowledges that, in spite of everything, he still loves Catherine and feels responsible for her well-being. Although David and Marita would prefer to go to Africa, they discuss taking Catherine to Switzerland to a mental sanitarium where she can be cured. At that point the manuscript does not indicate whether Catherine actually will return to David. Hemingway might have intended to write more material to explain what happened next, but his labelling the seven-page final chapter "Provisional Ending" makes it seem more probably that he felt that he could drop the story at the point where Catherine might return and then append the ending, using its abruptness for its shock value. There are, after all, similar gaps of time between some of the books in the earlier parts of the novel.

The provisional ending begins with a man and a woman revisiting the south of France. The woman says that what happened there "seems so long ago," and that they were "strange children" (422b.5, p. 1) then. They lie in the sun on the beach and reminisce about their trip to Madrid and the sexual games they played so that eventually the reader realizes that it is Catherine, not Marita, who is with David. Attempting to blot out the tragedies the couple has endured, Catherine talks about how "comic" things were in the old days, but David's response is restrained irony: "We were a yell of laughter" (p. 1).

As the chapter progresses, it becomes apparent that David has become a caretaker as well as a husband; he resembles Fitzgerald's Dick Diver. His ministrations to Catherine, coating her body with oil to keep her from burning and telling her when to move out of the sun or when to enter the water to cool off, are clinical. David and Catherine's relationship has become a parody of the one they shared in the early pages of the novel, furthering the theme that the discovery of evil makes it impossible to dwell in the Garden of Eden.

Other manifestations of the lost Eden are evident in this ending. David rubs oil into Catherine's breasts, a lover's action in the early chapters but a nurse's ministration in this ending. Catherine reflects the same clinical attitude when she looks down at her breasts and observes, "They're still good. . . . Though good for what is something else" (p. 2). The suggestion is that her breasts no longer attract David nor will they ever feed a child in this sterile marriage. Catherine has to acknowledge the losses they have suffered, asking David, "Why did we run out of things? There was everything and we ran through it in a year? (p. 3). Later she asks David if he remembers the time when "I used to talk about anything and everything and we owned the world?" (p. 4).

Gradually, it becomes apparent that Catherine still shows signs of her mental illness. She forgets major details of their life together, saying that it was too bad they never went to Africa, though David reminds her that they have been there. Too often she refers inappropriately to "comic" things in life; love is a comic word, old friends are recalled as comic characters; finally she reassures David that she "won't try anything comic. . . . You don't have to worry about that" (p. 4). Evidently one of her "comic" tricks has been a suicide attempt.

David tries to reassure Catherine. When she talks of having gone away, he tells her that she has come back.

> "Not really."
> "Yes you did and you will."
> "Not really. They don't know. They just say they know. That's all Switzerland is except cows and timepieces and goiters is people that don't know saying they know. Next time it will be worse."
> "They learn new things all the time. They really are lea[r]ning."
> "Too late for me. Don't let's be comic." (P. 5)

Catherine finally tells David she loves him, then asks him to promise her something without asking what it is. Even though David knows what the promise will entail, he agrees. Catherine's request is a predictable one.

> "If it goes bad again so I'd have to go back to the place can I, may I, do it the way Barbara did? I don't mean in a dirty place like Venice."
> "I couldn't let you."
> "Would you do it with me?"

"Sure."
"I knew you would," she said. "That's why I didn't like to ask." (P. 7)

She tries to reassure David that she will probably never ask him to join her in death, and in the end, the two agree to go for a swim, but experienced readers of Hemingway will not be reassured.

The fact that this ending was labelled "provisional" by Hemingway suggests that he had some reservations about it, but it is more artistic than the story of Barbara's suicide. Rather than closing with a shocking incident involving violent death, this ending would have concluded with the sort of falling action more in keeping with the rest of the novel. It would have had the advantage, like so much of Hemingway's work, of leaving many important facts beneath the surface of the story like the unseen portion of an iceberg so that the reader must infer their existence and their exact nature. Like the open ending of *The Sun Also Rises*, the provisional ending would have left many questions about the future of the major characters unanswered, perhaps a virtue in itself.

IV

The Jenks edition of *The Garden of Eden* has rendered a valuable service to Hemingway readers and scholars and should be acknowledged for the good work that it contains. However, in the handling of the ending, Jenks altered the novel so that it runs counter to the pattern of tragedy Hemingway had been preparing as he worked through the different versions of the massive manuscript. For Hemingway had very deliberately been constructing a tragic novel with his multiple tales of betrayal, jealousy, and guilt. Even in the simplified version as published, the only discernible direction of events leads toward tragedy. Catherine's growing sexual instability, her increasing jealousy of David's work, and her introduction of Marita into the Bournes' marriage—all prepare the reader for a darker conclusion than the soothing ending that sees Catherine out of the picture, David blessed with a new supportive mate, and the lost manuscripts freely flowing out of his memory and onto the paper.

Hemingway wrote chapter 30, in which all these positive things happen, but he wrote it only to intensify the shock of an ironic ending that would remind readers of a theme that had resounded through his work from its beginning: In the real life of the twentieth century, the winner takes nothing.

Notes

1. *Misadventures of a Fly Fisherman: My Life With and Without Papa* (New York: McGraw-Hill, 1987), p. 322.
2. Patrick Hemingway, in conversation with members of the Hemingway Society, 29 December 1987, Corte Madera, California.
3. *The Garden of Eden* (New York: Scribner's, 1986), p. 247. Hemingway was not usually so sanguine on the subject of lost manuscripts. In *A Moveable Feast* he lamented that he was unable to rewrite the stories stolen from Hadley or to write anything for some time after the loss—(New York: Scribner's, 1964), pp. 73–75. In an unpublished section of *Islands in the Stream* writer Roger Davis, who suffered a loss similar to Hemingway's, can never reconstruct the lost stories, and like Hemingway was inconsolable for a long time—Item 102–3, pp. 30–43, Ernest Hemingway Collection, John F. Kennedy Library, Boston.
4. *The Garden of Eden* manuscripts in the Ernest Hemingway Collection at the John F. Kennedy Library are not yet as fully catalogued as the other materials, and their temporary cataloguing system does not follow the same format as that for the other materials in the collection. The manuscript is broken down into the following categories:
    1. Item 422. Twenty-six pages of miscellaneous notes and fragments, all holograph except for a single page of typescript.
    2. Item 422a-1 through 422a-37. Folders containing all manuscripts from Book One, Chapter One through Book Three, Chapter Forty-six, mostly holograph, with a few pages of typescript heavily corrected with pencil in Hemingway's hand. This material, 1117 pages, covers the same ground as the published version of *Garden of Eden*: Book One, Chapter One through Book Four, Chapter Thirty, as well as much of the material on Nick and Barbara Sheldon and Andy Murray.
    3. Items 422a.1 through 422a.5, an additional 69 pages of holograph, consist of the "Provisional Ending" and four separate stories involving Nick, Barbara, and Andy.
    4. Items 422b-1 and 422b-16 are a 459-page typescript, partially corrected, of Items 422a-1 through 37.
    5. Items 422b.4 and 422b.5 are a 58-page typescript of the holograph Items 422a.1 through 422a.5.
    6. Ten folders of miscellaneous fragments, 130 pages in all. All references to the manuscript employ the Kennedy item numbers and are inserted parenthetically in the text. Previously unpublished material included in this article is copyright 1988 by the Ernest Hemingway Foundation and is printed by permission.

5.   See the headnote to *Islands in the Stream* (New York: Scribner's, 1970), p. [vii],
     and Mary Hemingway, *How It Was* (New York: Knopf, 1976), p. 520. Whether
     Mary Hemingway scrupulously followed her own principles has been ques-
     tioned by Gerry Brenner in "Are We Going to Hemingway's *Feast?*" *American
     Literature*, 54 (1982), 528–44.

HEMINGWAY'S *THE GARDEN OF EDEN:* WRITING WITH THE BODY

Kathy Willingham

"Gentlemen, you are criticizing my arithmetic when I am long ago into calculus."

—Hemingway[1]

Though critics sympathize with the character of Catherine and with feminist concerns in general, response to *The Garden of Eden* still largely fails to acknowledge the significance of Hemingway's theoretical prescience in terms of a feminist hermeneutic. A close examination of the novel reveals that *Garden* clearly addresses a number of issues receiving increasing amounts of attention from a diverse range of perspectives, namely gender roles and particularly questions concerning the relationship between gender and creative processes such as authorship. The novel, seen alone or in tandem with the manuscript, not only serves as an exemplum of the debilitating anxieties which the woman artist experiences, but also prefigures many contemporary theories concerning *l'écriture féminine*, as articulated in particular by Hélène Cixous. Viewed from this perspective, *Garden* not only contributes to our understanding of important gender-related issues, but moreover demands a revaluation of Hemingway's literary treatment of women, for *Garden* vividly calls into question previous critical charges of misogyny.

As numerous critics have pointed out, a major focus of both the published version of *Garden* and the original drafts pertains to artistry and creativity. Moreover, the novel explores the evolution of the characters' creative impulses from psychic or libidinal origins to practical or actual manifestations. On one hand, *Garden* offers access to the creative life of the novelist, David Bourne. Not only do we witness his struggle with such external obstacles as financial and marital considerations, but we are also privy to the internal or psychological variables. As I have previously suggested in "*The Garden of Eden:* Challenging Faulkner's Family Romance," Bourne engages in a psychic process which Richard H. King terms "monumental historical consciousness," whereby the individual, particularly the writer, "works through" a psychic/creative dilemma. Of historical consciousness, King says that it involves "repetition and recollection, the allure of the family romance, the difficult attempt to tell one's story and to be freed of the burden of the past . . . " (10). As evidenced by the interpolated African tale, Bourne painfully but successfully transcends his psychological heritage, and his demystification of these psychic dilemmas enables him to tell his story.

It is important to note, though, that Bourne's struggle with authorship constitutes only a portion of *Garden*'s plot, for Hemingway comments equally on Catherine's artistic odyssey. His treatment of Catherine reveals several surprising insights into the creative struggles of the female artist. Catherine clearly desires to be an artist, yet is riddled by feelings of inadequacy. She manifests, in fact, an attitude about authorship which clearly resembles the findings by Cixous throughout her *oeuvre* and by Sandra M. Gilbert and Susan Gubar in "Infection in the Sentence: The Woman Writer and the Anxiety of Authorship." Catherine's suffering and presumed descent into madness relate directly to her debilitating insecurities in the face of the patriarchal dominance of the arts.

Throughout the novel Catherine struggles heroically to legitimize her creativity, and she does so by using her physical body. Repeatedly the novel demonstrates her sense of inadequacy regarding the employment of language. Having no confidence in, nor because of her gender, full access to the traditionally male-controlled tool of literature, she turns to an alternative medium of expression—her own body. She literally embraces the avenue of artistic expression which *l'écriture féminine* advocates. Catherine creates a text, not with language, but with her body, as signified by such actions as cutting and bleaching her hair and insisting, first, on a transsexual relationship with her husband and, later, on a *ménage à trois* involving Marita. Moreover, all these actions signify what French feminist theorists call "*jouissance*."

Catherine expects David to act as a scribe. That is, she wants him to transfer to paper or to translate into language the story that she physically creates, and she provides the plot by living it moment to moment. Catherine's refusal to write the text herself can be explained not only by Cixous' belief that the phallocentric control of letters produces insecurity in the female writer, but also by two other interrelated Cixousian positions—the idea that the female libido and not the written word best expresses reality, and the aversion to text reification. Cixous' writing has produced its own body of criticism, and succinct descriptions of her theories by Leslie W. Rabine and Morag Shiach show why her feminist hermeneutic seems tailor-made for interpreting Hemingway's Catherine. According to Rabine, Cixous aspires to create a language which is "non-phallic" and "non-fetishistic" (42), realizing the contradiction if not impossibility of such a task. Cixous thoughtfully assesses her "'relation to the law of meaning in language'" and recognizes, says Rabine, the inability of written discourse to mirror reality accurately (38). Rabine argues that for Cixous, "the only reality is that spoken by the feminine unconsciousness and its drives" (38). As Cixous says, "woman's flesh speaks true" ("Sorties" 92). Cixous flatly rejects the mind over body hierarchy in Western thought and emphasizes, as Morag Shiach says, that "writing is produced, and understood, in relation to the body" (70). Shiach adds, "This interest in the relation between language and the body leads her to an engagement with the unconscious, as the locus of that which has been repressed by the brutal severing of the corporeal and the linguistic, and by the very process of sexual differentiation" (70).

Although Cixous believes that the ultimate text is the libidinal one, she nevertheless recognizes the need to employ, manipulate, and sabotage the very language system which she knows paradoxically entraps her. Catherine's refusal to write the text herself could, therefore, be interpreted as a purist affirmation of the belief in the libido's ability, as opposed to the written word, to articulate truth. Catherine cares little for how the text actually reads, just one indication that she privileges a libidinal text over a written one.

Cixous sees publishing as a phallocentric tool within a "biblicocapitalist society" (95). She understands but simultaneously dislikes that her work will be "transformed from a writerly process into a 'published text,' a book, an object of exchange, fetish or false phallus, that consumers will treat as a mirror of an objectified author" (Rabine 42). In *Garden* Catherine reflects a similar point of view about text fetishism and publishing. For instance, she objects to David's tendency to fetishize his clippings, and in one very telling scene says, "but what are you to do if you discover that the man's illiterate and practices solitary vice in a wastebasket full of clippings ... " (216). That she wishes to avoid reification of her own creative output is indicated by her resistance to writing her text herself and by her initial reluctance to publish the text.

Catherine's attitudes towards her text by no means signify an indifference on her part. Upon discovering that David has abandoned the task of transcribing her text and chosen, instead, to work on a narrative of his own creation, she destroys his manuscripts. Without question, this act (as well as all others leading up to this point) is subversive, yet as such it fulfills the central criterion which Cixous insists is integral to the creation of a feminine text. Cixous emphatically maintains that a feminine text must sabotage phallogocentrism, and a primary agenda of a feminine text is to "smash everything, to shatter the framework of institutions, to blow up the law, to break up the 'truth' with laughter" ("Laugh of the Medusa" 316).

Garden unequivocally constitutes a unique and moreover, dual, *Künstlerroman*. That it traces the development of David's artistic life is an idea which most critics enthusiastically embrace. However, *Garden* also portrays Catherine's artistic odyssey, and this becomes evident by analyzing the components of the novel which Hemingway suppresses. By submerging Catherine's artistic quest beneath aspects of the narrative foregrounding David's development, Hemingway mirrors a central thematic concern, namely the suppression of female creativity. To focus only on David's narrative and point of view not only neglects Catherine's artistic evolution, but constitutes a failure to acknowledge the text's "Other" where free play and creativity exist.

From the very outset of the novel, Hemingway places subtle signposts which guide us to see Catherine as a formidable character and a legitimate artist. In the opening chapter Hemingway describes the room where the couple resides as one which "looked like the painting of van Gogh's room at Arles" (4). Hemingway uses the mad artist stigma commonly associated with van Gogh and the ultimate and presumed insanity of Catherine to ask us to acknowledge Catherine's role as an artist. The symbolic alignment between Catherine and van Gogh signifies Hemingway's great sympathy for her aesthetic trials and sufferings. In *Less Than a Treason*, Peter Griffin says that as a result of reading van Gogh's letters in 1924, Hemingway became so touched by the artist's trials that he made a "pilgrimage" to his home and to the asylum where van Gogh had been institutionalized (72). Griffin suggests that Hemingway was moved by van Gogh's "suffering and sacrifice for the truth" (72), and adds, "Ernest returned to Paris filled with compassion for the long-suffering artist who had wagered his life on his work" (72). As evidenced by his treatment of Catherine, Hemingway shows a similar compassion for Catherine's aesthetic struggles.

Several critics acknowledge Catherine's artistry, but only tentatively. In *Hemingway's Quarrel with Androgyny*, Mark Spilka calls Catherine "the conversational artist . . . the talkative waitress of *The Torrents of Spring* (a teller of literary anecdotes!) come back to haunt or 'spook' her cruel creator" (12). Spilka notes Catherine's competitive nature and says that she tries "to assert some comparable form of creativity and self importance" (307). In spite of recognizing Catherine's artistry, Spilka ultimately fails to acknowledge that her actions comprise a legitimate artistic text, for he maintains that the character essentially serves a dual biographical function. On one hand she represents "an amalgam of many women in Hemingway's life" (305), and secondly, she symbolizes "the androgynous lesbian muse" within Hemingway's own psyche—"that secret female version of himself against whom his masculine artistry had always been opposed" (305).

Although Spilka's biographical explanation here undermines the legitimacy of Catherine's artistry, his labeling of her as a conversational artist has, nevertheless, significant implications in terms of a Cixousian hermeneutic. Feminist theorists have long addressed the position of silence which women have occupied socially, politically, and linguistically. Cixous, in particular, works to locate a place from which they can speak. Cixous believes that feminine writing provides such a site, and it does so, in part, by sabotaging the hierarchical relation between writing and speech and favoring the latter. In "Sorties" and elsewhere, Cixous emphatically asserts a "privileged relationship with voice" (93). Cixous' ideas about voice and the plurivocity of *l'écriture féminine* enable us to see the theoretical significance of Spilka's label.

John Raeburn and Robert Gajdusek are two other critics who, at least marginally, recognize Catherine as an artist. Gajdusek begins his article, "Elephant Hunt in Eden: A Study of New and Old Myths and Other Strange Beasts in Hemingway's Garden," by pointing out the similarities between Hemingway's *Garden* and Thurber's "Unicorn in the Garden," and he calls attention to both works' thematic exploration of sexual politics, competition, and creativity. He examines Catherine's dissatisfaction with the arbitrary, socially constructed gender roles to which she is expected to conform and says that she actively rebels. Moreover, Gajdusek recognizes the artistry inherent in her actions:

> David clearly sees, and with guilt, the source of Catherine's dilemma in his exclusionary art. The imaginary world of his art *does* exclude her— he is the creator whose creative act seems to replace her own biological function—and only his "narrative" of their life together gives her what she feels is a participatory role. She, in retaliation, becomes creator in the real, unnaturally manipulating life into fictive postures, creating drama. "I've invented you," she says of David and Marita, reciprocally trying to control destiny. (12)

Raeburn believes that Catherine "lacks the artistic talent," but, nevertheless, "possesses the artist's disposition" (115). He, like Gajdusek, points out Catherine's frustration with restrictive gender codes and "her sense of powerlessness in the world" (114). Raeburn says, "Catherine has no work to do— she would like to be a painter or writer but knows she lacks talent—and thus she is forever inventing projects, studying Spanish or undertaking reading and self-improvement regimens, or finally and disastrously, making plans for David's narrative of their lives together to be published" (115).

Although these three critics recognize that Catherine manifests an artistic sensibility, they fail unequivocally to call her an artist in the strict sense of the word. As a result of Cixous' insight into the "feminine practice of writing," we can not only understand such a critical reaction, but can also see that a feminine text such as Catherine creates clearly defies a traditional or phallocentric definition. According to Cixous, feminine writing "will always surpass the discourse that regulates the phallocentric system; it does and will take place in areas other than those subordinated to philosophico-theoretical domination" ("Laugh" 313). Cixous calls for a revaluation of criteria defining authorship, creativity, texts. She explains that writing has always been defined by phallocentric laws, and she encourages women "to write and thus to forge" for themselves "the antilogos weapon" (312). According to Cixous a feminine text is free to define itself, free to refuse to comply with or conform to phallocentric definitions, expectations, or limitations.

Repeatedly and emphatically Cixous also emphasizes the role that the physical body must play in the creation of a feminine text. She says, "Write your self. Your body must be heard" (312). She points to repressed libidinal desires as seats of great creative strength, and she explains that women have been indoctrinated to deny their eroticism, hence have been dispossessed of a major source of creativity (312). Cixous says, "In body.—More so than men who are coaxed toward social success, towards sublimation, women are body. More body, hence more writing. For a long time it has been in body that women have responded to persecution, to the familial-conjugal enterprise of domination, to the repeated attempts at castrating them" (316).

Throughout *Garden* we repeatedly witness Catherine's attempts to write with her body and successfully tap libidinal creativity. From the outset Catherine struggles painfully with logocentric discourse and only gradually realizes that the libido not only provides an effective measure of self-expression, creativity, and art, but also serves as the locus of her psychic, spiritual, and sexual liberation. In the opening chapter of the novel, for example, Catherine fears that her conversation strikes David as inadequate, uncreative. Both of their reactions here and in the subsequent scene are noteworthy:

> "We're not great conversationalists at meals," the girl said. "Do I bore you darling?"
> The young man laughed.
> "Don't laugh at me, David."
> "I wasn't. No. You don't bore me. I'd be happy looking at you if you never said a word." He poured her another glass of wine and filled his own.
> "I have a big surprise. I didn't tell you, did I?" the girl said. (11)

We learn next that the "surprise" involves changing herself. After making love, Catherine tells David that "it's for you. It's for me too. I won't pretend that it's not. But it will do something to you" (12). The surprise involves a hair style which is "cropped as short as a boy's," cut "with no compromises" (14–15). The haircut signifies a creative, sexual, and very public expression of her artistry. The same holds true of all subsequent acts, from bleaching her hair and enticing David to change his coiffure, to engaging in transsexual and bisexual relations. These juxtaposed scenes illustrate clearly that Catherine compensates for her insecurities about expressing herself with language by asserting her creativity and ingenuity physically.

Throughout the novel Catherine prefers physical to linguistic expression; moreover, she derives both self-respect and sexual satisfaction from communicating with her body. For instance, upon cutting her hair for the first time, she boldly displays this physical manifestation of her artistry in a local café. She tells David that "stupid people will think it's strange. But we must be proud. I love to be proud" (16). Besides deriving a sense of self-assurance from her bodily expression, she also experiences sexual gratification or *jouissance*. Each creative act of self-expression—the hairstyles, the bleachings, the transsexual and bisexual acts—manifests sexual pleasure, what Cixous calls autoeroticism. Catherine clearly speaks a libidinal language and often lets her body express her thoughts, as evidenced when she tells David, "I'll put on one of my tight shirts so you can tell what I think about things" (175–76). As this line indicates, Catherine's body communicates ideas while simultaneously manifesting sexual pleasure.

The self-confidence Catherine feels when exercising her physical or libidinal form of artistic expression contrasts with the stifling insecurities she experiences when trying to communicate with language. While David writes, Catherine often spends time reading books, writing letters, and, more notably, studying languages, as indicated by her reading of the "Spanish-English method book" (51). Even though such activities signal an active engagement with traditional phallocentric discourse, she never feels that she has full access to or command over such modes. Throughout the novel Catherine demonstrates her frustration with or alienation from language. In a very telling scene, David says that "bore" is "the one damned word in the language" that he "can't stand," and Catherine responds, "Lucky you with only one word like that in the language" (41). Catherine's inability to access language, or to enter into the Symbolic smoothly, in the Lacanian sense, is further reinforced by Catherine's obsession for gazing into mirrors. She is so fascinated with observing herself that she suggests purchasing a mirror to hang in the bar so that the three of them "can all see each other when we talk rot and know how rotty it is. You can't fool a bar mirror" (103). Cixous repeatedly speaks of alienation from the Symbolic as advantageous, and Catherine's interest in mirrors shows a similar satisfaction with existence in the Imaginary or pre-Symbolic condition.

Chapter six most vividly exposes Catherine's aesthetic frustrations and anxieties. She again expresses doubt about the quality of her conversation and says, "I'm sorry I'm talking so much. I'm sorry if I talk stupidly. I usually do" (53). She continues:

> "It's (wine) a different sort of talkative than absinthe," Catherine said. "It doesn't feel dangerous. I've started on my good new life and I'm reading now and looking outward and trying not to think about myself so much and I'm going to keep it up but we ought not to be in town this time of year. Maybe we'll go. The whole way here I saw wonderful things

to paint and I can't paint at all and never could. But I know wonderful things to write and I can't even write a letter that isn't stupid. I never wanted to be a painter or a writer until I came to this country. Now it's just like being hungry all the time and there's nothing you can ever do about it." (53)

This confessional speech reflecting her frustration with writing occurs when she has been struggling to control her creative, libidinal urges. When David tries to console her by telling her that "the country is here. You don't have to do anything about it," Catherine responds, "There's nothing except through yourself . . . and I don't want to die and it be gone" (53). As he has done here, Hemingway frequently juxtaposes Catherine's thoughts about artistry with ideas about death and madness. In doing so, he prefigures a number of feminist theorists about the anxieties highly imaginative women face upon contemplating an artistic endeavor.

According to Cixous, the artistic woman experiences fear, shame, and insecurity about her ability to create. She even doubts her own sanity, just as others also question her mental health. Cixous writes that the woman who internalizes phallocentric criticisms begins to accuse herself "of being a monster" (309). She writes, "Who, feeling a funny desire stirring inside her (to sing, to write, to dance, to speak, in short, to bring out something new), hasn't thought she was sick? Well, her shameful sickness is that she resists death, that she makes trouble" (309).

Cixous' insights into the effects of phallocentric dominance of literature and aesthetic value mirror Gilbert and Gubar's findings in "Infection in the Sentence." According to these two critics, the patriarchal control of literature has profoundly crippled the female psyche. Their thesis expands upon and revises the Bloomian notion of "anxiety of influence," and they argue that "in comparison to the 'male' tradition of strong, father-son combat, however, this female anxiety of authorship is profoundly debilitating" (293). They explain that the highly creative woman suffers from mental diseases or "diseases": agoraphobia, anorexia, claustrophobia (295).

Both the Bloomian theory and its revised feminist version provide paradigms applying to Hemingway. For instance, Hemingway's writing *The Torrents of Spring* in an attempt to invalidate Sherwood Anderson's influence confirms Bloom's ideas about an oedipal/literary complex, and helps to explain Hemingway's reaction to literary influences and mentors. His treatment of Catherine in *Garden* also reflects his understanding of the anxiety of authorship felt by women. He exposes Catherine's insecurity, alienation, and fear as well as other emotions which plague the woman artist. Gilbert and Gubar point out that a woman artist experiences "a radical fear that she cannot create, that because she can never become a 'precursor' the act of writing will isolate or destroy her" (291). They maintain that women believe "that if they do not behave like angels they must be monsters" (294). Cixous, of course, also points out that a woman's artistry, hence nonconformity, signals a sort of deviant behavior to all who conform to or internalize phallocentric views (309). David's calling Catherine "Devil" in response to her creative expressions manifests such an attitude.

A great disparity exists between what David says to Catherine and what he actually thinks. His reactions to her, as well as his attitudes, should be carefully scrutinized. As Raeburn says,

> David complacently if regretfully seems to accept pathology as an accurate diagnosis [of Catherine's behavior] but in doing so reveals his own myopia. David's point of view dominates *Garden of Eden*, but a dialogic subtext undermines to some extent the credibility of his perception. The specific circumstances of the marriage spur Catherine as much or more than any putative psychological trauma. (114)

Repeatedly in the novel Hemingway reveals that Catherine's aesthetic insecurities are justified. Not only does David fail to recognize Catherine's artistry, he actually casts them both into traditional roles of domesticity, with Catherine as the passive, submissive wife and David as the active, aggressive professional. Realizing the role to which she has been assigned, Catherine consequently desires to perpetuate the free play of the honeymoon in order to delay the closure and restriction of the marital life to come.

When the couple sit in the café, David reading his clippings and Catherine her mail, Hemingway writes that, as she reads her letters, "the young man looked at her and thought she looked a little as though she were shelling peas" (25). David perceives Catherine here in an unartistic, even degrading manner. Moreover, as the scene develops, David continues to privilege traditional domestic roles while Catherine desperately struggles to resist them. The couple begin to discuss Catherine's money, and her economic independence threatens David by subverting his role expectations. He responds defensively (to learning that she has received money), and noting his reaction, Catherine says, "Don't go away like that. You always said it never made any difference" (25). She recognizes David's conventionality concerning finances and other aspects of marital life. In a desperate plea, she says, "Why do we have to do other things like everyone else does?" (27). Catherine strongly advocates using her money to perpetuate the honeymoon, for its end will halt the narrative which she is creating. The honeymoon, as she deliberately guides it, provides the atmosphere, setting, and, above all, plot. Furthermore, upon ending the honeymoon, Catherine must submit to David's expectations concerning the nature of their future marital life, and the life style he envisions leaves her flat:

> "But we'll spend it [the money] and I think it's wonderful. You can write afterwards. That way we can have the fun before I have a baby for one thing. How do I know when I'll have a baby even: Now it's all getting dusty and dull talking about it. Can't we just do it and not talk about it?" (27)

Catherine's resistance here to David's desire for a traditional marital life (one which means forsaking an artist's life for herself) signifies a subversive discourse largely submerged beneath a narrative foregrounding David's professional life. On the surface this scene highlights David's artistic productivity, his success and reviews, and as such it literally and figuratively suppresses Catherine's artistic life. She sees his reviews not from the standpoint of jealousy but as symbols of his fetishism and of her own aesthetic death. As she says, "I know you have to read them. But even in an envelope it's awful to have them with us. It's like bringing along somebody's ashes in a jar" (24).

The motifs of money, spending, and gift giving which pervade *Garden* have great significance in terms of a feminist and post-structuralist hermeneutic. The novel contrasts Catherine and Marita's attitudes towards money and spending with David's, and these two disparate views correspond to Cixous' male and female economies. Throughout her work, Cixous argues that gift-giving regulates all relations—political, social, economic, aesthetic, linguistic, and libidinal. Although both a male and female economy exist, the former dominates, and Cixous denounces its emphasis on return, exchange, repayment, and debt ("Castration or Decapitation?" 48–50). She criticizes the male economy for associating gift-giving negatively with loss of power, self, and sexual potency, and she accuses it of leading towards psychic, social, philosophical death (48–50).

Cixous praises female economy for its unrestricted, unlimited expenditure, expecting nothing in return (50). The female economy dispenses gifts freely, and rather than fearing loss, embraces it (54). Cixous says, "[woman] basically *takes up the challenge of loss* in order to go on living: she lives it, gives it life, is capable of unsparing loss" (54). Cixous believes that all symbolic structures and relations can be transformed by appropriating the female economy (53–55).[2]

In *Garden* Catherine and Marita practice female economy. Catherine not only wishes to support David financially, she repeatedly buys him gifts such as the "Dent edition" of the Hudson text he so desires (14). Marita also reflects a generous attitude towards expenditure. As Catherine says, "She spends money like a drunken oil-lease Indian" (111). When Marita enters the relationship, she brings a special gift—a case of 1915 Bollinger Brut (122). Both women give and spend freely, and their behavior contrasts sharply with David's. Despite resistance to Catherine's financial support, David actually possesses a very acquisitive attitude towards money, as evidenced in Chapter Two by his miserly and methodical calculations of his book sales. Hemingway devotes two full paragraphs to describing David's rather obsessive assessment of the sales. David manifests the male economy in other ways as well. For him, money is a commodity to be possessed and a signifier of power and sexual control. He equates Catherine's financial support with loss of psychosexual dominance and wishes throughout the novel to be free of this perceived debt.

Beginning with Mauss' study of the potlatch in *The Gift* (1925), a number of French theorists have used the idea of the gift as a trope in discourse ranging from psychoanalysis to economics (Pefanis 33–5). Georges Bataille's usage signified a radical departure from the more mainstream school of thought represented by Lévi-Strauss who in *The Elementary Structures of Kinship* suggested that women signify the ultimate gift in a structure which depends on exchange, reciprocity, and endless payment (33–58). Catherine's behavior throughout the novel, her relation to the themes of gift giving and exchange relations, and her transgression of taboos signal a literary representation closely paralleling Bataille's interpretation of the potlatch, a reading largely reappropriated by Cixous and Catherine Clément (co-author with Cixous of *The Newly Born Woman*).[3] Cixous and Clément challenge the idea of woman's passivity which forms the matrix of Lévi-Strauss' interpretation of exchange relations, and both women work to deconstruct the assumption of passivity informing this and all other phallocentric structures. Clément points to the hysteric and sorceress who clearly "violate exogamous exchange and transgress kinship" (53), championing their refusal to comply with the masculine dictate demanding that "*woman must circulate, not put in circulation*" (53). In *Garden* Hemingway offers a presentation of kinship relations and exchange which clearly deviates from phallocentric representations. Catherine actively puts a woman into circulation by offering Marita to David. Moreover, she literally calls Marita "a present" (103). While some may see this gesture as Catherine's adoption of a male economy leading to the objectification of Marita, from a French feminist perspective, it challenges the traditional active/passive coupling as well as an act disrupting a phallocentric structure.

That Hemingway has, indeed, offered a revolutionary representation of woman is further illustrated by a comparison between Catherine's portrayal and Bataille's interpretation of the potlatch. The novel foregrounds the honeymoon as the setting, and Catherine's behavior during and attitude towards the ritual is of great significance. The potlatch often evolves around marriages, occasions which, Bataille says, provide for the giving of gifts, the tremendous display of generosity, excessive and orgiastic behavior, and even the transgression of taboos. ("The Notions of Expenditure" 120–25). Bataille relates such rituals to sacred time and says, "profane time being ordinary time, the time of work and of respect for the taboos, and sacred time being that of celebrations, that is in essence the time of transgressing taboos" (*Erotism* 257). Bataille valorizes the excess inherent in nonproductive expenditures such as the potlatch, for he believes that excess leads to revolution—dialectically, politically, economically ("Notions" 116–29). He includes other activities as nonproductive expenditure—"luxury, mourning, war, cults, the construction of sumptuary monuments, games, spectacles, arts, perverse sexual activity (i.e., deflected from genital finality)" (118). In *Garden* Catherine spends generously, expenditures involving literal gifts as well as orgiastic energy. She violates both heterosexual and exchange taboos, and she demonstrates an attitude towards the honeymoon which contrasts vividly with David's. Catherine reflects a reverence for the ritual of the honeymoon while David manifests a compulsion towards work, a desire to adhere to taboos, and a tendency to accumulate rather than spend. Catherine's behavior during the honeymoon ultimately leads to the transformation of sexual, social, and linguistic structures and mirrors Bataille's observations about excess and revolution.

It should be noted that Catherine also perceives her book as a gift. When David tells her that he is "through with the narrative," Catherine says, "that's dirty . . . that was my present and our project" (188). Marita understands the importance of Catherine's offering and tells David, "You must write it" (188). Catherine's reference to her novel as a gift is significant, for Bataille and Cixous both relate their theories of economy to writing. Cixous clearly states that although her theory of economy applies to concerns ranging from ontology to economics it above all applies to feminine writing. She maintains that feminine writing manifests all the characteristics of a feminine economy capable of initiating great psychic, social, linguistic changes.

Although Catherine persistently works on her narrative throughout *Garden*, she initially is uncomfortable about publishing it. Midway through *Garden* she asks David, "Can you publish it or would it be bad to?" (77). Interestingly, she hasn't even read what he has written, a clear indication that her attitude about the text stems from a disinterest in logocentric discourse. She tells David, "I'm so proud of it already and we won't have any copies for sale and none for reviewers and then there'll never be clippings and you'll never be self-conscious and we'll always have it just for us" (77–8). She obviously does not feel vulnerable about her own behavior being exposed and subsequently criticized, for she tells David, "No matter if it's where I've been bad put in how much I love you" (77). Catherine's initial reluctance to publish stems, then, from something other than shame or modesty concerning her sexual behavior. Cixous' analysis of the creative woman's relationship with publishing helps to illuminate Catherine's attitude. Cixous maintains that "publishing houses are the crafty obsequious relayers of imperatives handed down by an economy that works against us and off our backs . . . Smug-faced readers, managing editors, and big bosses don't like the true texts of women—female-sexed texts. That kind scares them" ("Laugh" 310). Cixous urges women to write and publish, nevertheless: " . . . let no one hold you back, let nothing stop you"—not even phallocentric institutions such as publishing houses, literary reviewers, and the like (310).

As the novel progresses Catherine overcomes her timidity about publishing and becomes determined to see her novel realized, and her change in attitude about publishing co-exists with a social and psychological transformation. She becomes increasingly self-assertive, independent and forceful in every respect, reflecting sexual, psychic, and artistic liberation. When David questions her about her publishing directives, she says, "they're straightforward plans . . . You don't have to groan about them. You've been doing just whatever you wanted to do all day and I was pleased. But I have a right to make a few plans" (188).

Despite Catherine's lucidity throughout this scene, David interprets her plans as a sign of madness, or irrationality, and he conveys a condescending attitude towards her plans, yet his response, ironically, indicates that her ideas are not unrealistic:

> "You've had a very busy day," David said. "You know, don't you, that you don't get manuscripts typed until whoever writes them has gone over them and has them ready for typing?"
> "That isn't necessary because I only need a rough draft to show the artists."

"I see. And if I don't want it copied yet?"

"Don't you want it brought out? I do. And someone has to get started on something practical."

"Who are the artists you thought up today?"

"Different ones for different parts. Marie Laurencin, Pascen, Derain,
Dufy and Picasso."

"For Christ sake, Derain." (188–89)

In *Garden* we can see that Catherine's commitment to publishing her narrative leads to radical measures. She openly and vehemently begins to criticize not only David's character but his writing ability as well. She subsequently divorces herself from the bonds of her relationships with David and
Marita. Tired of their criticisms and resistance to her plans, she tells them,
"You can spend the rest of your lives together . . . If you don't bore each other.
I have no further need of either of you" (191). She soon destroys David's
manuscripts in a final, radical effort to ensure work on her own narrative.
She never backs down from her publishing intentions, for near the novel's
end we learn that she has left for Paris "to do all the things" necessary for the
illustration and publication of her "book" (237).

Throughout the novel Catherine undoubtedly exhibits unorthodox
behavior regarding both her marriage and her relationship with Marita. She
defies old social and sexual taboos and initiates new parameters for relationships. In every respect Catherine's personal actions signify the larger political revolution which Cixous maintains results inevitably from a woman's liberation. She says that "her libido will produce far more radical effects of
political and personal change than some might like to think" (313), and adds
that "her liberation" will "modify power relations" and "bring about a muta-
tion in human relations, in thought, in all praxis . . . " (313).

Cixous explains that integral to the "new history" ushered in by liberated
woman is the nature of feminine language, the catalyst which "will wreck
partitions, classes, and rhetoric, regulations and codes" (315). Feminine language promises revolution on two levels. Extrinsically it triggers social and
political changes. Intrinsically it undermines phallocentric expectations and
demands concerning syntax, grammar, linear thought, Aristotelian unity,
and narrative teleology. Catherine's revolutionary use of language reflects
both levels. That the creation of her narrative substantially alters social,
political, and sexual codes is evident in the nature of her relationship with

David and Marita. Catherine also employs a language which clearly opposes phallogocentric discourse. In addition to communicating with her libido, she uses atomized, nonlinear, unorthodox patterns of speech. Her speech typically includes contradictions, circumfluent logic, fragmented sentences, irregular syntax and punctuation. It is also important to note that Marita, not David, appreciates Catherine's mode of expression—"She tells things very well you know" (184).

Cixous links questions of identity with language usage, arguing that feminine language subverts phallocentric binaries and ushers in *différence* and open-ended signification. Rabine tells us, for instance, that in "Laugh" Cixous employs continually changing pronouns: "I, you, she, they, and we merge into each other, change places, give each other to each other, and in general deny the stable positionality of the phallic subject" (31). This type of "rhetorical play," says Rabine, "contributes to her inscription of feminine desire" and "plays into her strategy of undoing phallocentric discourses" (31). In *Garden* Catherine also attempts to project a diffused subjectivity, evidenced by the various declarations of identity that she makes throughout the novel. She has atomized her identity to include such labels as "sister," "brother," "husband," "boy," "girl," and "Peter." She adamantly despises being assigned a set identity, as indicated when she tells David that being a "girl" exclusively is "a god damned bore" (70).

Catherine's desire to see her text ultimately realized is, ironically, gratified, for it constitutes the central part of Hemingway's *Garden of Eden*. Her actions provide the bulk of the novel's plot. Although the interpolated African tale evolves exclusively around David (at least on the surface), it metaphorically addresses David's problems with Catherine, according to critics. David's perspective on Catherine further draws us toward Catherine's role, and his attitudes, responses, and thoughts raise important questions about his reactions to and assessments of Catherine. The action involving David, then, in no way diminishes Catherine's importance to the novel.

Garden also forces us to take a closer look at Hemingway himself. His treatment of Catherine challenges numerous critical charges of misogynistic insensitivity, for in *Garden* he provides a sympathetic portrait of a creative woman who, contrary to critical assumptions, does not victimize the male protagonist; rather, she enables him to see beyond restrictive binaries: male/female, homosexuality/heterosexuality, passive/active. Catherine enriches David's life; she does not destroy it. She also enriches our understanding of Hemingway, for her portrait explains, perhaps, why he said, "'Things may not be immediately discernible in what a man writes, and in this sometimes he is fortunate; but eventually they are quite clear and by these and the degree of alchemy that he possesses he will endure or be forgotten'" (quoted in Lynn, 574).

Notes

1. Solomon says that *Garden* represents Hemingway's effort "to experiment, to move away from his early style; and he struggled with it from 1946 until his death in 1961" (31). She identifies this quotation as something he was "fond of saying to critics" during this period (31).
2. Cixous' definition of economy does not suggest biological difference. *Différence* exists at the level of *jouissance*. A male, in other words, can reflect a feminine economy.
3. Not only did Bataille and Hemingway share the same friends and acquaintances in Paris, Bataille's theories were widely discussed in the prominent aesthetic journals of his day. It is very likely, therefore, that Hemingway had either met Bataille or had heard of a number of his concepts.

Works Cited

Bataille, Georges. *Erotism: Death and Sensuality*. Trans. Mary Dalwood. San Francisco: City Lights, 1986.

———. "The Notions of Expenditure." *Visions of Excess: Selected Writings, 1927–1939*. Trans. Allan Stoekl, Carl R. Lovitt, and Donald M. Leslie, Jr. Minneapolis: U Minnesota P, 1985.

Cixous, Hélène. "Castration or Decapitation?" Trans. Annette Kuhn. *Signs: Journal of Women and Culture in Society* 7.1 (Autumn 1981): 41–55.

———. "The Laugh of the Medusa." *Critical Theory Since 1965*. Ed. Hazard Adams and Leroy Searle. Tallahassee: Florida State U P, 1986.

———, and Catherine Clément. *The Newly Born Woman*. Trans. Betsy Wing. Minneapolis: U Minnesota P, 1986.

Gajdusek, Robert. "Elephant Hunt in Eden: A Study of New and Old Myths and Other Strange Beasts in Hemingway's Garden." *The Hemingway Review* 7.1 (Fall 1987): 15–19.

Gilbert, Sandra M., and Susan Gubar. "Infection in the Sentence: The Woman Writer and the Anxiety of Authorship." *Feminisms: An Anthology of Literary Theory and Criticisms*. Ed. Robyn R. Warhol and Diane Price Herndl. New Brunswick: Rutgers U P, 1991. 289–330.

Griffin, Peter. *Less Than a Treason: Hemingway in Paris*. New York: Oxford U P, 1990.

Hemingway, Ernest. *The Garden of Eden*. Ed. Tom Jenks. New York: Scribner's, 1986.

King, Richard H. *A Southern Renaissance: The Cultural Awakening of the American South, 1930–1945.* New York: Oxford U P, 1980.

Lynn, Kenneth. *Hemingway.* New York: Simon and Schuster, 1987.

Pefanis, Julian. *Heterology and the Postmodern: Bataille, Baudrillard, and Lyotard.* Durham: Duke U P, 1991.

Rabine, Leslie W. "*Ecriture Féminine* as Metaphor." *Cultural Critique* 8 (1987–88): 19–44.

Raeburn, John. "Sex and Art in *The Garden of Eden.*" *Michigan Quarterly Review* 29 (Winter 1990): 111–122.

Shiach, Morag. *Hélène Cixous: A Politics of Writing.* New York: Routledge, 1991.

Solomon, Barbara Probst. "Where's Papa?" *The New Republic* (9 March 1987): 30–34.

Spilka, Mark. *Hemingway's Quarrel with Androgyny.* Lincoln: U Nebraska P, 1990.

Willingham [Cackett], Kathy. "*The Garden of Eden:* Challenging Faulkner's Family Romance." *The Hemingway Review* 9.2 (Spring 1990): 155–168.

OPENING BLUEBEARD'S CLOSET: WRITING AND AGGRESSION IN HEMINGWAY'S *THE GARDEN OF EDEN* MANUSCRIPT [1]

Steven C. Roe

Is the writer insensitive to the wife's plight? Could an insensitive man create such a structure? Is not one of the most interesting aspects the extent to which the story invites the pillorying of the character who seems biographically an extension of the author? In these stories, as in all his work, Hemingway is harder on himself and more rigorously moral than the vast majority of his readers. Such stories come out of the artist's careful, meticulous consideration of the relations between life and art and also out of guilt for his art's effect upon his life.

—Robert E. Gajdusek on "An Alpine Idyll" and other Hemingway short stories

Since Charles Perrault's inclusion of "Bluebird" in his book of "fairy tales," *Histoires ou Contes du Temps Passé avec des Moralités*, published in 1697, Bluebeard's exploits have been retold many times, in a variety of genres, with numerous modifications.[2] Perrault's fairy tale, however, stands as the definitive version of "Bluebeard." The basic plot of the story is simple: a powerful man with an unsightly blue beard marries a young woman, brings her to his mansion, gives her his key ring and tells her that she may "open everything [and] go anywhere," but "absolutely forbid[s]" her to "so much as open the door" of the room "at the end of the long gallery on the ground floor"; tormented by curiosity, the young bride unlocks the door of the forbidden chamber and finds the butchered corpses of Bluebeard's previous wives lying in pools of "clotted blood"; upon discovering his wife's transgression, Bluebeard draws his cutlass, preparing to kill again; yet, at the last moment, the young bride is rescued by her two brothers (Carter 31–40). Perrault, a seventeenth-century bourgeois, tailors the folkloric sources of his tale to suit the salon sensibilities of his audience. Through judgmental narrative commentary and "Moral" codas, he shifts attention away from Bluebeard's hideous crimes, focussing, instead, on the purported evils of female curiosity. Whereas Bluebeard's cutlass threatens decapitation, Perrault's quill pricks the female conscience; blood-and-gore savagery becomes an occasion for tongue-in-cheek urbanity. As Maria Tatar has recently observed, the brutalized victim is recast as a chastised villain (159).

In *The Garden of Eden* manuscript, Hemingway employs the story of "Bluebeard" less evasively, to render the disturbing psychological truths of yet another honeymoon world. That is, Hemingway stands at an ironic distance from the centralized consciousness of his newly married fictional persona, the writer-protagonist David Bourne, portraying him as a Bluebeard figure. David's "Bluebeardism" lies primarily in his creative vanity, in the self-absorption, detachment, and pride that inform his compulsion to write. Not coincidentally, Catherine, David's troublesome bride, accuses him of appropriating her unruly banter for his artistic ends, of "storeing it away [*sic*]" in the dark recesses of his own mind (3.15.12). Even at his most affectionate, David is stifling, and must be reminded by Catherine that they cannot keep their love "*locked up* like <*del.*: jewels; *rev.*: something> in a vault" (3.4.4; emphasis added). There is, to be sure, a despotic brutality in David's character, a desire to master and control otherness, to preside over the world rather than participate in it. A la Bluebeard, David Bourne emerges as an artist who derives his creative inspiration from a stratum of egocentric desires rooted in hostility and self-aggrandizement. Accordingly, David, with a heavy conscience, asks himself if "[i]t is possible that the only creation that is a moral act is pro-creation and that is why all other kinds are suspect? [*sic*]" (3.23.9.i). Still, despite his self-consciousness, David remains an oppressive and violent figure, obtusely prone to self-delusion. Indeed, Hemingway's Bluebeard bloodlessly commits the atrocities of his fairy-tale predecessor, evincing the monstrous potentialities of writerly introversion.

But whereas Perrault adopts a cavalier attitude toward femicide, insinuating that Bluebeard's disobedient bride deserves her husband's punitive maltreatment, Hemingway portrays feminine recalcitrance as a necessary countermeasure to male tyranny. That is, the author of *Eden* sympathetically embraces Catherine, the marginalized female "other," suggestively individualizing her character. Most notably, Hemingway conceives of Catherine as a woman who suffers from an hereditary mental illness (likely a form of schizophrenia), and whose past implicitly includes treatment in a Swiss sanitorium (3.13[b].22–23; 3.26.21; etc.). A deceptively perfect "twenty one" (<*rev.*> 1.1.19), Catherine equates her disorder with spiritual dissolution, and is haunted by the thought of dying (3.9.10–12; etc.). Meanwhile, if David cannot prevent Catherine's biological fate, he remains morally culpable precisely because his insularity precludes the compensatory *togetherness* that his fragmented wife so desperately requires, hastening her decline. Hemingway reinforces the destructiveness of David's artistic posture by imbuing the image of Bluebeard with a social and political trajectory, raising the motif into an overarching metaphor for patriarchal oppression. In her anguish, Catherine relentlessly exposes the monstrous selfishness of her writer-husband, wittily mocking the variable guises of masculine "author-ity." On most occasions, her devilishly feminine voice is closest to Hemingway's own, and accurately articulates the moral concerns of *Eden*. Inevitably, though, Catherine, to a lesser degree, becomes "monstrous" herself (3.43.5), turning into a vindictive savior who re-enacts the murderous egoism she detests. Thus, in the final analysis, Hemingway literally and figuratively weds two human types, the artist and the neurotic, leaving little to choose between the two. Through the focal image of Bluebeard, writing and aggression figure in an irresolvable drama of male power and female victimization.

The Bluebeard motif is explicitly introduced early, in the Grau du Roi section of the manuscript. One May morning, after the arrival of the mail, Catherine joins David at a café, where he is intently reading reviews of his newly published novel. According to David's publisher, who has sent the material, "[m]ost of the reviews [are] excellent" (1.2.5), and David himself describes them as "good" (1.2.8). Nevertheless, Catherine is "*frightened* by them" (1.2.7). "They do a terrible thing to me," she says (1.2.7). When David reminds her that she "asked to see them," Catherine, in a passage excised from the published version of the manuscript, replies: "I know. And people open the door into <*del.*: ~~Blue~~> Bluebeard's closet <*acc.*: They always do it. Look at Landru even>" (1.2.8). Catherine's noteworthy response to the reviews far exceeds petty wifely jealousy: she is, very explicitly, "*frightened* by them" (emphasis added). That is, Catherine perceives the clippings as portents of aggression. More pointedly, she implies that the reviews of David's novel involve a Bluebeardesque atrocity. Concomitantly, Henri Désiré Landru, the Frenchman to whom Catherine refers in the cited accretion, was popularly known in the twenties as "the modern Bluebeard," or "the Bluebeard of Gambais." Between 1915 and 1919, Landru swindled and murdered at least ten women, allegedly using an oven to dispose of their bodies (MacKenzie 15–22; 183–207). A great deal of publicity surrounded Landru's eventual trial, which may explain why Catherine chooses him to support her claim that people are "always" intrigued by Bluebeardesque crimes.

Here, as elsewhere, Catherine's strange associations, which she confesses *seem* "crazy" (1.3.3), deserve careful consideration. For, as someone who "really feel[s] things" (3.18.10), she often knows David better than he knows himself. Indeed, in keeping with Catherine's "feeling," David wields a "sharp knife blade" to open the "fat" envelopes containing the clippings (1.2.8). The danger of David's pocket knife is implied in his recommendation that Catherine use a dull "table knife" to open her letters (1.2.8). Thus, metaphorical details subtly corroborate Catherine's inexplicable "feeling" of dread (1.2.7), suggesting that the clippings do, in fact, embody a murderous secret. For Catherine, as for Hemingway, they reveal the monstrous vanity of David's writerly quest for self-validation. The reviews, all of which bear the same picture of David (1.2.6; 3.39.12) and flatter him with what Catherine calls "niggledy spit falseness" (1.2.8), feed his voracious ego, whose incessant devouring annihilates otherness, posing a threat to Catherine's own fragile sense of identity. "[B]ecause the primary thrust of the libido is towards the ingestion of all realities into the self," George Steiner claims, "there runs through human relations a drive towards the pulverization of the rival persona" (52). It is precisely this drive towards "*pulverization*" (emphasis added) that Catherine senses in her review-reading husband. For, to borrow Catherine's phrase, insofar as David chooses "to live in the clippings" (1.2.6)—to indulge the presumption of monolithic authorship—he can be neither a loving husband nor a loving friend. In his writerly role, David stands alone and aloof, viewing all things with a "*deadly* clarity" (1.1.15; emphasis added).

Moreover, as Catherine sees things, the clippings are a double-edged sword, posing a threat to David as well. "They could destroy you if you thought about them or believed them" (1.2.7), she says. "I wouldn't want to

die of eating <*acc.*: a mess of> dried clippings" (1.2.8). Thus, Catherine portrays David, the review-reader, as someone who fatally ingests scatological
refuse. Further still, she correctly perceives an element of hero-worship in the
reviews, a cult of personality that enshrines David as a veritable god.
Appropriately, David's review-reading is itself a kind of mass-like ceremony:
with a tumbler of vermouth and soda on the table before him (1.2.6), he
unfolds and refolds the clippings, protectively, it would seem, then places
them back in their envelopes, as if they were of sacramental value. David,
however, is a poor priest, engaged in a form of self-worship. He is so totally
absorbed by his own literary accomplishments that he is unaware of anything else, including what he is drinking. Catherine obliquely alludes to the
flavor of self-immolation that haunts the clipping ritual: "I don't want to be
stupid about them," she says. "But even in an envelope it's awful to have them
with us. It's like bringing along somebody's ashes in a jar" (1.2.7). To para-
phrase, David, the writer-god, is depersonalized even as he is immortalized.
In savoring such homage, he becomes public property, a mere museum-piece
in a pantheon of heroes. "How can we be us and have the things we have and
do what we do," Catherine asks, "and you be this that's in the clippings?"
(1.2.7). In effect, Catherine is asking David to exchange collective narcissism
for genuine interaction and intimacy. Interestingly, David concedes that
there may be a kernal of wisdom in Catherine's apparent madness: "They're
bad for you," he admits, but maintains, somewhat unconvincingly, that "it
doesn't last" (1.2.7).

Over the remainder of the *Eden* manuscript, Hemingway develops the
Bluebeard motif more indirectly, through a mosaic of oblique parallels and
inversions. Bluebeard, of course, tells his wife that she may "open everything
[and] go anywhere," but mitigates his generosity with a severe restriction.
This conflictual premise of permission and prohibition engenders the crisis
of transgression around which the tale revolves. Hemingway's heroine, however, does not await the measured favors of a law-giving husband. Given the
availability of her "spendable" family-trust money (1.3.3), Catherine proposes that she and David should enjoy unconditional freedom: " . . . now we can
do whatever we want let's do it now," she tells David, "and you can write
afterwards and probably better than if you just tried <*acc.*: now> and worried" (1.3.4–5). There is a spontaneous, orgasmic urgency about Catherine's
"plan," a sense of liberation that suggests the unfettered "*now*" (emphasis
added) of sexual release. Indeed, her flexible "idea," which eludes definitive
prescriptions, indirectly functions as a verbal mandate for the androgynous
lovemaking that occupies much of the manuscript. In effect, then, Catherine

displaces the gender hierarchy of the fairy-tale precedent, opening previously closed doors. Her "project" (1.3.2)—which she mysteriously describes as
"terribly constructive and even sound" (1.3.3–4), and as "a very trusting
thing" (1.3.7)—ultimately stands as an attempt to ameliorate the burden of
individuality through the rapture of togetherness. An advocate of understat-
ed "fun" (1.3.5), Catherine yearns for emotional fulfillment. "We'll do everything you want" (1.3.5), she assures her husband, forsaking authority for an
implied reciprocity.

Unable to grasp Catherine's mental shift, David remains mired in exclusionary precepts, assuming that if they are going to do everything *he* wants
they will not be able to do anything *she* wants." "What about us doing something that *you* want to do?" he asks (1.3.5; emphasis added). In response,
Catherine unequivocally and vituperatively rejects traditional patterns of
female subjugation: "Darling," she says, bristling, "don't don't don't ever
worry about me not doing what I want to do" (1.3.5). Threatened by his
wife's forceful rebuttal, David simply reverses the exclusionary model. "What
if I want to write?" he asks, implying that Catherine has prescribed otherwise. "The minute you're not going to do something it will make you want to
do it," he says (1.3.6), truly enough, alluding to the Edenic paradigm of forbidden fruit. Thus, David interprets Catherine's "idea" in oddly familiar
terms, as a permission-prohibition statement. More pointedly, he puts
Bluebeard's words into Catherine's mouth, painting her as the tyrant and
himself as the disenfranchised spouse. The ironic twist reveals an
entrenched, victor-victim ideology whereby power is monopolized rather
than shared. Not surprisingly, Catherine immediately points out David's
dualistic misreading of her verbal text: "If you feel like writing write," she
says. "All we said was that we'd do what we wanted and go where we wanted
and not worry about money or not writing. Nobody said anything about
worrying if you wrote. Did they?" (1.3.7). "No," David concedes, uncomfort-
ably. "I don't have to leave you when you write do I?" Catherine asks (1.3.7).
Significantly, David changes the subject. For, in actuality, it is *he* who must
leave when he writes, and, after three weeks of marriage, he is already anx-
ious to depart, eager for the distant heights of authorial omnipotence.

As the dangerously prolonged honeymoon stretches into August, the
nomadic Bournes return to the relative tranquility of the French Riveria,
where they tenant a remote and otherwise uninhabited hotel at La Napoule.
Interestingly, the long, low-lying building—situated high atop a coastal "hill"
(3.16.1; 3.20.4.i; etc.), exhibits the symbolic characteristics of Bluebeard's
equally removed country manor. Indeed, both residences contain a series of

rooms, holding numerous riches and diversions. At the "Casa Longa" hotel, David, the reclusive patriarch who is never without his "key ring" (3.26.19; 3.37.24; etc.), oversees access to "three rooms" (3.16.1): a "storeroom" (3.16.17), which, as the proprietress observes, is "full of tinned and bottled treasures" (3.29.14), some of which Catherine herself gathers on "collecting trips" to Cannes and to Nice (3.16.4); a bedroom, another place of mysterious delights; and a work room. The last of these, perhaps the most intriguing compartment of all, David habitually locks (3.38.1; etc.), reserving it exclusively for himself. A more remarkable confluence of meticulous detail makes the possibility of a consciously drawn parallel difficult to discount: for just as Bluebeard's secret room lies at "the further end of the long gallery on the ground floor" (Carter), David's work room is located "at the further end" (3.16.2) of the "long low hotel" (3.16.1; 3.40.1). Here, in the sanctity of his private chamber, David, the writer, will finally begin to vent his anger and aggression.

Appropriately, the inception of David's Bluebeardesque creativity coincides with the appearance of Marita, the new "wife" (3.21.6; 3.22.3; etc.) whose arrival marks a serial-marriage pattern. A sinister version of a seemingly idealized character-type in Hemingway's earlier work, Marita is a sycophantic mistress who meets the needs of a burdened male. Her abject subservience bespeaks a fanatical, soul-less longing for self-abasement, a desire, actuated by lostness, to prostrate herself before an omnipotent authority. "[A] certified book reader" (3.21.40), awed by the power of David's art, Marita has read his first novel (3.21.14), and is quite possibly "in love" with him *before* they meet (3.21.11; etc.). As David's self-described "business partner on writing" (3.37.40), Marita has a "project" of her own (3.20.27) and is inclined to "take" David away from Catherine, who meddles in his vocational secrets (3.21.10). Exhibiting unscrupulous fealty to an author-god, Marita, with cunning proficiency, undermines Catherine's tenuous sanity by enticing her into a spiritually damning lesbian affair (3.20.25–27; etc.). Concomitantly, as Catherine's replacement, Marita indulges David's darkest and most authoritarian sexual fantasies. Revealing the sadomasochistic nexus of her personality, she poses as David's captive "boy" or catamite (3.45.4–5), studiously recreating a pederastic fantasy that David, invoking his writerly talents, "invent[ed]" one night in Madrid with an unusually passive and boyishly shorn Catherine (3.14.19–20). Marita's imitative endeavors lead away from the intersubjective, androgynous intimacy that excites Catherine, toward one-sided and cruelly exploitative sexual relations, based on privileged usership and hierarchical mastery. Indeed, the abusively "rough"

(<*rev.*> 3.45.2) flavor of David's pederastic involvements may even imply a bizarre parallel with Gilles de Rais (the medieval baron popularly viewed as the real-life Bluebeard), who ritualistically molested and murdered scores of children, primarily small boys. Thus, under Marita's influence, David's closet-self takes on a starkly repugnant meaning, evoking an horrific tableau of savagery.

David's renascent creativity, fostered by Marita's support, entails a triptych of stories[3] about his boyhood in Africa, and his father's bloody exploits there. Throughout the tales, David's unnamed father figures as a ruthlessly egomaniacal man, exemplifying the most horrifying aspects of the Bluebeard archetype. There are, to be sure, shades of Bluebeard in Mr. Bourne, a rogue male whose misogynistic relationship to the feminine is implied by his debauched treatment of native women (3.32.3; 3.32.8; etc.). As a colonial buccaneer involved in the ivory trade, Mr. Bourne signals Hemingway's synoptic conception of Perrault's murderous tyrant, belying an implicit connection between egoism and imperialism. Indeed, the overarching spectrae of Bluebeard figures in a thematic design that ultimately implicates political ideologies of appropriation and domination. David, meanwhile, by alternately standing with or against his father in the stories he writes, unconsciously dramatizes the feelings of rage and remorse that inform his marriage. More pointedly, the stories themselves function as quasi-confessional, proto-psychoanalytic revelations. They are, in fact, disguised wishes, fantasies that express aggression and contrition through an elaborate network of contrapuntal imagery, turning violent emotions into narrative energy. Events of the past are superimposed upon the present, engendering a palimpsestic symbolism that amounts to a form of mutilation. As a writer of boyhood tales, David becomes enmeshed in self-fondling memories whose objectively naturalistic detail masks subjectively wrought distortions.[4]

David's second story, his "hardest," warrants careful consideration as one that he has "always put off writing" (3.21.5). Curiously, he depicts his decision to write the story as an altruistic exercise: "Write the hardest one there is," he tells himself. "Go ahead and do that . . . You have to <*del.*: ~~save~~; *rev.*: last> yourself if you're to be any good to [Catherine]" 3.21.4). And yet, David's noble pretenses are compromised by an underlying hostility. For in choosing to write about his African boyhood, David tells himself that he has, as he puts it, "locked out" Catherine and all of her problems (3.21.3). As already suggested, though, Catherine is still very much on David's mind as he writes. More accurately, then, à la Bluebeard, David, the artist, manages to "lock her up." He is, in fact, "completely detached" (3.23.1) as he writes, and tells himself that he must work in order to "fort up" (<*acc.*> 3.22.27) against Catherine's disintegration. The other-annihilating aggression implicit in David's militaristic posture is evident in the writing process itself, which becomes a kind of combative enterprise, demanding the violent exertion of creative power. In a deleted passage, for example, David tells himself that the "problem" presented by the story must be "faced and *conquered*" (3.21.5; emphasis added). Accordingly, he works slowly, "*attacking* each thing he [had] put off facing" (<*acc.*> 3.22.1: emphasis added). David's embattled manipulation of aesthetic form evokes his desire to twist all possible dimensions into his own, providing a paradigm for his attitude toward Catherine. Not coincidentally, the connection between authorial omnipotence and marital despotism is highlighted by the recurrence of distinctly Bluebeardesque images. Elsewhere, David tells himself that he must not worry about his writing anymore than he would "*open up the door of a dark room* to see how a negative was developing [*sic*]." (3.39.2.ii–iii; emphasis added). The photographic cast of the metaphor suggests among other things, the extent to which David's "camera"-like eye (3.39.2.ii) mechanically arrests an ongoing reality, affording a petrified iconography whose "negative" origins tend toward mythological absolutism and permanence.

The plot of David's "new and difficult story" is only partially rendered, through intermittent discussions about the tale, and through David's compositional reveries. "It's a story about Africa back before the 1914 war," he informs Catherine. "In the time of the Madji-Madji war [*sic*]. The native rebellion of 1904 in [German-occupied] Tanganyika" (3.26.16).[5] John Iliffe, in *A Modern History of Tanganyika*, describes the uprising as "an explosion of African hatred of European rule" (168), portraying the conflict as an especially bloody one, typified by horrible acts of cruelty on both sides. John Hatch, in *Tanzania*, further explains that the native rebels, inspired by a religious mysticism, fought with a millennial fervor, believing that they would attain "a kind of utopia governed by a new god who would banish all evil" (80). "It was," therefore, as David claims, "a very odd rebellion" (3.26.19). More pointedly, in the story itself, David's father learns, "too late" (3.23.2), of a native attack or "raid" (3.46.2). The conclusion of the tale is carefully veiled, but Mr. Bourne implicitly responds to the raid in a deeply disquieting way. Catherine, for example, alludes to "the massacre in the crater and the heartlessness of [David's] own father" (3.40.11). The human massacre to which Catherine refers might describe the initial native attack, or, alternatively, "the massacre" may provide a clue to the nature of Mr. Bourne's "heartless" retaliation. Either way, Mr. Boune's response to the attack, *the thing left out,* emerges as the crucial aspect of the story. "Was this when you stopped loving [your father]?" Marita asks David, after reading the tale (3.26.3). "It's a terrible story," she adds, "and its wonderful" (3.26.4). Much later, David and Marita, alluding to the story, recall how his father "took up the march immediately after he had eaten the [thirteen] bad eggs" (3.42.11). Broadly viewed, then, the story of the raid stands as a tale of vengeance, involving untold atrocities.

The psychoanalytic significance of the Maji-Maji story hinges upon David's complete identification with his father (3.23.2.i–ii; 3.25.5–8; etc.). David, in fact, *becomes* his father as he writes: "He only wrote what his father did and how he felt and in all this he became his father and what his father said to Molo [his native foreman] was what he said" (3.25.3–4). In effect, then, David vicariously participates in his father's implied punishment of the African rebels, thereby satisfying a wish to aggressively assault his recalcitrant wife. Thus, Mr. Bourne, the anonymous fantasy figure, vividly embodies the reckless masculine self-determination that David lacks. Catherine makes the charge of egoic gratification explicit. Alluding to David's African stories in general, she tells him: "The worst thing was the dirt and <*acc.*: the flies and> the cruelty and bestiality. *You seemed almost to grovel in it*" (3.40.11; emphasis added).

Concomitantly, Catherine's status as a victimized rebel, implicit all along (3.3.3–4), is now framed in a specifically contrapuntal context: when she returns from her initial lesbian foray with Marita, David, having just begun the story of the raid, observes, in a deleted accretion, that she looks "darker than ever and very excited and defiant" (3.21.8); and when David subsequently attempts to quell her elation, Catherine looks at him "lovingly but *rebelliously*: (3.21.8; emphasis added) Moreover, Catherine and the Maji-Maji warriors share insurgent aims. Professing to "hate evil" (3.21.16), Catherine, too, is animated by a fervent idealism, and entertains utopian hopes in her attempt to overthrow the imperialistic ego of her writer-husband. Further still, in her zeal, she, too, carries out a series of offensives that are ultimately self-destructive. For after Catherine consummates her relationship with Marita, David is "shocked at <*del.*: ~~how~~; *rev.*: the *dead* way> she look[s] and at her toneless voice" (3.21.28). The complex interrelationship between the story of the "massacre" and the story of the honeymoon is pointedly reinforced as David compares the devastating psychological effects of Catherine's lesbian insurrection to a "big disaster or a tragedy" (<*rev.*> 3.22.10).

But it is David's retaliatory brutality, like his father's, that ultimately stands out as the most disturbing fact in a gruesome cycle of violence. For David becomes coldly inhumane when Catherine tries to explain that she must "go through with it" (3.21.18). "I'm going up to Paris," he says. "You can reach me through the bank" (3.21.18). In actuality, David goes only as far as Cannes, but his emotional distance is, indeed, great. "Don't you want to take care of her?" Marita asks when David returns. "Not particularly," he answers (3.21.21). Later that night, when Catherine pathetically tries to justify her actions, David launches a verbal attack of his own. "Perversion's dull and it's very old fashioned," he quips. "I didn't know people like us even kept up on it" (3.21.32–33). Marita, meanwhile, smiles knowingly at David's cutting commentary, looking, we are told, "as a very young owner might seeing her horse start to make his move at the three quarter pole [sic]" (3.21.33). Hardened by his "hardest story," David, in effect, *breaks away*, demonstrating the resolute invulnerability of his father.

The Bluebeardesque aspect of David's writerly triumph is especially apparent when Catherine, unable to resist the temptations of the forbidden chamber, insists upon reading the Maji-Maji story (3.26.17). "It starts very well," she tells David, adding that his "handwriting is *atrocious*" (3.26.17; emphasis added), a comment that innocuously hints at the emotional atrocities that inform David's creative process. Indeed, as Catherine reads on, she is overcome by terror. In disgust, she "[tears] the cahier in two and [throws] it on the floor" (3.26.18). "It's horrible," she says. "It's bestial. So that was what your father was like" (3.26.18). "It's <acc.: even> more horrible written in that child's notebook," Catherine continues. "You're a monster" (3.26.19). The carefully orchestrated folkloric resonance of the scene is intensified by Marita, who, retrieving the torn manuscript from the floor, asks David for "the key" to his room so that she can "lock [the story] up" (3.26.19). Afterwards, when the Bournes are alone, Catherine characteristically regrets her macabre accusations, which, nevertheless, hold a good deal of truth. For even as she deprecates her own violence, Catherine accurately intuits David's underlying desires: "You'll have me *shut up* or *put away*," she says (3.26.21; emphasis added). Disingenuously, David tries to allay Catherine's fears, claiming that they could "see a good doctor . . . "[t]he same way" they might "go to the dentist" (3.26.21), an analogy that coldly and absurdly paints Catherine's prospective treatment as a simple clinical procedure. David's peculiar brand of emotional terrorism shows through as he brutally attempts to impress the idea upon Catherine in a scene that echoes "Hills Like White Elephants," where "the man" pressures "the girl" to have a "perfectly simple"

abortion (277). In a near-hysterical effort to silence her selfish and insensitive male companion, Catherine, like the cornered "girl" in the earlier work,
threatens to "scream" (3.26.22; 277).

The very next morning, David begins his final African tale. Troubled, as
always, about the ethicality of his "grade" and his life, he now writes with
greater detachment about his father. That is, whereas in writing the Maji-
Maji story David *became* his father, he now *watches* his father, through the
eyes of young "Davey," his boyhood self. This third story, which is fully rendered as it develops in the mind of the writer, begins with Davey's solitary,
nocturnal discovery of a bull elephant. The initial, moonlit sighting of the
bull constitutes a radiant, visionary moment of awe and wonder: "covered"
by the passing shadow of the massive animal, Davey experiences an ecstatic
sense of oneness with something far greater than himself (3.26.24). Trained
in his father's ways, though, young Davey reports the presence of the elephant to his father, who embarks upon a hunt for the ivory-laden animal. As
the hunt progresses, Davey comes to resent his father's rapacious egoism:
"Many times during the [first] day [of the hunt] he had wished that he had
never <del.: s̶e̶e̶n̶; rev.: betrayed> the elephant and in the afternoon he
remembered wishing that he had never seen him" (3.30.43). On the second
day, when Juma, Mr. Bourne's native tracker, claims, in effect, that he does
not care about the elephant's feelings, Davey flatly opposes the thoughtless
brutality of the hunt: "*I care*," he tells himself. "I saw [the elephant] in the
moonlight and he was alone but I had [my dog,] Kibo . . . The bull wasn't
doing anyone any harm . . . and now we're going to kill him. It's my fault. I
betrayed him" (3.22.6–7).

The psychological configuration of the elephant story, considered amid
an array of contrapuntal image patterns, imparts a symbolic equivalence
between the elephant and Catherine, whereby the former functions as a
"cover figure" for the latter.[6] David's obsessive insistence upon Catherine's
"ivory" beauty is merely the most obvious clue to her disguised presence in
his final story: "You're just like ivory," David tells his blonde-haired wife.
"*That's how I always think.* You're smooth as ivory too" (3.39.31; emphasis
added). The imagistic confluence of mysterious "others" is, in fact, subtly
pervasive: while David attributes anthropomophic feelings to the elephant,
he conceives of Catherine as a "wild animal" (1.1.24; 3.16.15), and Marita
compares her to a "brave animal that will not die" (3.24.21) ; whereas the elephant has "great," "slowly moving" ears (3.26.26), Catherine, in her own way,
has bewitchingly "perfect ears" (3.5.7); while the elephant travels in search of
his "dead friend" (3.32.56), Catherine, who is also in search of togetherness,

wants [to] "be friends" with David (3.38.5); whereas the elephant is very old (3.26.24), Catherine, as her illness progresses, also begins to feel "old" (3.27.22); while the dying elephant loses all its "dignity and majesty and . . . beauty" (3.37.10), Catherine hopes that she will not "get ugly" in the throes of her own demise (3.27.29); and whereas Davey bemoans the loss of the elephant, David, as he puts it, "embalm[s] the dear dead days [with Catherine] like a bloody *taxidermist*—" (3.29.27.i; emphasis added). The litany of contrapuntal connections, only touched upon here, culminates in the motif of brotherhood: while young Davey comes to think of the elephant as his "brother," Catherine repeatedly beseeches David to think of her as a brother. "[W]e are brothers aren't we?" she asks (1.2.1; etc.).

Interestingly, David himself consciously acknowledges the interplay of past and present, telling himself that he must "use the sorrow that [he has] now" (the sorrow of losing Catherine), "to make . . . [himself understand] how the early sorrow came" (the sorrow of losing the elephant) (3.29.9). Similarly, David associates his painstaking fictional portrayal of the elephant with his love for Catherine: "In the story he had tried to make the elephant alive again as he and Kibo had seen him in the night. . . . Maybe I can, he said. Maybe I can make Catherine whole again and happy too" (3.29.7–8). Elsewhere, though, David speciously attempts to deny Catherine's submerged presence in the story: "Don't confuse things," he tells himself. "You're not that tired because you've done a day's work" (3.29.11). Later still, when David openly asserts that he does not "want to get the [African] work mixed up" with the honeymoon, Catherine authoritatively challenges the purity of David's supposedly self-contained creativity: "But it's you who mix it up," she says. "Can't you see?" (3.39.44–5). At best, then, David possesses an occluded understanding of his writerly motivations and deliberately chooses not to analyze (or psycho-analyze) his African material, fearing that he will damage his ability to write it (3.29.11; 3.39.2.ii–iii).

As David obliquely realizes, the subjacent import of the elephant story is both self-incriminatory and self-serving. For, on the one hand, of course, young Davey betrays the elephant just as David betrays Catherine. Indeed, Davey poses a redolent question, one that resonates beyond the immediate frame of the hunt: "Why didn't you help the elephant when you could?" he asks himself (3.32.8). And yet, on the other hand, the story simultaneously affirms young Davey's bond with the forsaken brother. Paradoxically, that is, Davey is redeemed by his own guilt, which brings him to a conscious realization that he cares for the elephant, a realization that sets him apart from his brutal father. In effect, Davey becomes a helpless spectator, forced to witness an event that he abhors. His remorse spawns a conscience-soothing perception that transcends betrayal and death: "[the elephant] didn't look at *me* as though he wanted to kill *me*," Davey thinks, while the slaughtered animal lies dying, after having charged Juma. "He only looked sad the same way that I felt" (3.37.14; emphasis added). Thus, David, under the guise of his boyhood persona, accomplishes in art what he fails to accomplish in life: he spiritually marries the victimized "other," ensuring an unbreakable, brotherly union. "Davey," the sympathetic jungle boy, is not, after all, very far from "Davie" Crockett, the affectionately nicknamed husband who agrees to accompany Catherine into the moral wilderness of androgyny (1.3.4–5). In the solipsistic realm of his imagination, David exonerates himself for his own crimes: the betrayed but beloved elephant functions as a forgiving surrogate for a more accusatory wife. Despite his rekindled boyhood empathy, then, David remains guilty of his father's "professional" savagery (3.30.37). For, in the very act of writing, David, another consummate professional (3.32.12), practices an *ivory trade* of his own, imperialistically exploiting the ivory-like Catherine as a material resource, transforming her, as it were, into a mere "art-i-fact."

The Bluebeard parallels culminate in David's *murderous* response to his wife's most serious transgression, the retaliatory burning of his African manuscripts, which she astutely characterizes as "intolerable little essays in juvenile sadism and bathos" (3.38.14). Barely able to control his rage, David, in total earnest, threatens to kill her: "All I want to do is kill you," he says. "And the only reason I don't do it is because you're crazy" (3.40.11–12). On a verbal level, though, the murder takes place. For David, in a gesture of obliteration, politely and viciously *shuts up* Catherine after all: "Shut up please," he says. "I'm sorry your mother ever met your father and that they ever made you. <acc.: I'm sorry that you were ever born and that you grew up. I'm sorry for everything we ever did good or bad—" (3.40.13). David's "deadly" (3.38.8) intentions are latent in his subsequent neglect. After Catherine, in a dangerously unstable condition, announces that she plans to drive to Paris alone, David offers little in the way of resistance (3.41.3–11). "Do you think it's murder [to let her go]?" he asks Marita (3.42.3). Later still, after Catherine wisely departs by train, David sardonically dismisses the possibility of "bring[ing] her back" (3.46.26). In fact, as the manuscript concludes, David's only "duty" (3.44.27) lies in the rewriting of his stories, and, significantly, he returns to the story of the raid, identifying, more strongly than ever, with his vengeful father (3.46.1–4).

The interminability of the Bluebeard paradigm is apparent as Marita, the willing catamite, revises Catherine's boyish passivity in an attempt to re-empower the stricken writer (3.44.31–32; 3.45.1; 3.45.4; 3.45.16; etc.). "We don't have to play charades," he tells her, "and you don't have to be Scheherazade [sic]" (3.45.29). Scheherazade, the heroine of the *Thousand and One Nights*, is the yarn-spinning wife of King Schariar, Bluebeard's counterpart in Eastern folklore. Convinced that all women are unfaithful, Schahriar vows to take a new bride every night and execute her the following morning. Scheherazade, however, curbs her husband's murderous policy by perpetually exciting his curiosity with titillating stories. Literary criticism being what it is, scholars have interpreted Scheherazade's role in different ways. For Ferial Jabouri Ghazoul, Scheherazade speaks with a feminist voice, asserting female subjectivity in a male world (43–44); alternatively, for Maria Tatar, Scheherazade objectifies herself, becoming a passive yet beguiling instrument of male pleasure (163). Marita, who promises to be David's "street Arab" (3.45.25[b]), clearly fits Tatar's profile. But there might well be *two* Scheherazades in *Eden*, the second of whom more closely resembles Ghazoul's feminist heroine. For Catherine attempts to preoccupy her tyran-nical husband by asking him to transcribe the ongoing "narrative" of her honeymoon adventures (3.16.27–29; 3.40.9; etc.), hoping, all the while, to assuage his stifling egoism.

Nor, finally, should one overlook the connection between Perrault's fairy tale and the biblical tale Hemingway's title invokes. For "Bluebeard" is often regarded as a folkloric retelling of the "Eden" myth. On a structural level, both stories turn upon the prohibition-transgression dynamic that Hemingway so artfully exploits; just as Jehovah carefully guards the fruit of certain trees, Bluebeard guards his secret closet; and just as Eve is tempted to taste the forbidden fruit, Bluebeard's wife is tempted to peer into the forbid-den chamber. Moreover, both Jehovah and Bluebeard are jealous rulers who issue severe punishments. But the similarities between the two stories are less remarkable than their differences: if Eve's transgression stands as the original sin that plunges mankind into the nightmare of human history, Bluebeard's wife reveals the Janus-faced duplicity of a human law-giver whose sins are far greater than her own. Indeed, while Perrault tries to imbue his fairy tale with a biblical ethos, the tale itself bespeaks a more subversive, pre-literary histo-ry, rooted in the irreverent laughter of folkloric irony. Hemingway, the skilled allusionist, taps this oral spirit of exposure, complicating his "Edenic" story of an unruly and aspiring woman with disquieting insinuations. In particu-lar, he pillories his own deific pretenses in the figure of David Bourne, a post-

Romantic author-god of high modernism, who egomaniacally regards his métier as a religious mystery (3.37.54–55; etc.). Thus, whereas Keats, in his letters, compares human life to a "Mansion of Many Apartments" whose furthest chamber is "a lucky and a gentle one—stored with the wine of love— and the bread of Friendship" (Bush 274), the claustrophobic mental rooms in *Eden* negate promise. Hemingway, a "white beard" of many wives, conveys, through Bluebeard, the murderous polygamist of folklore, what he feared most about himself.

Notes

1.   This paper is based on Item 422.1 in the Hemingway Collection (J.F.K. Library), the only extant version of *Eden* that has not undergone posthumous editorial revision. Parenthetical citations to the manuscript identify book, chapter, and page number[s]. Authorial revisions and other textual irregularities are noted by abbreviation: *acc.* (accretion); *del.* (deletion); *rev.* (revision).

2.   For scholarly perusals of "Bluebeard" retellings, see Sherrill E. Grace, "Courting Bluebeard with Bartok, Atwood, and Fowles: Modern Treatment of the Bluebeard Theme," *Journal of Modern Literature* 11.2 (July 1984), 245–262; Juliet McMaster, "'Bluebeard at Breakfast': An Unpublished Thackeray Manuscript," *Dickens Studies Annual*, 8 (1981), 197–230; and Maria Tatar, *The Hard Facts of Grimm's Fairy Tales*, Princeton: Princeton UP, 1987.

3.   Hemingway may have been confused about the number of stories David writes. While David claims to have written "four" stories (3.27.20), the chronological sequence of his writing sessions seems to allow for only three stories. The first of these, not dealt with here, is minimally rendered in evocative, fragmentary images (3.20.1–2).

4.   Thus far, *Eden* criticism—dealing either with the published novel or the manuscript or both—tends to treat the African stories very differently, as mythopoeic tales of spiritual development. With varying degrees of enthusiasm, critics have argued that Hemingway idealizes David's self-directed creativity as an example of masculine heroism.

5.   Hemingway occasionally misspells "Maji Maji" as "Madgi-Madgi." The rebellion actually occurred between 1905–07.

6.   While *Eden* criticism frequently posits a thematic interrelationship between the hunt and the honeymoon, little has been said about the specific link between Catherine and the elephant. Frank Scafella's "Clippings from The Garden of Eden," *The Hemingway Review* 7.1 (Fall 1987): 20–29, offers the most pointed commentary thus far, but expressly precludes the equivalence posited here. Approaching David's writing on a mystical level, Scafella observes that "they [Catherine and the elephant] are one in David's longing to make them as they

were." Scafella, however, makes a distinction that befits his view of David's transcendent function as an artist: "[This] is *not* to say that the elephant is Catherine in disguise, but that in the elephant is embodied the deep hollow feeling that David has from Catherine . . . " (28).

Works Cited

Bush, Douglas. Ed. *Selected Poems and Letters by John Keats.* Riverside Editions. Boston: Houghton Mifflin, 1959.

Carter, Angela. Tr. *The Fairy Tales of Charles Perrault.* London: Gollancz, 1977.

Gajdusek, Robert E. "'An Alpine Idyll': The Sun-Struck Mountain Vision and the Necessary Valley Journey." *Hemingway's Neglected Short Fiction: New Perspectives.* Ed. Susan F. Beegel. Ann Arbor: UMI, 1989. 63–183.

Ghazoul, Ferial Jabouri. *The Arabian Nights: A Structural Analysis.* Cairo: Cairo Associated Institution, 1980.

Hatch, J. C. *Tanzania: A Profile.* New York: Praeger, 1972.

Hemingway, Ernest. *The Garden of Eden* Mss. Item 422.1. Hemingway Collection. John F. Kennedy Library, Boston.

———. "Hills Like White Elephants." *The Short Stories of Ernest Hemingway.* New York: Scribner's, 1966.

Iliffe, John. *A Modern History of Tanganyika.* London: Cambridge UP, 1979.

Mackenzie, F. A. Ed. *Landru.* Famous Trial Series. New York: Scribner's, 1928.

Steiner, George. *In Bluebeard's Castle: Some Notes Towards the Redefinition of Culture.* New Haven: Yale UP, 1971.

Tatar, Maria. *The Hard Facts of Grimm's Fairy Tales.* Princeton: Princeton UP, 1987.

"COME BACK TO THE BEACH AG'IN, DAVID HONEY!": HEMINGWAY'S FETISHIZATION OF RACE IN *THE GARDEN OF EDEN* MANUSCRIPTS

Carl Eby

All of us, readers and writers, are bereft when criticism remains too polite or too fearful to notice a disrupting darkness before its eyes.

—Toni Morrison, *Playing in the Dark*

In 1950, reminiscing about his youth in Paris, then a quarter of a century behind him, Ernest Hemingway, using the clipped pseudo-"primitive" language he was so fond of in his later years, told his friend and crony A. E. Hotchner a curious yarn about one of his adventures at the club, *Le Jockey:*

> Was in there one night with Don Ogden Stewart and Waldo Pierce when the place was set on fire by the most sensational woman anybody ever saw. Or ever will. Tall, coffee skin, ebony eyes, legs of paradise, a smile to end all smiles. Very hot night but she was wearing a coat of black fur, her breasts handling the fur like it was silk. She turned her eyes on me—she was dancing with the big British gunner subaltern who had brought her—but I responded to the eyes like a hypnotic and

cut in on them. The subaltern tried to shoulder me out but the girl slid
off him and onto me. I introduced myself and asked her name.
"Josephine Baker," she said. We danced nonstop for the rest of the
night. She never took off her fur coat. Wasn't until the joint closed she
told me she had nothing on underneath. (Hotchner 52–53)

Hemingway of course, like so many writers, was a notorious liar. Famous
both for mythologizing his genuinely remarkable life and for trying to live up
to that myth, Hemingway, in spite of his reputation as a hard-boiled realist,
was frequently less than diligent when it came to distinguishing between fantasy and reality in his own life. His evening with Josephine Baker, reeking as
it does of the men's locker room and stale detective novels, is surely one of
his lies. Baker's 1925 debut in *La Revue Nègre* had made the exotic African-
American dancer literally an overnight sensation in Paris: Hemingway could
not have failed to recognize her. Hemingway's major biographers apparently
agree, for none of them even allude to the story, much less credit it.[1]

The Baker story *does*, however, bear a more than suspicious resemblance
to a passage in Hemingway's heavily autobiographical story, "The Snows of
Kilimanjaro." Gangrenous and dying in remote Africa, Harry recalls his trip
to Constantinople years before, and how, angry with his wife and lonely for
an earlier love, he had slept with "a hot Armenian slut" whom he "took away
from" a "British gunner subaltern" at a dance hall (SS 65). Hemingway, like
Harry, quarreled with his wife before his 1922 trip to Constantinople to cover
the Greco-Turkish war, but whether the story about the Armenian woman has
its origin in fact or fantasy is unclear.[2] If the passage is pure fiction, we are left
wondering why Hemingway felt inclined first to invent it and then to pass it
off as the truth in another guise. If, on the other hand, the passage is ground-
ed in autobiographical truth, its connection to the Baker story does more than
demonstrate how Hemingway used the raw material of his life to forge fiction
only to use that fiction to reinterpret and fictionalize his life (a process which
bedeviled him and continues to bedevil all but the most careful of his critics).
Troubling questions remain. Why does Hemingway substitute Josephine
Baker for the "Armenian slut," and why the attention to her dark skin, her
nakedness, and her fur coat? Why does he compare himself to a "hypnotic"?
If, as Byron in a Freudian mood once quipped, a lie "'tis but / The truth in
masquerade," what do we ultimately make of the details of the Baker fantasy?

There is surely nothing so extraordinary in a man's comically cliché-rid-
den fantasy about a beautiful woman, but Hemingway's fabricated evening
with the beautiful, dark-skinned, short-haired, fur-clad Baker seems to be

something more than this; it reads like the raw stuff of his daydreams. Perhaps we should not be surprised to discover, then, that the concerns of Hemingway's fantasy bear a remarkable resemblance to those of one of his major projects of the forties and fifties, the posthumously published, fantasy-laden, novel *The Garden of Eden*. The Baker story in fact reads like a crystallization of those concerns—concerns which, if understood psychoanalytically, clarify, without resolving, indeterminacies central to the dynamics of *The Garden of Eden*—concerns which, moreover, both invoke and clarify an eroticization of race by white male authors which has inspired studies of American literature from Leslie Fiedler's seminal 1948 essay, "'Come Back to the Raft Ag'in, Huck Honey!'" to Toni Morrison's recent and equally important *Playing in the Dark* (1992).

Morrison herself explores some of these concerns in *The Garden of Eden* brilliantly but without the full evidence of the manuscripts at her disposal or an explicitly psychoanalytic framework for her ideas. With the aid of such evidence and such a framework, I hope to extend her analysis into new territory and to clarify how the socio-psychology she explores, a psychology by which American authors have traditionally defined themselves as "white" and "male" in relation to an insistent and ever-present racial and sexual otherness, relates to the individual psychology of Ernest Hemingway.

Nancy Comley and Robert Scholes have attempted a similar project in their recent book *Hemingway's Genders*; yet driven by a laudable distaste for reductivism, Comley and Scholes explicitly avoid a psychoanalytic interpretation of Hemingway's work, opting instead to study Hemingway's unique deployment of cultural codes. However, I hope—by revealing some of Hemingway's personal codes—to show precisely how such a Freudian (or post-Freudian) reading can be useful *without* being reductive. Thus I use psychoanalysis not to reveal the *real* or *essential* truth about my subject (for I realize that no such thing exists), but rather to reveal a different, more theorizable, pattern uniting what Comley and Scholes call the "threads" of the Hemingway Text.

I

"Isn't it nice our dark things are so simple and so complicated too?"
—Ernest Hemingway, *The Garden of Eden* Manuscripts

The "sea changes" undergone by the various lovers in *The Garden of Eden* manuscripts have understandably received a good deal of attention from Hemingway scholars in the past few years. Yet while the experiments of

Catherine, David, Marita, Nick, and Barbara with gender swapping and uni-
sex hairstyles have provoked much commentary, only recently has any significant attention been paid to their obsession with sun-tanning—an obsession which, though superficially innocuous, is in fact integral to their metamorphoses. David acknowledges as much when (in some lines which incidentally read like a gloss of Hemingway's 1931 short story "The Sea
Change") he lies awake one evening pondering Catherine's transformation:

> She changes from a girl into a boy and back to a girl carelessly and
> happily and she enjoys corrupting me and I enjoy being corrupted. But
> she's not corrupt and who says it is corruption? . . . All you know is that
> you feel good after it. . . . So we must have the sun to make this sea
> change. The sea change was made in the night and it grows in the night
> and the darkness that she wants and needs now grows in the sun.
> (KL/EH 422.1, 2.4.4)[3]

The fact that all of the major characters in *The Garden of Eden* are well-
tanned, that brown skin is one of the most pervasive images in the manuscripts, that Catherine, David, and Marita spend endless hours tanning at the
beach, and that Nick and Barbara even tan on the ski slopes during the winter, may seem like nothing more than a quirk of personal taste, coming from
an author who spoke of his wives "when things were going well . . . in a standard phrase: they were happy, healthy, hard as a rock, and well-tanned"
(Baker, *Life* x). Yet in this novel, and for Catherine in particular, a tan is clearly *more* than a tan. As Morrison has argued, the "sea change" is racial as well
as sexual.

The skillfully but radically edited version of the novel published by
Scribner's in 1986 mutes Hemingway's concern with race considerably, but
the concern is hardly subtle in the original. Throughout the manuscripts,
Catherine seems desperately concerned with being "dark enough not to be
white" (KL/EH 422.1, 4.3.1). Tanning on the beach at the Grau du Roi,
Catherine claims she wants to be as "brown as a Kanaka" (KL/EH 422.1,
2.1.1). In Madrid, she is delighted when a bootblack mistakes her for a Gipsy
and when the Colonel tells her she looks like "the young chief of a warrior
tribe" and calls her "the darkest white girl I've ever seen" (KL/EH 422.1, 6.9.2;
GOE 62–63).

After waking up late one morning, she calls herself David's "lazy naked
octoroon half-caste wife" and "wild girl" (KL/EH 422.1, 5.5.2).[4] She provides

an exceedingly odd excuse for her jealousy about David's success as a writer: "I can't help it any more than if I were a negro" (KL/EH 422.1, 2.3.3). Later she tells David, "I'm your Kanaka and when we go to Africa I'll be your African girl too" (KL/EH 422.1, 2.4.1). Even David wonders why his "wife want[s] to seem to be of a different race and have completely different pigmentation" (KL/EH 422.1, 2.2.3). When lying in bed one night, he finally asks her why she wants to be so dark, she gives an interesting but vague reply:

" . . . Right now it's the thing that I want most. . . . and we're so far along now. I don't know why I want it so much. It's like I wanted to have my hair cut. But this takes so long. Maybe that's part of it. It's like growing something. But it makes me excited too. Just good excited all the time. The fact that it's happening. Doesn't it make you excited to have me getting so dark?"

"Uh-huh. I love it. . . . But we have to be careful with you."

"You *are* so careful and good. Look how nice it is against the sheets with only this much light."

"It's lovely."

It was too and strange in the small light.

"I don't want to be a white girl anymore and I'm half-caste already and I think I can be darker and it still be good. Did you think I could ever be this dark?"

"No because you're blonde."

"I can. . . . But I want every part of me dark and it's getting that way and you'll be darker than an Indian and that takes us further away from other people. You see why it's important. . . . I wish I had some Kanaka blood or some Indian blood but then it probably wouldn't mean anything. It's the changing that is as important as the dark. But I'm going to be so dark you . . . won't be able to stand it and you'll be helpless. White women will always bore you."

"They bore me already." (KL/EH 422.1, 2.4.3–4; portions qtd. in Comley and Scholes; see also *GOE* 30–31)

For the others as well, a tan isn't simply a tan. Nick is described repeatedly— by himself, by Barbara, by Andy, and by David—as looking like a "reservation Indian." David jokes about being a "half-assed Tahitian," and Catherine, who calls him a "renegade Kanaka," plans to make him "darker than an Indian" (*GOE* 154; KL/EH 422.1, 4.3.4). When Hemingway introduces us to the Italian

heiress, Marita, she isn't only the "dark girl"; she is so dark that her skin
seems almost "Javanese" (*GOE* 236). And while Marita initially imagines that
David might like one of his "girls lighter than the other" (*GOE* 101), after
constant gender-flipping drives Catherine mad, Marita decides to fill
Catherine's old shoes, getting her hair cut to become David's "M'Bulu girl"
(KL/EH 422.1, 36.45.25). In David's opinion, she ends up looking more like
"a Bizerte street urchin" or "water front Arab," but he assures her, "You do
look like Africa. . . . But the very far north and you mix up the genders"
(KL/EH 422.1, 36.45.1–2). Marita is hardly particular, though, and tells her
"Effendi," David, "we can be people from the Gobi desert" or, if that fails,
"Cossacks" (KL/EH 422.1, 36.45.16, 22).[5]

This racial transformation, like all aspects of the "sea change" the characters undergo after seeing Rodin's statue, *The Metamorphoses of Ovid*, is radically overdetermined, partaking of manifold cultural, literary, and psychological associations and numerous—almost always troubling—racial stereotypes. On the surface, both Catherine and Marita want to fill in for David's
boyhood African sweetheart. But Hemingway also clearly associates racial
otherness with a primitivism which must have struck him as only appropriate for his theme: *The Garden of Eden.* When Andy tries to relate the story of
Nick and Barbara, he insists that the "things they did were primitive. . . . It
was all very primitive" (KL/EH 422.2, 40.inserts.10). Lurking behind Andy's
assertion are all the stereotypes by which the West has traditionally constructed the "primitive" as something "original," "simple," "spontaneous,"
and "pure," yet simultaneously "mysterious," "lustful," "irrational," and
"defiled" (Torgovnick 19, 80). This interest in the "primitive," however, is as
characteristically modernist as it is Edenic. In a sense, the wealthy white
woman Catherine, who expresses an interest in the "primitive" art of Picasso,
plays at being a Kanaka much like whites played at being black in their visits
to the night clubs of Harlem in the twenties and thirties.

Yet Catherine isn't *simply* playing, nor is she searching for some sort of
Lawrentian or Andersonian mythical authenticity lying just beyond the col-
orline; she sees her dark skin as an integral part of her identity. When the
Colonel asks her what she plans to do with her tan, she replies: "Wear it. . . .
It's very becoming in bed. . . . I don't really wear it. It's me. I really am this
dark. The sun just develops it. I wish I was darker" (*GOE* 64). Catherine's
dark skin, like that of all the other characters, signifies her alienation from
"proper" (read *white*) society and her transgression of social taboos. It also
clearly signifies what Hemingway regarded as her moral "darkness," a moral
darkness in us all just waiting to be "developed." If Catherine's insistence on

being "Kanaka" clearly connects her to the supposedly innocent, Edenic, sexually liberated, tropical islands of Margaret Mead's Pacific, it also carries an implicit threat so long as we remember Captain Cook's reputed fate at the hands of cannibal Kanakas. And while Catherine's "honorary" status as a Kanaka links her to Richard Henry Dana's Kanaka companion Hope, likewise a sick friend who must be cared for, her darkness may as well link her to the Babo of Melville's "Benito Cereno," the supposedly subservient partner who, like Bugs in Hemingway's story "The Battler," in fact commands the ship.[6] Yet the obvious titillation she derives from tanning, her repeated insistence that her tan looks wonderful in *bed*, and her tendency to link her obsession for tanning to that obvious signifier of gender status in *The Garden of Eden*, her obsession for hair-cutting, all suggest (as do Morrison and Comley and Scholes) that Catherine's racial transformation also has to be read as part and parcel of her psychosexual transformation.

II

> Everybody has strange things that mean things to them and we have to understand them....
> —Ernest Hemingway, *The Garden of Eden* Manuscripts

According to Leslie Fiedler, "When ... the [white male] American writer does not make impotence itself his subject, he is left to choose between the two archetypes of innocent [racially charged] homosexuality and unconsummated incest: the love of comrades and that of brother and sister" (348). Whatever we may think about the breadth of this claim, in *The Garden of Eden* Hemingway seems to take up both of these archetypes which Fiedler aptly enough describes as "Edenic affair[s] ... lived out in a Garden in the process of being destroyed" (351). More importantly, Hemingway takes up the two archetypes in a manner which ultimately clarifies how they form— at least in his case—part of a unified psychology.

In *The Garden of Eden*, the friendship between the native hunter, Juma, and the boy, David, in the story of the elephant hunt fits nicely (at least initially) into Fiedler's litany of innocent homoerotic lovers, one white and the other dark: Dana and Hope; Leatherstocking and Chingachgook; Ishmael and Queequeg; Huck and Jim; Ike McCaslin and Sam Fathers. We might easily add to Fiedler's list such colonial British duos as T. E. Lawrence and Ali or Kipling's Kim and the old lama—duos which Fiedler with his American emphasis ignores but to which Hemingway plainly alludes in *The Garden of Eden* manuscripts (KL/EH 422.1, 36.45.19). In this archetype, Fiedler explains, dark skin signifies for the white male imagination, among other things, an escape from feminine civilization and the super-ego into the mythical masculine wilderness and forbidden sexuality of the uncivilized id.

Kipling's *Kim* both exemplifies this archetype and holds a key to Hemingway's treatment of the elephant story. Kim repeatedly flees the constraints of British decorum and feminine society for the freedom of the Indian road with the beloved old Tibetan lama, changing races like a chameleon—*or like Catherine*—all the while. And in one scene which must have appealed to Hemingway immensely—for reasons which should grow still clearer—the Irish boy, Kim, has his hair cropped and his face painted by a prostitute so he can pass as a "low-caste Hindu boy" on the road, though he tells the prostitute that he does this to visit his twelve-year-old Hindu lover. But even more importantly for understanding *The Garden of Eden*, the power of male bonding in Kipling's novel is conveyed most poignantly in the old lama's comparison of himself and the boy to the two elephants who save one another in Buddhist legend, Shakyamuni and his disciple Ananda in earlier lives. Hemingway, moreover, evidently recognized the homoerotic undertow of this bonding: "Andy do you believe it about women for breeding, boys for pleasure, and melons for delight?" Catherine asks. "I always thought of it as everything that Kipling left out. . . . Imagine how he would have been with all that in. Sometimes it's almost there but then it moves away. He knew it for a while and then he was ashamed of it" (KL/EH 422.1, 6.9.14).

In *The Garden of Eden*, the old lama's parable lurks behind the story the adult David writes of the old elephant's return to the bones of his long deceased friend and partly explains the boy David's break with his father and Juma, the "god damned friend killers" (*GOE* 198).7 The elephant's final charge, which almost kills Juma, who "had always been David's best friend and had taught him to hunt," seems a sort of wish fulfillment aimed both at Juma and, indirectly, at David's father, signifying a failure, or rejection, of the homoerotic bonding of Fiedler's archetype (*GOE* 171).[8] Homoeroticism thus seems for David, through his identification with the elephant, to be linked inextricably with death—either his father's or his own at the hands of his father. It is linked as well with a sort of primal repression: "I'm going to keep everything a secret always," he tells himself. "Never tell anyone anything again" (*GOE* 181).

Gender affiliation, however, is never stable in this novel, and the old bull elephant who becomes David's "hero" and "brother" in the place of his father and Juma is symbolically as feminine as it is masculine. Thus, the killing of the elephant with his oversized tusks, which the adult David clearly associates with the "ivory"-haired Catherine, and David's subsequent boyhood rejection of his father and Juma, force the adult David into Fiedler's second archetype, an incestuous love for a woman who looks just like him and repeatedly calls him "brother," a love blending innocence with an overwhelming sense of sin. David may jokingly assure Marita (whose brother "was in love with her") that he "never minded incest if it was in the same family," but he can never entirely shake the feelings of "corruption" and "remorse" which follow his sexual experiments with Catherine (KL/EH 422.1, 33.42.22). Yet if Hemingway manages to link both of Fiedler's archetypes, one nevertheless suspects, given the recent biographical scholarship of Mark Spilka, Michael Reynolds, and Kenneth Lynn, that the connection Hemingway establishes has little (if anything) to do with any sort of Jungian collective unconscious and quite a lot to do with the vicissitudes of his own boyhood.

A work of as much importance to the background of *The Garden of Eden* as *Kim* is Proust's *Remembrance of Things Past*, which Catherine is reading in the Madrid section of the novel. True to form, she skips immediately to Book Four, *Sodome et Gomorrhe*. The biblical allusion to the cities of the plain is rich enough in itself, suggesting a homoerotic and "perverse" parallel for the more epistemophilic/narcissistic/oedipal loss of Eden.[9] (In *The Garden of Eden* Nick is afraid that his hair cut makes him look like a "sodomite," so, using what he calls an "Indian trick," he hides his hair under his hat.) The connection to Proust is important, however, not only for the allusions to sodomy, not only because Proust shares Hemingway's interest in male and female homosexuality, not only for the weight Proust gives to loss and the impermanence of love, but also for what it suggests about the importance of involuntary unconscious memories (both David's and Hemingway's) in the genesis of *The Garden of Eden*. (The importance of such memories is further underscored by still another book on Catherine's reading list, W. H. Hudson's memoir of his boyhood, *Far Away and Long Ago*.)

As Toni Morrison and Marianna Torgovnick have so convincingly demonstrated, white male authors have traditionally constituted and shored up their own egos in dialectical relation to racial and sexual "otherness," but Hemingway seems to have been particularly driven to do so due to an intensely fragile ego troubled by his own remembrance of things past.

David's attachment to the "African girl" of his boyhood (like Nick Adam's memories of his "Indian girl" Prudie/Trudy) suggests a fascination with "original love objects" more complex than simple nostalgia. In fact throughout Hemingway's fiction, the actual representative of the "original love object"—whether it be Hadley, Agnes von Kurowsky, Marjorie Bump, Prudy Boulton, David's African girl, or Nick's little sisters—often seems to matter less than the position that she occupies in the male hero's psyche; all later love is portrayed as a reaction to, or imitation of, some original affair in the distant past. And if Hemingway's concerns strike us as "archetypal," I would like to suggest that, aside from his sheer verbal artistry, some element of Hemingway's vast cultural appeal may reside precisely in how the psychosocial dilemmas of his age—an age in which many of his white male compatriots felt challenged by the rising power of racial and sexual "others"— found an intensified mirror-image in Hemingway's personal psychology.[10]

The now famous early "twinning" of Hemingway and his older sister, Marcelline—whom Hemingway as a boy nicknamed significantly enough "*Ivory*" (Mellow 22)—with its concomitant gender-flipping and hair-matching, seems to have profoundly disturbed the early formation of Hemingway's ego, gender identity, and body-image. Having a "matching" sister must have, among other things, led to a prolonged and intense stage of primary identification as well as an intense and irreconcilable need to individuate, casting doubt upon such fundamental questions as "Am I a boy or a girl?" and "What is me and what is not me?" This upbringing seems to have given Hemingway both his tremendous ability to identify with others and equally powerful need to fend off exactly this sort of identification through the process of objectification.

These abilities, desires, and anxieties surface in *The Garden of Eden* when Catherine flip-flops between genders and (like her namesake in *A Farewell to Arms*, like Maria in *For Whom the Bell Tolls*, and like her replacement, Marita, in *The Garden of Eden*) tries to merge identities with her lover. She dresses like David, talks him into having his hair cut and dyed to match her own, and insists that she wants to be exactly like him. Such unity between lovers clearly had a symbolic and spiritual significance for Hemingway, who apparently strove for a similar unity in his relationships with Hadley and Pauline (Diliberto 79), but it just as clearly invokes psychosexual concerns which partly explains the feelings of "remorse" and "corruption" which David associates with this unity. Like infants narcissistically trapped in the Lacanian mirror stage, David and Catherine stare endlessly into mirrors to confirm and constitute their body images and egos. Their love itself is such a mirror, but in trying to forge their own egos in relation to nearly identical "others," Catherine and David seem to intensify the very anxieties which they, or Hemingway, are trying to escape.

Hemingway apparently tried to confront these anxieties like a colonial magistrate, by making color the signifier of "otherness." Yet this doesn't solve David's, or Hemingway's problem: David himself tans like Catherine and becomes, after Catherine takes him to the coiffeur's, a "white headed Indian" (KL/EH 422.4, 4.inserts.18). In a sense he becomes other than himself. Insofar as Marita allows David to play the "sahib" or "effendi" to her "Arab street urchin," insofar as she promises to leave David unchanged in her attempts to look and be just like him (KL/EH 422.1, 35.44.31), she seems less threatening than Catherine. Yet she resembles Catherine more closely than she would have David believe. Thus when Marita looks at David's "whitish" hair against his "dark face" she thinks, "I wish I'd done that to him" (KL/EH 422.1, 36.45.14).

By turning Catherine into David's "African girl," Hemingway may allow David (who imaginatively "becomes his father" in the process of writing the African story) to identify with his father, the seducer of African girls, when David with his gender status challenged needs such an identification most (GOE 147). Yet as he grows darker himself, and as Catherine tempts him to play games with his own gender, he perhaps also becomes his father's African girl. Such narcissistic indeterminacy is all the more frightening for Hemingway's characters since the otherness against which the ego defines itself seems absolutely yoked to sexual otherness—invoking the most frightening aspects of masculine anxiety about body image. Thus, while Mark Spilka wonders whether the narcissism which has long been recognized in Hemingway's fictional romances "altogether explain[s] these relations," claiming that "feminization, or better still androgyny, might further explain them" (217), I want to suggest that (while they by no means explain anything altogether) what Spilka calls "androgyny" in Hemingway's texts is largely the result of precisely such narcissistic desires and anxieties.

According to classic psychoanalytic studies by Phyllis Greenacre, boys frequently cope with fragile body-images and the resultant intensification of castration anxiety by adopting a fetish—an object, which as Freud observed, can paradoxically both stand in for and confirm the absence of the maternal or female phallus, the absence of which seems to confirm the possibility of masculine castration. In Freud's words, the fetishist has not

preserved unaltered his belief that women have a phallus. He has retained that belief, but he has also given it up. In the conflict between the weight of the unwelcome perception and the force of his counter-wish, a compromise has been reached, as is only possible under the dominance of the unconscious laws of thought—the primary process. Yes, in his mind the woman *has* got a penis, in spite of everything; but this penis is no longer the same as it was before. Something else has taken its place, has been appointed its substitute, as it were, and now inherits the interest which was formerly directed to its predecessor. But this interest suffers an extraordinary increase as well, because the horror of castration has set up a memorial to itself in the creation of this substitute. (157)

For the fetishist, then, women must be both "other" and not entirely "other." Fixated at the phallic stage or "position," he can only conceive of the female genitalia as a disconcerting "lack." By endowing women with the fetishized object (or substitute female phallus), Freud explains, the fetishist simultaneously denies the possibility of his own castration and turns women into "acceptable," less threatening partners, warding off the apparent threat of homosexuality while covertly preserving an outlet for homoerotic desire in his female but phallic object. In just this way, by endowing the old elephant with the enormous, overstated tusks which David associates with the ivory-haired Catherine, which Hemingway must have associated with his troublingly identical "twin" sister, "Ivory," and which David's father and Juma will hack off the dead animal in an act confirming their presence/absence, David denies and displaces his own attachment to a homoerotic male bonding. The roots of the fetishism which allow him to do this, moreover, lie precisely in the narcissistic anxieties inherent in the innocent brother-sister love of Fiedler's second archetype.

Post-Freudian psychoanalytic theory suggests that fetishism originates not so much in a subsequent reaction to oedipal castration anxiety, as Freud suggested, as it does in the vicissitudes of preoedipal separation and individuation (Greenacre, Stoller, and Roiphe and Galenson). If a male child is confused about the boundaries of his own ego and body and his own gender status, he is particularly susceptible to the terrifying fantasies of dismemberment which call into being intense pre-oedipal and oedipal castration anxiety. (And the intensity of Hemingway's castration anxiety is difficult to ignore given stories such as *The Sun Also Rises* or "God Rest You Merry, Gentlemen.") As Greenacre explains, there is even a particular predisposition to fetishism among men raised in households, like Hemingway's, "in which there are two children of opposite sex, either twins or only a year or two apart in age, who are constantly cared for together, daily bathed and dressed together" (54), since this leads to confusion about the status of the ego, gender identity, and body image.

One hardly needs to read *The Garden of Eden*, with its overt linkage of gender-swapping and hair-cutting, to notice Hemingway's now famous obsession with hair. Remember Frederic Henry's excitement as he watches Catherine Barkley getting a marcel wave in *A Farewell to Arms*; or Harry Morgan's almost identical excitement when Maria gets her hair bleached in *To Have and Have Not*; remember those other short-haired women in his novels, Brett Ashley in *The Sun Also Rises*, or Maria in *For Whom the Bell Tolls*. This eroticization of hair has long been acknowledged by Hemingway's critics (though I haven't read anything about the form it takes in disguise: a fur-fetish or, odd as it may seem, a fetish for small furry animals, particularly cats), but it is generally understood as a simple re-enactment of Hemingway's twin-like relation to Marcelline and is seldom if ever treated as a true fetish in the Freudian or post Freudian sense with all the psychoanalytic baggage that this entails. Yet we cannot understand much about Hemingway's fascination for hair without this baggage, nor can we understand his fascination with racial transformation. After all, Catherine can only compare her obsession for tanning, which she insists is like "growing something"—a female phallus we might presume?—to her obsession for hair-cutting.

The fetish, as a marker of both absence and presence, is an inherently paradoxical, unstable object. As Catherine, that daughter of a "dark" father and "fair" mother (*GOE* 63), explains herself, her darkness would signify nothing if she were *really* Kanaka: "It's the *changing* that is as important as the dark" (my emphasis). Catherine isn't simply "the darkest white girl in the world," she is also "the blondest," with hair "just like ivory." Her dark skin always has to be counterpointed against the whiteness of sheets, her pearls, her clothes, or her hair. The fetish, as imaginary female phallus, is a marker of gender difference which paradoxically somehow fails to mark exactly this difference. One hardly needs to grope to find phallic women in Hemingway's texts: Catherine Barkley with her riding crop, Pilar with her scepter-spoon, Margot Macomber with her Mannlicher, or Brett Ashley with Jake's missing phallus. Catherine Bourne, oscillating between boyhood and girlhood, in possession of the fetishized but closely cut ("phallic" yet "castrated") hair, both has and does not have the female phallus, she is both other than David and yet paradoxically identical to him. Her racial transformation, which is not really racial transformation (she both "wears" her tan and yet really is this dark), is the marker of precisely this difference/non-difference.

Yet not only are Hemingway's female characters, with their fetishized hair and suntans, simultaneously both phallic and castrated, David and Nick in their games with hair-cutting and sunbathing, in their willingness to "go native" (to use a very problematic phrase), assume the fetishized items themselves in what Otto Fenichel would define as subtly transvestic acts; that is, they identify themselves with the phallic woman. Thus when the "wild girl," Catherine, becomes the phallic "Peter" in bed, David *becomes* Catherine:

"Now you can't tell who is who can you?"
"No."
"You are changing," she said. "Oh you are. You are. Yes you are and you're my girl Catherine."
"You're Catherine."
"No. I'm Peter. You're my wonderful Catherine. You're my beautiful lovely Catherine. You were so good to change." (*GOE* 17)[11]

Such transformations, moreover, are hardly confined to Hemingway's fiction. Like Marita, who speaks of sharing the same "tribal rules" with David (KL/EH 422.1, 36.45.35), Hemingway, in the manuscripts to *A Moveable Feast*, describes his sexual experiments with Hadley (experiments which apparently involved identical haircuts) in almost exactly these terms: "We lived like *savages* and kept our own *tribal* rules and had our own customs and our own standards, secrets, *taboos*, and delights" (qtd. in Kennedy 135, my emphasis). On his last trip to Africa, Hemingway not only appears to have had a dalliance with a Wakamba girl, Debba—whom he called his "fiancée" and compared to Nick Adam's boyhood love, Prudy—he tried, in Carlos Baker's words, "to go native" himself, shaving his head "to the scalp, like a Masai girl's," dying his clothes various shades of Masai rusty pink ochre, and taking up spear hunting (Baker, *Life* 517; Mary Hemingway 367). Yet in spite of the seemingly macho spear-shaking, Hemingway's attempt to go native, insofar as it involved a sort of fetishistic cross-dressing, was, like David Bourne's transformation, inherently transvestic. The spear-throwing itself seems to be on some level but a playful game of *fort!/da!* through which Hemingway could attempt to master the anxiety inherent in playing the role of the phallic/castrated "Masai girl." If such an interpretation seems far-fetched, the following entry in Mary Hemingway's diary, written by Ernest during this "native" period, should make it less so:

We decided last night to lay off all huntings and shootings today . . . and *devote the day to rest and Miss Mary's Christmas haircut. . . .* Her hair is naturally blonde to reddish golden blonde to sandy blonde. Papa loved it the way it looked naturally, but Miss Mary had made him a present of saying to make her hair really blonde a couple of weeks ago, and this made him want to have her as a *platinum* [ivory?] blonde, as she was at Torcello where we lived one fall and part of a winter, burnt the Beech logs in the fireplace and *made love at least every morning, noon and night* and had the loveliest time Papa ever knew of. . . . Loving Mary has been such a complicated and wonderful thing for over nine years. . . . Mary is . . . [a sort of] prince of devils . . . and almost *any place you touch her it can kill both you and her. She has always wanted to be a boy and thinks as a boy without ever losing any femininity.* If you should become confused on this you should retire. *She loves me to be her girls, which I love to be, not being absolutely stupid.* . . . In return she makes me awards and at night we do every sort of thing which pleases her and which pleases me. . . . Mary has never had one lesbian impulse but has always wanted to be a boy. *Since I have never cared for any man and dislike any tactile contact with men* except the normal Spanish abrazo or embrace which precedes a departure or welcomes a return from a voyage . . . , *I loved feeling the embrace of Mary* which came to me as something quite new and *outside all tribal law.* On the night of December 19th we worked out these things and I have never been happier. (Hemingway 20 Dec. 1953, qtd. in Mary Hemingway 370, my emphasis)[12]

If the act of writing in Mary's diary doesn't in itself strike us as vaguely transvestic, it is hard to overlook Ernest's desire to be one of *Mary's* "girls." More importantly, though, the above passage allows us to glimpse some of the complexity behind Hemingway's desire. In it we can trace how he used his fetishistic relationship with Mary, a relationship mediated by ivory hair and tribal law, a relationship which under the pull of narcissism turns *both* partners into masculinized feminine objects, as a defense against and substitute for the embrace of a homoerotic desire which itself stemmed in part from the dangerous power of a feminine whose touch can "kill both you and her." It is in this edenic, polymorphously perverse, yet anxiety-laden desire that we should look for Hemingway's quarrel with what Spilka defines more vaguely as "androgyny."

The dynamic instability of Hemingway's desire is reflected in a dynamic structural instability running throughout *The Garden of Eden*—an instability which suggests the ultimate inadequacy of the ending chosen by Scribner's editor Tom Jenks for the published version of the novel. In the manuscripts, the short-haired Bournes must always be played against the long-haired Sheldons. Each of the central characters is riven internally; yet they nevertheless seem more aspects of a single psyche than individual agents. Given the radical instability of the fetish and the splitting of the ego that both engenders it and is perpetuated by it, there simply is no happy escape from *The Garden of Eden.* To dispense with the fetish is unacceptable since it would expose Hemingway to intolerable castration anxiety—making women "inadequate" and forcing him towards what he would consider an unacceptable homosexuality. Yet to keep the fetish is to keep a fundamental split in the ego which must remain irresolvable. Even if Catherine *could* simply go away as she does at the conclusion of the Scribner's edition, Marita is too similar for comfort, and the phallic woman represented most clearly by Catherine forms part of David as well. As Robert Fleming has suggested—though for very different reasons—the double suicide contemplated by Catherine and David in the "provisional ending" of Hemingway's manuscript is unfortunately the only way to resolve the irresolvable and achieve some sense of an ending.

Only now can we understand Hemingway's daydream of Josephine Baker and its relationship to the passage from "The Snows of Kilimanjaro." Baker (pronounced as "Bak*hair*" by the French) was the quintessential *garçonne* (French for "flapper"), and she was virtually an ambassador for the sexual adventurousness of bohemian Paris in the 1920s (Rose 11; Haney 69). As Marjorie Garber notes in *Vested Interests,* cross-dressing was a staple of Baker's shows, and Baker's associations with transvestism were "ubiquitous":

> When she danced the Charleston onstage Baker "sang in a man's voice." She described herself as having "pointed knees and the breasts of a seventeen-year-old-boy." Her famous banana skirt, worn at the Folies-Bergère, is unforgettably described by Phyllis Rose as looking, when she danced, "like perky, good-natured phalluses" in "jiggling motion"; later, when she appeared with the Ziegfeld Follies, the bananas had transmuted into tusks. (279)

The tusks (which in period photographs look more like spikes to me) may be little more than a happy coincidence, but I am less inclined to find coincidence in the scandal surrounding her appearance in a blonde wig to sing "*Si j'étais blanche!*" a satirical song about the then new (1932) French fad for sunbathing:

Moi si j'étais blanche
Sachez qu'mon bonheur
Qui près de vous s'èpanche
Gardr'ait sa couleur
Au soleil, c'est par l'extèrieur
Que l'on se dore
Moi c'est la flamme de mon coeur
Que me colore. (qtd. in Hammond 91)

In Hemingway's fantasy, Baker, the phallic/castrated boy/girl, is clearly more than a glamorous substitute for an anonymous racial other who in turn functioned as a substitute or "cure" for an original love. When Hemingway, at a club which Robert McAlmon equated with transgressive sexuality (92), driven by a "hypnotic" unconscious attraction, "cuts in" on Baker, separating her from the big phallic gunner subaltern, he confirms her psychosexual castration; yet Baker, perhaps like Hemingway's "hard-as-rock" wives,[13] functions as a walking—or, rather, dancing—fetish. Hemingway's daydream of her "coffee skin," short hair, and "coat of black fur," not only collapses his favorite fetishes into a single icon, it exposes the very nature of the fetish—it is that which like Baker's fur coat both stands in for and conceals a lack, the "nothing underneath." Beneath Hemingway's tie to this presence and lack, beneath the narcissistic tension between his inseparability from Baker with whom he dances all night and his contradictory need to objectify her entirely, beneath the noun-clipping pseudo-primitive language which allows him to transvestically "go native" in the very act of telling his story, lurks a gangrene that both reveals the fragility of Hemingway's body-image and symbolizes his fear of moral "corruption." Hemingway confronts these anxieties courageously in his sprawling manuscript about the Sheldons and the Bournes, but these are the demons which ultimately drive him beyond the gates of Eden.

Notes

1. While I don't believe this story, I recognize that Baker and Hemingway were friends. Sorting out the exact nature of Hemingway's relationship with Baker, however, is difficult if not impossible, since Baker was even more prone to

self-mythologization than was Hemingway. According to Phyllis Rose, Baker "tried on different pasts as though they were dresses, to see which suited her" (114).

2. Michael Reynolds doubts the authenticity of this story (*Paris Years* 77). James Mellow, however, is less inclined to dismiss it (197). It seems fair at least to say that the incident formed part of Hemingway's psychological autobiography whether it actually happened or not.

3. For *The Garden of Eden* manuscripts, I cite item number, folder, chapter, and page. Thus "(KL/EH 422.1, 4.3.1)" means Kennedy Library item 422.1, folder 4, chapter 3, page 1. Wherever possible I try to quote from the published version of the novel (indicated simply by "*GOE*") instead of the manuscript.

4. As a demonstration of how, in editing the manuscripts, Tom Jenks muted Hemingway's concern with race, we might note how this line appears in the published version of the novel: "I'm your lazy naked wife" (43).

5. I realize that Cossacks are Caucasian, but ethnic otherness clearly substitutes here for Hemingway's ongoing interest in racial otherness. His inclusion of "Arab street urchins" invokes the strong associations in *fin de siècle* Europe (most notably in the work of Gide) between North Africa and pederasty.

6. Michael Reynolds includes Dana's book in *Hemingway's Reading, 1910–1940: An Inventory.*

7. Mark Spilka, who has written eloquently about Kipling's influence on Hemingway's work, claims that the elephant story in *The Garden of Eden* is indebted to the dancing elephants in Kipling's Mowgli stories, but Hemingway's debt to Kim (which Spilka curiously ignores) strikes me as far more profound. Reynolds includes a nine volume set of Kipling in *Hemingway's Reading, 1910–1940: An Inventory.*

8. David more or less admits as much when he says he wishes the elephant had killed Juma (*GOE* 202). David's reaction could also be prompted in part by homoerotic jealousy; David thinks to himself, "Juma will drink his share of the ivory or just buy himself another god damn wife" (*GOE* 181).

9. The loss of Eden is "epistemophilic" and "narcissistic" insofar as it evokes the child's first recognition of sexual difference. (The narcissist longs for a world anterior to such recognition, but such a world, like Eden, is always-already-lost.) The loss of Eden is "oedipal" insofar as it is the consequence of a transgression against God the Father.

10. Not only do I suspect that Hemingway's desires and anxieties were unusually intense due to the vicissitudes of his childhood, I suspect as well that his expression of these desires and anxieties was (frequently) unusually intense due to the influence of his bipolar disorder. During a manic or hypomanic phase, one is more inclined to "act out" one's fixations. We see this phenomenon clearly in the cyclical nature of Catherine's unusual behavior: "It lasted a month, [David] thought, or almost. And the other time from le Grau du Roi to Hendaye was two months" (*GOE* 57).

11. Hemingway emphasizes the phallic implications of the name "Peter" in a fragment among the *GOE* manuscripts: "I'd never known anyone named Peter that wasn't a prick" (miscellaneous notes and fragments KL/EH 422).

12. I should also call the reader's attention to the following anecdote in Lynn's biography: "In early 1947 [nearly seven years before Ernest wrote the cited entry in Mary's diary], Hemingway urged Mary to have her hair bleached silver and gave his own a henna rinse. To the servants at the Finca he explained the change in his appearance by saying he had doused his hair with what he thought was a bottle of shampoo left behind by Martha" (543). Here, again, Hemingway assumes the fetishized item himself in a subtly transvestic act. I must, however, be absolutely clear about the difference between *performing* what I call a "subtly transvestic act" and *being* a transvestite.

13. See Otto Fenichel's well-known 1936 paper, "The Symbolic Equation: Girl = Phallus." We see another instance of this when, in further allusion to *Sodome et Gomorrhe*, David calls Catherine's white sharkskin dress her "pillar of salt suit" (KL/EH 422.1, 8.13.37).

Works Cited

Baker, Carlos. *Ernest Hemingway: A Life Story.* New York: Scribner's, 1969.

Comley, Nancy R. and Robert Scholes. *Hemingway's Genders: Rereading the Hemingway Text.* New Haven: Yale U P, 1994.

Diliberto, Gioia. *Hadley.* New York: Ticknor & Fields, 1992.

Fenichel, Otto. "The Psychology of Transvestism." *The Collected Works of Otto Fenichel.* Vol. 1. New York: Norton, 1953. 167–180.

———. "The Symbolic Equation: Girl = Phallus." *The Psychoanalytic Quarterly* 18 (1949): 303–324.

Fiedler, Leslie. *Love and Death in the American Novel.* 3rd edn. New York: Anchor, 1992.

Fleming, Robert. "The Endings of Hemingway's *Garden of Eden.*" *American Literature* 61.2 (1989): 261–70.

Freud, Sigmund. "Fetishism." *The Standard Edition of the Complete Psychological Works of Sigmund Freud.* Trans. James Strachey. Vol. 21. London: Hogarth, 1963. 147–58.

Garber, Marjorie. *Vested Interests: Cross-Dressing and Cultural Anxiety.* New York: Harper Perennial, 1992.

Greenacre, Phyllis. "Perversions: General Considerations Regarding Their Genetic and Dynamic Background." *The Psychoanalytic Study of the Child* 23 (1968): 47–62.

Hammond, Bryan, and Patrick O'Connor. *Josephine Baker.* London: Jonathan Cape, 1988.

Haney, Lynn. *Naked at the Feast: A Biography of Josephine Baker.* New York: Dodd, Mead, 1981.

Hemingway, Ernest. *A Farewell to Arms.* New York: Scribner's, 1929.

———. *For Whom the Bell Tolls.* New York: Scribner's, 1940.

———. *The Garden of Eden.* Ed. Tom Jenks. New York: Scribner's, 1986.

———. *The Garden of Eden* Manuscripts. Hemingway Collection, John F. Kennedy Library, Boston, MA. Quoted by permission.

———. *The Short Stories of Ernest Hemingway.* New York: Scribner's, 1938.

———. *To Have and Have Not.* New York: Scribner's, 1937.

Hemingway, Mary Welsh. *How It Was.* New York: Knopf, 1976.

Hotchner, A. E. *Papa Hemingway: A Personal Memoir.* New York: Random House, 1966.

Kennedy, J. Gerald. *Imagining Paris: Exile, Writing, and American Identity.* New Haven: Yale U P, 1993.

Lynn, Kenneth. *Hemingway.* New York: Simon & Schuster, 1987.

McAlmon, Robert. *Being Geniuses Together: 1920–30.* Revised with Supplementary Chapters and an Afterword by Kay Boyle. San Francisco: North Point, 1984.

Mellow, James. *Hemingway: A Life Without Consequences.* New York: Addison-Wesley, 1992.

Morrison, Toni. *Playing in the Dark: Whiteness and the Literary Imagination.* New York: Vintage, 1993.

Reynolds, Michael. *Hemingway's Reading, 1910–1940: An Inventory.* Princeton: Princeton U P, 1981.

———. *Hemingway: The Paris Years.* Cambridge, MA: Basil Blackwell, 1989.

Roiphe, Herman, and Eleanor Galenson. *Infantile Origins of Sexual Identity.* New York: International U P, 1981.

Rose, Phyllis. *Jazz Cleopatra: Josephine Baker in Her Time:* New York: Doubleday, 1989.

Spilka, Mark. *Hemingway's Quarrel with Androgyny.* Lincoln: U of Nebraska P, 1990.

Stoller, Robert. *Presentations of Gender.* New Haven: Yale U P, 1985.

Torgovnick, Marianna. *Gone Primitive: Savage Intellects, Modern Lives.* Chicago: U of Chicago P, 1990.

HEMINGWAY'S BARBERSHOP QUINTET: *THE GARDEN OF EDEN* MANUSCRIPT

Mark Spilka

I

In 1946, when Ernest Hemingway began writing *The Garden of Eden*, Scott Fitzgerald had been dead for nine years, Rudyard Kipling for ten. Both writers were much on Hemingway's mind as he fashioned what now seems to be his most experimental and easily his most ambitious novel. Fitzgerald's life and work, particularly *Tender is the Night*, would offer precedents for the troubled triangles in Paris and on the Riviera which dominate the main narrative; Kipling's *Jungle Books* would inspire the African tale of an elephant hunt, the composition of which becomes a dynamic counterpoint to that narrative Hemingway would measure himself, as always, against expired and admired competitors and try to beat them at their own games; but it would be his game, as always, that mattered.

As early as May 28, 1934, Hemingway had written Fitzgerald a predictive letter, complaining about his tragic stance in *Tender is the Night*, his failure in that novel to use rather than abuse his personal dilemma in caring for his mad wife Zelda:

Reprinted as excerpted[1] with permission from Novel, *21 (1987), pp. 31–45.*

Forget your personal tragedy. We are all bitched from the start and you especially have to be hurt like hell before you can write seriously. But when you get the damned hurt use it—don't cheat with it. . . . You see, Bo, you're not a tragic character. Neither am I. All we are is writers and what we should do is write. Of all people on earth you needed discipline in your work and instead you marry someone who is jealous of your work, wants to compete with you and ruins you. It's not as simple as that and I thought Zelda was crazy the first time I met her and you complicated it even more by being in love with her and, of course you're a rummy. *But you're no more of a rummy than Joyce is and most good writers are. . . . All you need to do is write truly and not care about what the fate of it is.* (Emphasis mine)[2]

By 1946 the Fitzgerald dilemma, as Hemingway saw it, became the basis for his own novel about artists with mad wives who must learn to stick to their jobs in the face of "tragic" circumstances. But it was the curious late sequence from *Tender is the Night*—the "lesbian lark" and the "barbershop showdown"—that seems to have set him off.

There were, of course, still other and much more private urgencies. According to Jeffrey Meyers, Hemingway's second wife, Pauline Pfeiffer, had become disillusioned with men in the years following their divorce in 1940, and "about 1946 . . . [had] turned to her own sex" for love.[3] By this time Hemingway had been divorced by his third wife, Martha Gellhorn, for whom he had left Pauline, and had just married his fourth wife, Mary Welsh. His sympathies with Pauline had been reawakened by his rueful experience with the fiercely independent Martha, and perhaps also by his new marriage to a better caretaker, a petite, devoted, and rather boyish woman like Pauline. By 1947 Pauline herself was in Cuba, helping him to cure their ailing son Patrick in Mary's absence, and on such good terms with Mary when she returned as to become her nurse and host in Florida, later that same year, while Mary was recuperating from the flu. The good relations between these wives, as colored by Pauline's emergent lesbianism, and perhaps also by the resumption of androgynous sexual practices with Mary that recalled Pauline, seem to have confirmed and perhaps even shaped his decision to create fictional versions of his first and second marriages with Hadley Richardson and Pauline: for in those marriages two good relations with lesbian shadings had seemed to obtain between paired wives, and the hair fetishisms from childhood (which Pauline especially had exploited) had similarly led to or been bound up with androgynous experiments.

His first awareness of such connections seems evident in the fiction written during the early years with Pauline. Thus, late in *A Farewell to Arms* (1929), ex-Lieutenant Henry describes in oddly suggestive terms his visit to the hairdresser's in Switzerland where his common-law wife Catherine is having her hair waved:

> *It was exciting to watch and Catherine smiled and talked to me and my voice was a little thick from being excited. The tongs made a pleasant clicking sound and I could see Catherine in three mirrors and it was pleasant and warm in the booth. Then the woman put up Catherine's hair, and Catherine looked in the mirror and changed it a little, taking out and putting in pins; then stood up. "I'm sorry to have taken such a long time."*
>
> *"Monsieur was very interested. Were you not, Monsieur?" the woman smiled.*
>
> *"Yes," I said.*
>
> *We went out and up the street. It was cold and wintry and the wind was blowing. "Oh darling, I love you so," I said.*[4]

The sexual excitement recorded here seems to have been based on Pauline's early efforts to distinguish herself from Ernest's first wife, Hadley, through tonsorial stylings and seductions. She had apparently sensed a similar excitement in Ernest, a kind of secret identification with her own three-mirrored stylings that she might appropriate for herself, even as Catherine appropriates it, a few pages later in the novel, when she asks Henry to let his hair grow longer while she shortens hers:

> *"Then we'd both be alike. Oh, darling, I want you so much I want to be you too."*
>
> *"You are. We're the same one."*
>
> *"I know it. At night we are."*
>
> *"The nights are grand."*
>
> *"I want us to be all mixed up. . . . "* (299–300)

The androgynous direction of these early romantic scenes—even their latent threat of male unmanning and female manning—now seems clear. What Hemingway had brought to Fitzgerald's novel, what he had pieced together for himself over the years with Pauline and Martha and in the new life with Mary, was his own understanding of why Fitzgerald had put lesbian and tonsorial fiascos in zany sequence and what he himself might make of such conjunctions out of his own long-nurtured hunches.

II

Among Fitzgerald scholars the connection between his homosexual anxieties and his writing problems has become a critical commonplace. In a recent contribution to this view Angus Collins speculates that certain homosexual sequences in "The World's Fair," an early version of *Tender is the Night*, are "projection[s] of vocational insecurity." Fitzgerald's paralyzing fear of "vocational emasculation" had become identified in his mind with gay and lesbian sexuality; he had in effect chosen a homosexual vocation whereby his notoriously "insecure masculinity" had become "related to matters of craft"; and only when he "had mastered any suspicions of himself as emasculate artist" could he make significant progress on *Tender is the Night*:

> *Homosexuality therefore defines the circle of his creative difficulties in that he is homosexual both in his moral and artistic commitment and in his proneness to moral collapse: homosexuality can convey to him both his own much greater emasculation (the attenuations of art) and his own capacities for self-abandonment (the perils of self-indulgence). The novel is completed only when the sense of apostasy begins to predominate, when Fitzgerald learns that his choice of career is far less reprehensible than his failure to practice it.[5]*

Here Collins argues that, in writing *Tender is the Night* (1934), Fitzgerald would break the homosexual circle, resolve his creative difficulties, and so exercise the very discipline that Hemingway had denied him. But as Arthur Mizener notes in *The Far Side of Paradise*, Hemingway would soon modify his original harsh judgment, and in 1935 would tell Maxwell Perkins of how strange it was that "in retrospect" the novel "gets better and better."[6] Meanwhile he had correctly identified Fitzgerald's "dangerous self-indulgence," his importation of "feelings about his own decline" into the character of Dick Diver, as a problem he would himself have to face in his own version of the writer's struggle with "tragic" circumstances (238). Thus David Bourne, his chief persona in *The Garden of Eden*, would make of the act of writing a stoic buffer against such circumstances and would stubbornly resist their debilitating power. He would confront the hazards of androgyny that Fitzgerald (though he had oddly caught their form) had only dimly understood, and would overcome them through courageous masculine artistry.

The interesting point in this standoff with Fitzgerald is that Hemingway .sensed how lesbianism connects with soldier Tommy Barban's barbarian triumph over the Divers' barbershop androgyny—their oddly tonsured harmony, their symbiotic alliance as Riviera prima donnas. He would give Barban's healthy claims a far less cynical twist in his own view of masculine artistry, and would exploit the Divers' civilized shavings far more deviously than Fitzgerald had imagined. Whether he understood that Abe and Mary North were based upon his boyhood hero, Ring Lardner, and his wife Ellis, or that Fitzgerald's barbershop scene was surely influenced by Lardner's "Haircut" (that famous early narrative model for his own juvenile style), or that Abe and Mary together offer fictional analogues for the Divers' decline and fall—whether or not he understood all this, he decidedly sensed that Mary North's emergent lesbianism after her husband's death was like Pauline's after her divorce, that it reflected upon Nicole Diver's man-hating propensities, and Pauline's too, and upon Nicole's previous madness, and Zelda's too, and that of his mistress Jane Mason during the troubled years with Pauline: for this would be the pith and point of his own adventures into barbershop disharmonies in *The Garden of Eden* with the fictional likes of Pauline, Zelda, Hadley, Jane, even of later loves and wives like Adriana and Miss Mary, perhaps Miss Martha too. More interesting still, he seems to have understood that in all this biographical scramble, androgyny, and not homosexuality per se, was Fitzgerald's underlying problem as well as his own, many critics of both writers and much patriarchal and even feminist sentiment to the contrary notwithstanding.

All of which helps to explain why *The Garden of Eden*, in its roughly completed manuscript form, is chiefly a novel about haircuts—or about haircuts and the narratives and counter-narratives they inspire. Ring Lardner's talkative barber has in this respect little or nothing upon Hemingway's talkative heroines and their emotional investments in hair styles. Indeed, the first chapter of the 1500-page manuscript swings upon newlywed Catherine Bourne's account of her "dangerous" surprise for her husband David, her trip to the barber shop for a boy's haircut like his—an account excised like so much else from the 247 pages of the printed version of the novel issued by Scribner's in May 1986.[7]

One can understand the excision. The account is not on the surface the "dangerous" adventure that Catherine makes of it as she tells of her fright when the barber holds "everything out to one side" and goes "snip-snip-snip," then does the back and the other side, and explains that she felt confident nonetheless about going on because she had seen him cut David's hair the week before and had now told him "to cut mine just the same as yours" (Ms. 1/1/insert 18). But the excision of this "little drama" is in fact a violation of the novel's manuscript style, its attempts to get at unsuspected depths through selective descriptions of supposedly insignificant (even silly) actions, its claustrophobic concentration upon the surface details of eating, drinking, swimming, diving, tanning, barbering, bantering, bickering, but above all talking, and below all, writing and making love—a violation, then, of the novel's narrative status as an expansive account of an inner journey, a "sea change" as seen from inside the iceberg, and therefore not an ordinary novel at all, like his own early icebergs, or his recent war epic, *For Whom the Bell Tolls*, or for that matter, Fitzgerald's *Tender is the Night*, with its solidly realized social context and wide cast of characters—as Hemingway's persona almost explains ("It's not a novel . . . It's an account. Travels and Voyages," (Ms. 3/16/27) in one of many excised implications of the author's conscious intent.

One of the nicer signposts of that inner journey, the Rodin statue from "The Gates of Hell," based on Ovid's *Metamorphoses* and Baudelaire's *Les fleurs du mal*, has also been removed from the opening chapter, quite possibly because it ties in directly with the Paris couple, Nick and Barbara Sheldon, whom Scribner's editor, Tom Jenks, decided he must remove along with the subplot they enliven starting with Book Two in the manuscript. Thus, on the evening after her barbershop story, when the newly shorn Catherine asks David to make love to her as she is, she also asks him in an excised passage if he remembers "the sculpture in the Rodin museum," and with that in mind, if he will now "try and be good and not think—only feel." A moment later she asks, "Are you changing like in the sculpture? . . . Are you trying to?" Then, as his resistance slackens until they cannot tell "who is who," she becomes even more insistent:

> "Now will you please be that way now? . . . Will you change and be my girl and let me take you? Will you be like you were in the statue? Will you change?"
>
> He knew now and it was like the statue. The one there are no photographs of and of which no reproductions are sold. (Ms. 1/1/170)

The statue in question, from a group sometimes called "The Damned Women," consists of two lesbians making love, the more active of whom looks (in the bronze version in the museum) like a naked man with a woman's breast plainly visible on his chest as he enfolds a naked woman, but who proves on closer inspection to be a naked woman with a short haircut like Catherine's. About the lack of photographs and reproductions in the 1920s David may be right; but in 1939 and again in 1953, while Hemingway was writing the novel, a reproduction did appear in a German edition of Rodin's work and others have since become available.[8] Still, whatever its accessibility, the important point is that Hemingway chose not to describe it, even as he chose not to describe with any exactness the lovemaking between his sexual seekers after dangerous knowledge. For them as for us, it is the edenic invitation to forbidden mysteries and disturbing sexual ambiguities that matters. As Catherine tells David, she has thought about the statue "Ever since. . . . that day in the Rodin," and though she doesn't understand why "it works," she knows that it does; and David too not only feels its metamorphic powers but admits them to himself while struggling with his conscience:

> *You know the statue moved you and why shouldn't it? Did it not move Rodin? You're damned right it did and why be so holy and so puritanical? You're lucky to have a wife that is a wild animal instead of a domestic animal and what is a sin what you feel bad after and you don't feel bad.* (Ms. 1/1/23–24)

In Book Two, which consists solely of the excised Paris chapter, we learn more about this "moving" statue, this public inspiration for troubling private changes. Indeed, the book opens with a clumsy overview of its effect on both couples:

> *With the other two it had started at the end of February. It had really started long before that but there had been no actual date, as there was for the day in May that Catherine had ridden up to Aigues Mortes and back to Le Grau de Roi* [sic], *until this night and the following morning at the end of February in Paris. None of them remembered the actual dates of commitment and none of them remembered the dates on which they had first turned in off the rue de Varennes to the Hotel Biron with the beautiful gardens and gone into the museum where the changings had started. One girl had forgotten that it had started there and, for her perhaps, it had not but she too had seen the bronze long before.*
>
> *"Let's think of something fun to do that we've never done that will be secret and wicked," the girl had said.* (1)

Hemingway's revision here of the biblical Garden of Eden plot seems plain enough: two couples pass through the beautiful gardens at the Hotel Biron, enter the Rodin Museum, and are so moved by the statue there of metamorphic love that they begin their own androgynous experiments; and in each case the "girl" is the active agent, the Eve-like tempter. The editorial loss of this magic matter seems sad enough; but the loss too of the Paris plot with its lively change of pace and its range of useful meanings, is perhaps sadder. We soon learn, for instance, that Nick and Barbara Sheldon are poor but happy artists and therefore healthy foils to the rich unhappy Riviera Bournes. Indeed, they have experienced androgynous love without previous qualms, and as the chapter opens they experience it again, in their cold and barren Paris flat, with Barbara pressing down lightly but firmly upon her supinely cooperative spouse. Thus it is not androgynous love per se that causes trouble ("We've always done that when you wanted to," says Nick on p. 2 in response to his wife's enticement), so much as its public expression through statues, hair styles, and conversations—especially as they convey controlling female power. And even then a thoughtful, cooperative, and sympathetic spouse like Nick can let his hair grow long over a five-month period as a surprise present for his wife, without her discovering it, in true O. Henry fashion. We witness a second excised barber scene, at any rate, as—after their simple breakfast of brioche, ham and eggs—Barbara shapes Nick's hair to resemble hers, then shares the excitement of his gift by making more androgynous love:

> "It ruins work," she said, "but it's so exciting. Why should something so simple be so exciting?"
> "I'm not sure it's so simple."
> "It's so much fun it must be very wicked."
> "I'm pretty sure it's wicked."
> "But Nickie how did you get it so long?"
> "It took five months."
> "It must have. But how did you do it?"
> "Don't you remember when you asked me to?"
> "I always asked you to."
> "Well anyway this time I told the barber I wanted to let it grow because you liked it. The same barber that cuts yours. The Spanish one. He said how long? I said like yours." (12–13)

How Nickie did it is indeed a mystery (and perhaps cause in itself for Jenks' editorial clippings), but presumably he combed it back and up rather than out and down, and so hid the change from Barbara. What counts is the liveliness of the telling, the cheerfulness of these loving American babes in foreign woods who "go to sleep like good children" after another crazy day (19, 23), who seem at ease with androgynous changes ("It's just like all the Indian kids were," says Nick on p. 15 as if recalling his namesake's life in northern Michigan), and whose inner life seems only mildly troubled with thoughtful moments at night and ebullient stream-of-consciousness wonderment.

In Book Three of the manuscript, however, when the Sheldons meet the Bournes and Barbara and Catherine respond to each other with erotic intensity, the latent danger of "possession" by androgyny is openly acknowledged. Thus, in a confessional passage, Barbara tells David of her troubled feelings about herself:

> "I know I'm strange. But I'm not a queer or I never was. Crazy if you like and with special things or one thing that I wanted and got it or have it or had it. It was just a simple delight or ecstasy. It was private but I made it public. That's the danger, the necessary danger. And I didn't know things took possession of you. There's where you've gone wrong of course." (Ms. 3/4/8 bis 1)

The "necessary danger" of making things private public—that's where, according to Barbara, they've all "gone wrong." Their experiments with androgynous coiffures—long for the Sheldons, short for the Bournes—are public expressions, then, of private love modes which now possess them, and which ultimately lead to sexual betrayals and beckoning disasters—madness for Catherine, suicide for Barbara, accidental death for Nick, expulsion from Eden for David and his new "girl" Marita. From such impending consequences, moreover, the explicit barbershop scenes acquire their curious resonance.

Where David and Catherine are concerned, the Scribner's edition does some justice to this fateful dimension. For them it may be enough that we hear Catherine's account of her Eton haircut in Chapter Five and witness the coiffeur's artistry in Chapter Nine as he bevels and blonds the couple's hair to make them look alike. Catherine's hysteric fear of death, and the meeting with their common mistress Marita, follow hard upon these public expressions of androgynous "possession," and after they dye their hair again in another elided scene in Chapter Twenty-One they both feel appropriately "damned." Still, the riskiness of art itself—the coiffeur's, David's,

Catherine's—is lost by the disconnection of such scenes from the Rodin statue's fatality, and from Marita's recognition too (another sad excision) of how
well Catherine's artistry in talking matches David's writing skills. And again
the editor shears too close, in Chapter Twenty-Nine, where Marita loses her
African haircut and the novel ends without the fateful implications of *her*
impending possession by androgyny.

She has by this time shown extraordinary sympathy for David's work, and
thereby won his love, and Catherine herself has numbed his loyalty by burning his African stories so as to leave unrivaled his narrative account of their
"journey" into androgynous wilds. Marita has become the good wife, then,
the one who admires all his writing and shares with him its mystery (another excised dimension). Further, he has rescued her from her purely lesbian
past (also excised) and converted her to heterosexual love of the missionary
as well as the androgynous order, as if to counteract his own conversion to
androgyny and his wife's to lesbian love. All the more "dangerous," then,
when Marita tells David, at the end, that she wants her hair cut to resemble
that of his first girlfriend during his African boyhood. If she in turn has converted him from a sick sense of severe "perversion" to a healthy sense of
"variety," the signs of her own Catherine-like obsession with androgyny bur-
geon in the late chapters—largely excised, alas, along with the complexities
of her nature and her alarming African haircut which, as it turns out, makes
her look more like a street Arab than a tribal princess.

III

*We are all bitched from the start and you especially have to be hurt like
hell before you can write seriously. . . .*

Was that "all-American bitch" Grace Hall Hemingway on Ernest's mind
when he admonished Scott Fitzgerald with such a grim view of childhood
and its painful aftermath? Certainly his mother had twinned him from the
start with his older sister Marcelline, dressing them alike in infant smocks
and frocks, arranging their hair in matching Dutch-length cuts, holding
Marcelline back a year so they might start school together, and when Ernest
received his first boy's haircut that pre-school summer, giving Marcelline a
boy's haircut too. Was Ernest in that sense *paired* with a bitch from the start,
or paired with one bitch by another, as he later saw it? Or was that triangulated pairing in fact edenic at first and only gradually too grim and painful

to acknowledge? It is at any rate to Marcelline and Ernest, their mother's twin Dutch dollies in infancy, at seven and six her grade school gamins, that we must turn for childhood models of the longhaired Sheldons and shorthaired Bournes—even for the painful aftermath of such dangerous stylings. As Marcelline herself reports, her hair grew out unevenly that fateful summer, after her first boy's haircut, and was further botched in the fall by a helpful scissors-wielding playmate. As punishment her mother sent her to school in sister Sunny's baby bonnet until a wise teacher intervened, some two weeks later, and persuaded Grace to remove the bonnet and let Marcelline escape to the second grade, where she belonged.[9] No wonder then that hair styles became the observant Ernest's lifelong measure of female manipulations, androgynous twinnings, arrangements of the heart and breasts and loins; no wonder that the Bournes in *The Garden of Eden* see themselves as brother and sister as well as brothers with matching hair styles, or that Pilar sees the cropped Maria and Roberto as brother and sister in *For Whom the Bell Tolls*, or that Littless cuts her hair short to become Nick's forest brother in "The Last Good Country," or that Catherine Barkley proposes matching hair styles to Lieutenant Frederic Henry in *A Farewell to Arms*, or that Marie Morgan dyes her hair blond to excite her pirate husband Harry in *To Have and Have Not*—even as Pauline surprised Ernest by dyeing her hair blond on her thirty-fourth birthday in July 1929, or indeed, even as Ernest first urged his fourth wife Mary to bleach her hair blond, then doused his own hair copper bright, during the composition of *The Garden*, claiming that he had mistaken the bottle for his ex-wife Martha's "old shampoo."[10] As his frequent chapter notations—"Hair," "Hair Cutting," "Hair Symbol"—attest, hair was for Hemingway the public expression of his own private obsession with androgyny, his easy imaginative access to a woman's manipulative, talkative, stylistically inventive powers, his secret envy of her breasts and womb, his unconfessed desire to rest confident in her supine passivity, and his honest awareness of her oppression by men much like himself. Beyond that he obviously liked women, liked having them around as adoring wives or "daughters": indeed, he desperately needed their attentive presence, and in *The Garden of Eden* he finally attested to that terrible dependency, as when the betrayed David tells his returning wife Catherine and future mistress Marita, after their first lesbian experiment, "I missed you both" (Ms. 3/21/31).

Vulnerability and dependency, then, were the blissful conditions that "hurt like hell" after four serial marriages, and that moved Ernest to write about "the happiness of the Garden that a man must lose."[11] His ambivalent feelings about androgyny had become the very subject of his novelistic search, his three-mirrored account of inner voyages, his condensation of successive marital and extra-marital entrapments, with only his African pennings to pull him through his own Ulyssean weakness for long- and short-haired sirens, his own Samsonian blindness and loss of hairy strength (cf. Ms. 3/25/29). As we shall see, these inner weaknesses are intimately bound up with the hero's writing skills and with the novel's curious construction as an account that could only have been written by David Bourne, whom we constantly observe either in the act of writing something like it or of living what he writes. This is Hemingway's most self-reflexive novel about the art of and need for writing his own kind of "found" and "invented" fictions; and that art is intimately bound up with his life and work during all his marriages, but especially his first and second as measured by and through his fourth.

One biographical question this novel speaks to, for instance, is what kind of husband and lover was Ernest Hemingway? The complicated answer—since Ernest plays all the main male roles, assigning aspects of himself or stages of his life to Nick Sheldon (Paris), David Bourne (the Riviera), Andrew Murray (Spain), and David's unnamed father (Africa)—can be put into simple if painful terms: he was an extremely dependent man in all these roles. As Chapter Seven in the Scribner's edition opens, for instance, the editor excises a long passage from Book Three, Chapter Thirteen, of the manuscript in which David muses over the word "Innocence" on which the previous chapter ends, his friend Andy Murray—a square character who refuses to change his hair style and whose initials point in this respect to Archibald MacLeish and to Hadley's second husband, Paul Mowrer—his friend Andy having held there that the Bournes bring more saving innocence to the time they're in than he does. Certainly David's musings over their life together are at this point innocent enough, that is to say honest and to the heartfelt point, as he makes "a head for a coin" (p. 6) out of his sleeping wife's face, imagining lines and angles like a sculptor, then acknowledging that "She's the sculptor with her lovely head. I see why she likes to do it" (p. 7). Then, having emulated her close-cropped artistry with loving and imaginative care, he reviews his own emotional progress, his new freedom from remorse, his lessened anxiety about where they're heading and about his continuing failure to write, his concern all the same with the danger of such heady freedom, and with the lack of helpful "signals from the pits" to "tell you where you stand" ("or maybe there are and you can't read them," p. 9); and then thinking of their latest experiments—

The only signal was she asked you this time and you said yes. And do you still say yes? I said yes and I neither apologize nor explain. You know the danger? All right what would be the danger of No? You don't think it would be greater? How do I know? I didn't say no. You don't think that you will have to learn to say it? Very possibly. (9)

The danger of saying no, then, as reviewed by a man who obviously can't say no, or who says it rather so that it always means yes—as both his wife and mistress understand. Thus when David calls her "an intriguing corrupter" after she provides them with a common mistress, Catherine tells him "an old secret": "You aren't very hard to corrupt and you're an awful lot of fun to corrupt" (*GE* 150). And when she persuades him to dye his hair once more to resemble hers, she says, "I love to make you do things you really and truly don't want to and then you like them when we do them"—at which point David begins to realize "what a completely stupid thing he had permitted" (*GE* 178). And again, as her illness increases and David becomes "sick of crazy things," she repeats what he also knows: "You always do everything I want because you really want to do it too" (*GE* 196). Even his mistress Marita tells him playfully and definitively, late in the novel, that she loves to hear him say no: "It's such a non-definite word the way you say it. It's better than anybody's yes" (Ms 3/45/5); and then, being a better and more protective caretaker than Catherine, she reassures him that she loves his weaknesses as much as his strengths, for "they're what makes the strengths."

That seems to be the second self-revelation from Hemingway: that his emotional dependency on his wives and mistresses, his androgynous complicity with their several obsessions with hair, skin, dress, gender, and lesbian attachments, is what makes for his strength as a creative writer. That crucial argument occurs again and again in the actual manuscript, as when in Book Three, Chapter Twenty-Three, David ponders the division between his life with Catherine and Marita, whom he sorely misses though he knows it is wrong "to want them both," and his creative work:

If you live by the senses you will die by them and if you live by your invention and your head you will die by that too. All that is left entire in you is your ability to write and that gets better. You would think it would be destroyed. By everything you have been taught it should. But so far as you corrupt or change, that grows and strengthens. It should not but it has. Is it possible that the only creation that is a moral act is pro-creation and that is why all other kinds are suspect? It could be but it seems too simple and too much like a justifying. All you know is that you have written better, clearer and plus net, he used the French phrase in thinking, as you have deteriorated morally. But that could be temporary or it could be a building up and strengthening by what good there is trying to build against the destruction. That could be. Don't apportion blame for the destruction now. It will all be apportioned in due time and not by you. (9)

Scribner's editor elides this passage, and all others like it, and appropriates only the ending as it applies to David's newly triangulated love (*GE* 132); but in the actual manuscript it is the entanglement of the *ménage à trois* with the writing process that matters, the complicity in "corruption" that increases creative strength. Thus in Book Three, Chapter Twenty-Seven of the manuscript, when Marita tells David that he writes now in his own defense "and under impossible conditions," David thinks that "maybe the impossible conditions make it [possible for him to write]" (12); and again in Book Three, Chapter Twenty-Nine of the manuscript, as he thinks about another African story, he speculates on the probable androgynous sources—whether disastrous or enabling—of his new effectiveness:

> *It is going to be rough to do but so far they have gone well and maybe you can thank Catherine and her disasters for them. Not her disasters, her disaster that embraces everything. You can thank the other girl who loves you and handles and canalizes you like an engineer or tries to when you don't impede her. You probably would have blown up with Catherine here alone. . . . But would any of it have happened if you'd been alone? Of course it would. It had built steadily to happen. Don't go into that now. That is as useless to go into as to think what would have happened if you and Kibo had not learned to hunt at night with the full moon. How wrong that was to do. If life was only conducted for survival . . . how much you would have missed. What happened with Catherine goes in the narrative. Don't confuse things.* (10–11)

The extension of the fateful principle to his African boyhood, and the imagination of his own passivity in the hands of the two women he loves, are instructively alike. He understands his complicity in the events of the "found" narrative we read—the one Catherine has asked him to write about their life together—and in the boyhood events of the counter-narrative we read in either case becomes strikingly evident in Book Three, Chapter Three, of the original manuscript, in which David and Catherine run into the Sheldons at Hendaye and David starts to write about events in their lives that we have already witnessed in Book Two, the Paris chapter.

He had started to write about the Sheldons, taking it up when he had seen them in the bistrot [sic] together at dinner on a cold night in Paris at the end of last February and how excited and happy they had looked and how absorbed they had been in each other. He put down how Barbara had smiled at him as though he were a co-conspirator and he remembered being in the coiffeur's when they had come in together. It had gone simply and easily. So easily that it was probably deceptive and that, having seen them only the day before, he saw them so vividly himself that he might not be making them come alive to some one else. But as he read it over it seemed to be what he had tried to get in its complex simplicity and he thought that perhaps he was writing so easily because, not having tried to force any writing before, he was coming fresh to it now. If it is worthless, he thought, it will be good five finger exercises to get started with. God knows I do not have to write about them nor the length at which they choose to wear their hair while living in the Vth arrondisement [sic] in Paris. That's banal enough. Certainly I am not limited to that as a subject and what importance has it? He is a painter and a damned good painter and what difference does it make, any of it. (1)

The effect of this passage is startlingly reflexive, perhaps because it is more detailed than the similar moments when David indicates how he writes about himself and Catherine, but more probably because it involves other characters whose lives he must invent from the few events he has witnessed—and that five finger exercise in complex simplicity, as he calls it, is not a bad description of the Paris chapter and its lively change of pace, its bed and brioche harmonies. But the point is that David fuses at such moments with his own creator, Ernest Hemingway; he becomes an aspect of his creator's life and work in the way Stephen Dedalus figures as the young artist who will eventually write *Ulysses* and *A Portrait of the Artist*, only now our portrait is of the artist as a young newlywed on a disastrously overextended honeymoon, and that too is not a bad description of Hemingway's life with Pauline, or with his later wives, once the purifying poverty and cultural richness of the Paris years with Hadley were over. As with Joyce, at any rate, the invitation to read the novel, or the account of inner journeys, biographically is a built-in aspect of the text. And in that light the connection between androgynous "corruptions" with wives and mistresses and the author's writing strengths becomes a matter of critical speculation and concern.

Whether in the printed or manuscript version, that connection is conveyed by the two kinds of narrative David writes, the main narrative on which Catherine wants him to concentrate, and for which she tries to find illustrators like Picasso, Marie Laurencin, and Nick Sheldon, and the African tales that she resents so much she ultimately burns them. One can see, from the tension between these narrative impulses, why the Sheldon subplot remains unfinished in the manuscript, only sketchily continued in three later fragments called "Andy's Story," and why Scribner's editor decided to scrap it: for how could David continue to speak for the Sheldons, in his ongoing account of his own triangulated troubles, without altogether becoming Ernest Hemingway? It was a problem in point-of-view narration that Hemingway himself could not altogether solve, as his decision to let Andy Murray solve it suggests. What Andy tells us about Nick's accidental death while Barbara and Andy make love, and about Barbara's eventual suicide while under Andy's care, David could not have witnessed, and therefore could not reinvent as a plausibly imagined part of the main narrative, an integrated part of his own ongoing quarrel with androgyny. And the alternative device of a story within the story—the old Fielding strategy—must have seemed a bit too tired to pursue. So the later Sheldon story was left in fragments and could not be salvaged by Scribner's editor without connecting links of his own invention. Nor could he answer for himself the questions David initially raises about the subplot—"what importance has it? . . . and what difference does it make, any of it?"

A great deal, of course, for Hemingway scholars, or for any biographical critic with half an eye for literary dynamics. For plainly the Sheldon subplot was Hemingway's substitute for the missing link in David and Catherine Bourne's life history: David's previous marriage to another woman, someone like Barbara Sheldon, whom he had betrayed at Catherine's urging in order to marry Catherine herself. David Bourne—whose very name suggests (among other things) that hidden burden[12]—was instead created "innocent," that is to say previously unmarried and therefore free of Hemingway's guilt in leaving Hadley for Pauline, again at Pauline's manipulative urging ("You aren't very hard to corrupt"). And Catherine too was created free of Pauline's previous manipulations. The "innocent" Bournes, then, who just happen to begin their honeymoon year at Grau du Roi, as did Ernest and Pauline Hemingway in 1927, are juxtaposed with another happily married pair of "innocent" Americans, painters Nick and Barbara Sheldon, who just happen to live in Paris in the manner of Ernest and Hadley Hemingway, circa 1925. And these fictional versions of Hemingway's second and first marriages just happen to cross paths at Hendaye Plage, in the south of France, before going their separate ways!

Hemingway's pleasure in creating such conjunctions seems evident enough, as when Barbara Sheldon smiles at David Bourne in that Paris restaurant in February "as though he were a co-conspirator" (Ms. 3/3/1); or when Barbara and Catherine regard each other with mutual admiration and desire, upon meeting at Hendaye (Ms. 3/1/2–3), or wish each other well, upon parting, and Barbara says, "Have . . . a lovely life, and take good care of David" (Ms. 3/8/4); or similarly when Barbara advises David to get Catherine out of the Riviera ambiance if he loves her (Ms. 3/5/7). These moments are not surprising, given Ernest's continuing use of Hadley, long after their divorce, as friendly adviser and admired first-married love, and given also her relieved and friendly transfer of Ernest into Pauline's hands, as those of a better, richer caretaker, back in 1926. But the insistence upon the mutual lesbian attraction between Barbara and Catherine, or Hadley and Pauline, is indeed surprising. We know from recent biographical diggings that Hadley left Bryn Mawr because of her mother's grim suspicions of her roommate's overly fond mother, Mrs. Rapallo, whom she naively admired.[13] We know that Pauline's sister was a lesbian, and that Pauline became one after her divorce from Ernest; and we know from the Hadley tapes preserved by her biographer that Pauline liked to crawl into bed with Ernest and Hadley in the mornings during her visits with them at Schruns and Juan-les-Pins.[14] We know also that Ernest was obsessed with lesbianism, that he considered his mother "androgynous"—probably because of the newly discovered incident in the summer of 1919 when his father banned from the house for unspecified reasons his mother's adopted protégé and "girlfriend," the young and pretty family helper Ruth Arnold, and because of Ruth's return in later years as his mother's paid companion.[15] And, finally, we know he was sexually drawn to Gertrude Stein as to a literary version of his "androgynous" mother during the Paris years with Hadley.[16] From all of which we may surmise, more broadly, that Ernest was drawn to women with lesbian and/or androgynous propensities, as with Hadley, Pauline, Gertrude, and Mary, and perhaps also Martha, Jane, and Adriana.

In this light the lesbian link between Barbara and Catherine is itself the missing link in the Bournes' life history, the sanctioning of real betrayal by fictional admiration and desire—as if Ernest had simply acted out the desires of Pauline and Hadley in leaving one wife for another. "Do you have the faintest idea how beautiful you are and what you are doing to people?" asks Barbara/Hadley of Catherine/Pauline upon seeing her latest haircut (Ms. 3/7/3). What she has already done to David/Ernest is thus blessed, forgiven, exonerated, if not altogether explained. One possible explanation—that

Ernest identified with supposedly lesbian lovers, or projected his own
androgynous feelings upon them—must wait till we discuss the *ménage à
trois* between Catherine, David, and Marita—whose very name compresses
those hitherto missing wives, Martha and Mary, into verbal complicity with
these strange arrangements.

IV

Meanwhile there is the counter-impulse to consider, the Kipling impulse, the
writing of the African tales. Just before his honeymoon with Pauline Ernest
had put together a collection of stories called *Men Without Women* from
which he said "'the softening feminine influence' was missing . . . whether as
a result of 'training, discipline, death, or other causes.'"[17] While at Grau du
Roi with Pauline he had then completed two new stories for the collection,
one about Nick Adams' boyhood called "Ten Indians," the other—called
"Hills Like White Elephants"—about an insensitive man who tries to persuade his lover to have an abortion. The African tales that David Bourne
composes on the Riviera are invented boyhood stories like those that
Hemingway wrote about Nick Adams in northern Michigan, and David's
disillusionment with his father in the crucial elephant tale is like Nick's disillusionment with Dr. Adams in tales like "Indian Camp," "The Doctor and
the Doctor's Wife," "Ten Indians," and much later, "Fathers and Sons." The
lovely metaphor of "hills like white elephants," which the woman faced with
abortion voices as the second story opens, suggests also the violation of the
sacredness of life that young David witnesses in the elephant hunt; but that
mystery and that sacredness derive as well from Kipling tales like "Toomai
and the Elephants" and "The White Seal" from *The Second Jungle Book*, "My
Lord the Elephant" from *Many Inventions*, and "Letting in the Jungle" and
other Mowgli stories from *The Jungle Book* itself.[18] Indeed, Hemingway's
favorite poem from *The Jungle Book*—the animals' lament when Mowgli
leaves the jungle to get married—is a childhood paradigm of the tension in
this late novel between the "marriage" story on the Riviera and the boyhood
tale of men without women in Africa; and the writing of the latter tale is an
act of manly resistance to the "corruptions" of the androgynous married life
which apparently make it possible. For unlike Fitzgerald's Dick Diver, who
accedes to his own corruption through triangulated love, David Bourne
resists his complicity in things feminine by writing manly tales about African
wars and hunting expeditions. His preoccupation with African stories is like
Hemingway's preoccupation with such stories in the 1930s, or with sporting

tales about bullfighting, skiing, boxing, and fishing in the 1920s; and his oscillation between such stories and the main narrative is like Hemingway's oscillation between novels of failed sexual relations (*The Sun Also Rises, A Farewell to Arms*) and tales of stoic male endurance; indeed, it constitutes a curious paradigm, a defensive rationale for the manly author's creative history and its apparent source in reactive strength, in self-defining resistance to his own androgynous propensities, his own failed or failing marital and/or extra-marital relations. The long unhappy strenuous playboy life of Ernest Hemingway becomes more devious and more valiant than we have supposed, given this resistive creative strength and its frank location in his own androgynous weakness, his own dependency and openness to the manipulations of many wives and mistresses whom he desperately needs, and with whom he secretly identifies.

E. L. Doctorow's puzzlement over the hero's curious passivity, in his review of the published novel, is in this light relevant to our understanding of the manuscript version and the life behind it.[19] Doctorow locates "the ultimate deadness of the [published] piece" in David's character: "His incapability in dealing with the crisis of his relationship does not mesh with his consummate self-assurance in handling the waiters, maids and hoteliers who, in this book as in Hemingway's others, come forward to supply the food and drink, the corkscrew, and ice cubes and beds and fishing rods his young American colonists require." Doctorow goes on to mock this evidence of travel writing for provincial American readers, the lack of any substantial disaster like war or postwar disorientation to lend plausibility to the characters' suffering, the consequent "tone of solemn self-attention" which rises to unjustified "portentousness" over 70,000 words of text. But then he also speculates about the missing 130,000 words, the excised subplot, the clear evidence of Hemingway's attempt to transcend the limitations of his famous pared down early style, and to remake himself on a grand scale after recognizing the stylistic insufficiencies of his previous epic venture, *For Whom the Bell Tolls.* This seems to me exactly right, though Doctorow's further guesses about "a large cast and perhaps multiple points of view" in the actual manuscript lead us toward his kind of ambitious fiction rather than Hemingway's. But the exciting evidence of Hemingway's attempted new development as a writer is decidedly there; and Doctorow is again right to dismiss his failure in this regard, and the novel's failure also, as beside the point. What matters is "that he would have tried, which is the true bravery of a writer, requiring more courage than facing down an elephant charge with a .303 Mannlicher."[20]

That is indeed the point. *The Garden of Eden* is a novel about a writer's bravery—about Hemingway's bravery as he saw it in the daily struggle to transcend his own terrible dependencies and passivities. This is Hemingway's testament to the writer's trade as he practiced it, using his own hurts and weaknesses, his being five times bitched from the start, and then four and more times bitched again, by his own need to compete with women on honeymoon grounds, and to redefine himself therefrom by resistant actions and resistant writings, whether of found or invented fictions. The traveler's daily record of meals, bars, beaches, beds, and barbershops is there because that is how he chiefly lived, under "the softening feminine influence" of married love that he sorely needed to exist at all; and his bravery consists mainly of stripping away his daily portion of manly sports (save one marvelous fishing scene and much androgynous swimming), and of collapsing the essential isolation of his post-Hadley marriages into a single honeymoon year of touring, tanning, eating, drinking, and making androgynous love— as if to force the lonely essence of the writer's inner life into felt existence for us, while at the same time indicating, indeed demonstrating, the power, range, and varied richness of his writing.

The most direct demonstration comes from the tale of the elephant hunt, the writing and reconstruction of which (after Catherine burns the African tales) constitute the writer David's comeback, his triumph over those "tragic" circumstances to which Fitzgerald supposedly succumbs in *Tender is the Night*—or at least Dick Diver does. Lacking the revelations about art and androgyny in the actual manuscript, Doctorow suggests that Hemingway might have succumbed in a different way:

> David Bourne's passivity goes unexamined by the author, except as it may be a function of his profession. But the sad truth is that his writing, which we see in the elephant story, does not exonerate him: it is bad Hemingway, a threadbare working of a theme of a boy's initiation rites that suggests to its own great disadvantage Faulkner's story on the same theme, "The Bear."[21]

Hemingway would have hated that last comparison, especially with regard to the one novel wherein he tries courageously to do new things, as Faulkner once said he never did; but there is a bit of "The Bear" in this initiation story, and some Sherwood Anderson too, and a great deal of Kipling, about whom Doctorow fails to speculate. Moreover, other reviewers— notably John Updike—found the elephant tale engaging.[22] Certainly it is a new kind of animal story for Hemingway, who prided himself on avoiding sentimental identifications with animals as in the Mowgli stories, but who here unashamedly allows his young protagonist to find in the elephant a hero and brother, to resist and resent his killing (though he has himself enabled it by discovering the elephant at night while hunting with his African dog Kibo), and to react to the elephant's feelings as to human feelings.

At stake here is the alliance between children and animals that Kipling assumes in the Mowgli stories, the assumption of common ground as sub-human, prehuman, or demonic species, and the acquisition of animal power and mystery in the vengeful struggle against adult inequities, as when Mowgli directs the elephants to trample down the native village in "Letting in the Jungle," or when Toomai rides his musty elephant far into the jungle at night to watch the wild elephants dance, and returns from the forbidden ground to tell his tale in triumph. Hemingway tries to temper and improve on such assumptions through his characteristic theme of dillusionment; and in fact the alliance between the boy and the dying elephant does improve on Kipling, and on Faulkner too, in that it aligns the killing of such jungle monarchs not simply with the breakdown in trust between boy and man, father and son, but also between male friends. For the odd anthropomorphic point of the tale is that the old, tired, great-tusked elephant had been visiting the grave of a friend whom David's father and the native hunter Juma had killed the previous year, so that David thinks of the latter pair as "the god damned friend killers" (*GE* 198) and relishes the elephant's revenge when he throws Juma aside—as if recognizing his friend's killer—while charging off to his death, leaving David with "the beginning of the knowledge of loneliness" (*GE* 201) as recalls the lapse of "dignity and majesty and . . . beauty" from the dying beast's sad eyes (200).

"It was a very young boy's story," thinks David as he finished it (*GE* 201), thus underscoring the Kipling connection. Given its placement as the "hard story" David has wanted for a long time to write, it seems to me also a very self-critical story, in that David's father is more obviously based on Hemingway himself as a hardened big game hunter and an insensitive father to three sons, than on his own father; and yet Hemingway's lifelong problem with male friendships does seem to be attributed here to his father's "friend-killing" role. Was the elephant's death, and the boy's reaction to it, a kind of breakthrough then of boyhood resentment against Dr. Clarence Hemingway for teaching his son how to kill rather than love, how to suppress rather than share his deepest feelings? If so, it provides some balance to the indictment here of Grace's androgynous ways, and indicates—perhaps for the first and

only time—how much he felt his father—an obtusely sentimental if not a
ruthless man—had failed to teach him how to be a friend. And perhaps also
how much that hurtful failing had helped to shape his early stoic style. As
David puts it in the tale, "I'm going to keep everything a secret always. . . .
Never tell anyone anything again" (*GE* 181).

Notes

1. The omitted opening to this essay treats Hemingway's fascination with F. Scott
    Fitzgerald's *Tender is the Night*, in *The Portable F. Scott Fitzgerald*, intro. John
    O'Hara (New York: Viking, 1945).
2. *Selected Letters*, p. 408. A version of this passage also appears in Arthur Mizener's
    biography of Fitzgerald, *The Far Side of Paradise* (Boston: Houghton Mifflin,
    1951) pp. 238–39, which Hemingway received from Mizener in January 1951
    and read with mixed feelings (*Letters*, pp. 716–19).
3. Jeffrey Meyers, *Hemingway: A Biography* (New York: Harper & Row, 1985), p.
    346.
4. *A Farewell to Arms* (New York: Scribner's, 1929), pp. 292–93.
5. Angus P. Collins, "Homosexuality and the Genesis of *Tender is the Night*,"
    Journal of Modern Literature 13 (March 1986), 170–71.
6. Arthur Mizener, *The Far Side of Paradise*, p. 239. In this 1951 biography Mizener
    had reviewed Hemingway's relations with Fitzgerald, quoted from Hemingway's
    letters, and opened up slants on Fitzgerald's work and world that seem to have
    figured in Hemingway's ongoing work on *The Garden of Eden*. See for example
    the poem "Do you remember . . . That I hated to swim naked from the
    rocks/While you liked absolutely nothing better?" p. 235, which Hemingway
    would reverse for David and Catherine; or Zelda's "empty shell" letter, p. 236,
    which becomes a model for Catherine's farewell letter, in *The Garden of Eden*. In
    his correspondence with Mizener Hemingway grudgingly admitted that "your
    book did tell me many things I did not know. . . . I learned a lot and I was very
    grateful." *Letters*, p. 718.
7. *The Garden of Eden* (New York: Scribner's, 1986), 247 pp., cited hereafter in the
    text as GE plus page numbers. References to the manuscript version of the novel
    are from the 1500-page copy in the Hemingway Collection at the Kennedy
    Library in Boston, Mass., and will be cited in the text as Ms. plus
    Book/Chapter/Page number.
8. "The Metamorphoses of Ovid," *Rodin Sculptures*. Phaidon Edition (London and
    New York: Allen and Unwin Ltd., Oxford University Press, 1939), plate 62:
    (London: Phaidon Press Ltd., 1953), plate 52; and in the white plaster version,
    Rodin Sculptures, ed. Jennifer Hawkins (London: Her Majesty's Stationery

Office, 1975), plates 10–11; and *The Sculpture of Auguste Rodin,* ed. John Tancock (Philadelphia Museum of Art, 1976), plates 3601, 3601. Interestingly, 36-3 is called "Daphnis and Chloe," as if the figures were male and female.

9. Marcelline Hemingway Sanford, *At the Hemingways: A Family Portrait* (Boston: Little, Brown, 1962), pp. 109–11.

10. Jeffrey Meyers, *Hemingway,* pp. 435, 437.

11. Carlos Baker, *Ernest Hemingway: A Life Story* (New York: Avon, 1969) pp. 583, 891. Hereafter, *A Life Story.* From a letter to his friend Buck Lanham, June 19, 1948, on the novel's theme.

12. The name Bourne contains "born," "burn," "borne," and "bourn" as its obvious implied meanings, with borne suggesting either bearing burdens or being carried along passively. Hemingway himself plays with the second and fourth meanings late in the novel, as David and Marita find relief in verbal banter from the burning of the African tales: "Who burned the Bournes out? Crazy woman burned out the Bournes," says David, and then decides "I'll write in the sand. . . . That's my new medium. I'm going to be a sand writer. The David Bournes, sand writers, announce their unsuccessful peek into that undiscovered country from whose bourne no traveler returns who hasn't been there. That's from a poem Shakespeare and I wrote together. He was extremely talented and Duff Cooper believes he was a sergeant. . . . It's a very convincing theory" (Ms. 3/44/24–25).

13. Peter Griffin, *Along with Youth: Hemingway, the Early Years* (New York: Oxford University Press, 1985), pp. 142–43, 184–85; Jeffrey Meyers, *Hemingway,* pp. 58, 346.

14. According to Peter Griffin, in private conversation, October 1986, on the tapes taken by Emily Hahn. See also *A Life Story,* pp. 221–22.

15. Michael S. Reynolds. *The Young Hemingway* (Oxford and New York: Basil Blackwell, 1986), pp. 78–81, 105.

16. Ct. Meyers, *Hemingway,* pp. 76–77, and *Letters:* "I always wanted to fuck her and she knew it and it was a good healthy feeling and made more sense than some of the talk," p. 650.

17. *A Life Story,* p. 234; *Letters,* p. 245.

18. Hemingway read Kipling in boyhood and later owned all these works, but "The White Seal" reference requires some explanation. In Book Three, Chapter Forty-Four, Marita and David see each other as seals in the water or on the beach (pp. 13–14). When Marita asks "Are seals nice?" David replies: "Did you read the Naulahka by Kipling? . . . That's all I know about them except in arctic and antarctic chronicles and circuses and zoos" (p. 14). Hemingway's mistake is interesting: there are no seals in *The Naulahka: A Story of East and West,* the action of which takes place in India and the American West; but its plot—the persuasion of an American woman to give up her independence, her mission work in India, for marriage—is decidedly relevant to Marita's voluntary status as an adjunct wife in *The Garden of Eden.* The Kipling work that Hemingway

misremembers here is "The White Seal" in *The Second Jungle Book*, about the search by a white seal for a safe haven for his much-hunted species—hence Marita's remark in the chapter: "When he kissed me he looked like a white-headed seal" (p. 13).

19. E. L. Doctorow, "Braver Than We Thought," *The New York Times Book Review*, May 18, 1986, pp. 1, 44–45.
20. Doctorow, p. 45.
21. Doctorow, p. 45.
22. John Updike, "The Sinister Sex," *The New Yorker*, June 30, 1986, pp. 85–88. See especially p. 88, where Updike finds the elephant's shooting "horrendous and moving" and the tale's "splicing and counterpoint" with the main narrative "quite brilliantly" managed. For Faulkner's criticism of Hemingway for staying within known limits, see Meyers, p. 432.

PART V

The Inevitable Consideration of Hemingway's Biography

HEMINGWAY AND HEMOCHROMATOSIS

Susan Beegel

Our bodies all wear out in some way and we die.

—Hemingway (*DIA*)

Several biographers have noted the probability that Ernest Hemingway suffered from a disease called hemochromatosis, but to date none has explored the matter in any detail. The question of whether Hemingway had hemochromatosis has attracted little attention in part because it cannot be definitively answered with existing evidence. Yet the very real probability that he did suffer from this disease holds so many implications for our understanding of his life, and particularly his death, that it deserves extended consideration.

Also known as "bronze diabetes" or "iron storage disease," hemochromatosis is an inherited metabolic disorder present from birth and causing an increased absorption of iron in the gut. Over the years, massive iron deposits accumulate in the body's organs, eventually causing irreversible damage to the pancreas, joints, glands, liver, and heart (Eichner, "Many Faces" 115). Such damage can produce an array of physical symptoms, increasing in number and severity as the patient ages. Although a study of young people with hemochromatosis shows that abnormal amounts of iron are present in the body by the late teens, most sufferers do not experience recognizable symptoms before their 30s and 40s, and are seldom diagnosed before the disease becomes full-blown between the ages of 50 and 60 (Rowe 201: Motulsky 1161: Eichner, "Times of Plenty" 83).

The onset and severity of symptoms vary greatly from patient to patient, because the amount of iron absorbed by a person with hemochromatosis varies greatly according to his or her diet, ingestion of alcohol, and sex. The use or avoidance of cast-iron cookware, iron-rich food and water, iron-fortified cereals and medications, and vitamin C supplements all influence the amount of iron a given individual has available for absorption (Motulsky 1161; Eichner, "Times of Plenty" 79 and 81). Overeating increases the volume of dietary iron, as does the ingestion of alcohol. Because women with hemochromatosis lose iron periodically during menstruation and occasionally during pregnancy, they generally take ten years longer than men to develop clinically apparent symptoms (Eichner, "Times of Plenty" 79).

Diagnosis is usually based on the classic clinical triad of diabetes mellitus, cirrhosis of the liver, and excessive skin pigmentation. Ernest Hemingway had diabetes mellitus, diagnosed by doctors at the Mayo Clinic, when he committed suicide at the age of 61 (Baker 556). His tendency to diabetes was certainly inherited. His father Clarence developed diabetes near the end of his life, as did at least two—Marcelline and Leicester—of his five siblings (Reynolds 16). Although adult onset diabetes is not an uncommon disorder, when accompanied by liver disease and increased skin pigmentation it may indicate hemochromatosis.

At the time of his suicide, Ernest was also suffering from cirrhosis of the liver, "a chronic disease characterized by fibrosis and nodule formation distorting liver architecture and by impaired liver function" (Holvey 776). In giving his medical history upon his admission to the Mayo, Hemingway noted his repeated bouts with jaundice and his enlarged liver (Baker 667). Other people had noted his enlarged liver as well, including his son, Gregory Hemingway, M.D., who commented that "his liver had been in poor shape for years . . . badly damaged" (15), and George Plimpton, who observed that "his liver was bad. You could see the bulge of it stand out from his body like a long fat leech" (Lynn 529). Dr. Hugh R. Butt, a liver specialist at the Mayo, found a "'palpable left lobe of the liver . . . with a round edge,'" and other symptoms indicative of impaired liver function (Baker 667).

Alcoholism is a well-known cause of cirrhosis of the liver, and that Hemingway was a heavy drinker is equally well-known (Dardis 157–207;

Goodwin 50–72). However, Hemingway's drinking habits do not rule out the possibility that hemochromatosis was the underlying cause of his liver disease. Because alcohol actually stimulates the body's absorption of iron, and because some alcoholic beverages, like the red wine Hemingway loved so well, are rich in iron, a heavy drinker with hemochromatosis runs a far greater risk of developing cirrhosis of the liver than a non-drinker with iron storage disease (Motulsky 1161). Various studies indicate that between 30 and 40 percent of patients with diagnosed hemochromatosis consume more than 100 grams of ethyl alcohol a day, and that heavy drinkers with the disease develop symptoms earlier than non-drinkers (Powell 132; Rowe 240).

Hemochromatosis is sometimes called "bronze diabetes" because iron storage disease causes hyperpigmentation, or bronzing of the skin (Eichner, "Many Faces" 115). This bronzing, caused both by excessive deposits of iron and of melanin (the same pigment that causes tanning on exposure to sunlight), is most pronounced in exposed areas and scars (Holvey 1488–9; Motulsky 1161). In some patients, bronze pigmentation is particularly pronounced in the skin around the eyelids and also appears in the conjunctiva, the mucus membrane that covers the exposed surface of the eyeball (Motulsky 1161).

Because Hemingway was deeply tanned by his years of deep-sea fishing, it's difficult to say whether he experienced this diagnostic skin pigmentation, but a close-up color photograph of the author taken a few months before his death and reproduced on page 156 of Barnaby Conrad's *Hemingway's Spain*, is suggestive.[1] The photo clearly shows distinctive brown stains around the eyes and margins of the eyelids, and, arguably, intruding on the conjunctiva. The scar on Hemingway's forehead incurred in an accident in 1928 also shows a small area of dark pigmentation. The presence of these brown areas is emphasized by the author's otherwise unhealthy pallor, a pallor which, if the photo's color reproduction is true, has a grayish undercast also characteristic of hemochromatosis (Motulsky 1161).

In the male patient with hemochromatosis, iron-induced damage to the hormone-producing cells of the pituitary gland can also cause hypogonadism, a condition whose symptoms include loss of libido, impotence, loss of bodily hair, enlargement of the breasts, and testicular atrophy (Eichner, "Many Faces" 118; Motulsky 1162; Milder 43; Kelly 629–32). Biographer Norberto Fuentes records that "Hemingway was the patient and friend for many years of Dr. Frank Stermayer" a distinguished Cuban physician who intimated to colleagues that Hemingway suffered periods of impotence, "'a chronic condition that came and went'" (69–70). A few months before his death, Hemingway told A. E. Hotchner that he could no longer "enjoy himself in bed," and when psychiatrist Howard Rome asked Mary to visit a locked wing of the Mayo Clinic to tender to her husband's allegedly reviving "sexual impulses," the "reunion" meant to reassure Hemingway was "not entirely satisfactory" to either partner (Hotchner 229; Mary Hemingway 633).

More compelling is evidence that Hemingway used methyltestosterone, a synthetic male hormone. David Nuffer, a scholar exploring the author's history of drug use, has generously directed my attention to the following 24 February 1952 letter from Hemingway to Harvey Breit:

> Then if you are really run down and fatigued and gloomy there is no reason why you shouldn't take Methyltestosterone. You don't have to take it as a shot in the ass. And it is not to make you fornicate more. Paul explained to me that it was good for the head and for the whole general system. He gave it to me in the form called Metandren Linguets put out by CIBA Pharmaceutical Products Inc. Summit N.J. They are small tablets and I am supposed to take one a day dissolveing it under the tongue. Actually I forget to take them for several months and then if I start to feel low, or tired or drag ass I start them again. When Paul wanted me to take them I explained to him that I had no need for sexual stimulation and didn't want to take anything that would get me into any more trouble than I got into already. But he explained that this was something that kept your head in good shape and counter-acted the gloominess everybody gets (*Letters* 753).

It isn't clear why the Paul of this letter (Paul De Kruif, the bacteriologist author of *The Microbe Hunters*) wanted Hemingway to take methyltestosterone. Hemingway insisted that he was using the drug to combat fatigue and depression, but according to pharmacist Allen Bell, methyltestosterone's psychological effects can include habituation, anxiety, depression, excitation, and sleeplessness. The drug is generally prescribed for hypogonadism, impotence, and the male climacteric (change of life), so Hemingway's use of methyltestosterone does suggest that he was experiencing sexual difficulties, perhaps related to the hypogonadism of advancing hemochromatosis.

The 1952 letter has other disturbing implications. Users of methyltestosterone can become addicted to the drug, which is widely used as an aphrodisiac in Spanish cultures, and may have been available on the street in Cuba (Bell). The drug can cause hepatitis, from which Hemingway suffered repeatedly in the 1950s, as well as other forms of potentially life-threatening liver disease (Fuentes 65–66; Bell). Given the probability that Hemingway had hemochromatosis and the certitude that he drank too much (he boasts in the same letter of consuming 17 double frozen daiquiries), methyltestosterone was the last thing his beleaguered liver needed. De Kruif also increased Hemingway's iron intake with vitamin and mineral supplements.

Metabolic disorders like hemochromatosis are common causes of organic brain syndromes and can produce alterations in mental function, behavior, and neurological processes. One psychiatric textbook warns that an underlying metabolic disorder should be considered "whenever rapid changes in behavior, thinking and consciousness"—like those afflicting Hemingway near the end of his life—"have occurred" (Dale 1406). According to the same text:

> the earliest signs are likely to be impairment of memory, particularly recent memory, and orientation. Some patients become agitated, anxious, and hyperactive; others become quieter, withdrawn, and inactive. Perceptual errors—such as illusions, delusions, and hallucinations . . . —often heighten anxiety and agitation (1406).

There is disagreement among experts about the nature and extent of the mental and behavioral changes characterizing the latter stages of hemochromatosis. Dr. Michael Milder, on the basis of a 20 year study involving 34 patients, feels that an identifiable syndrome does exist:

> the most frequent complaints [are] marked lethargy, psychomotor retardation, and inability to think clearly . . . in several [patients] the condition progressed to frank disorientation and confusion with intermittent stupor and decreased responsiveness to external stimuli (Milder 38).

The average age of onset for these symptoms is 59; Hemingway was 60 years old when his personality began to show noticeable signs of disintegration (Milder 38; Baker 550–554). Both lay and medical observers have commented on Hemingway's profound depression in the months preceding his suicide, his difficulty in walking and speaking, his complaints that he could not concentrate, his delusions characteristic of disorientation and confusion, and his failures to respond to those around him (Baker 550–564); Hotchner 264–304; Mary Hemingway 619–637; Betsky 22; Fiedler 395–405; Brian 248–263).

However, hemochromatosis cannot be singled out as the sole cause of Hemingway's fatal depression. Doctors at the Mayo Clinic attributed Hemingway's depression to his medication for high blood pressure and to contributing psychological factors that will probably remain privileged communications between the author and his psychiatrist, Dr. Rome (Gregory Hemingway, 15; Baker, 556; Brian, 253). Biographer Michael Reynolds has offered compelling evidence that the author suffered from an inherited manic-depressive illness. Withdrawal from alcohol or an organic brain syndrome characteristic of liver failure may also have been at fault. Some individuals have speculated that the shock treatment Hemingway received at the Mayo may have brought about his death, by adding anxiety about permanent memory loss to his already precarious mental state (Meyers 550; Hotchner 293; Brian 22). Any or all of these problems, including hemochromatosis, may have precipitated Hemingway's suicide.

William B. Ober, M.D., a pathologist specializing in "medical analyses of literary men's afflictions," has wisely cautioned those bent on similar enterprises about the dangers inherent in paleodiagnosis (xi–xii). However, the expert on diseases of the liver who actually examined Hemingway near the end of his life did not rule out the possibility of iron storage disease. According to Carlos Baker, Dr. Hugh R. Butt of the Mayo Clinic told Hemingway that he "'might possibly have a very rare disease called hemachromatosis [sic],'" but decided not to perform the liver biopsy necessary to confirm such a diagnosis (Baker, 556). Butt's caution is understandable—liver biopsy is an invasive procedure posing a real risk of hemorrhage to the patient (P. M. Beegel; Kent 837–40).

In *My Brother, Ernest Hemingway*, Ernest's only brother Leicester records that "tests at the Clinic had uncovered the possibility that Ernest might have hemochromatosis, a very rare disease that could bring an end to the functioning of various organs" (255). When interviewed by Denis Brian several years after the publication of this memoir, Leicester Hemingway believed without reservation in his brother's illness:

> He [Ernest] had hemochromatosis. It's rare, but not a killer disease. It's a condition wherein the blood picks up more iron than normally and you eventually become more loaded with iron than a normal male. It's something that females almost can't get. They [the staff at the Mayo Clinic] were undoubtedly doing the best they knew how, but I don't think they were going deeply enough into the chemical imbalance that probably was hitting him. They went heavily into shock treatment,

which they probably thought was going to fix him up immediately . . .
(Brian 252)

In Gregory Hemingway's *Papa: A Memoir*, Ernest's youngest son, an M.D.,
recalls that in 1960 his father telephoned him from Cuba to say "I saw a good
doctor today who told me I had a rare disease that makes you blind and permanently impotent" (13). Gregory, who had just started medical school and
ignored his father's use of the adjective "rare," could think of "no common
medical condition besides diabetes mellitus . . . that causes both impotence
and blindness" (14). He did not know then that his father had diabetes, felt
there was nothing seriously wrong with his eyesight, and attributed his difficulties with impotence to a damaged liver and his medication for high blood
pressure (14–15). Although diabetes mellitus, impotence, and liver damage
are among the major clinical manifestations of hemochromatosis, Gregory
did not believe his father when he wrote from the Mayo Clinic to say that he
had "hemachromatosis [sic], a rare and eventually fatal form of diabetes"
(114).[2]

In *How It Was*, Mary Welsh Hemingway cites as one of her husband's
delusions his belief that he was suffering from "an imagined dread disease"
(633). However, at least one other of Hemingway's alleged "delusions," his
insistence that he was being persecuted by the F.B.I., has since proved to be
founded in fact.[3] As Dr. Butt told Hemingway that he might have hemochromatosis, the author's belief that he was suffering from a "dread disease" was
probably more rational than delusory.

Dr. Herrara Sotolongo tells us that in the late 1950s Hemingway "became
interested in the medical literature on the subject of diseases of the liver"
(Fuentes 65–66). If Hemingway read about hemochromatosis, he would have
known that once the disease has become full-blown and cirrhosis of the liver
has manifested itself, the prognosis is poor. In patients with hemochromatosis, the most common cause of death is cancer of the liver (Eichner, "Many
Faces" 122). According to Carlos Baker, Hemingway told at least one family
friend that he feared his weight loss was due to cancer (559). Other causes of
death from hemochromatosis are cirrhosis of the liver, followed by congestive heart failure and complications of diabetes (Eichner, "Many Faces" 122).
The belief, real or mistaken, that he was terminally ill may have contributed
to Hemingway's suicide. Studies suggest that fear of death, pain, and illness,
as well as the social isolation that accompanies illness, may cause a depression predisposing the terminally ill to suicide (Lester, 26). The same studies

also warn that suicides among the terminally ill may be prompted by changes in biochemistry like those accompanying hemochromatosis (26).

Hemingway's family history of diabetes, depression, and suicide is not incompatible with an inherited metabolic disorder like iron storage disease. When Ernest's father, Dr. Clarence Hemingway, shot himself in 1928, he was suffering from diabetes so severe that he believed he might face the loss of a leg from gangrene caused by circulatory problems (Sanford, 231). His daughter Marcelline records that even before things reached this pass, Dr. Hemingway underwent a profound personality change like that later experienced by his son:

> . . . my father changed from his high-strung, active, determined, cheerful self—the self with a twinkle in his eye—to an irritable, suspicious person. He was quick to take offense, almost unable to let himself believe in the honesty of other people's motives. He began to spend long hours alone in his office with the door closed. He kept his bureau drawers and his clothes closet locked. It was an agony for my mother, who shared the bedroom with him, to think he must be distrusting her (Sanford 228–9).

In *Alcohol and the Writer*, Donald Goodwin, M.D. observes that because Dr. Hemingway, unlike his son, was a strict teetotaller, the similarity between their breakdowns seems to preclude any possibility that Ernest's fatal depression was alcohol-induced (68).

In addition to Ernest, at least three of Clarence Hemingway's other five children experienced similar difficulties. After developing cancer, Ursula committed suicide with a drug overdose in 1966 (Brian 309; Reynolds 16). When Leicester, who seemed so certain that his older brother had diabetes and who knew so much about it, shot himself in 1982, he was suffering from depression and from diabetes so severe that he faced the amputation of one or both legs (Reynolds 16; Brian 261). Marcelline suffered from diabetes and depression, and although her death in 1963 was reported to be from natural causes, her brother Leicester suspected suicide (Brian 309; Reynolds 16).

In Hemingway's day, hemochromatosis was believed to be a rare disease, and his biographers have been repeating the adjective "rare" throughout the nearly 30 years since his death without consulting the advancing state of medical knowledge about this disorder (Lynn 530; Meyers 539; Leicester Hemingway 255; Gregory Hemingway 114; Baker 556). However, today's methods of genetic testing indicate that "the gene for hemochromatosis is common," perhaps "the most common abnormal gene in the United States" (Eichner, "Times of Plenty" 77; "Many Faces" 115). According to specialist Edward R. Eichner:

> About 10 percent of the population are heterozygotes (carry one gene for hemochromatosis). But recent genetic research has shown that it takes two genes, one from each parent, to develop the disorder. In other words, hemochromatosis is an autosomal recessive disease. If 10 percent of persons have one gene, it is estimated that 0.3 percent have two genes (are homozygotes). Thus, in a city of one million persons, 3,000 will have hemochromatosis—an 'epidemic' ("Times of Plenty" 77).

This means that if Clarence Hemingway had hemochromatosis, all of his children would have inherited one gene for the disease from him, making them carriers. But if any of the children were to develop the disease, they would have had to inherit a second gene for hemochromatosis from their mother. So Grace Hall would need to be at least a carrier, transmitting the second gene necessary for hemochromatosis to some of her children. Current research indicates that such marriages are "not so rare an occurrence when 10 percent of us are heterozygotes," and "in such a family, each child has a 50 percent chance of inheriting hemochromatosis . . . " (Eichner, "Times of Plenty" 81). The fact that at least three of the six Hemingway children inherited diabetes and accompanying changes in mental status is consistent with a family history of hemochromatosis.

It's the diagnosis of hemochromatosis, rather than the disorder itself, that is rare (Eichner, "Many Faces" 115–122). Iron storage disease is tragically difficult to diagnose because the disorder often presents no obvious symptoms until irreversible organ damage has taken place. Some sufferers are never diagnosed at all, as diabetes, cirrhosis, or congestive heart failure may be mistaken for the patient's primary problem, rather than the symptom of an underlying disorder. It's because this disease is so difficult to diagnose that its prevalence among the population was only recently suspected. In 1961, the belief expressed by Hemingway's liver specialist, Dr. Hugh Butt, that hemochromatosis was "very rare," further impeded prompt diagnosis.

All of this is tragic because, if detected early via a simple blood test, hemochromatosis can be controlled by phlebotomy-induced anemia, or, in plain English—bleeding—perhaps the oldest and simplest treatment in the medical repertoire. Regular bleeding can deplete the body of excess iron and prevent its accumulation. If begun early enough in the course of the disease, it can reverse or prevent organ impairment by iron overload (Neiderau 335–336). In addition, patients can be warned to avoid alcohol and iron-rich foods and medications. And finally, all of this is tragic because, if Hemingway had hemochromatosis, early diagnosis and treatment of this metabolic disorder might have enriched American literature.

The grave's a fine and private place, and at present we may never know for certain whether Ernest Hemingway had hemochromatosis. The cause of his death was so obviously a self-inflicted shotgun wound, that no autopsy was required after his suicide (Baker, 667; Meyers, 561). However, improved understanding of the Hemingway family's medical history and increasing medical knowledge of the disorder may eventually answer the question once and for all. In the meantime, scholars should be alert for developments in these areas, and the very real possibility that Hemingway had an inherited metabolic disorder should give us pause for thought.

Doctors have long known that organic and mental processes are tightly interwoven, but Hemingway's biographers and critics have focussed on the psychological dimensions of the author's suicide to the exclusion of its physiological causes. The possibility that Hemingway had hemochromatosis should at least caution us against the dangers inherent in interpreting his life and work in the light of his death. If his suicide was indeed precipitated by advanced iron storage disease, the unwary may find themselves unwittingly psychologizing an organic brain syndrome rather than uncovering what Leon Edel has called "the hidden personal myth" (162).

We might also be cautioned against omitting the body from the mind-body problem when studying the life as well as the death. For example, although the early natural history of the disease is poorly understood, young men with hemochromatosis "may complain of lost libido and impotence and may have testicular atrophy and low plasma levels of testosterone" (Eichner, "Many Faces" 118). The prevalence of a lack of passion, impotence, androgyny, and masculine overcompensation as themes in Hemingway's work, as well as his now celebrated "sexual confusion," may be more symptomatic of iron storage disease than of an overbearing mother. Sexual dysfunction is caused by iron deposition in the pituitary gland, the same process which causes the changes in mental status characteristic of iron storage disease (Eichner, "Many Faces" 118). Future medical research may uncover an inheritable organic basis, perhaps hemochromatosis, for the recurring depressions endured by many members of the Hemingway family.

In *Illness as Metaphor,* Susan Sontag warns us that

Psychologizing seems to provide control over the experiences and events (like grave illnesses) over which people have in fact little or no control ... For those who live neither with religious consolations about death nor with a sense of death ... as natural, death is the obscene mystery, the ultimate affront, the thing that cannot be controlled. It can only be denied. A large part of the popularity and persuasiveness of psychology comes from its being a sublimated spiritualism: a secular, ostensibly scientific way of affirming the primacy of "spirit" over matter. That ineluctably material reality, disease, can be given a scientific explanation. Death itself can be considered, ultimately, a psychological phenomenon (54).

Hemingway biography and criticism of late seem particularly afflicted by psychologizing, by what Hemingway himself would call "unavoidable mysticism," "pseudo-scientific jargon," and "pretty phallic images drawn in the manner of sentimental valentines" (DIA 53). Perhaps this affliction, our willingness to psychologize Hemingway without reference to "material reality," is symptomatic of our unwillingness to accept his death, and not coincidentally our own deaths, as inevitable and ultimately necessary.

The Blaine County Coroner's Office lists the cause of Ernest Hemingway's death quite simply as a "self-inflicted gunshot wound to the head" (Baker 668). Yet whether or not he had hemochromatosis, at the time of his suicide Hemingway was suffering from high blood pressure, diabetes, cirrhosis of the liver, depressive illness, and the ravages of alcoholism, dying proof of his own assertion in "The Art of the Short Story" that "Longevity, gentlemen, is not an end. It is a prolongation." (130). In many respects, then, Hemingway's suicide was a death from natural causes. Perhaps it's time his biographers and critics evolved a more natural history of the dead.

Notes

1. Exposure to sunlight also obscures evidence of hyperpigmentation in the case of Ernest's father, Dr. Clarence Hemingway. His daughter, Marcelline Hemingway Sanford, reports that he "grew tanned" on a 1928 trip to Cuba after developing the symptoms of depression and diabetes that would end in his suicide later that year (227).
2. "I don't know where he found out about that disease," says Gregory, but it's interesting to note that Hemingway's son misspells hemochromatosis exactly as

did Carlos Baker in quoting Dr. Butt's written report to Ernest (Baker, 667). If Gregory copied the spelling mistake from his father's letter, that would suggest that Ernest was simply forwarding his son information received from his physician. On the other hand, Hemingway is purported to have told Gregory: "I doubt if you'll ever make much of a doctor—you can't even spell the word medicine correctly" (Baker 556 and 667; Gregory Hemingway 13).

3. Michael S. Reynolds was the first to recover Hemingway's F.B.I. dossier. Jeffrey Meyers has demonstrated that the F.B.I. did in fact track Hemingway to the Mayo Clinic, and that his psychiatrist, Dr. Howard Rome, communicated with the F.B.I. about his registration under an assumed name (542–544). In *Dangerous Dossiers*, Herbert Mitgang quotes uncensored portions of Hemingway's 122-page file, and postulates that his support of the Spanish Loyalists, his WW II intelligence operations, and his connections with Fidel Castro made Hemingway of special interest to the F.B.I.

Works Cited

I would like to thank my father, Dr. Paul M. Beegel, for his assistance in acquiring and interpreting the medical literature on hemochromatosis, and for his patience in answering my myriad questions about the disease. He has been my partner in this enterprise. My physician, Dr. Timothy Lepore of Nantucket Cottage Hospital, and Dr. Edward R. Eichner, a specialist on hemochromatosis at the Oklahoma Health Sciences Center, have also given generously of their time and expertise. My pharmacist, Allen Bell, R.P.H., was of great help to me in exploring the use and abuse of methyltestosterone, and the staff of the Central Maine Medical Center Health Sciences Library assisted cheerfully with obtaining and photocopying articles. All of these people have made my layman's venture into the world of medicine instructive and pleasant indeed.

Baker, Carlos. *Ernest Hemingway: A Life Story*. New York: Scribner's, 1969.

Beegel, Paul M. Telephone conversation. 4 June 1989.

Bell, Allen. Telephone conversation. 2 May 1990.

Betsky, Seymour. "A Last Visit." *Saturday Review* 44 (29 July 1961): 22.

Brian, Denis. *The True Gen: An Intimate Portrait of Hemingway by Those Who Knew Him*. New York: Grove, 1988.

Conrad, Barnaby. *Hemingway's Spain*. San Francisco: Chronicle, 1989.

Dale, Allan J. D. "Organic Mental Disorders Associated with Disturbances in Metabolism, Growth, and Nutrition" in Freedman, et al. eds. *Comprehensive Textbook of Psychiatry*. Baltimore/London: Williams & Wilkins, 1980.

Dardis, Tom. *The Thirsty Muse: Alcohol and the American Writer*. New York: Ticknor & Fields, 1989.

Edel, Leon. *Writing Lives: Principia Biographica*. New York: W. W. Norton, 1984.

Eichner, Edward R. "Hemochromatosis in Times of Plenty." *New Developments in Medicine* 3.2 (Sept. 1988): 77–84.

———. "The Many Faces of Hemochromatosis." *Internal Medicine* 8.12 (Nov. 1987): 115–122.

Fuentes, Norberto. *Hemingway in Cuba.* Trans. Consuelo Corwin. Secaucus, N.J.: Lyle Stuart, 1984.

Goodwin, Donald W. *Alcohol and the Writer.* 1988. New York: Penguin, 1990.

Hemingway, Ernest. "The Art of the Short Story" in Joseph Flora, ed. *Ernest Hemingway: A Study of the Short Fiction.* Boston: G. K. Hall, 1989.

———. *Death in the Afternoon.* New York: Charles Scribner's Sons, 1932.

Hemingway, Gregory H. *Papa: A Personal Memoir.* Boston: Houghton Mifflin, 1976.

Hemingway, Leicester. *My Brother, Ernest Hemingway.* 1962. New York: Fawcett Premier Library, 1967.

Hemingway, Mary Welsh. *How It Was.* 1976. New York: Ballantine Books, 1977.

Holvey, David N., and John H. Talbott, eds. *The Merck Manual of Diagnosis and Therapy.* Rahway, N.J.: Merck, Sharp & Dohme Research Laboratories, 1972.

Hotchner, A. E. *Papa Hemingway.* New York: Random House, 1966.

Kent, Geoffrey and Hans Popper. "Liver Biopsy in Diagnosis of Hemochromatosis." *American Journal of Medicine* 44.6 (June 1968): 837–40.

Kelly, Thomas M., et al. "Hypogonadism in Hemochromatosis: Reversal with Iron Depletion." *Annals of Internal Medicine* 101.5 (Nov. 1984): 629–632.

Lester, David, and Gene Lester. "Heredity and Environment in the Causation of Suicide" in *Suicide: The Gamble with Death.* Englewood Cliffs: Prentice-Hall, 1971.

Lynn, Kenneth S. *Hemingway.* New York: Simon & Schuster, 1987.

Meyers, Jeffrey. *Hemingway: A Biography.* New York: Harper & Row, 1985.

Milder, Michael, et al. "Hemochromatosis: An Interim Report." *Medicine* 59.1 (1980): 34–49.

Mitgang, Herbert. *Dangerous Dossiers: Exposing the Secret War Against America's Greatest Authors.* 1988. New York: Ballantine, 1989.

Motulsky, Arno G. "Hemochromatosis" in James Wyngaarden and Lloyd H. Smith, Jr., eds. *Cecil Textbook of Medicine.* Philadelphia: W. B. Saunders, 1985.

Neiderau, Claus, and Georg Strohmeyer. "Hemochromatosis" in Robert Rakel, ed. *Conn's Current Therapy.* Philadelphia: W. B. Saunders, 1988.

Nuffer, David. Letter to author. 25 June 1989.

Ober, William B. *Boswell's Clap and Other Essays.* 1979. New York: Perennial Library, 1988.

Powell, Lawrie W. "The Role of Alcoholism in Hepatic Iron Storage Disease." *Annals of the New York Academy of Sciences* 252 (1975): 124–134.

Reynolds, Michael S. "Hemingway's Home: Depression and Suicide" in Linda W. Wagner, ed. *Ernest Hemingway: Six Decades of Criticism.* East Lansing: Michigan State U P, 1987.

Rowe, John H., et al. "Familial Hemochromatosis: Characteristics of the Precirrhotic Stage in a Large Kindred." *Medicine* 56.3 (1977): 197–211.

Sanford, Marcelline Hemingway. *At the Hemingways: A Family Portrait.* London: Putnam, 1961.

Sontag, Susan. *Illness as Metaphor.* 1978. New York: Vintage, 1979.

Editor's note: This article is a revision of a paper presented at the "Hemingway in Idaho" Conference, June 9–11, 1989, a conference supported in part by a grant from the Idaho Humanities Council.

THE HEMINGWAY-STEIN STORY

Linda Wagner-Martin

Early in 1922 Ernest Hemingway sent Gertrude his letter of introduction from Sherwood Anderson, asking whether he and his wife, Hadley, might call. To Stein's prompt response inviting them to tea, Hadley wrote cordially that Sherwood had told them many nice things.[1] Arriving in Paris a few weeks earlier, Hemingway had written Anderson, "In a couple of days we'll be settled and then I'll send out the letters of introduction like launching a flock of ships."[2] Through the letters, Hadley and he met Sylvia Beach, Ezra Pound, James Joyce, Matthew Josephson, and Alfred Kreymborg; by being friendly in cafés, Hemingway also met Blaise Cendrars, the poet visible in 1920s theater,[3] and other French writers, as well as Leo Stein, Morrill Cody, and a sea of other would-be artists. And by reading Apollinaire, Gide, Wilde, and Stein at Shakespeare and Company, the couple was beginning to understand literary Paris.

They were clearly impressed with the chance to meet Gertrude. In addition to Anderson's praise of her and the near-reverence with which she was held among some café crowds, Hemingway saw the power she had in the art world. As one American observed, after the war Gertrude "became an unofficial pontiff and she could make or mar an exhibit with little more than a movement of her thumb."[4] The always ambitious Hemingway saw her as a

Excerpted and reprinted with permission from Linda Wagner-Martin, "Favored Strangers": Gertrude Stein and Her Family (Rutgers University Press, 1995).

means into the avant-garde art world as well as the literary one. He trusted
his boyish good looks to make a favorable initial impression and then—
charming her from the start—defined his role in their friendship as that of
listener. On March 9 he wrote Anderson, "Gertrude Stein and me are just like
brothers and we see a lot of her."[5] Alice and she took the Hemingways along
on their monthly visit to Mildred Aldrich, where they picnicked for the day.
Mildred was also enthusiastic about the deferential, "extraordinarily good
looking"[6] American.

From late March into June Hemingway traveled in Italy and Switzerland,
covering the world economic conference for the *Toronto Star*, but during the
summer he and Hadley resumed their intimacy with Gertrude and Alice.
They grew to appreciate the women's joy in their paintings and to see how
serious Gertrude was about her writing. When she offered to read Ernest's
work—sitting on the bed in the Hemingways' small apartment—he was
ecstatic. True to her method, she gave him little specific criticism but praised
his "direct" poems and worried that the beginning of his fiction was prolix
("There is a great deal of description in this . . . not particularly good description. Begin over again and concentrate").[7] She liked all his stories except "Up
in Michigan." Antagonized by the blatant pun of the title, she warned him
that writing "inaccrochable"[8] fiction was pointless. Just as a shocking painting could never be hung, this seduction story could not be published. What
she failed to tell him, though she probably thought he could figure it out
from reading her work, was that writing could be filled with sexuality, so long
as it was disguised.

Pleased with what he had written, Gertrude urged Hemingway to give up
journalism. Not only did he spend much of his time covering stories for the
Toronto paper, but such reporting entailed extensive travel. If he were going
to learn to write from the center of his being, he would need permanence—
a stable place, tranquil surroundings. To that end Gertrude urged him to buy
good paintings, explaining that most expatriates' money went into women's
clothing, which had a short life. If he could encourage Hadley to dress comfortably rather than fashionably, as Alice and she did, the Hemingways might
then be able to make such purchases.

More important than Gertrude's suggestions for living, however, were her
prolegomena about the way a writer's work had to come from, and also
absorb, the best part of the psyche. Hemingway could see that Alice arranged
the days to support Gertrude's brief period of writing. Her work, then, could
flow unimpeded because her mind was not clouded with trivia. That
Hemingway began to understand Stein's process of good writing is clear

from a summer letter: "I've been working hard and have two things done. I've thought a lot about the things you said about working and am starting that way at the beginning. If you think of anything else I wish you'd write it to me. Am working hard about creating and keeping my mind going about it all the time. Mind seems to be working better."[9] Comparisons between his early newspaper columns and his stories from 1922 and 1923 show dramatic changes.

During the summer of 1922 Gertrude varied her routine by sitting for sculptor Jo Davidson and writing a portrait of him in turn. She continued proselytizing for her own importance in literature even as she wondered at the praise both Joyce's *Ulysses* and Eliot's *The Waste Land* were garnering. (As she said of the latter, "The trouble with Tom Eliot is that he tries too hard to be British. That absurd umbrella he totes about—and why not face the fact that splitting an infinitive is American?")[10] For all their love of meeting new people, however, Gertrude and Alice felt that Paris was wearing thin, and in August they drove south to help their sculptor friend Janet Scudder find a house near St. Rémy in the part of France they thought most beautiful, "between Avignon and Aix-en-Province, Orange and the sea."[11] Locating a good hotel for themselves, the two stayed on through the autumn and into winter; Gertrude later said that the peace made her feel as if she had finally recovered from both the stresses of war and worries about her health.[12]

That fall Hemingway covered the peace conference in Germany, Lausanne, Bulgaria, and Constantinople. He complained to Hadley, "I'm so sick of this—it is so hard. Everybody else has two men or an assistant, and they expect me to cover everything by myself—and all for one of Masons little baby kike salaries."[13] (Disillusioned with reporting, Hemingway wrote his father that he had had "a belly full of travelling . . . nearly 10,000 miles by R.R. this past year. Been to Italy 3 times. Back and forth Switzerland-Paris 6 . . . Constantinople-Germany-Burgundy-The Vendee [*sic*].") In November Hadley thanked "Miss Stien and Miss Toclaz" (she sometimes spelled the name *Tocraz*) for their gift of an "ambrosiac melon," saying that she and Ernest were leaving for Switzerland and hoped to spend January in Italy.[15]

It was during 1923 that Gertrude gave Hemingway "the run of the studio": she told him that when they were out, he should have a drink and wait for them.[16] Gertrude and he took long walks and discussed writing and art, with her telling stories about Picasso, Rousseau, Braque, Matisse, and other painters; Hemingway recalled that her conversation was "more about them as people than as painters."[17] As part of his indoctrination into becoming a writer, Hemingway (under orders from both Gertrude and Leo Stein, a café friend of his) read Jane Austen—for her conversation. By reading aloud the first chapter of *Pride and Prejudice*, he learned the same thing he did from reading Gertrude's *The Making of Americans*—that conversation written to be read is not the same as what one hears. A friend quoted Hemingway as saying, "Stein made me see that written conversation is primarily for the eye. It is something that has to be contrived in its own right.... Mostly you've got to make out a written conversation so that it will seem natural in the imagination of your reader without benefit of his sense of hearing."[18]

Although he had been doing some work that satisfied him, Hemingway had had a frustrating winter and spring. In January Hadley had packed all his writing—including carbon copies—to bring to him in Austria. When her suitcase was stolen, nothing survived from his first years in Paris but a few stories out in the mail. Hemingway made no secret of his agony over this loss. A few weeks later he was again unhappy because Hadley was pregnant; at the close of a long visit to the rue de Fleurus, he announced sadly to Gertrude that he was too young to be a father. (Although she feigned sympathy, she later told Hadley about his comment—which she thought was "hilarious.")[19] Resentful about the impending changes in his lifestyle, Hemingway took two trips to Spain. On one, he "lived in a bull fighters [*sic*] pension . . . and then travelled all over the country with a crew of toreros." On the second, with Hadley, he took in "the big Feria at Pamplona." After seeing these twenty bullfights, Hemingway claimed to be an expert and announced that the sport was "a great tragedy—and the most beautiful thing I've ever seen." Far from a brutal pastime, he said, bullfighting "takes more guts and skill and guts again than anything possibly could."[20]

The range of emotions Hemingway experienced during this year contributed to the strength of the fiction he was writing using the methods Gertrude urged him to try. As he learned to go inside himself, to find a key image or scene to convey the feeling that drove the narrative, Hemingway wrote some of his best stories. The purity of the distillation of his emotions into words pleased Gertrude, and she continued to encourage him. But unlike Pound, who gave him high praise, Gertrude played the role of hard-to-please teacher. Janet Flanner remembered her being very critical of Hemingway, and another friend recalled a day when he was leaving the salon and Gertrude kidded him by saying: "I've been trying to persuade Hem to omit that fishing episode he's used twice already, but he maintains that he has no imagination and must use what happened to him." As Hemingway left, Alice interjected, "And what happens to his friends. Well, so far, Lovey, he's kept you out of it." Stein's reply was not complacent: "Oh, I won't escape, I'm not deluding myself. . . . But if only Hem would give up that show-off soldiering, that bogus bull fighting, the lowdown on his friends and forget that phoney grace under pressure and just be himself, he'd turn out a real book."[21]

Gertrude believed in Hemingway's talent, and she was also attracted to him. But Alice, who never hid her animosity toward the young American, was becoming more overt about her dislike. To avoid conflicts with Alice, Gertrude often saw Hemingway in the Luxembourg Garden rather than at home; some evenings they met at the Brasserie Lipp, where they ate the heavy German food and discussed religion. A friend recalled that Hemingway was fascinated with Catholicism as he had observed it in Spain and impressed with the bullfighters' reverence for it. "Deeply interested in the problem of redemption," Hemingway was searching for what his friend called "a theory of grace."[22]

Problems

On August 17, 1923, the Hemingways sailed for Canada so that their child could be born closer to home. John Hadley Nicanor Hemingway (Bumby) arrived October 11, with Hemingway absent from the birth because he was traveling for the *Toronto Star*. In late November Hadley wrote Gertrude about their "healthy and happy and really dreadfully handsome" son, who is also "a tremendous smiler." She lamented the distance between Paris and Toronto and promised that the family would return to France in January, saying "You've no idea how we miss you two."[23]

In November Gertrude sent Hemingway her review of his *Three Stories and Ten Poems* from the Paris edition of the *Chicago Tribune* and in December a copy of her portrait "He and They, Hemingway" from the little magazine *Ex Libris*. While Stein had meant her review to be positive, she had unfortunately used the word *turgid* to describe his fiction (she preferred his poetry). When Hemingway replied, he assured her that he would "try not to be turgid,"[24] saying that he had "some good stories to write." He also showed his nasty side, mentioning: "They [readers in the States] are turning on you and Sherwood both; the young critical guys and their public. I can feel it in the papers etc."[25] Throwing down a seemingly innocent gauntlet, Hemingway was playing his game of exercising power, keeping people beholden to him: his letter suggested further that, because Pound had asked him to work with Ford Madox Ford on the new *Transatlantic Review*, he might be able to shore up the older writers' reputations. Perhaps he did not know that *Geography and Plays* had been widely reviewed, receiving high praise from Edith Sitwell, Ben Hecht, and Van Vechten as well as more moderate reactions from Kenneth Burke in *Dial* and Edmund Wilson in *Vanity Fair*.

Hemingway quit the *Toronto Star* on December 31; by then Hadley, Bumby, and he were back in Paris, reconciled to living on Hadley's trust income until his writing brought in money or he began receiving a salary from Ford Madox Ford. When his poems had appeared in Harriet Monroe's *Poetry*, Hemingway had been described as "a young Chicago poet now abroad,"[26] but now his identity had changed to fiction writer. The publication of a single story in *The Little Review* was now augmented with monthly contributions to *Transatlantic Review*, beginning with the April 1924 issue, in which "Indian Camp" (titled "Work in Progress") appeared. For much of 1924 the "Chroniques" section of the journal featured his brief items about artists, writers, bullfighters, and boxers. In December "The Doctor and the Doctor's Wife" appeared. But other than these, Hemingway in 1924 had no publications besides a few poems published in the German *Querschnitt*, one other story in *The Little Review*, and *in our time*, the pamphlet of prose sketches. He made very little money from his writing. Rather, the satisfaction he found in his new life as writer and editor stemmed from wielding power; in his role at *Transatlantic Review*, he wrote Gertrude that they would use excerpts from *The Making of Americans* at a rate of thirty francs a page.[27]

Hemingway may also have seen his connection with *Transatlantic Review* as a way to counter the influence on Gertrude of Harold Loeb, the editor of *Broom* (where Stein's "If You Had 3 Husbands" had appeared). Hemingway observed with jealousy Gertrude's friendship with Loeb, especially the recent portrait she had written of him; he was also watchful of her affection for Jane Heap, coeditor with Margaret Anderson of *The Little Review*. Heap was both a close personal friend and the agent for Gertrude's work. Her obvious lesbianism and cross-dressing, like that of Romaine Brooks, marked a new trend toward visible sexual markers at the rue de Fleurus, and Ernest—like his close friend Pound—was uncomfortable. For Hemingway, being a self-confident male meant being in charge—sexually, physically, emotionally; he often talked about his boxing and skiing. Elizabeth Anderson—when

Sherwood and she visited Paris—ridiculed his poses. She described Hemingway's "bouncing into the room, beating his chest and loudly boasting: 'I can walk like an Olympic marathoner. I just walked all the way over here—fifteen blocks—and I'm not a bit tired.'" Elizabeth had just walked twenty blocks, and she wasn't winded either.[28]

Another way of ingratiating himself with Gertrude was asking her and Alice to be Bumby's godmothers. While the Hemingways may have honestly thought the women's support would be helpful to their baby, there was an element of opportunism in the invitation: it suggested Ernest's jealousy of Picasso, whose young son was already Gertrude's godson. On March 16, 1924, with Chink Dorman-Smith as godfather and Alice and Gertrude as godmothers, the youngest Hemingway was baptized at the Episcopalian chapel of St. Luke's in the Luxembourg Garden. On Bumby's six-month day (April 10), they all celebrated again. Although lukewarm about her role, Alice knit the child a sweater and a chair cover, and Gertrude brought a silver cup and rubber animals for his bath.[29]

Hemingway was satisfied that he had made Gertrude happy by involving her in his family and by helping to publish her writing. For her part, however, she had more to do in life than oversee the Hemingways; as she wrote a friend, the spring had been "very hectic" because of relatives visiting (her nephew Allan had married in February) and "young admirers" dropping in. Of the two groups, she said, she preferred the latter.[30] Hemingway knew he had competition, and he vowed to earn her praise someday by improving his writing. His August letters to her in Belley, which she called the "enchanted" valley,[31] showed his pride in his new long story, "Big Two-Hearted River": "I'm trying to do the country like Cézanne and having a hell of a time and sometime getting it a little bit. It is about 100 pages long and nothing happens and the country is swell, I made it all up, so I see it all and part of it comes out the way it ought to . . . but isn't writing a hard job though?" He praised her tutelage: "It used to be easy before I met you. I certainly was bad, gosh. I'm awfully bad now but it's a different kind of bad."[32]

In other of his August letters, showing his tendency to spread tales, Hemingway rehearsed his version of what was wrong with Ford's *Transatlantic Review*. Originally using his own capital for the journal, Ford soon had to find patrons, and the resulting partnership meant the end of the short-lived magazine. While Hemingway played the innocent bystander, attributing all kinds of misbehavior to Ford and those who bought stock, his version of the muddle didn't fool Gertrude: she was one of the stockholders. She knew that if the journal folded, she would lose her outlet for *The Making of Americans* and her monthly payment. Always cognizant of finances, she wrote: "That little check comes in handy, anything comes in handy." She also reminded him, kindly, to "tell Hadley and Goddy [her nickname for her godson] that we speak of them all the time."[33]

Seeing Hemingway's manipulative comments in the wider context of the Paris literary world, Gertrude was happy to do what she could for him, but she also remained friends with Ford and Stella Bowen, continuing her visits to their afternoons and Christmas parties for the young children of the quarter and inviting Bowen to "drop in after dinner." Stella recalled that the three women "would sit beneath the Picassos and the rest of the collection and discuss methods of dealing with one's concierge, or where to buy linen for sheets, or how to enjoy French provincial life."[34] Gertrude saw no need to choose between Ford and Hemingway.

During 1924 Gertrude's hopes for advances died as both Knopf and Liveright rejected *The Making of Americans,* but the appearance of excerpts in *Transatlantic Review* had created interest. Later in the year, when Robert McAlmon offered to do the book as part of his Three Mountains Press series, Gertrude accepted readily. She may even have puffed the amount of attention she thought the book would receive, just as she had exaggerated possible reviewers for *Geography and Plays,* but her point was that there was an audience, though small, for her work, and she would use whatever means she could to take advantage of that interest.

Five hundred copies of *The Making of Americans* appeared in 1925, co-published by McAlmon's Contact Editions and Three Mountains Press. Because sales were small, McAlmon's recriminations were vociferous. Before it was obvious that the book would not sell, Hemingway blamed McAlmon's drinking for the problems. "It's hard to see your editor throw up your royalties," he said on one occasion.[35] In the eventual struggle over who owned the remaining unbound pages, Stein almost succeeded in selling the book to Charles and Albert Boni, but the deal fell through. Her friendship with the volatile McAlmon was over, but as a result of the novel's availability, Gertrude's name began appearing elsewhere—and made her a more of a threat to Hemingway's own burgeoning reputation.

Hemingway's chief motive throughout his life was to make himself into a successful writer—no matter what the cost. When critic Edmund Wilson, in a 1924 review of Hemingway's early work, linked him with both Stein and

Anderson,[36] he planted the seed of rebellion in Hemingway, who would not accept being called anyone's pupil. It was only another year before he wrote the scurrilous *The Torrents of Spring,* a parody of both Anderson's novel *Dark Laughter* and Gertrude's writing. While Hadley and most of his friends told him that he should not publish this two-week effort because it would hurt Anderson and Stein terribly, Hemingway insisted that *Torrents* was good writing. As Hadley watched her husband's judgment disintegrate, she wondered whether his malice was new or had only been well disguised. She continued to take Bumby to visit Gertrude and Alice, but there was a tense undercurrent to the friendship.

Ernest, however, went on bringing Americans to Gertrude's salon; the connection was eminently useful to him as he stormed the citadel of literary acceptance. With him came John Dos Passos, Archibald and Ada MacLeish, Donald Ogden Stewart, Nathan Asch, Ernest Walsh, Evan Shipman, and F. Scott Fitzgerald, whose earlier books Gertrude admired because they captured the spirit of American youth. Predictably, Hemingway resented the achievement of Fitzgerald's 1925 *The Great Gatsby,* and he became even more jealous when he saw how much Gertrude liked Fitzgerald. She was attracted by his modesty, his handsomeness, and his talent, and he responded—with some disbelief—to her praise of his work.

During the mid-1920s Stein established herself in a great many new relationships with protégés.[37] But as she turned fifty and saw that, despite all her contacts with writers, publishing remained illusive, even *her* confidence ebbed, and she resumed her interest in painters. If Hemingway thought he was the chief attraction in the salon, he was wrong: Gertrude paid as much attention to her friendship with the young Russian Pavlik Tchelitchew, whose exuberant laughter—like his long yellow gloves—seemed freshly innocent. She also held court for Bébé Berard, Kristians Tonny, and musician Allen Tanner, as well as Bravig Imbs, Böske and George Antheil, Eugene Berman, Pierre Charbonnier, Elliot Paul, and the handsome René Crevel.[38] (Crevel, a leading surrealist known for his ability to go into trances, was a favorite with both women.) Although Gertrude was never officially a surrealist, she knew of their manifesto and their experiments and was the only woman (with sixteen men) to have signed the verticalism manifesto in *transition* 21.[39]

Another stream of American visitors to the salon came recommended by Carl Van Vechten—Blanche Knopf, singer Nora Holt, novelist Nella Larsen, and, in the fall of 1925, Paul and Essie Robeson. Gertrude's friendship with Paul was immediate, and she and Toklas entertained for the talented black

Americans. Gertrude later wrote Van Vechten that they both liked "niggers" not because of primitivism but "because they have a narrow but a very long civilisation behind them. . . . Their sophistication is complete and so beautifully finished and it is the only one that can resist the United States of America."[40] Also in 1925 Elmer Harden, a long-time Massachusetts friend, brought poet Edith Sitwell to the salon, and the meeting of the two wildly experimental women writers was a success. Sitwell's *Facade*, an operetta with lines spoken through megaphones, had made headlines since its first performance in 1922, and her recent praise of Stein in journals and in her book *Poetry and Criticism* had already endeared her to Gertrude, who never forgot a favorable comment. As friendship with Sitwell broadened to include her brothers and others of their circle and the possibility of Gertrude's lecturing in England was often mentioned, Hemingway felt abandoned.

Angry over Gertrude's fascination with the British and resentful that her friendship toward him was cooling, Hemingway one evening came drunk to the rue de Fleurus. It was almost as if he were delivering a challenge: if Gertrude and Alice were so class-conscious and thought of themselves as superior, let them see what their young American friend was really like. Another visitor to the salon described the scene: "The door opened and Hemingway reeled in, accompanied by two buddies also the worse for drink. 'Hi, Gertie,' he bellowed. 'Ran into a couple of your fans at the Dôme who wouldn't believe I was a friend of yours so I brought them over to prove it.'" Stein's reply, according to the observer, was, "I'm not at home to anyone in your condition and don't call me Gertie. Now get out and what's more, stay out!"[41]

The sulking Hemingway did not return, but he did frequently walk in the Luxembourg Garden. Happy that he was in disfavor, Alice urged Gertrude not to allow him back. In several weeks, however, admitting her "weakness" for him, Stein appeared with him in tow, and the friendship resumed. The young author knew that he needed Gertrude's help as he rewrote the first draft of his Pamplona novel, *The Sun Also Rises*, which he had finished in September. On their autumn walks, they discussed the Jewish character Robert Cohn and the dialogue in what would be key scenes of the novel. It was at this point, however, that Gertrude let him know that she thought him ninety percent Rotarian and agreed with Alice that, while he seemed to be modern, he did smell of the museums.[42] Years later, Alice explained her objection to Hemingway on the grounds that—unlike Picasso, Gris, or Fitzgerald—he was never a serious artist: "Neither reading nor writing is a natural inevitable necessity for him."[43]

Sometime later, Hemingway was waiting downstairs at the rue de Fleurus when an argument between the women exploded in the bedroom, and he heard the "terrible things" Toklas said "and Gertrude's pleading." Returning home, he told Hadley that he had never heard such language and that he could never have anything more to do with the women.[44] Whether he was truly shocked, or whether he could not bear having Gertrude reduced to pleading with a woman he so disliked, or whether Alice's tirade included him and his relationship with Gertrude, Hemingway chose to use this event to distance himself from the two. When Hadley next took Bumby to call, she was turned away by the maid. Terribly hurt, Hadley accepted the fact that the two women, realizing what Hemingway had heard, also felt that there was no way to save the friendship. The actual scene, however, with the words Hemingway claimed to have abhorred, is lost to history.

Notes

1. Ernest Hemingway to Gertrude Stein, no date, Hemingway Collection, John F. Kennedy Library (Boston). This and subsequent material, used by permission of the Hemingway Society, Robert Lewis, President.
2. Hemingway to Sherwood Anderson, Dec. 23, 1921, in Carlos Baker, ed. *Ernest Hemingway, Selected Letters, 1917–1961* (New York: Scribner's, 1981), p. 59.
3. Blaise Cendrars, "Interview," *Paris Review*, 10 (Spring 1966), pp. 105–132.
4. Bravig Imbs, *Confessions of Another Young Man* (1936), quoted in Linda Simon, *The Biography of Alice B. Toklas* (Garden City, NY: Doubleday, 1977), p. 167.
5. Ernest Hemingway to Sherwood Anderson, March 9, 1922, in Baker, *Ernest Hemingway, Selected Letters, 1917–1961*, p. 62.
6. Gertrude Stein, *The Autobiography of Alice B. Toklas* (NY: Random House, 1933), p. 212.
7. Ibid., p. 213.
8. Recounted in Ernest Hemingway, *A Moveable Feast* (NY: Scribner's, 1964), p. 15.
9. Ernest Hemingway to Gertrude Stein, February 18, 1923, in Baker, *Ernest Hemingway, Selected Letters, 1917–1961*, p. 79.
10. Quoted in Alix Du Poy Daniel, "The Stimulating Life with Gertrude & Co.," *Lost Generation Journal*, 6 (Summer 1979), p. 18.
11. Alice B. Toklas, *The Alice B. Toklas Cook Book* (Garden City, NY: Doubleday, 1954), p. 94.
12. *Gertrude Stein, The Autobiography of Alice B. Toklas*, pp. 209–210.
13. Ernest Hemingway to Hadley Hemingway, November 28, 1922, in Baker, *Ernest Hemingway, Selected Letters, 1917–1961*, p. 73.
14. Ernest Hemingway to Clarence Hemingway, March 26, 1923, in Baker, *Ernest Hemingway, Selected Letters, 1917–1961*, p. 81.

15. Hadley Hemingway to Gertrude Stein and Alice Toklas, November 25, 1922, Hemingway Collection, Kennedy Library.

16. Ernest Hemingway to Donald Gallup, September 22, 1952, in Baker, *Ernest Hemingway, Selected Letters*, 1917–1961, p. 781.

17. Ernest Hemingway, *A Moveable Feast*, p. 17.

18. Ralph Church, "A Rose Is a Rose Is a Rose" (memoir), Bancroft Library, University of California at Berkeley, pp. 24–25.

19. Alice Hunt Sokoloff, *Hadley, The First Mrs. Hemingway* (NY: Dodd, Mead, 1973), p. 61.

20. Ernest Hemingway to W. Home, July 17–18, 1923, in Baker, *Ernest Hemingway, Selected Letters*, 1917–1961, pp. 87–88.

21. Alix Du Poy Daniel, "The Stimulating Life with Gertrude and Co.," *Lost Generation Journal*, 1979, p. 17.

22. Ralph Church, Memoir, p. 29.

23. Hadley Hemingway to Gertrude Stein, November 28, 1923, Hemingway Collection, Kennedy Library.

24. Ernest Hemingway to "Dear Friends," November 9, 1923, in Baker, *Ernest Hemingway, Selected Letters*, 1917–1961, p. 102.

25. Ibid., p. 101.

26. In *Poetry*, 21 (January 1923), p. 193.

27. Ernest Hemingway to Gertrude Stein, February 17, 1924, in Baker, *Ernest Hemingway, Selected Letters*, 1917–1961, p. 111.

28. Elizabeth Anderson and Gerald R. Kelly, *Miss Elizabeth, A Memoir* (Boston: Little, Brown, 1969), p. 169.

29. Gioia Diliberto, *Hadley* (NY: Ticknor & Fields, 1992), p. 173.

30. Gertrude Stein to H. P. Gibb, August 18, 1924, Yale American Literature Collection.

31. Alice B. Toklas, *The Alice B. Toklas Cook Book*, p. 100.

32. Ernest Hemingway to Gertrude Stein, August 15, 1924, in Baker, *Ernest Hemingway, Selected Letters*, 1917–1961, p. 122.

33. Gertrude Stein to Ernest Hemingway, no date, Hemingway Collection, Kennedy Library.

34. Stella Bowen, *Drawn from Life*, 1941 (reprinted, London: Virago, 1984), p. 171.

35. Quoted by Alice Toklas to Donald Gallup, April 29, 1951, in Toklas, *Staying On Alone*, ed. Edward Burns (NY: Liveright, 1973), p. 229.

36. Edmund Wilson, "Mr. Hemingway's Dry Points," *Dial*, 77 (October 1924), pp. 340–341.

37. Interview with Virgil Thomson in Frederick W. Lowe, Jr., "Gertrude's Web, A Study of Gertrude Stein's Literary Relationships" (Ph.D. Dissertation, Columbia University, 1956), p. 170.

38. See Matthew Josephson, *Life Among the Surrealists* (NY: Holt, Rinehart and Winston, 1962).

39. Shari Benstock, *Women of the Left Bank: Paris,* 1900–1940 (Austin: University of Texas Press, 1986), pp. 380–381.

40. Martin B. Duberman, *Paul Robeson* (NY: Knopf, 1988), pp. 92–93.

41. Alix Du Poy Daniel, "The Stimulating Life with Gertrude & Co.," *Lost Generation Journal,* 1979, p. 17.

42. Gertrude Stein, *The Autobiography of Alice B. Toklas,* p. 220 (from 216–220).

43. Alice B. Toklas, "They Who Came to Paris to Write," *New York Times Book Review* (August 6, 1950), p. 25.

44. Ernest Hemingway to Donald Gallup, September 22, 1952 in Baker, *Ernest Hemingway, Selected Letters,* 1917–1961, p. 781; also in Diliberto, *Hadley,* p. 191.

HEMINGWAY: THE 1930s (EXCERPT)

Michael Reynolds

For a month they disappear into the daily routine of the ranch: early breakfast in the lodge, writing all morning for Ernest, fishing on the river after lunch, early-evening supper in the lodge with Lawrence and Olive Nordquist attending to the several paying guests, and whiskey afterward in the heavy chairs around the fireplace. Situated at 6,800 feet on the floodplain of the Clarks Fork of the Yellowstone River, the ranch is sheltered by Squaw Peak rising to ten thousand feet behind it and the Beartooth Mountains at eleven thousand feet across the river. Along the Fork, creeks enter the flow, their names speaking of earlier days: Crazy Creek, Pilot Creek, Ghost and Beartooth creeks, Blacktail, Timber, and Hoodoo creeks. Here every turn and rise has its particular name, given to it by men and women now forgotten: Sugarloaf Mountain, Cathedral Cliffs, Painter Gulf, Beartooth Butte, Dead Indian Ranch. River and valley take their name from Lewis and Clark, whose expedition first brought eastern eyes to rest on this country whose richness exceeded all expectations.

Terrain maps, filled with detail, are Hemingway's travel companions, even in this newfound country where the geodetic survey is quite recent. Names of creeks, heights of mountains, distances between ranches, the direction of roads and rivers all matter to him. It is good to know where you are, where

Reprinted with permission from W. W. Norton Company from Hemingway: The 1930s *by Michael Reynolds (1997), pp. 45–58.*

you have been, where you are going. It is even better to have some detail of it afterward: he records mileage driven, money paid, books read, and fish caught. He does not need a compass or a map to tell him the river runs east-southeast in front of the ranch. But afterward the map will be there to confirm memory and aid creation if he is writing. Having fished one steep canyon with gravel siding impossible to climb, he can read the map of a never-fished river canyon and understand it almost as well as the first. In his new fishing log, Ernest makes detailed notes on each day's catch, baits used, numbers taken, weights, and stream conditions. Rain or shine he fishes the river, horsing in the trout, netting small trout high out of the water without bending to meet them. His form is a little disappointing. When it rains, he notes how long it takes the river to clear. On his birthday, July 21, he and Pauline release fourteen and keep eighteen cutthroat trout. The next day, Pauline's birthday, returning from the river they see a fat black bear walking down the dirt road.[1]

On a marker tree beside One-Mile Creek where it passes a few hundred yards above the Hemingways' cabin, a bear's claw marks reach higher than a man's head. In mid-August, according to Hemingway's hunting log, a local rancher needed help with a "large old male bear" who was killing cattle high up off Crandall Creek. How much help was needed may be questioned, but that was the excuse for outfitting Ernest for a bear hunt out of season. On August 17, well attended by Nordquist's cowhand, Ivan Wallace, Ernest rode the now familiar pack trail southeast along Squaw Creek to the Crandall Ranger Station. From there the North Fork trail rising into mountains narrows as it passes under Hunter's Peak and into a rugged forest of fir, white-bard pine, and spruce based on volcanic rock. The trail, becoming little more than an animal path, crosses Blacktail and Cow creeks before it drops down through switchbacks to the North Fork of Crandall's Creek. Here Ernest and the redheaded Ivan shoot the old horse they brought in for bait and leave it to "rise." That was on Sunday. By Wednesday morning, predators are feeding on the carcass; in that rare air at eight thousand feet, odors intensify and the heart pounds, but no bear shows. By Tuesday night, Ernest is back at the L-Bar-T, without a bear but still eager for the hunt. Friday morning, reoutfitted with fresh supplies, his new Springfield rifle, Zeiss field glasses, and a raincoat, he and three ranch hands set out again for the bear bait. Before they reach the ranger station, Ernest's horse bolts, lurching him through a pine thicket that lays open the left side of his face, blood dripping and the horse spooked. A bandage won't do. He needs stitches, and the closest doctor is fifty miles away in Cody. By midnight, having traveled the unspeakable dirt ranch road, through countless gates in a car rented from the ranger, they are in Dr. Trueblood's office, where the veterinarian turned doctor sews up Hemingway's wound with six stitches, using a little whiskey taken internally as anesthetic. A white bandage now swaddles his jaw and the left side of his face. The resulting scar will add to his bulging forehead scar from the falling Paris skylight, the one on his finger from the Key West punching bag, and the scars on his rebuilt right knee and his right foot from the war.

Returning through the Wyoming night, they are back at the ranger station by morning. That evening at the horse bait, as the light is about to fail completely, with the brown bear in the telescopic sight of his new rifle, Ernest is letting out his breath slowly and squeezing the Springfield's trigger with an even pull, and then the bear falling in slow motion. A week later, on the same ripe bait, he kills a second bear. Ernest, camera-shy and proud, stands beside the huge black pelt stretched upon the cabin wall. Admirers stroke the glossy fur.[2] Nine years later he will remember Clarks Fork Valley with trout rising to dry flies, remember waking in the cold night with coyotes howling. "You could ride in the morning, or sit in front of the cabin, lazy in the sun, and look across the valley where the hay was cut so the meadows were cropped brown and smooth to a line of quaking aspens along the river, now turning yellow in the fall." The years blend together into one year with all the good days combined: "all the hunting and all the fishing and the riding in the summer sun and the dust of the pack-train, the silent riding in the hills in the sharp cold of fall going up after the cattle on the high range, finding them wild as deer and as quiet, only bawling noisily when they were all herded together being forced along down into the lower country."[3]

Evenly spaced along the Fork are ranches similar to Nordquist's, most of which were homesteaded at 320 or 640 acres: not enough land to raise cattle and too far from the market if you did. Some raised horses, but with little profit. Others, like Nordquist, caught hold of the dude-ranch craze bringing soft-seated East Coast families west for summer vacations. By putting on a little show for the summer dudes and picking up some hunters in the fall, a man could get by. Give the guests an evening cookout on the trail, ponies tethered and campfire smoking, or a makeshift rodeo in the high meadow where bangtails buck the boys about faster than a dude's camera can pan the field.[4]

Rising up under blankets to the odor of pine smoke and frying bacon, the air cool and resinous, Pauline standing there with her hands in her hip pockets, ready for whatever, Ernest watches the wranglers get dudes saddled up for the morning run, smells horse piss in the straw. This is country without a phone or electricity where the mail comes once a week, and no one particularly cares one way or another if Ernest spends his mornings writing, afternoons fishing, evenings reading. His contemplative and his active life are jammed together so tightly that only minutes separate them. By the end of July he is talking about having his bullfight book finished before the November snows force him out. Brave self-promises on a difficult book. He takes time to write Louis Cohn, promising that as soon as his "book trunk" arrives he will send a page of manuscript for the Hemingway bibliography Cohn is putting to press. "Thank you so much for the offer of the Galsworthy Conrad," he tells Cohn, "but it is doubtless too valuable for you to give. I'll take the Scotch or Rye and let the first editions go." Then he adds, "nor heed the rumble of the distant drums."[5]

The Nordquist ranch provides the conditions in which he works best and steadily, for he prefers to write in transient places, close to the natural world. *The Sun Also Rises* was written on the road in Spain, following the bullfights; *A Farewell to Arms* was drafted under transatlantic and transcontinental circumstances. At Nordquist's, five minutes after setting down his pencil he can be on a horse, or within twenty minutes his line is in the water. He arrived at the ranch with seventy-four pages of manuscript drafted on a book without a title and with problems to solve about the new edition of *In Our Time*. A month later he tells Max Perkins he is writing six days out of seven and has forty thousand words done, roughly another fifty pages of manuscript. By early September he is on page 174 or about sixty thousand words.[6] Max wants new material added to *In Our Time*, but Ernest is uncomfortable jazzing up an old book with new stories written in a different manner. Nor does he want Max Perkins rearranging the stories or grouping together all the vignettes which divide the stories: "Max *please believe me* that those chapters are where they belong."[7] However, his earliest story, which he was forced to cut out of the 1925 version of the book—"Up in Michigan," a brutal seduction story told from the woman's point of view—he tries to revise, but the scene with the drunken Jim Gilmore forcing himself on Liz Coates and her being left with the pain and the ignorance becomes less readable the more he fiddles with it. Finally he gives up, telling Perkins, "I know you will not publish it with the last part entire and if any of that is out there is no story." He has promised Max to have mailed the book with corrections, including the original, uncensored version of "Mr. and Mrs. Elliot" and "with or without a couple of short pieces of the same period depending on how these seem in the book between now and then."

But he cannot write the preface Max wants for the collection of short stories. "I am too busy," he said, "too disinterested, too proud or too stupid or whatever you want to call it to write one for it." Determined to resist as much of the whoring expected of "Professional Writers" as he can, Hemingway suggested Edmund Wilson for the job.[8] Looking for other material from the 1922–25 period which might honestly meld into *In Our Time*, Hemingway remembers "The Death of the Standard Oil Man," an unpublished story set during the Greco-Turkish War of 1922. But in August when his "book trunk" arrives from Piggott, the manuscript is not there. Instead he finds a story about the Greeks at Smyrna in 1922 when the Turks were about to burn that town, a story written in late 1926.[9] Its doubled narration—a reporter telling the reader what a British officer at Smyrna said—pulls the reader quickly through the page into the fiction. Ernest, who was never in Smyrna, knew reporters who saw and wrote of the Greeks breaking "the legs of the baggage and transport animals" and shoving them "off the quay into the shallow water."[10] It was a strong piece with refugees jammed on the quay and Greek mothers refusing to give up dead babies and "nice" debris floating in the water. It fit with the other stories like the Elliots trying but unable to have a baby, and the bloody cesarean operation at the Indian camp, war sketches with the dead in the street, and Nick having to return to the States because of his pregnant wife, the punchy boxer that night by the rail line, and Nick ending up after the war not quite right on Big Two-Hearted River.

On September 3, Hemingway mailed Perkins a corrected copy of *In Our Time*, including a somewhat sanitized version of "Mr. and Mrs. Elliot" and the Smyrna sketch, which he agreed to call "Introduction by the Author," which would follow the introduction he hoped Edmund Wilson would write because someone had to explain that this was an early book. His accompanying letter was a confusion of disclaimers: reissuing the book was Scribner's idea, not his, although it was a good book, but should not be called a "new" book; however, they could say it had new material, yet giving the readers an old book now would probably hurt sales of his bullfight book to follow (174 pages written). And Scribner's better check for libel, because they published this book at their own risk; he would give no guarantees against lawsuits. Sick of the interruptions caused by this reprint of *In Our Time*, he would take days to get back into the bullfight book.[11]

He was also working on an experimental story told in two voices and several parts, a story not unlike the bullfight book. The story began with a naturalist commenting, tongue in cheek, on the work of earlier observers of flora and fauna, complaining that war dead were ignored by natural historians. "Can we not hope to furnish the reader with a few rational and interesting facts about the dead?" he asked. The second paragraph, which he lifted word for word from Bishop Stanley's *A Familiar History of Birds* (1881), told of Mungo Park, on the brink of death in the African desert, finding God's fingerprints in a small moss-flower. Hemingway's naturalist asks, "Can any branch of Natural History be studied without increasing that faith, love and hope which we also, every one of us, need in our journey through the wilderness of life? Let us see what inspiration we may derive from the dead."[12]

Similar in theme to the vignette of the refugees on the Smyrna quay, which it references, but written in a different style, "A Natural History of the Dead" was an experiment in both structure and voice. The first half developed the premise; the second half illustrated the premise with an example. The narrator, a veteran out of the last war, speaks in a sardonic voice and with the detachment of a natural historian observing the dead bodies on the Italian front of 1918. Bodies left unburied go from "white to yellow, to yellow-green, to black." Left long enough in the sun, "the flesh comes to resemble coal tar," and swells inordinately, straining at the confining uniform. Everywhere there is paper of the dead blowing in the wind. And the smell of the unburied dead, mixed with the lingering odor of mustard gas, one cannot forget.

Nothing the narrator has seen gives him much cause to rejoice in God's presence in the natural world. Soldiers die like animals, some from wounds seemingly slight but deep enough to serve. Others "die like cats: a skull broken in and iron in the brain, they lie alive two days like cats that crawl into the coal bin with the bullet in the brain and will not die until you have cut off their heads." This observation leads him to an extended illustration: a mountain field station with wounded bodies and an overworked doctor. The dead are carried into a cold-storage cave; one of the badly wounded, "whose head was broken as a flower pot may be broken" and who was presumed dead, lies in the dark, moaning, like the cat refusing to die. Under pressure of the wounded crowding the station, the doctor refuses to move the dying man out of the cave, having no way of making his suffering less nor the faintest hope of saving his life. No, he will not give him an overdose of morphine, he tells a wounded artillery officer. He has little enough to operate with now. The officer can shoot the man if he wishes. Doctor and patient trade insults until the artilleryman loses all composure. "Fuck yourself," he said. "Fuck yourself. Fuck your mother. Fuck your sister. . . . " At which point the doctor throws iodine into his eyes, disarms him, and has him restrained. Meanwhile the moaning man in the cave of the dead has become permanently quiet. "A dispute about nothing," the doctor calls it.[13]

The story was not finished on September 13, when Ernest and Pauline, preparatory to her going east with Bumby, signed new wills. His money went to Pauline, Patrick, and John, in that order. If they were dead, the estate was payable in equal shares to his first wife, Hadley, and his sister-in-law, Jinny Pfeiffer. His Italian war medals should go first to John and then to Hadley. The will did not mention Hadley's divorce settlement—all the income from *The Sun Also Rises*—nor did it mention what he expected her to do with the war medals.[14] Two days later in Billings, Pauline and Bumby boarded the Burlington train for Chicago and from there, connections to St. Louis. It was time for her stepson to return to his mother in Paris; Henrietta, their French nursemaid, would act as his traveling companion. That same day the fall hunting season opened, and Ernest's bullfight book was 188 pages of dense manuscript.[15] In two months at the ranch, he averaged about two pages a day. Over the next forty-five days, with only one fruitless hunt in the high mountains and customary afternoons of grouse shooting to take his mind off the book, Ernest completed another hundred pages of manuscript. He was close to the end: two more chapters and the appendix, he told Max.[16] Meanwhile, his public visibility was increasing dramatically: *A Farewell to Arms* was being translated into French and German; the Lawrence Stallings stage version of the novel was about to open on Broadway; and Paramount Pictures purchased the film rights to the novel for $80,000.[17]

November 1, Route 10 outside of Park City, Montana. Gently rising and falling as it follows the north bank of the Yellowstone out of sight in the dark, the two-lane road is empty except for a Ford roadster with two bearded men in the front seat and a third in the rumble seat. Hemingway drives. Next to him sits John Dos Passos, on his way to Billings to catch the night train east. Floyd Allington from Red Cloud is hunkered down in back. A diminished bottle of bourbon is shared against the cold, as the sun sets behind them and blue shadows go black. Fresh gravel laid down the day before is not yet properly rolled or settled, and the center line is not marked. With the lights of Laurel faint over the far hill, a car approaches, its lights bright; Hemingway, his night vision marred by a weak eye, blinks and moves the Ford as far right as seems safe. Someone is speaking, but with the noise of the engine and tires on gravel, it is difficult to hear.[18]

In the Saturday-night emergency room of St. Vincent Hospital, Dorothy Buller checks in for her night shift duties to find three strangers, two in pain, one of them seriously hurt. Bob Bass is telling someone how he helped pull the big fella from the overturned Ford out on the Livingston road and gave all three a ride into Billings. The Red Lodge cowboy, with a dislocated right shoulder and a few scratches, is taped up and sedated. The larger, darkly bearded man with the broken arm is being taken to x-ray. The third man, also bearded but unhurt, his glasses unbroken, wants to know if his friend's money belt is missing. Nurse Buller assures him that no one has touched anyone's money belt.[19]

On Sunday morning in Piggott, Arkansas, Pauline receives the telegram from Dos Passos telling her that Ernest is in the hospital injured. Packing quickly and putting her own problems on hold, she leaves Piggott Monday morning, reaching Billings on the Tuesday-evening train.[20] By this time Ernest is no longer in the three-person ward where he spent his first night. When Dr. Louis Allard, an orthopedic surgeon recognized nationally for his work on polio victims, discovered that his patient was Ernest Hemingway, he immediately moved him into a private fourth-floor room; when Pauline arrives, he moves him again, across the hall to 421, so that she can stay in the adjoining room. On Thursday, Dr. Allard operates to restructure the oblique spiral fracture three inches above Ernest's right elbow. Using kangaroo tendon to bind tight his bone work, the surgeon sews up his nine-inch incision and immobilizes Hemingway for three weeks to let the fracture heal properly.

That afternoon the *Billings Gazette* announces that Sinclair Lewis has won the Nobel Prize for literature, and off-year election results are being posted across the country. Democrats are close to breaking the Republican control in both houses of Congress, and Governor Franklin Roosevelt of New York is returned to Albany by a record plurality.[21] In steady, gnawing pain from the repaired fracture, Hemingway is not particularly interested in literary or political prizes. After the fifth day, the doctor takes him off the morphine, leaving him alone with the pain and his night thoughts.[22] For three weeks unable to move for fear of ruining his writing arm, he has plenty of time to think, too much time. He has been there before, badly wounded in the Milan hospital twelve years earlier, worrying then whether he might lose his leg, and sometimes now in the night he wonders which hospital he is in this time. He is, Pauline says, "pretty nervous and depressed from the pain and worry." Once again he is sleeping fitfully by day and lying awake in the night. Not even Pauline, with her seemingly inexhaustible capacity for tending to his needs, can stay on his schedule. Tall, stately Harriet O'Day, the special nurse assigned to him, provides the small bedside radio that, along with a little prohibition whiskey from his well-stocked bar, gets him through the nights.[23]

Three days after Hemingway's operation, two new patients, Martin Costello and Alec Youck, are moved into the ward across the hall from Hemingway's room. In the Surita Café, Costello and Youck had been shot by an unknown assailant. Youck, a Russian farm worker, was hit in the thigh, but not seriously. The *Gazette* said that Costello, a Mexican beet worker, might die from the bullet that passed through his stomach. The newspaper said:

> Two men . . . were arrested . . . Thomas Hernando, restaurant cook, and Joe Aglo, who lived in a room above the restaurant. A box of cartridges was found in Aglo's room. . . . Arriving at the café, [Constable] Thomas found Youck on the floor in a rear room. At the foot of the stairs . . . Thomas found Aglo and Hernando supporting Costello who was bleeding profusely. . . . Costello . . . refused to talk of the shooting. Officers recalled that three years ago when a bullet wounded the arm of a girl with whom he was walking and tore into his coat sleeve, he also refused at that time to name the person who fired the shot. . . . Joe Diaz, operator of the Surita café and the rooms above . . . said he knew nothing about any quarrel in which Costello might have figured. Mrs. Diaz was at the café when Constable Thomas arrived, but she, too, said she knew nothing of the shooting. Questioning of persons in the vicinity elicited no further information.

The cartridges found in Aglo's room were .32 caliber, the same caliber as the slug removed from Costello's stomach, but no weapon was recovered. Four days later, the police gave up their investigation. The beet worker, the cook, the Russian, and the boarder all said they had no idea who the gunman might have been.[24]

Now Hemingway has something new to think about as he gets regular reports from the nurses on Costello's condition and his continuing refusal to name his attacker. The Russian groans a good deal the first few days, but Costello, with drain tubes hanging from his stomach, keeps his suffering to himself. Sometimes the wounded man's Spanish-speaking visitors share drinks with Ernest; sometimes they borrow his Spanish newspapers. Eventually they will all become part of his fiction, but then in the cold November, with the days beginning below zero and the light failing early, the wounded Mexican and his friends are a pleasant break in the monotony. By the end of the month, his pain has subsided enough for him to become difficult and abrasive: he dictates a querulous letter to Max Perkins, wondering if there is some special reason they are keeping Edmund Wilson's introduction from him, and where are the books he ordered?[25]

Hemingway's prominence and sometimes good humor, which he is able to maintain for the nurses and doctors, make him a remarked-upon and pampered guest for whom the Catholic sisters of Charity who operate the hospital cannot do enough. Particularly drawn to him is Sister Florence Cloonan, who brings in his daily mail and who, in her "tin Lizzie," is well known on the streets of Billings. "When you saw her coming," one of the nuns said, "everybody moved to the other side of the street." With Ernest, Sister Florence speaks passionately about the baseball season past and the college football season just closing. Connie Mack's Philadelphia Athletics and Knute Rockne's Notre Dame are the two teams upon whose success her life seems to depend as she followed them religiously on the radio. "Because of a heart condition, she wasn't supposed to become excited. When a baseball game became particularly unnerving, she'd take refuge in the hospital chapel and pray until she was calm and could return to her post beside the radio."[26]

As November turns into even colder December, Hemingway is finally able to move about, his arm tightly wrapped and immobilized in a sling that looks as if it were made from bedsheets. The damaged nerves which have made his writing hand useless keep him ever edgy. By a low light, he reads late, devouring the book shipment from Perkins: Somerset Maugham's *Cakes and Ale*; Arthur Train's mystery *The Adventures of Ephraim Tut*; Dorothy Sayers's *Omnibus of Crime; The Real War 1914–1918*; and O'Flaherty's *Two Years*.[27] From Billings and Denver newspapers and from sketchy radio news, he is more in touch with his native land than he was during the previous four months at the ranch. In Cuba and Spain, revolutions flare up with the governments killing their own people in the streets. President Hoover, in his State of the Union address, tells the nation that it faces an enormous $180 million deficit, making any tax relief unlikely. Moreover, he asks Congress for an extra $150 million to spend on public works to reduce rising unemployment. Smelling fresh pork in the barrel, congressmen and senators bicker for almost two months over where the money will be spent. Meanwhile, no one in or out of the government can say exactly how many people are "idle," or how many banks have already closed.[28] In spite of which, radio crooners urge the country to sing "Bye, Bye Blues" and "Get Happy" because everything is "Fine and Dandy" "On the Sunny Side of the Street."[29]

Neither fine nor sunny could describe Hemingway's mood as the year's end approaches. His right arm remains splinted and useless in a sling, his wrist paralyzed from a stretched or pinched nerve, and the pain still a steady throb. Under the green fluoroscope, Dr. Allard shows him where the bone is mending, but when the feeling in his wrist will return is anyone's guess.[30] His few letters are dictated to Pauline, who types them as he speaks, but it is impossible for him to dictate the bullfight book.

Being a doctor's son, he always exaggerates his illnesses and is quick to project the worst possible scenario—traits which sometimes lead those who know him well to underestimate the seriousness of his condition. For the nurses he can always joke, but when Archie MacLeish, alarmed by the accident, flies into Billings from New York to comfort Hemingway, a hazardous two-day trip on Northwest Airlines, Ernest is surly and suspicious, accusing his friend of coming only to be present at his death. Maybe it was a joke, but Archie does not think so. The next day, he is a different Ernest, the one who would never have said such a thing and who carries on, in fact, as if he had not. A month later, MacLeish gave Max Perkins his report on Hemingway:

> He suffered very real & unrelenting pain over a long time. I went out because I know how his imagination works when his health is concerned & because I thought any normal event such as the arrival of a friend might give him some kind of a date to hold on to. When I got there the pain was largely over & the wound beginning to heal. . . . I think all his friends can do is to keep him cheerful in idleness—a hell of a job. Poor Pauline.[31]

A friend of Max Perkins who was visiting while Archie was there found Hemingway "pale and shaky although cheerful. . . . We drank a couple of bottles of Canadian beer. . . . I sent him up four mallards and some trout again."[32]

Facing what might be six months of physical therapy to rehabilitate his badly weakened arm, Hemingway finally admits to himself and MacLeish, whom he invited along all expenses paid, that he will not be able to go on an African safari in 1931. Gus Pfeiffer, his private banker, put up $25,000 of stock to underwrite Ernest's dream of African hunting, a dream he has nurtured since, as a ten-year-old, he followed in the magazines and on the movie screen the African hunting adventures of his hero Teddy Roosevelt. Now in Billings, with snow falling and Christmas decorations up in the halls, Africa is as remote as the moon. Ernest dictates a letter to Henry Strater, the New York painter, saying his promise of a paid-up safari is still good, but they will have to put it off for a year. In letters he can joke about being an "ex-writer," but it is a hollow joke.[33]

Early on the morning of December 21, Ernest and Pauline warm themselves in the Billings railway station, waiting for the eastbound Burlington train to arrive. Late the next evening they will be in Kansas City, and the following morning in St. Louis, to be met by Pauline's father, who will drive them on to a Piggott Christmas. Outside falling snow is accumulating in empty streets as the Zephyr pulls into the station. On Christmas Eve when they arrive in Piggott, he is running a fever; weak from two months in the hospital bed, he goes back to bed in his in-laws' house, where he never felt at home, not that feeling "at home" was ever a particularly calming experience for him. He cannot write left-handed, nor can he dictate. This he tells Owen Wister in a letter dictated to Pauline, who types as he talks. As for writing about a real person, as Wister did in his Roosevelt book, it could not be done well. "You can't recreate a person," Ernest says, "you can only create a character in writing. You can record an actual person's actions and recreate them in a sense, i.e. present them through this recording but it takes great detail."[34] As a constant reader of histories and biographies, he speaks as much to himself as to Wister, and speaking, perhaps, to others to follow. His book in progress, a study of the bullfight and a good deal more, is built on details small, numerous, yet selective, and didn't he always work that way, choosing the telling detail from the welter of possibilities?

Notes

1. The Hemingway Fishing Log, 1930–34, John F. Kennedy Library Hemingway Archive; Eaton film, DPS 28: c, John F. Kennedy Library.
2. Hemingway Hunting Log, 1930–34, John F. Kennedy Library; Carlos Baker, *Ernest Hemingway: A Life Story* (New York: Scribner's, 1969), pp. 212–13. See also Hemingway to Louis Cohn, Sept. 3, 1930, University of Delaware, Cohn Collection and Hemingway to Henry Strater, June 20, 1930 in *Selected Letters*, ed. Carlos Baker (New York: Scribner's, 1981), p. 324.
3. "The Clark's Fork Valley, Wyoming" first published in *Vogue*, February 1939, reprinted in *By-Line: Ernest Hemingway*, ed. William White (New York: Scribner's, 1967), pp. 298–300.
4. Eaton film, John F. Kennedy Library Hemingway Archive.
5. Hemingway to Louis Cohn, July 29, 1930, University of Delaware, Cohn Collection.
6. Hemingway to Maxwell Perkins, August 23, 1930, in *Selected Letters*, ed. Carlos Baker, pp. 326–28; Hemingway to Henry Strater, Sept. 10, 1930 in Ibid., pp. 328–29.
7. Hemingway to Maxwell Perkins, July 24, 1930, Princeton University Library.
8. Hemingway to Maxwell Perkins, August 12, 1930; Hemingway to Louis Cohn, Sept. 3, 1930, University of Delaware, Cohn Collection. See also Paul Smith, *A*

Reader's Guide to the Short Stories of Ernest Hemingway (Boston: G. K. Hall, 1989).

9. Hemingway to Louis Cohn, Sept. 2, 1930, University of Delaware, Cohn Collection; Paul Smith, "The Bloody Typewriter and the Burning Snakes," *Hemingway: Essays of Reassessment*, ed. Frank Scafella (New York: Oxford University Press, 1991), pp. 81–3.

10. *Death in the Afternoon*, typescript, p. 1, John F. Kennedy Library Hemingway Archive.

11. Hemingway to Maxwell Perkins, Sept. 3, 1930, Princeton University Library. One attempt to revise "Mr. and Mrs. Elliot" became the verso of MS p. 189 of *Death in the Afternoon*, University of Texas Harry Ransom Humanities Research Center.

12. Edward Stanley, *A Familiar History of Birds* (London: Longmans, Green, 1881), pp. 1–2; Ernest Hemingway, "A Natural History of the Dead," *Winner Take Nothing* (New York: Scribner's, 1933), pp. 97–98.

13. "A Natural History of the Dead," pp. 97–106.

14. Patrick Hemingway Collection, Princeton University Library.

15. Hemingway to William Horne, Sept. 12, 1930, Baker Collection, Princeton University Library.

16. Hemingway to Maxwell Perkins, Oct. 28, 1930, Princeton University Library.

17. Assignments of Copyrights, vol. 786, pp. 97–110, Library of Congress. Contract is dated Sept. 17, 1930, and signed for Hemingway by Matthew G. Herold, attorney in fact. Hemingway's share was $24,000.

18. "Noted Novelist Is Injured in Auto Accident," *Billings Gazette*, Nov. 2, 1930. Carlos Baker interview with Floyd Allington, July 20, 1964, Princeton University Library.

19. Mary Pickett, "Hemingway in St. Vincent: The Booze Also Rises," *Billings Gazette*, April 8, 1983, 2-D/6, interview with Dorothy Buller and Bernardette Martin; "Noted Novelist Is Injured in Auto Accident," *Billings Gazette*, Nov. 2, 1930.

20. Carlos Baker, *Ernest Hemingway: A Life Story*, p. 217; *Billings Gazette*, Nov. 5, 1930.

21. "Hemingway in St. Vincent"; Carlos Baker, *Ernest Hemingway: A Life Story*, p. 217. Kangaroo tendon, which was packaged in hermetically sealed glass tubes, was one of several binding materials in medical use in 1930. *New York Times*, Nov. 6, 1930.

22. Hemingway to Archibald MacLeish, Nov. 22, 1930, *Selected Letters*, p. 330.

23. "Hemingway in St. Vincent." See also Pauline's appended note to the Hemingway letter she typed to Waldo Peirce, Nov. 28, 1930, copy at John F. Kennedy Library Hemingway Archive and in Carlos Baker, *Ernest Hemingway: A Life Story*, p. 217.

24. "Two Wounded in Mystery Shooting," *Billings Gazette*, Nov. 10, 1930, pp. 1, 2; "Sunday Fracas Still a Mystery," Nov. 13, 1930. Billings was and remains a center for processing sugar beets.

25. Hemingway to Archibald MacLeish, Nov. 22, 1930 in Carlos Baker, *Ernest Hemingway: A Life Story*, p. 218. Hemingway to Maxwell Perkins, Nov. 24, 1930. Princeton University Library.

26. "Hemingway at St. Vincent." In 1943, Florence Cloonan died in Denver from a heart attack.

27. See Michael Reynolds' *Hemingway's Reading* (Princeton, NJ: Princeton University Press, 1981).

28. *New York Times*, Nov.–Dec. 1930.

29. Among the most popular songs of 1930, according to Roger Lax and Frederick Smith, *The Great Song Thesaurus* (New York: Oxford University Press, 1984), pp. 55–56.

30. Hemingway to Henry Strater, Dec. 15, 1930, *Selected Letters*, ed. Carlos Baker, p. 335.

31. Archibald MacLeish to Maxwell Perkins, Jan. 4, 1931, *Letters of Archibald MacLeish*, p. 31; Scott Donaldson, *Archibald MacLeish: An American Life* (Boston: Houghton Mifflin, 1992), p. 207.

32. A letter from a Mrs. Snooks quoted in Maxwell Perkins-Henry Strater (December, 1930), Baker Collection, Princeton University Library.

33. Hemingway to Archibald MacLeish, Dec. 15, 1930, *Selected Letters*, ed. Carlos Baker, p. 335; Hemingway to Archibald MacLeish, Dec. 15, 1930, Library of Congress.

34. Hemingway to Owen Wister, Dec. 26, 1930, University of Virginia Alderman Library. In his next book, *Green Hills of Africa*, Hemingway attempts what he says here cannot be done.

INDEX

417

Grebstein, Sheldon 104
Greenacre, Phyllis 339–41
Greenblatt, Stephen (*Marvelous Posses-sions*) 33–35
Griffin, Peter (*Less Than a Treason*) 296–97
Gris, Juan 398
Gubar, Susan 246–47 ("Infection in the Sentence," 294, 301–2)
Gurko, Leo 153–54

H
Haas, Adelaide 83
Halliday, E. M. 104
Hamill, Peter 1135
Hampshire, Stuart 191–92
Harden, Elmer 398
Harris, Daniel 243
Hatch, John (*Tanzania*) 318
Hawthorne, Nathaniel 30
Hayes, Helen 177
Heap, Jane 22, 394
Hecht, Ben 394
Hemingway, Dr. Clarence E. (father) 1–2, 369–70, 376, 382–83, 391
Hemingway, Ernest:
  African stories 317–25, 332–45, 349, 362, 364, 366–70
  African-American issues 8–9, 29–30, 226, 329–45
  alcoholism 9, 102, 376–77, 385
  ambition 219, 221–22, 396–97
  as an American writer 4–5, 19–20, 225–26, 335
  anti-Semitism 7–8, 391, 398
  autobiographical writing of 6, 213–34, 253, 330, 363–64
  biography of 1–4, 7, 23–26, 174, 176, 332, 338–41, 350, 353, 358–60, 363–64, 366, 369–70, 375–85, 389–401, 403–16
  cats 341

as celebrity 5–7, 213–14
"code" 4, 7–8, 46, 112, 214
craft as writer 2–3, 6, 23–26, 214–18, 220–24, 269–81, 293–308, 390–91
criticism of 4–12, 171–84, 240–55
expatriation 4, 216–34
F. B. I. investigation 381
gender considerations 9–10, 30, 45–48, 61–67, 81–94, 171–84, 240–63, 293–308
heroes in fiction 4, 8, 46–51, 143–44, 214, 267–81
illness (hemochromatosis, manic depression) 7, 375–85
language in writing 81–94, 139–40, 295–307
macho attitudes of 2, 9, 46–59, 69, 74, 99, 101, 176–77, 214, 241, 342, 394–95 (*see also* heterosexuality, homosexuality)
manuscripts of work 119–34, 283–92, 293–308, 311–27, 329–48, 349–72
at Mayo Clinic 376, 378, 380–81
as modernist 5–6, 9, 114, 135–47, 220, 223–26, 326
misogyny; *see* gender, women charac-ters
Native American issues 29–41, 47–50, 220, 224–25, 227, 304, 333, 337, 357
nature writing 3, 10, 214, 226–28, 271–81
Nobel Prize in Literature 10, 269
racial considerations 9, 29–41, 47–50, 220, 224–25, 227, 304, 331–45 (*see also* Native American issues)
as realist 2, 136, 224
relationships with parents 1–2, 239–40, 258–59, 366, 369–70, 383–84
religion in work of 39–40, 54, 109, 119–34, 224–25, 315, 393

Works

Oldsey, Bernard 11
Omi, Michael 39
O'Neill, Eugene 5
O'Sullivan, Sibbie 61–79
Othello 152

P

Paris Review 12, 41
Parker, Dorothy 11
Paul, Elliot 397
Peele, George ("A Farewell to Arms")
    151
performance as a component of literary
    text (performativity) 46–53, 57, 227–28,
    232, 234, 279
Perkins, Maxwell (Max) 352, 406–7,
    409–10, 413
Perrault, Charles (*Histoires ou Contes du
    Temps Passé avec des Moralitiés*)
    311–12, 318, 325
Pfeiffer, Gus 413
Pfeiffer, Jinny 25, 365, 409
Pfeiffer, Pauline; *see* Hemingway, Pauline
    Pfeiffer
Phelan, James (*Narrative as Rhetoric*) 12,
    174, 178
Picasso, Pablo 334, 364, 392, 395–96, 398
Pierce, Waldo 329
Plimpton, George 12, 41, 376
Poetry, 394
political considerations in art 185–210,
    224, 228, 277, 295–308
Pound, Ezra 23–25, 119–20, 125–26,
    129, 134, 136, 143, 271–72, 389, 392,
    394 (*Hugh Selwyn Mauberley,* 271)
Price, Reynolds 115
primitivism 334, 342–43, 345, 398
Prince, Gerald 7
Proust, Marcel (*Remembrance of Things
    Past*) 337
psychoanalytic criticism 330–45
Pullin, Faith 178

Q

Quershnitt 394

R

Rabine, Leslie W. 295, 308
Raeburn, John (*Fame Became of Him,
    Hemingway as Public Writer*) 6,
    297–98, 302
Real War 1914–1918, The 412
Reardon, John 11, 269, 280
regionalism 225
Renza, Louis A. 213–38
Reynolds, Michael 11, 152, 178, 243,
    337, 380, 403–16
Rich, Adrienne 243
Richardson, Hadley; *see* Hemingway,
    Hadley Richardson
Robeson, Essie 397–98
Robeson, Paul 397–98
Rodin, Auguste (*The Metamorphoses of
    Ovid*)("The Gates of Hell") 334,
    354–56, 358
Roe, Steven C. 311–27
Roiphe, Herman 340
Rome, Dr. Howard 378, 380
Roosevelt, Theodore 2, 17, 413–14
Rose, Phyllis 344
Rosenfeld, Paul 11
Roth, Philip 135
Rousseau, Henri (*Le Douanier*) 392
Rousseau, Jean-Jacques 204–6
Rovit, Earl 46, 104, 241
Rubin, Gayle 32

S

Sanford, Marcelline Hemingway (*At the
    Hemingways: A Family Portrait*) 1,
    239–40, 338, 341, 358–59, 376, 382
satire 21–26
Sayers, Dorothy (*Omnibus of Crime*) 412
Sarry, Elaine (*The Body in Pain*) 35
Schneider, Daniel J. 178

191912⁊   h.1/